D1070806

# THEATRE MANAGEMENT IN AMERICA

# STEPHEN LANGLEY

# THEATRE MANAGEMENT IN AMERICA

WAGGONER LIBRARY
DISCARD

## PRINCIPLE AND PRACTICE

Producing for the Commercial, Stock,
Resident, College and Community Theatre

MACKEY LIBRARY
TREVECCA NAZARENE COLLEGE

**DRAMA BOOK SPECIALISTS / PUBLISHERS**

Copyright © 1974 by Stephen Langley

All rights reserved. No part of this publication may be reproduced or
transmitted in any form or by any means, electronic or mechanical, including photocopy, recording, or any information storage and retrieval
system now known or to be invented, without permission in writing
from the publishers, except by a reviewer who wishes to quote brief
passages in connection with a review written for inclusion in a magazine,
newspaper, or broadcast.

All rights reserved under the International and Pan-American Copyright
Conventions For information, address: DRAMA BOOK SPECIALISTS/
PUBLISHERS, 150 West 52nd Street, New York, New York 10019.

**Library of Congress Cataloging in Publication Data**

Langley, Stephen.
    Theatre management in America.

    1.   Theatre management—United States.   I.   Title.
PN2291. L3          658'. 91'7920973          73-13886
ISBN 0-910482-45-4

First edition

Printed in the United States of America, by
Noble Offset Printers, Inc. New York, N.Y. 10003

This volume
is dedicated
to dedication itself,
without which
there could be
no theatre to manage.

The author gratefully acknowledges permission to reprint granted from the following:

Brooks Atkinson (Letter to the New York Board of Estimate).

David Merrick (*Hello Dolly* address form).

The National Ticket Company, New York, New York (ticket samples).

Excerpt from *Light Up The Sky* is reprinted by permission from Mrs. Moss Hart. (© copyright by Moss Hart 1948, 1949.)

Excerpt from *Ellen Terry and Bernard Shaw, A Correspondence* is reprinted by permission of The Society of Authors (London, England) on behalf of the Bernard Shaw Estate.

Excerpt from *The Performing Arts: Problems and Prospects* is reprinted by permission of The Rockefeller Brothers Fund, New York, New York.

Offering Circular for the Broadway production of *And Miss Reardon Drinks A Little* is reprinted by permission of Producing Managers Company, New York, New York.

# TABLE OF CONTENTS

APPENDICES:

# PREFACE

Until recently, a volume dealing with theatre management would have seemed a rare curiosity. Now, however, it is increasingly apparent to laymen and professionals—and alarmingly apparent to both incipient and established arts organizations themselves—that the business of organizing, funding, managing and sustaining almost any given artistic enterprise requires executive leadership of a special kind.

This book attempts to outline a comprehensive view of theatrical producing in America: its history, theory and practice. It deals exclusively with live theatre. More specifically, I have tried to define theatrical producing and management as a profession, to describe how the various branches of the profession are currently structured and to suggest a few principles that might strengthen theatre practice both economically and artistically.

Most facets of theatre—architecture, scene design, literature, acting and staging techniques—are well documented historically and in terms of current practice. Comparatively little, however, has been published about the history and practice of theatrical producing and management. The memoirs of a few dozen eighteenth and nineteenth century actor-managers, chronicles that record production casts and statistics, of which George Odell's *Annals of the New York Stage* is the most impressive example, and bits of information that can be snatched from a variety of other sources comprise but a meager library on the history of American theatre management. In the present century Alfred Bernheim's *The Business of the Theatre,* together with several other pioneering studies, such as Baumol and Bowen's *Performing Arts: The Economic Dilemma*, Thomas Gale Moore's *The Economics of the American Theatre* and Jack Poggi's *Theatre in America*, have begun to fill gaps that have existed much too long. In terms of practical guides and hard-core information, other recent books have finally provided interested readers with sound reference material, most notably *Performing Arts Management and Law*. edited by Joseph Taubman, and Donald Farber's *Producing on Broadway* and *From Option to Opening.*

Each chapter in this book could be expanded into a full volume and it is hoped that such volumes will be forthcoming. In my opinion, however, the forest should be viewed before the trees. Consequently, I have tried to convey a comprehensive picture of what is, by all counts, a highly diversified industry. So diverse, in fact, that it can't even decide how to spell its own name. (These pages favor *theatre* as opposed to *theater*.) But there is also a great, if largely invisible, interdependence among the different branches of American theatre. Community theatre contributes to the nature of broad-based attitudes and support for professional theatre; college theatre is an increasingly substantial factor in the determination of professional standards and practices; and resident theatres are setting new trends that are restructuring and revitalizing the profession. The commercial theatre is reflecting all of this, indeed is dependent on it, while it continues to serve as showcase and wholesaler for the entire industry.

It is a good time to ponder the whole industry from a structural point of view—precisely because it is changing—and it is always wise to ask: What are we moving away from and what are we moving toward?

Recently, a colleague of mine said that the best thing about working in theatre is never having to worry about what to do on a day off—there are none. It could also be said that, despite demanding work and twenty-five-hour days, every one of them is a holiday. This is true because theatre is a profession that abounds with an unusually high number of wonderfully kind and interesting people. I have been fortunate to know many of them. I have avoided the use of footnotes in this volume because I would not know where to stop: each and every sentence was, I suppose, inspired by somebody. Naturally, it is impossible to acknowledge everyone who has contributed in some way to a book of this size, but several people should be mentioned.

I wish to thank Professor Edward O. Lutz of Brooklyn College for his assistance on Part III and Willard Swire of Actors' Equity Association for his helpful comments regarding Part II. Among many whose friendship for me was severely and unfairly tested by my constant requests for commentary and editorial assistance, I am especially grateful to Jane Graham, James Fiore, David Conte and Edelmiro Olavarria. During the past two years, my work on this book has enjoyed the assistance and protection that only a loyal and efficient secretary can provide and I must thank two such women: Sally Feigen (winters) and Judith Watson (summers). And thank heavens I found Barbara Spencer Mack, a typist who can spell!

Much material in this book is based on lecture notes prepared for my graduate students in theatre management at Brooklyn College, who should be praised for tolerating me while they taught me how much I didn't know. Similarly, I must thank several thousand professional performers and hundreds of other employees who have labored under my administration without once taking me to court. By way of gratitude, I have been careful to disguise any people or places I have used to illustrate my points in this manuscript.

For better or for worse, my career as a theatre manager would never have continued without encouragement from many, many people. First and last, I am grateful for having been blessed with parents and grandparents who knew how to encourage and strengthen my fondest dreams. I must thank the late Mrs. Florence B. Pegram for providing the resources for my early European travels. I am grateful to my longtime friend and employer, Mrs. Sidney Gordon, a motivating force of no mean proportion. So often, while sitting at my desk and wondering how to explain something, I have thought back to the words of colleagues and teachers who have been an influential part of my life. And of the many, my heartfelt gratitude compels me to mention Mary Porter, Herman Krawitz, Tom DeGaetani, Joseph W. Scott, Edward Lutz, Rudolf Bing, the late Stephen Joseph, the late Willian Van Lennop, Elliot Norton, Charles Shattuck and the man who taught me by his own example the definition of humanist, Dante Negro.

Of course the greatest blessing any author can have is an association with an editor who can make deadlines sound as enticing as an ice cream sundae. Ralph Pine, the Managing Editor of Drama Book Specialists/Publishers, was a fellow student in Boston. He directed a play I had written in college and inspired me to stay at home on my twenty-first birthday—which also happened to be Christmas Day—doing rewrites. Now he has succeeded in keeping me off the streets for over two years. But we are still talking and still missing the same cocktail parties.

While many people, both knowingly and unknowingly, have contributed to the contents of this work, and my indebtedness to them is considerable, any errors, omissions or misconceptions are, of course, my own responsibility. I do not doubt for a moment that someone else could have written a more definitive book on this subject. But until that book is published, I can only hope that mine will assist those people—God bless them all—who labor for the living theatre.

# THEATRE MANAGEMENT IN AMERICA

## PRINCIPLE AND PRACTICE

# Part I

# Fundamentals of Theatrical Producing

# CHAPTER ONE

# The Idea for Theatre

*Why* a theatrical production is originated often determines its success. Thousands of plays are produced in America every year. Some engage professionals who earn their living in the theatre, most utilize students or amateurs; some are laudable examples of theatre art, the vast majority range from mindless diversion to worthless spectacle. Some producers and managers become involved in theatre almost by accident, some as the result of long and careful preparation. Compared to other professionals, such as lawyers, teachers and economists, it seems evident that too many producers and managers begin their careers haphazardly. Why? What motivates people to seek a career in the theatre business?

## ▪ GETTING THE IDEA

The idea behind a theatrical career, production or organization is the *why* of it. Every theatre, play or production begins as one man's idea. But ideas have a life of their own. They are subject to very unscientific and unpredictable behavior as they are passed from person to person. Yet, few people succeed without the initial impetus of a reasonably clear idea. If a project fails—and failure occurs frequently in theatre—it is probably because the original idea was lost, misguided or compromised along the way.

3

An idea for theatre requires that certain fundamental decisions be made before it is put into action. These will be related to at least one of the following questions:

| | |
|---|---|
| *Why?* | The idea |
| *What?* | The artistic form it will take |
| *Where?* | The place where it will be expressed |
| *When?* | The time when it will be expressed |
| *Who?* | The people who will express and manage it |
| *Wherewith?* | The cost |

The present chapter deals with the first of these questions.

### THE PROFIT MOTIVATION ▪

To the serious artist and to many societies throughout history, the notion of reaping financial profit from art has been either secondary or nonexistent. It is nonetheless a very old notion that, for theatre, dates back to ancient Rome when state-appointed impresarios were given a budget to produce a particular spectacle which they attempted "to bring in under budget" and thus "pocket" the remainder. In contemporary America at least half of all theatrical productions are originated primarily to "make money." Profit is not a very good primary motivation if one hopes to produce something of artistic merit. It is also a rather peculiar motivation in light of statistics that prove how few theatrical productions show any real profit, whether on Broadway, on the campus or in a community theatre. From the investor's viewpoint, theatre is a highly speculative venture. It has about the same potential for realizing a return as one might expect, say, from betting on horses. Obviously, there are some differences in the theatre and some benefits that might not result from a day at the races. For one thing the loss of money in a theatrical enterprise is tax deductible for the investor and, at least for the very wealthy, may be a more interesting way to accumulate deductions than investing in other businesses. For the Broadway producer and his backers there may be psychic rewards associated with involvement in a creative project, social rewards resulting from acquaintanceships with interesting and celebrated people or cultural rewards when the project is artistically successful.

Like gambling on horses, theatrical investing involves a high degree of risk. But there is a big difference between the professional investor or gambler and the neophyte. In the commercial theatre there are producers, playwrights, designers and actors who possess high qualifications and sound backgrounds. That makes their ventures a better risk than others, just as some jockeys, horses and racetracks are, to the person who takes the trouble to study them, better than others. Yet, both fields are littered with stories of dark horses that have won as well as highly qualified contenders that have lost. The theatrical investor should know the odds against him and—in the case of commercial New York theatre—the law now requires that he be informed of them through a prospectus or offering circular. This document states the probability of success for theatrical ventures in general and, in specific terms, gives the backgrounds of the principals in the venture and their plans for the production in question. Despite such formalities, most investors base their decisions upon intuition or upon a friendship with someone connected with the production.

If a majority of professional theatre productions in New York are originated for financial gain, it is equally true that countless stock, community and amateur plays produced across the nation begin for the same reason. Many professional stock theatres, as well as college and civic theatres, merely engage plays or musical groups that have been pre-packaged. Their productions arrive at the theatre just minutes or hours before the first performance, travel complete with their own performers, costumes, sets and special equipment and usually feature well-known stars. In such cases the producer serves merely as a wholesaler who is buying a finished product and attempting to resell it at a profit, whether for himself or for an organization. This process eliminates the creativity involved in originating a production, but it may provide the satisfaction of exposing a community to professional theatre of a higher quality than is otherwise available to it. When profit is the primary motive for importing packaged shows—which is more often the case with theatre productions than, say, with touring operatic or symphonic productions—the producer tends to engage what is most popular or faddish rather than what is artistically viable. And because profit *is* the stimulant most of the time—from both the producer's *and* the performer's point of view—an enormous amount of second-rate theatre is packaged and sent to the hinterlands. Broadway hits, performed with skill if not always with genius, are transformed into touring vehicles for film and television personalities unused to live audiences and untutored in the art of acting, though their salaries may be so astronomical as to make the producer's margin of profit negligible.

On the amateur level, including schools, clubs, charities, social organizations and some community theatres, most plays or "shows" aim to raise money for a favorite local cause: new uniforms for the football team, instruments for the school band, the senior class trip to Washington, a new dance floor for the Elks Club. It is more than a little depressing to realize that the overwhelming majority of Americans who have seen any live theatre at all have seen only amateur performers with little if any previous experience, groups organized for one production alone and motivated by reasons that bear only the most casual relationship to the art and craft of theatre.

Broadway tycoons, then, are not the only people who see theatre in terms of a dollar sign.

### THE SOCIAL MOTIVATION ▪

There is nothing reprehensible about the wish to achieve eminence in a chosen field or to earn a decent living in it. The person who lacks such motivation stands little chance for success. But as a primary reason for entering theatre, the social urge, like the financial one, is both superficial and selfish. Although ego is essential to the artist, so is a considerable selflessness. This is particularly true in the performing arts where quality depends on the collaboration of many people. Yet, this need for collaboration appears to be less understood in theatre than in other branches of the performing arts. It is easier to comprehend, for example, that a third violinist in a symphony orchestra must perform according to the dictates of the conductor and the score than to comprehend that a supporting actor must function in an equally disciplined and selfless manner. Is it because a sour note in the middle of a symphony is more obvious to us than a line that is slurred in the theatre? Are we more familiar with the works of Beethoven than with those of Shakespeare? Do we go more often to the symphony, the choral concert, the ballet than to the theatre?

Why does the public appear to expect less from actors than from other performing artists? Perhaps because our theatre expects less from itself. Generally, it expects that actors can perform with much less training if any at all, with a much shorter apprenticeship if any at all, and for a much lower salary if any at all, than it demands from other performers. Such attitudes are possible because so many young actors are more interested in approbation than in the art form they presume to serve. If a person wishes to succeed in serious music, opera or ballet, he must expend an enormous amount of time, money and energy before he even dares hope for an audition with a leading professional organization. The local Barrymore in Peoria, Illinois, however, can and often does go directly from the lead in a high school play to an audition in New York. Occasionally he may even land a role and become an overnight success. The theatre is the only branch of live performing arts in which this can happen (excluding the field of pop music), but it happens far less frequently than beginners would like to believe. Most stars and hits that are acclaimed an "overnight success" are, in fact, the result of long years of patience, faith and self-sacrifice. But the press, the public and the American temperament are fond of Cinderella stories and prefer to believe them, even to the detriment of their sense of reality. The need for recognition is a normal human trait. The belief that this need will be fulfilled by Prince Charming at a palace ball is not.

Apart from social or public recognition in a narrow sense, a number of people involve themselves in theatre to gain social prestige in a broader sense. Just as members of Louis XV's court were flattered to appear in Madame du Pompadour's theatricals, people today may feel social pride in being cast in a community theatre production, a conspicuous means of demonstrating one's sense of social or civic responsibility. (Richard Nixon's only direct experience in theatre, for example, came from joining a community theatre group in order to meet a girl named "Pat.") Either as a Broadway producer or as a member of a little theatre club in California, involvement promises entrée into social cliques. More than a few have become "angels," purchased a summer theatre or joined a local drama group for this reason alone. Many civic, college and community theatre buildings have been financed by generous gifts from wealthy benefactors who wished to assert their social prominence. Philanthropy is an admirable activity and theatre would be much poorer without it, but when a theatre building is merely the result of one man's desire to memorialize himself, when it does not coincide with a public and professional desire or when it is constructed in a manner that is not realistically suitable, it may prove to be mere folly.

Theatre is by nature and necessity a public activity but, paradoxically, when its participants attempt merely to use the public for personal gain the art of theatre is lost.

### THE EDUCATIVE MOTIVATION ▪

There are many ways theatre may be used to educate an audience. All art has the potential to influence public opinion. That explains why dictators of totalitarian governments are so quick to censor or ban artistic expressions that fail to conform with their own views. But there is a vast difference between art that educates and what might be called "educative art." It is the difference between a production of Shakespeare's *Henry I V*, for instance, and a session in psychodrama. The first is presumably motivated by a desire to achieve artistic standards (although a variety of secondary objectives are both possible and valid), while the second type is organized primarily to achieve some specific, nonartistic objective. So long as one has a clear understanding of the real purpose and value of educative theatre it can be a helpful and unique method of accomplishing a goal. Educative theatre includes such diverse forms as *the industrial show* (intended to demonstrate or promote manufactured products), *the psychodrama* (intended as a psychologist's device or type of therapy in which a patient is encouraged to "lose himself" in a role and thereby to express his problems subconsciously), *the role-playing exercise* (in which participants consciously assume roles in order to profit from a more lifelike situation than a book or lecture might provide), *the agit-prop production* (intended to disseminate propaganda by theatrically agitating an audience and thereby moving it to action) and *guerrilla theatre* (also political in content and propagandistic in purpose). In most instances these types of theatre do not employ professional actors (though the actors often possess well-tempered skills); performances do not take place in theatres or places ordinarily used; and the audiences do not pay an admission charge. Educative theatre, in short, deals first in the promotion of products or ideas or attempts to instruct through the medium of theatrical involvement. Artistic achievement in this type of theatre is secondary and sometimes even inappropriate.

### THE HUMANIST MOTIVATION ∙

A humanist is a man who believes that truth can be discovered at least as quickly and well through the medium of a painting, a symphony or a play as it can through the medium of a geological equation. An artist is a humanist who is as passionately committed to the discovery of truth as is the scientist. While not everyone who works in the theatre need strive to be an artist in the fullest sense, everyone should possess a notion of the humanistic nature of art and of its ultimate quest. This is the first requisite for serious theatre and it allows little room for self-centered social, financial or political motivation. Truth is fiercely impersonal. Because both the arts and sciences are committed to the same end, they have frequently been of great benefit to each other. In fact, it may be regretted that theatre does not more often approach its problems with scientific thoroughness and that aspiring actors are not more often imbued with the intellectual discipline common to the scientist. It would seem that any theatre practitioner motivated by a passion for truth and belief in the humanist approach would progress further than the person propelled by more selfish motivations. If something is not worth doing for its own intrinsic value—such as building a theatre or producing a play— then one should be honest about the limited and probably selfish reasons for doing it and seriously question whether it is worth doing it at all.

Unfortunately, the American penchant for practicality has tended to create a society driven by the need to "justify" everything that is not *obviously* practical, especially those things that give pleasure and joy. The Protestant Ethic, a force that kept America ticking for a long time, was, after all, established by the progenitors of men who went around smashing art works in the cathedrals of Europe. Anti-aestheticism is still manifest in the discomfort that many Americans experience unless they are able to attach a financial, social or political value both to their possessions and to their activities. But this attitude may be losing its dominance. New generations are measuring the quality of life according to the beauty and joy it contains as well as the material benefits. In search of a greater realization of life, more and more people are coming to understand—as some have always understood— the humanizing force of the arts and their ability to expand man's consciousness and sense of being human in a way that is both rewarding and penetrating. A humanist, then, is also a generalist, a person of deep intentions and broad horizons.

## ■ STATING THE IDEA

### CLARITY OF PURPOSE ■

After one has acknowledged what motivates a theatre project, more specific objectives should be formulated. In commercial theatre, where profit is the motive, the producer finds this unnecessary—though it should, of course, be practiced by the artistic personnel in commercial theatre. Administrators and artistic directors in all types of noncommercial theatre, however, must concern themselves with clarifying and stating their objectives, their methodology. To ignore this fundamental task (and many organizations do) is to risk the life of a project and to guarantee confusion. It is also to admit the absence of a plan. While the originating idea for theatre is likely to be the brainchild of a single person, it must eventually be discussed and subscribed to by others who will play leading roles in the project. There is bound to be disagreement regarding particulars. Any broad goal requires considerable thrashing out before all those who are a party to it arrive at mutual understanding. Those who remain in fundamental disagreement should be eliminated from the project as soon as possible. Human relations being what they are, such action is difficult and painful more often than not. Philosophical honesty is, unfortunately, rare, and unity of purpose among people a singular accomplishment. But it can be achieved if one is stubbornly unwilling to proceed without it—even at the risk of losing potential participants, diminishing initial enthusiasm or revising budgets and timetables. Unless agreement about the philosophy and objectives behind a project is reached and especially well understood between the artistic and administrative elements, at least half the organization will labor under false or wrongly construed assumptions or under none at all. The operational flaw that results when clarity of purpose is missing is the classic situation of people working at cross purposes. While formulating and publishing a clear statement of purpose may not guarantee a harmonious and successful operation, it is a vital first step in that direction.

### STATEMENT OF PURPOSE ■

After a tenable idea for theatre has been conceived and a sufficient number of key people who subscribe to it have been gathered, what is called for is a brief sentence or paragraph that clearly states the philosophical commitment of the group. It may include its primary objectives—the objectives by which the organization demands that its ultimate success or failure be measured. This embodiment of purpose should be the real tyrant of the venture. It should serve as a henchman, a chief of police that objectively, unceasingly, impersonally, demands obedience. Suppose the objective of a theatre is to produce new plays of significance but the directors of that theatre cannot discover any works they feel *are* significant. Their only honest decision is to produce no plays at all. On the other hand, if they manage to present plays that do measure up to their standards, though they meet low box office receipts and disdain from the press, they may consider their theatre a success and those who judge them honestly will respect their integrity.

While a primary goal of all theatre should be to establish and maintain standards of artistic excellence, the methodology for achieving this will vary. There are many instances in which the success of theatre is best served by compromise, but that does not include compromise in regard to fundamental goals and objectives. If this becomes necessary or desirable the original project should be dissolved and a new one organized from the beginning.

PUBLICATION OF PURPOSE •

To help maintain unity of purpose within a group, to keep a project on the road initially intended for it and to elicit germane criticism from its audience, a theatre group should take every opportunity to proclaim its objectives. Where are the most obvious and appropriate places for such statements of purpose to appear?

> The offering circular
> The charter for a theatre organization
> The constitution for a theatre group
> Brochures and other literature about the theatre
> Playbills
> Press releases
> Major advertisements
> Employment applications
> Appeals and applications for financial aid
> Operational manuals
> In the lobby
> Over the proscenium
> In the sky

If the primary motivation for theatre is the *why* of it, the declared set of objectives is the *how* of it.

## • ORGANIZING THE IDEA

When an idea for theatre can be clearly articulated and understood, when the primary motivation for activating the idea is also clear, then an appropriate type of theatre organization must be found (or founded) in which the concept may be produced in a manner consonant with the goals at hand. This is easier to accomplish if one is creating a theatre group from scratch than if one is producing within an existing organization. It is the difference between a custom-built house and a conversion job. The playwright, especially, may have considerable difficulty in finding a producer and a theatre that he considers appropriate for his work. Hence, new plays often begin on one level, in one type of organization and then move to others; or plays may be adapted to fit several different media. The problem is to find the ideal. It is not uncommon for a play to begin in an amateur theatre and then to be produced professionally. The reverse is also true.

Perhaps, like the physical law that dictates that water shall always seek its own level, it may be said that a play always finds *its* level of worth. *Waiting for Lefty, J. B.* and others may have been premiered on the amateur stage; they have since found a place in the repertory of professional theatres. Conversely, plays like *Time Out for Ginger* and *Never Too Late* were Broadway hits but have since established a life in amateur theatre and are unlikely to be revived by serious professional groups. The same rule holds for the work that goes through various media adaptations: novel, theatre piece, film, television series, *et cetera.* Several versions may prove satisfactory but in most cases only one is ideal, and this one usually works best because it most closely expresses the creator's original concept (even though it may be the adapter rather than the originator who discovers the ideal). The idea for theatre most likely to succeed, whether it is the idea behind a single production or the idea behind a producing organization, is the one that most nearly expresses or facilitates the original artistic concept.

This book defines four types of theatre organization, each with its own implicit goals, standards, motivations, administrative peculiarities and artistic potential: (1) commercial theatre, (2) stock and resident theatre, (3) college theatre and (4) community theatre. Later chapters will discuss each of these in terms of its economic and managerial structure. It is appropriate at this point to consider the broad artistic potential of each and how it may best serve an idea for theatre.

### THE COMMERCIAL THEATRE ■

How well can artistic excellence fare in a system that is tied to a profit-and-loss type of economy? Fitfully, at best. So long as a large number of theatre people place financial reward or self-recognition before the art itself, the commercial theatre will continue more or less as we know it today. The expertise of a producer in the commercial theatre lies primarily in his ability to prejudge the desires of his potential consumer market. The product itself may be good or bad. It is only necessary that the consumer market be sufficient to create a demand that will result in a profit. It is not the commercial producer's business to evaluate the quality of a product or the standards by which the public judges it; he is not concerned with the growth and development of talent or bothered about the spiritual and intellectual needs of the artist—not unless such matters, in his opinion, can be translated into profit. The commercial theatre industry, in comparison with others, spends little time and money on what is called "product development." While the automobile, cosmetic, drug and other industries consider it self-defeating not to invest in pure research, in a goodly amount of laboratory experimentation, the commercial producer who maintains a young playwright on stipend or underwrites a workshop theatre that may eventually turn out highly marketable plays or performers is rare indeed. In this regard, the commercial theatre is among our most irresponsible industries. Its practice is merely to skim the cream from the produce of noncommercial theatre and should it turn out to be sour, to throw it back. Nonetheless, the faults of the system cannot be blamed on producers as much as on the people whose participation in the system continue to make it possible. So long as people remain largely satisfied with the present quality of commercial productions, a great deal that is cheap and shoddy wlll continue to see the lights of New York, not to mention the rest of America. The challenge and responsibility for change does not rest with the public, the producer or the critic but with the theatre artist himself. The public demands what it has been taught to desire, the producer attempts to satisfy the desire, the critic attempts to explain the desire. Only the artist has any real power to initiate, interrupt, interpret or change the desire.

The financial and material resources of commercial theatre have long been legend. Broadway production budgets that approach a million dollars are not uncommon. An ever-increasing percentage of these budgets is drained by administrative, legal and inflationary costs; neither the artist nor the physical theatre plant has benefited significantly from higher expenditures or from higher profits. Due to this factor, the majority of New York's commercial theatres fall far below the physical standards of many noncommercial theatre plants and only a small percentage of performers in commercial theatre find it possible to make it their sole source of income. But, New York continues to function as the leading showcase for an impressive amount of talent in the performing arts; it continues as the leading supplier of talent for films, television and stock. In terms of supplying new plays, it services most of the nation's noncommercial theatres. This seems to prove that, despite almost overwhelming administrative and legal complexities, not to mention an extremely capitalistic distribution of profit, the system can still be mastered to advantage, and productions of considerable artistic merit can still result.

## STOCK AND RESIDENT THEATRE ▪

"Stock theatre" generally means those summer and winter seasonal operations that employ Equity actors. "Resident theatre" is a term commonly used to indicate those operations that maintain a permanent company of Equity actors who usually perform a number of different plays in series or in alternating sequence. Both systems evolved from the nineteenth century English and American stock companies of professional actors that performed in their own "home" theatre, retained the same actors for long periods of time and presented a standard number of plays in repertory while adding new ones on occasion. Most stock theatres today, however, do not maintain resident companies, do not perform plays in repertory and do not utilize stock scenery, costumes or properties with any real consistency. Many resident theatres today do not maintain a permanent company for more than a single season, frequently engage guest performers for specific roles and often do not present plays in repertory rotation or repeat a production after its first run of performances. Nonetheless, *stock, repertory* and *resident* are terms that have established meaning both within the industry and for the general public. The terms also connote the quality of what is produced. Stock, straw hat or summer theatre, as it is variously labeled, implies for many a kind of theatre that is "old hat" ' because it presents hits left over from Broadway featuring stars left over from television and Hollywood. The method of producing in such stock theatres as the Cape Cod Melody Tent in Hyannis, the Mineola Playhouse on Long Island and the Westport Country Playhouse in Connecticut have changed considerably over the past twenty years. But artistic quality remains at a low level. On the other hand, "repertory theatre" has come to possess a more sophisticated, serious and long-haired connotation. And theatres like the Tyrone Guthrie in Minneapolis and the American Shakespeare Festival Theatre in Stratford, Connecticut, do at least aim for higher artistic standards than the stock theatres.

There are numerous nonprofessional, non-Equity stock theatres that are designed along the same lines as theatres which employ Equity actors. The Provincetown Playhouse in Massachusetts is a good example. It employs a resident company of nonprofessional actors each season, operates in a small plant, is headed by a permanent producer and presents productions of a reasonably serious nature. The dinner theatres, which are invariably less serious and more commercially oriented and may or may not employ Equity actors, are also in this category.

Finally, operating in small houses, with flexibility of producing and casting and often under the continuing management of a highly dedicated and skilled artistic director, is that type of professional theatre in which the building it uses and the corporation that operates it remain permanent, though its plays are not repeated and many of the performers are employed for only one production. It may be a healthy sign that no label has yet been coined to classify this third derivative of the stock-repertory tradition. Of all segments of live theatre today, this type of management may come closest to offering a new and promising framework for artistic achievement. From an organizational viewpoint, it falls into the category of professional, resident theatre. Companies of this type include Joseph Papp's New York Shakespeare Festival, Paul Baker's Dallas Theatre Center, Michael David and Robert Kalfin's Chelsea Theatre Center in Brooklyn and Ellen Stewart's La Mama Experimental Theatre Club in Greenwich Village.

Within the wide spectrum of stock and repertory theatre, then, there is a great range of quality and purpose. Summer and winter stock theatres as well as the dinner theatres are, for the most part, blatantly commercial. Most are operated by private corporations for private profit. All other theatres of the stock-repertory type are operated by nonprofit corporations in which the profits, if any, are poured back into the organization (though not necessarily to the benefit of the participants).

While there is lots of room at the commercial end of the scale for the Establishment, as it were, there is also ample room at the other end for the radically experimental. As will be shown in chapter 6, the nineteenth century stock theatre never fulfilled its potential either artistically or economically and America has never been able to boast a repertory theatre of any national, much less international, significance. It is unlikely that the several types of theatre organizations that consciously seek to imitate traditional stock and repertory systems will succeed any better. The earlier stock companies are simply not worth imitating and the leading repertory theatres of the world, such as the *Comédie Française* and the *Kabuki,* are so steeped in indigenous cultural tradition that they are impossible to imitate—least of all in twentieth century America. The smaller professional groups, experimenting with new plays and new styles of production, are those most likely to influence the quality of American theatre and American drama, primarily because they possess the resources, the courage and the inclination to strike out in new directions.

## COLLEGE THEATRE ∎

If the much-publicized "cultural boom" of the sixties was anywhere realized, it was on the campus and in our public school systems. It has been estimated that as many as two thousand new theatres and auditoriums were constructed or under construction by the end of the 1960's, the vast majority built by schools and colleges. Many, of course, were constructed as multi-purpose affairs and include everything from theatres to gymnasiums. But an impressive number of new theatres, fine arts centers and performing arts complexes on the campus are first-rate facilities. Like the massive civic complexes (of which the John F. Kennedy Center for the Performing Arts in Washington will probably remain the most recent example for some time), the construction boom on the campus was a manifestation of what has been aptly described as "the edifice complex." At least each auditorium at Lincoln Center, except, most notably, the Vivian Beaumont, was originally designed to house an established artistic company. In too many cases new theatres have been planned, financed and nearly completed before—almost as an afterthought—it has occurred to someone to think seriously about the performance programs that should or might fill them. Ideally and realistically, this process should be reversed if the results are to be worthwhile.

College theatres not only offer lavish facilities but also provide a tie-in with larger institutions that can furnish an enormous amount of fiscal, administrative, material and human resources found in no other type of theatre organization. One could fill an entire volume simply by listing the vast variety of people, services and equipment that stand behind a small theatre on, for example, a campus of the University of California or of the City University of New York. But what of the artistic quality of most college theatre productions? Considering the available resources on the one hand and the fact that school plays are performed largely by amateurs on the other, the overall quality is disappointing. Although scenic and technical standards may be extremely high, the end result falls short. The reasons for this apparent paradox are mixed. The campus theatre may be attempting to appeal to too many types of audience or it may overly compromise its priorities, especially those between its obligation to teach and its obligation to entertain. Due to its affiliation with largely tax-supported and politically controlled institutions it may lack the freedom and independence required for artistic integrity or it may get bogged down in bureaucratic red tape. Whether or not related to such common frustrations, the lack of artistic achievement in college theatre stems fundamentally from an absence of clear and single-minded purpose. This is followed by a lack of sound theatre management so common that it appears to be endemic.

From the audience point of view campus theatre either provides performances that are not easily available elsewhere or a chance to see one's child "perform." From the faculty point of view it provides employment opportunities that are not readily available elsewhere. But what does it provide for its student-participants? Surely, the notion that aspiring professionals can be trained by amateurs is a perverse one. Is theatre a trade, an art or a profession? Do theatre courses belong with the liberal arts, the humanities or the fine arts? If an artist can be trained or "educated" in any ordinary sense, is this best accomplished in an institution or by apprenticeship to a master? What are the differences between the conservatory or specialized school approach in performing arts education and the liberal arts college approach? Judging from their nervous flirtation with performing arts curricula to date, most universities appear to lack clear answers to such questions. Yet, nothing will have a stronger impact on the future of the performing arts than how they are treated—or mistreated—by our educational institutions.

### COMMUNITY AND AMATEUR THEATRE ▪

A nonprofessional theatre is, simply, one comprised of people who do not derive their income from it and do not spend most of their time engaged in it. There are two distinct categories: (1) nonprofessional groups that present plays with some regularity and (2) nonprofessional groups that are organized on a one-time basis to present a play or a show for some special purpose. The former represents what is known as "community theatre" and the latter falls under the heading of "amateur theatre" (though both types are amateur, or nonprofessional).

In spite of limited resources and volunteer labor, the artistic quality of many community theatre productions can be surprisingly good. The first major concerted attempt to stimulate community theatre in America was the Federal Theatre Project, organized during the depression under the auspices of the Works Progress Administration Act. Although it ultimately collapsed under a barrage of political criticism and pressure, it did succeed in demonstrating that amateurs and professionals working together can make meaningful contributions to the art. The annual production of Paul Green's *The Lost Colony* in North Carolina, an outdoor symphonic drama similar in spirit to the passion plays presented at Oberammergau, represents community theatre in its truest sense, as do some of the emerging street and people's theatre groups. Often, however, the local theatre club tends to produce recent Broadway musicals and comedies and places little emphasis on the continuing development of its individual members, either in terms of their abilities or their knowledge of theatre and dramatic literature.

Children's theatre companies that utilize adult performers, though they are often headed by a full-time director, also fall into the category of amateur theatre. Even those that earn considerable income and operate under Equity contracts often possess the unmistakable mark of amateurism. In contrast to the commercially motivated companies is the professional group that presents performances specially adapted for children, such as the Metropolitan Opera Studio Company, the Joffrey Ballet or the children's concerts popularized by the New York Philharmonic under Leonard Bernstein. The artistic quality of these performances is strikingly superior to the trite and condescending quality of most troupes that call themselves "professional children's theatre."

When nonprofessional theatre operates under the guidance of a dedicated and knowledgeable leader, whether he is himself a professional or not, when work is carried on with an honest realization of the limitations at hand, when the group is dedicated to theatre for its own sake and not merely trying to ape the commercial stage, the results should at least prove satisfactory. Certainly, there is nothing heinous about amateur theatre as such, for it can provide a celebration of life that the average citizen may be missing in his other activities. This goal alone may justify the organization of an amateur group.

## ▪ FUNDING THE IDEA

Budgets and bookkeeping are not among the most glamorous aspects of theatre, but they represent the practical core of any production plan. If motivation is the *why* of an idea, and organization is the *how* of it, then money is the *wherewith*. It is axiomatic that money management is a necessary element in all types of theatre; it is also that aspect of theatre about which there is the smallest interest and skill among theatrical workers. Everyone is familiar with the saying that "if it is worth doing, it is worth doing well." Applied to theatrical production, adherence to this principle requires the expenditure of money. Just as it is dishonest to compromise the basic goals of an organization simply "to get something onto the boards," so it is foolhardy and self-defeating to begin a production knowing that funds for it will be inadequate. But this frequently happens because nobody associated with the project is capable of translating artistic goals into realistically estimated costs.

As the type of organization formed should directly relate to the goals of the venture, so the fiscal structure also must be consonant with the motivating idea. It would be hypocritical, for instance, to dedicate a theatre to civic or educational ideals and then to operate it as a profit-taking enterprise. Several Broadway producers are fond of arguing that when non-profit theatres, such as the Vivian Beaumont, the Ahmanson Theatre at the Los Angeles County Music Center or the Eisenhower Theatre at the John F. Kennedy Center for the Performing Arts present big stars in popular hits they offer unfair competition to commercial producers, who must operate without the subsidization or tax advantages enjoyed by nonprofit theatres. It poses an interesting question.

Whether the aim is to show a profit for individual investors or to achieve some higher goal, which methods of fiscal structuring are most commonly used in the theatre business?

PROFIT-TAKING VENTURES •

The main reason for forming a corporation as opposed to a company is to limit the personal liability of the owners and to insure the continuation of an enterprise beyond the natural lives of its founders. A corporation is a legal device that may show profit or go bankrupt, that may be sued or not or that may be sold in part or *in toto,* quite separate from the personal estate of the individual owner or investor. The two types of corporation discussed in this book are the privately-owned, profit-taking corporations and the public or private nonprofit corporation. The former is one that seeks to earn profits and then divide these among its investors in proportion to their investment or share in it; the latter also may show a profit but may not award its profits as such to corporate investors or officers (though it obviously may increase their salaries and benefits).

Commercial theatre productions in New York operate under a device known as the Limited Partnership Agreement.* Devised by Attorney John Wharton and sometimes called "the Wharton Agreement," the Limited Partnership Agreement is the simplest means yet invented for a commercial producer to cope with the law and with such agencies as the Securities Exchange Commission. Aside from the general partners, investors in this type of theatrical entity may not themselves be active participants in the project being financed. In previous centuries many theatrical companies were financed by means of a shareholding scheme. In early American theatre, the investors were usually actors in the company itself. Although this sys-

*See chapter 5.

tem creates a more personalized business and it is still practiced by a few theatre groups, it is not feasible as a method for financing extremely expensive ventures. Too, as the actor-managers of early American theatre companies learned, when a company is comprised of shareholding actors who possess the right to establish policy and make decisions by vote, the manager or artistic head is denied the autocratic power necessary in most theatrical endeavors. They learned, as Rudolf Bing once phrased it, that "a theatre should be a democracy—run by one man!" Using the Wharton Agreement, the producers (being the general partners) exercise total control.

Stock theatres, road houses and children's theatre companies that aim to make a profit are formed as private corporations, but the owners are usually limited to one or two persons who are the sole investors, officers and directors. Complete autocracy is again possible. But the profit motive, together with the fear of losing what may be a sizable personal investment, prevent much risk or experimentation and also much good theatre.

### NONPROFIT VENTURES ▪

Nonprofit corporations are not organized in order to go bankrupt or lose money any more than are the profit corporations. But they do confess a greater awareness of financial risk. While they aim to remain solvent, they vary in the amount of capital and collateral that they maintain—and their holdings are also dictated in varying degrees by government regulations. Recent laws, for example, have made it more difficult for nonprofit corporations to be used by wealthy individuals as a tax dodge. They must be active according to their stated objectives, which is to say that they must regularly expend a certain percentage of their holdings. All public or tax-supported institutions, religious organizations and charities—and hence all theatres associated with these—are nonprofit structures operated in trust.

Aside from being comparatively selfless in nature, the privately controlled nonprofit corporation possesses numerous advantages as a fiscal and legal structure for serious theatre projects. In contrast to profit-taking corporations the nonprofit corporation, for example, is free from the burden of considerable taxation, can more easily recruit volunteer help, will more likely receive gifts and donations from individuals, is eligible for financial assistance from private foundations and government agencies and stands a greater chance of establishing itself as an ongoing institution that will outlive its founders.

The most obvious disadvantage of operating a theatre as a nonprofit structure is that the artistic director will be required to function under a board of directors or trustees. If that usually austere and frequently uninformed body is willing to allow the director considerable freedom in dictating policy, the enterprise has a fighting chance to run smoothly and successfully. But, as is often the case, if there is a great deal of interference from the board, the result may be internal dissatisfaction and a low quality of stage production.

## ▪ WHEN THE IDEA BECOMES A WORKABLE PLAN

Any idea for theatre, be it for a play, a production, a building or an organization, is a special idea. Potentially, it can enlighten, enhance and expand the lives of many people. But is it a feasible idea?

The hopeful producer or several managers of a project will do well to reexamine the idea behind it before turning to the arduous business of staffing, casting, book-keeping and advertising; before getting lost in a hailstorm of decisions about dimmer boards, acoustics, air conditioning systems and ticket computers; before becoming upset over zoning laws, building permits, fire laws and labor unions. Are answers easily forthcoming to the six W's: why, what, where, when, who, wherewith? Has the idea been tested and tried as much as possible without actually being put into full operation? Surprisingly, as many "good ideas" are disallowed when put to the test as "crazy ideas" are proved workable. But no idea has the magical power to translate *itself* into action; this must be done by its agents.

# CHAPTER TWO

# The Manager
# for the Idea

Theatre became big business toward the end of the nineteenth century, when virtually all control rested in the hands of a few profit-minded producers. Predictably, the essential humanity of the theatre and its artists suffered considerably. The men who comprised the Theatrical Syndicate and the Shubert brothers were businessmen *in* the theatre but not *of* the theatre, a fact that formed a schism between the business and artistic elements of the profession. Exploitation of the many by the few was a widespread phenomenon that permeated every branch of the labor market and caused, by the late nineteenth and early twentieth centuries, a rash of worker demonstrations, strikes and the growth of labor unions. Symptoms of labor dissatisfaction occurred in theatre as in other industries.

But is theatre an industry? Until the invention and growth of electronic entertainment, it cannot be claimed that the machine age caught up with the performing arts, and it may still be argued that the incandescent light bulb was the last invention significantly to influence the art of live theatre. While machines may not at first have affected the art of theatre, however, they did affect theatre as a business, and this reality caught actor-managers so unawares that they soon lost all control over the enterprise. Suddenly, a new kind of expert was required—a man familiar with train schedules, geography, the national theatre map and other matters unknown to the average manager of a single acting company. Such an expert was a necessity because of changing times and an evil only because, as it happened, men who assumed the job were not "of the theatre."

Quantitatively, theatre activity increased manyfold under the guidance of business experts and with the advent of greater mobility created by a booming transportation industry. Qualitatively, it got nowhere. Today, the business tycoon is still a force to be dealt with in commercial theatre, but he is no longer the only force. Nonetheless, most theatrical artists continue to regard management (from the producer to the box office treasurer) with suspicion and distrust and most can cite numerous experiences with theatre administrators that illustrate the lack of sympathy and understanding between artists and management. Often, however, the blame should be shared. If only a minority of administrators possess an honest and selfless commitment to the theatre, so only a minority of performers possess even a rudimentary understanding of the theatre's economic and administrative realities.

## ▪ THE THIRD-CENTURY MANAGER

The actor-managers who controlled the first century of professional theatre in America, roughly from 1750 to 1850, were too naïve about business affairs to effect a successful transition from an agrarian to an industrialized America. The businessmen who replaced them and controlled professional theatre for the second hundred years, roughly from 1850 to 1950, eventually deserted live theatre for more lucrative enterprises when theatre ceased to offer easy profits. Beginning in the 1950s, a new breed of manager-producer started to evolve.

Several decades ago, Bernard Shaw defined the role of a manager by commenting that every artistic director in theatre should be followed around by a hard-minded businessman whose main job should be to cut all production budgets by half. And that is essentially what the second-century manager did, thereby creating a villainous, penny-squeezing, Scrooge-like image of theatre managers and producers which retains a certain validity to this day. But, more and more, we are coming to the realization that, while economy remains important, the manager must assume other responsibilities if live theatre is to survive and prosper according to the needs of society. The Rockefeller Panel Report, *The Performing Arts: Problems and Prospects,* published in 1965, shows cognizance of these new responsibilities by defining a good arts manager as

> a person who is knowledgeable in the art with which he is concerned, an impresario, labor negotiator, diplomat, educator, publicity and public relations expert, politician, skilled businessman, a social sophisticate, a servant of the community, a tireless leader—becomingly humble before authority—a teacher, a tyrant, and a continuing student of the arts.

Obviously, this is no ordinary man! But, of course, art is no ordinary business.

The arts manager today must be a man of taste, sensitivity and erudition whose inclinations and education enable him to search out, recognize and develop the genius of artistic originality in whatever guise it may appear. Because the guise is likely to be unusual, if not startling, he must also possess a lion's share of courage to support and promote it. He must be a Diaghilev. Administrative, financial and promotional know-how in the arts are wasted when not modified by such qualities. An enormous amount of goodwill must be extended to artists in faith that, eventually, the negative, nineteenth-century image of a theatre manager will be replaced by that of the third-century manager. The plain fact is that artists are still justified in their defensiveness toward representatives of management.

If a person is the manager for a theatre which he himself has founded, then he must seek others who can support the objectives of his administration. But, more often, a manager is likely to join an existing company or institution, in which case he should be cross-examined by both the institution and by himself as to whether his personality, experience and philosophy are in accord with the task at hand. Only if this is true will he be able to function as translator for goals and policies between the organization and the public and between factions within the organization itself. Like a good umpire, a good manager has the ability to keep his eye on the ball and on the goal lines. When leaders of any kind in any field lose their sense of vision and purpose, those below them almost invariably follow suit. Lack of purpose, an atmosphere of insecurity, pettiness, superficiality, infighting and disunity always reflect absence of or failure in leadership. To gain respect and establish authority by consensus an uncommon amount of fairness, manifested by a willingness to sacrifice personal reward for the good of others and for the success of artistic objectives, is necessary.

## ▪ EDUCATION AND TRAINING FOR THE THIRD-CENTURY MANAGER

Leaving aside the artist and the performer for the moment, what kind of person is the third-century manager? What type of background, training and education is apt to produce a person with the qualities and capabilities to guide theatre through the rest of this century and into the next?

### LIFE EXPERIENCE ▪

Basic patterns of behavior, sympathies and directions that will eventually comprise a lifestyle are developed early. Formal education gives one the time to grow, but not always the means; at most, formal education can draw out and broaden one's inherited or acquired characteristics. We can train doctors, musicians and managers in their respective crafts, we can develop their skills, but we cannot create a scientist or a humanist as such. In the arts the widest vocabulary of human sensitivities is desirable, the deepest awareness of the needs and feelings of life, an instinctual response to the heartstrings of humanity. An early and continuing exposure to the arts and confrontation with a variety of the world's cultures and societies viewed from the known bias of one's own inherited circumstances may also broaden the humanist orientation. Certainly, a person instinctually attracted to the arts feels an urge to explore life symbolically and universally and, if his explorations are to end in discovery, he must possess the kind of courage and vision we generally associate with history's great revolutionists. While only the true artist can *express* such humanistic vision, lesser artists as well as arts managers may at least be able to recognize the visionary insights of genius, feel comfortable in their presence and confident in leading others toward them.

It is not surprising when a child of twelve says he wants to be an actor, but it would be more than precocious of him to say that he wanted to be an arts administrator. It would seem premature for a person even as a college undergraduate to select a career in arts management. Educators who endorse undergraduate degrees with a specialization in arts management run a high risk of graduating students who are merely prepared as skillful bureaucrats. The difference between a professional and a skilled laborer is that the former is, or once was, a generalist, while the latter was never anything but a specialist. Just as the pediatrician must first learn general medicine, the theatre manager must first learn the arts. The first century of American theatre managers, like the first century of American physicians, had neither the resources nor the knowledge to indulge in much specialization. They were all generalists. Second-century American managers, rather like miracle-workers and quacks were outsiders from the professional point of view. They were specialists without portfolio. The third-century manager must come from the profession he serves and remain committed to the quest that it symbolizes.

FORMAL EDUCATION ▪

High quality education at any level and at any price is difficult to obtain. Up to the college years, a broad exposure to the basic disciplines, an accumulation of basic skills and a rough realization of one's intellectual and emotional characteristics are the minimum accomplishments to be desired. Most valuable of all is the development of a compulsive, intellectual curiosity, without which it is impossible to live a full and meaningful life. Indeed, curiosity is such a primary motivating force that it can impel a person to hurdle the most overwhelming odds, including those of disadvantaged background and poor education. If it is coupled with energy and determination then extraordinary achievement is not only possible but likely.

Although college degree requirements have been relaxed in recent years, it may be hoped that the value of a liberal arts education has not been forgotten and that a student majoring in theatre will not be discouraged from relating his special interest to the liberalizing forces of history, language, literature and the sciences. Conversely, if a special interest, such as theatre, can serve as a point of departure for exploring other areas, that is fine. One may progress inductively or deductively and arrive at the same point.

An undergraduate concentration in theatre management runs the risk of limiting the student's outlook too early, but a single course in the subject as part of an undergraduate theatre program is desirable and, for the theatre major, should be mandatory. A large portion of theatre students become teachers or become involved with educational, community and amateur theatre groups. The problems they are required to solve are often of an administrative nature. A typical high school drama instructor, for example, not only coaches plays but spends an equal amount of time securing a budget from the school principal, obtaining goods at a low cost, doing publicity and guiding the administrative affairs of the school drama club. Yet many such instructors, though they may have graduated from a good theatre program in which they studied theatre history, directing, design, acting, stagecraft and dramatic literature, have had no exposure at all to theatre management.

The syllabus in Appendix A suggests what units of study might be appropriate for an undergraduate course in theatre management offered by a department of theatre in a liberal or fine arts college. Such a course should be required for all theatre majors and could be adapted to fit the needs of a music or dance department or applied to the performing arts field as a whole. Combining class lectures with field experience related to the campus theatre, the course should provide the undergraduate student with an understanding of general operational procedures and economic principles and better prepare him for a career or involvement in theatre, especially in nonprofessional theatre. It should also offer the student an opportunity to consider the field of performing arts administration for future specialization and, from the college's point of view, it should help intensify student-faculty relations through meaningful administrative collaboration.

SPECIALIZED EDUCATION ▪

Among the first to offer full graduate programs in theatre administration were the Yale School of Drama, the University of California at Los Angeles and the University of Wisconsin. Others have since followed suit. How many such programs are desirable depends upon the type of education they aim to provide and the job market awaiting graduates. Certainly, the number of full-time, top-level performing arts administrative positions is well in the hundreds. Most are held by people lacking formal education and training in the field, although experience and general background have produced a number of outstanding leaders. A dozen or so well-planned and well-taught graduate programs offered by leading colleges could guarantee a more professional, ready and better-prepared pool of management talent than now exists.

A program of study in theatre administration on either the master's degree or doctoral level should require a minimum of two years' resident study, with a third year of field work or research a desirable supplement. Students should hold an undergraduate dossier that includes at least six or eight theatre courses and should be able to produce other evidence showing a serious interest in the arts. Entrance allowances should be made for life experience, giving equivalency credit to students who have worked professionally in the field. Only those colleges with a fairly active theatre complex should attempt a full graduate program in theatre administration, since work assignments should be an integral part of the program. While field work is important, a graduate program should aim to produce students who are potential leaders in their field, not just skilled practitioners. Classroom work should encourage analytical and original thinking; known practices should be challenged by new and different theories. The list of course titles in Appendix B suggests the nucleus of a four-semester graduate program in theatre management.

The program should be strengthened by the inclusion of guest lecturers of professional eminence, by intensive work in the campus theatre and by internship with a professional, off-campus theatre that accepts management apprentices. Ideally the internship should last a full year and offer experience with two different theatre organizations. Naturally, the quality of study is dependent upon the quality of the faculty, the amount of supervisory and tutorial guidance provided outside the classroom, the quality of students accepted for matriculation and the quality and type of campus and off-campus theatre with which the program is affiliated. Because theatre administration as an area of specialized study is quite new and skilled theatre administrators are presently in demand, many leading professional and community theatres are anxious to accept apprentices or interns, many will offer them a small salary (which might be supplemented by stipends from the college) and most will open their files and meetings so the qualified intern can gain the fullest comprehension of the organization. Internships should follow the completion of course work, although the student should be required to return briefly to his campus after the internship for final evaluation by a faculty committee and to submit a thesis report related to his field work.

Training required for part-time and second-level theatre management positions (such as public school arts coordinators, arts council members, theatre chairmen and managers of nonprofessional groups) might be accomplished by short training programs and special workshops sponsored by national organizations such as the Association for College and University Concert Managers, the American Theatre Association, the Theatre Development Fund and the Performing Arts Management Institute—if such organizations could expand and intensify their training activities. Or training might be sponsored by the adult education and university extension programs in leading colleges and institutes. (The Harvard Summer School Institute in Arts Administration established such a program in 1970.) There is tremendous need for such training programs to be increased, both in quality and quantity. Best devoted to a special aspect of management, workshops can provide a valuable opportunity for practicing managers to "brush up," to learn about new developments in the field and to exchange methods and techniques of administration with their colleagues.

CONTINUING EDUCATION ■

It is easy for a busy professional to become so wrapped up in day-to-day activities that he finds little time to devote to his continuing development, both as a professional and as an individual. In the arts it is particularly important to allow time for reading, traveling, attending theatres and museums, remaining active in at least a half dozen national organizations and in numerous local groups, attending seminars, institutes and workshops and otherwise keeping abreast of the times and the profession. While maintaining an objective overview of the manager's own operation is crucial, so also is the matter of developing and polishing a viable world view by allowing time for thought and reflection and for a full life emotionally.

## ■ FUNDAMENTAL TASKS OF THEATRE MANAGEMENT

In this day of large, flashy theatres, elaborate productions and dizzying budgets, it is tempting to forget that theatre is, fundamentally, a simple matter. Only four elements are necessary in order for a theatrical performance to take place:

1. *Creative raw material* (an idea, a scenario, a script)
2. *A person to refine the material* (an actor, a dancer, a singer, a priest, a witch doctor)
3. *A place to present the material* (a theatre, a church, a barn, a street, a clearing in the woods)
4. *An audience to witness the presentation*

The more this process, this act of theatre, is formalized, the more supportive personnel, equipment and money it requires. In short, the more management it requires. A theatre manager is any person who plays a part in bringing together or facilitating two or more of the above elements leading to a theatrical performance. From the economist's point of view, he may be regarded as any person who helps bring labor and capital together in order to produce an end product. From a landlord's point of view, he is any person who manages a theatre building. Thus, he may be an agent who finds performers to interpret a particular script; he may be a local benefactor who constructs or operates a building in which actors may perform; he may be a publicity director who finds an audience for the performers; he may be a general manager who supervises the entire process from beginning to end. He is a matchmaker bringing together the idea, the artist, the place and the audience. He is any person engaged in setting goals, selecting plays, raising capital, hiring personnel or supervising and controlling a theatrical operation. All such activities are basic management tasks. Hence, many people who work in theatre function as a manager in one sense or another.

### SETTING GOALS AND OBJECTIVES ▪

Chapter 1 deals with the importance of goals and objectives in the theatre, with whether a theatre organization can state its philosophy and whether it has a clear plan of action. When the answer is no, it may fall to a newly hired managing director to see that goals and objectives are decided upon and spelled out in black and white. The organization that hires him, probably represented most tangibly by a board of directors, has every right to question the applicant's philosophy of theatre. He should request a similar explanation from the board regarding its concept of theatre. If the board is ambiguous on this point, can it accept the manager's philosophy as its own? If there is disagreement between the two parties, is it merely a matter of semantics or are the two philosophies so far apart that they cannot be reconciled? Often, a theatre or institution is so anxious to hire a new manager or artistic director that probing discussions about these questions are put aside until after the person has been hired, when of course they are bound to surface and demand attention. Much aggravation would be spared if the leaders and directors of theatre groups agreed to basic philosophical terms and objectives before going to work on specifics.

### SELECTING THE PLAYS ▪

In commercial New York theatre it is the producer's first and most important chore to find a play, or "property," that is available to him and that he wishes to present on the stage. It is a responsibility he seldom shares with anyone. While other types of theatre should begin with goals and objectives, the commercial theatre begins with the play itself, from which, like buying land on speculation, one hopes to mine a fortune. Once the commercial producer has committed himself to a play that he believes will "make money," he must purchase an option on it, thereby legally obtaining the rights to produce it. Because promising new scripts are difficult to come by, the business of searching for a property can be a full-time occupation. The active producer may read as many as ten or twenty new scripts a week for many months before selecting one for production. Scripts may be sent to him by agents, they may arrive unsolicited from aspiring playwrights or the producer may request or commission them directly. Commercial producers keep a close watch on noncommercial theatres that produce new plays, on new plays being produced in Europe and many other less obvious sources for potential commercial hits.

Tracking down and buying plays has become such a science, literally extending to every corner of the globe where theatrical productions occur, that it is virtually impossible for any new play of actual or potential worth to be produced without coming to the attention of a commercial producer. Because of this and the fact that talented dramatists are rare, it may be that there is less playwrighting talent of potential worth that goes undiscovered than of any other type of talent in the performing arts.

In noncommercial ventures, where commitment is, hopefully, toward producing good theatre rather than toward presenting one property at a time in order to show a profit, the business of selecting plays is often a shared responsibility. The goals of many groups dictate a preference for certain types of plays—new plays of social "relevance," the classics or some other broad category. Play selection in noncommercial theatres may be restricted by limitations that would be of little or no concern to the commercial producer: the talents of a resident company of actors, the preferences of a resident stage director, the technical facilities of a particular theatre, the budget.

The one person who must feel real enthusiasm for the play is the person who will direct it. It is always a mistake to assign a director to a project in which he has little faith or understanding. For this reason, it is dangerous for a community or educational theatre to elect a "play selection committee" that has the power to choose plays for production unless the director can at least veto the selections.

Most resident, college, stock and community theatre groups that produce a series of productions each year select their plays from published manuscripts. The manager or landlord of a road house, a Broadway house or a commercial stock theatre is concerned with "booking" plays from those already in production or at least in the planning phase. His selection, then, is secondary, based on other people's choices. The owner of a Broadway theatre does not ordinarily entertain playwrights, he entertains producers who own a script that they wish to present in his theatre. A commercial stock manager selects a season of plays from productions offered by so-called packagers. The college theatre that presents a professional play series can only select from available touring companies that have been organized by someone else. In other words, the people in charge of theatres such as these are not producers in the usual sense, but managers and landlords.

### RAISING THE CAPITAL ▪

Whether organized as a profit-taking venture or as a nonprofit corporation, whether the project is a puppet show in a neighborhood garage or a grand opera in a three-thousand-five-hundred-seat theatre, a certain amount of capital and material resources will be necessary. Most theatre people have worked with sufficiently impoverished production budgets to know that necessity is the mother of invention and that inventiveness can play a large part in the magic of theatre. Indeed, there is a school of thought among theatre educators that professes students learn best when made to work with severely limited resources. Perhaps. But more important than the amount of capital available for a production is how that capital is used. Fabulous sums of money, as Hollywood has proved countless times, do not automatically insure good entertainment, much less great theatre. Money alone is no more magical than an empty theatre. One is only properly excited about such resources when one has an idea about how they might be used. When the idea is forgotten and one remembers only the excitement that money or some other resource once stimulated, resources tend to be used meaninglessly or haphazardly. Hence, money is frequently spent simply because it is available and theatres are used simply because they are there. Little satisfaction is likely to result.

In most cases, theatre production expenses are paid from money earned through ticket sales. Or, capital may be donated as a gift, invested in hopes of gaining a return or earned through fund-raising drives. Labor may be organized on a volunteer or low-salaried basis and material goods may be secured and space found without the expenditure of capital. However the talents, materials and facilities necessary for a theatrical performance are found, the process is a primary responsibility of management and a very time-consuming one.

## STAFFING AND CASTING ▪

Theatre is a human enterprise. It is also a highly creative one. These factors add an extra complexity to the challenge of management in theatre. One must not only cope with all the inevitable problems of trying to get a large number of people to work together as a team but also with getting this team to create one of the most intangible and delicate of all products, the theatrical moment. The first objective in staffing and casting for a theatre must be unity and teamwork. In both areas it is advisable to fit people to available jobs and roles rather than to try to fit overly defined jobs and roles to the people available. In other words, it is much easier to redefine job requirements or the untested interpretation of an acting role than it is to insist upon preconceived requirements. Naturally, there must be a degree of conformity to a central, motivating idea. The challenge of management is to discover a medium between rigid conformity to an idea or goal and the human requirement for flexibility. Creative energy is the most difficult of all forces to place in harness and put to work.

## SUPERVISING AND CONTROLLING ▪

A final primary responsibility of theatre management is that of guiding a project or production once it has been initiated. Close vigilance over each person and aspect of the project is necessary as a basis for responsible decision-making. After the major objectives have been set, the play selected, the financing secured and the staff and cast employed, all subsequent decisions are secondary. Like it or not, the major decisions have by this time been made and, short of starting all over again, are largely irrevocable. Many projects have met failure simply because their primary *raison d'etre* was forgotten or changed midway. The business of supervising and controlling a project, then, is a matter of analyzing and correcting the weak spots and of perceiving and bolstering the strong spots. It is a matter of checking and balancing, of shifting and adapting, of inspecting and evaluating, of slowing down and speeding up—but always of pushing the project toward its intended destination.

The ideal method for managing any project is to organize the fundamental elements so thoroughly and well that, once it is under way, its directors and managers can devote their full attention to coping with minor or unexpected developments— plenty of which are certain to arise.

The ideal manager for a theatre project is not necessarily a man with a Ph.D. in Arts Administration. He does not necessarily have a background in economics or management. The ideal manager for an idea is one who embodies it and makes it work.

## ▪ TYPES OF THEATRE MANAGERS

Many people in theatre hold positions that are primarily administrative. Often, a job title is misleading or fails to convey a clear indication of the person's true responsibilities. What are the most common job titles for leading management positions in the theatre and, briefly, what activities are most often associated with them?

### PRODUCER ▪
In the British theatre a producer is the person who stages and directs the play; on the continent he would be called a *régisseur* or *mettier en scène*. In the American theatre a producer is the person who raises money to finance a theatrical production. He may or may not be active in other aspects of theatre operations, but he is always the financier. He is the person who "presents" the production to the public. In institutional theatres the term "producer" is inappropriate because no single person is the financier; rather, the institution "presents" the production and is the financier.

### BOARD OF DIRECTORS ▪
All public profit-taking corporations are headed by a board of directors, the membership of which is elected by the stockholders by vote proportionate to the number of shares they hold. It is the primary function of a board to appoint the leading officers or managers and to set the governing policies of the corporation. Corporate officers may or may not also be members of the board. Depending on the bylaws of the corporation, the board usually meets annually at a general meeting of stockholders for the election of new board members and other affairs that require a general vote. It may also meet by itself on a more frequent basis. If a board of directors subverts the authority of its officers by overruling decisions or by creating an organization so loaded with checks and balances that the officers and managers cannot function with efficiency and reasonable independence, the organization —especially in the case of theatre—stands little chance for success. The burden of leadership and, frequently, the need to exert strength falls on the shoulders of the board chairman, who may often find that he must risk losing his position on the board in order to provide strong direction.

### BOARD OF TRUSTEES ▪
Except for the fact that, semantically, boards of trustees are more appropriate for nonprofit corporations than boards of directors, there are no practical differences between the two and a nonprofit corporation may call its board members "directors" instead of "trustees." The people who serve on both types of board usually work without salary, although they may receive an honorarium (often a fixed amount awarded for each meeting they hold). Both must bear a certain burden of liability if the actions they take can be proved negligent or if they act contrary to the better

interests of the corporation. Board membership may be regarded as an honor, but it is not a job to be accepted or executed lightly.

The manner by which board members for nonprofit organizations are elected or appointed varies so greatly that one system is seldom like another. Government-sponsored organizations, such as a state arts council or New York's City Center, are usually headed by a board of trustees, the chairman of which is a politically-appointed officer. Other organizations, such as the United States Institute for Theatre Technology, have boards that are elected by and from the general membership, although the executive directors for these organizations are appointed positions. Too, there may be several classes of membership, some with and some without voting rights. In other cases, a board may elect its own replacement members, and the director of the board may also be the president of the corporation as well as its general manager. The rules that determine the governance of nonprofit corporations are always stated in the charter or constitution and bylaws which, once adopted, may be changed only by membership vote or some other device that is almost certain to be complicated and time-consuming. This is another reason why care must be taken when formulating the founding policies of an organization.

∎

## BOARD OF ADVISERS ∎

Advisers are usually nonsalaried personnel who fulfill an honorary function that may be of considerable assistance to a theatre but whose advice the theatre is not obligated to follow. They may be businessmen whose association with a theatre may prove helpful in solving financial problems or patrons who have donated large sums of money to the theatre and whom it wishes to recognize and encourage in their generosity. In educational theatre they may be students and faculty members who are especially active in theatre and whose advice is deemed valuable. A board of advisers is often a good device for widening local involvement and support for an organization without at the same time limiting its powers of decision-making. But if an organization creates a board of advisers or consultants it should be prepared to treat its suggestions seriously. Everybody likes to be asked for opinions, but, once asked, nobody likes to have those opinions scorned or ignored.

∎

## EXECUTIVE DIRECTOR ∎

Very often the chairman of a board may appoint a salaried administrator to carry out the policies of the board and to serve as a liaison between it and the staff of the organization. This person is given the title of "executive director." That title also may be used for any other job that entails supervision of the business and administrative aspects of a theatre, exclusive of supervision over artistic affairs.

∎

## GENERAL MANAGER ∎

In commercial theatre a general manager is responsible to the producer. He has a broad range of responsibilities that concern every aspect of a given production or producing organization. In noncommerical theatre a general manager is responsible to the board of directors and should be given full authority over the entire operation, both administrative and artistic. The position of General Manager of the New York Metropolitan Opera Association provides a well-known example of how the job should work: he supervises the running of the house as well as the planning of each season of operas and the hiring of artistic talent. Authority and the chain of command are crystal clear. If the Metropolitan's board of directors decided to divide the General Manager's responsibilities between two people, it would almost certainly cease to function as efficiently as it has in the past. Yet, many organizations do exactly that, creating, in place of a single general manager, an artistic director and an executive director, each with supposedly equal but separate authority. The trouble is that the affairs of any institution are so interrelated that no decision or action is truly separate from the whole fabric of the operation. Also, it is nearly impossible to find two people of equally matched ability and strength who can maintain a harmonious working relationship for any length of time without one dominating or trying to dominate the other.

### ARTISTIC DIRECTOR ▪

While the title of "artistic director" may imply that the person has little to do with overall administration, it also may be used instead of "general manager" to emphasize that the job includes artistic as well as administrative responsibility. The artistic director may be at the top of the organizational structure with business managers and others below him. Whatever title is selected for the head of an organization, it should be clear to everyone that he is the man whose "yes" or "no" can make any decision a final one.

### PRODUCING MANAGER ▪

The financier in a commercial theatre who also serves as his own general manager may use the title of "producing manager" to indicate his total involvement in the enterprise.

### MANAGING PRODUCER ▪

When the financier in a commercial theatre is usually absent and does not participate very actively in most decision-making, "managing producer" is an appropriate title for the person who assumes the responsibilities of producership (selecting plays, hiring both management and artistic personnel and so on) and also supervises the overall operation.

### MANAGING DIRECTOR ▪

Often the same as a managing producer (though an appropriate title in both commercial and noncommercial theatre), a managing director has overall authority in supervising an organization and may play a considerable part in artistic decision-making, though he is never the financier.

### ACTOR-MANAGER ▪

The term "actor-manager" is seldom used today and few people really fit the nineteenth-century definition of it. Actors who manage their own companies, as did Herbert Beerbohm Tree, Henry Irving and Augustin Daly, are largely a past phenomenon, although a few more recent gentlemen, among them Laurence Olivier and the late Tyrone Guthrie, come close enough to keep the tradition alive. The rarity of actor-managers today may also be explained by the fact that artistic leadership in theatre has shifted during the last half century from the actor to the director, so that it is much more common to find stage directors establishing their own theatres. In this case they generally assume the title of "artistic director" for the organization as well as simply "director" for any production they stage personally.

### IMPRESARIO ▪

Also a rather outdated title, "impresario" indicates a person who works in the concert and opera field either as the manager of his own theatre or as an independent producer who organizes and sends on tour various performing artists. In recent times the title has been applied to such men as Florenz Ziegfeld, Billy Rose and Sol Hurok.

### DIRECTOR OF THEATRE ▪

Schools and colleges that are active in the several performing arts appoint heads for each division called, variously, "director of theatre," "director of music," "chairman of theatre" or another title of a similarly obvious nature. They are charged with the artistic and administrative leadership of the division but work under a higher authority and within institutional limitations of budget and organization.

### BUSINESS MANAGER ▪

Working under a general manager or artistic director, a business manager is responsible for the fiscal details of an organization.

### PRODUCTION MANAGER ▪

In a large operation it may be necessary to employ a person as a production manager or coordinator who is required to supervise backstage operations and to serve as a link with administrative personnel. In smaller operations these responsibilities are assumed by a production stage manager.

### COMPANY MANAGER ▪

In professional theatre, and usually associated with a single production rather than with a multi-production operation, a company manager serves as the producer's full-time representative. Unlike the general manager of a Broadway or touring production, the company manager stays with the performing company wherever it travels and copes with minute-to-minute administrative details. (He must also be a member of the Association of Theatrical Press Agents and Managers, ATPAM.)

### ADVANCE MANAGER ▪

Touring professional productions, both those on national tours of major houses and those sent out to stock theatres as "packages," require that the producer employ an advance manager or director to precede the production and handle such matters as company housing, transportation, advance publicity and the technical preparations required for each theatre that has engaged the production. (He must be a member of Actors' Equity Association.)

### HOUSE MANAGER ▪

In professional New York theatre a house manager is employed by and responsible to the landlord. He is the landlord's representative, responsible for upholding the terms of the producer's lease with the theatre. Also a member of ATPAM, he is the counterpart of the company manager, who is the producer's resident representative. In institutional theatre the house manager is simply a person who supervises the audience areas of the building, primarily during performance hours.

**PERSONAL MANAGER** ■

Be they producers or performers, the busier and more successful people in theatre may require the services of a full or part-time manager to supervise their professional and sometimes their personal lives. Unlike an agent, who has numerous clients and spends only a limited amount of time with each of them, a personal manager provides more individualized services and may attend to such diverse matters as promoting his client, handling personal appointments and serving as bookkeeper, banker and legal advisor.

**PUBLICITY DIRECTOR** ■

New York producers hire a professional press agent (a member of ATPAM) to take charge of all advertising and publicity needs for a given production. He is likely to operate his own agency with a small staff and numerous clients. Institutional theatres frequently employ a full-time public relations director or, in the case of educational theatre, may utilize the services of the college or university public relations office. The various people who work in this area under such titles as "press representative," "publicity director," "public relations director," "head of audience development" and "advertising director" are all managers in that they supervise, coordinate and make key decisions that will effect the success or failure of the project in question.

**STAGE MANAGER** ■

In professional theatres the stage manager must be a member of Actor's Equity Association. He assists the artistic director during rehearsal periods, but during performances he holds complete authority over the stage and backstage operation. This places him in a leading supervisory position and makes his job primarily administrative.

**TECHNICAL DIRECTOR** ■

Most productions and theatres require a person to supervise the many aspects of assembling the physical production and, perhaps, of managing a large staff and budget related to these. The technical director in many theatres may also serve in some other capacity—master carpenter, lighting designer, electrician—but still be given the responsibility of overall technical supervision. In other theatres the stage manager may have this responsibility, in which case he is given the title of "production stage manager."

■

The twenty-two titles described above are the ones most commonly used in commercial and noncommercial theatre and indicate the wide span of managerial positions necessary to most theatrical operations. There are numerous other job titles as well as other specific jobs that also qualify as administrative. The difference between titles and the responsibility they involve is essentially a matter of whether one is charged with managing the overall operation or only a single part of it. Although the titles and job responsibilities vary, the fundamentals of management and supervision in theatre are salient to all.

# CHAPTER THREE

# The Place for the Performance

As the number of Broadway theatres decreased in recent decades and commercial productions grew more infrequent and more costly, playwrights and producers began to seek professional outlets beyond Times Square. This resulted in the rapid proliferation of Off Broadway theatres during the 1950s and 1960s as well as the growth of off-Off Broadway (a reaction to the creeping commercialization of Off-Broadway). Experimental theatre came to be associated with non-theatres: churches, garages, lofts, storefronts—nothing radically new, for the history of theatre architecture is largely comprised of studies in how non-theatre places evolved into structures built exclusively as theatres: thrashing grounds into the classical Greek theatres, inn yards into the Elizabethan theatres, cathedrals and tennis courts into the eighteenth-century European theatres. The best of contemporary theatre architecture need not be examined too closely to see the influence of "loft theatre": the use of open space, the frequent omission of the proscenium arch, the more intimate relationship between performer and audience areas and the fondness for exposed brick walls and other raw materials. Other recently built theatres, especially the larger ones, merely continue in the tradition of nineteenth-century architecture as if neither theatre nor society had changed in the slightest. Whenever theatre becomes overly formalized and stuffy, creative artists instinctively seek other places to work.

Governments, architects and the general public may believe that performances can only be held in elaborate and enormous theatres, but theatre people themselves know better. Lord Kenneth Clark, the critic and historian, has wondered if any great humanist thought was ever conceived in a large room; one might also wonder if a huge auditorium has ever inspired any originality in the theatre. In this age of mass media and electronic entertainment, live theatre is all the more precious for its unique ability to reach people intimately, to address itself to small groups rather than to the masses and to deal with the unusual rather than the conventional. Most serious producers, dramatists and performers in non-musical theatre today are wary of bigness in whatever form it may appear.

Regardless of theatre size or the goals of its founders, there are numerous factors that must be taken into consideration concerning the community in which a theatre is located, the building itself and the manner in which these are apt to influence artistic objectives.

## ▪ THE LOCATION OF THE THEATRE

Ideally, each producer and artistic director should be able to select the community where he feels his theatre has the best chance to thrive, both economically and artistically. While the choice of location may be limited by circumstances, the brave people who search out performance places might often come closer to their ideal theatre if they searched a little longer and, perhaps, a little further afield.

Probably the most conscientious attempt in recent times to suit artistic goals to a community was undertaken by Tyrone Guthrie, Peter Zeisler and Oliver Rea in their methodical search of the country that culminated in the opening of the Tyrone Guthrie Theatre in 1963 and the establishment of the Minnesota Theatre Company at Minneapolis-St. Paul. It is a well-documented story that should lend encouragement to producers and artistic directors who are less than satisfied with utilizing theatre buildings merely because they are readily available. Of course, not everyone has the time and money to invest several years in a nationwide search for the ideal community in which to locate a theatre company. But anyone can scrupulously examine the community in which he finds an existing theatre and be apprised of the fact that many more theatres and performance places exist than the most obvious and convenient ones. When assessing a potential theatre site—the community, the audience potential, the building itself—the advice of professional consultants is often helpful in gathering information. However, like the business of selecting plays and casting actors, final decisions about the performance place may also, without apology, be based upon a degree of intuition, upon a "feel" one gets from a particular theatre or community. Consultants, feasibility reports, architects and the rest are helpful and often necessary adjuncts to the process of creating new theatres, but they should never be allowed to dominate this process. Having just been released from the hands of business tycoons, the American theatre must guard itself against another type of philistine, the corporate VIP manager, the expert with charts and graphs and complicated answers who is noted for his agility in heading or advising one large corporation and board of trustees after another. Artistic directors who attempt to establish their own theatre can often serve as their own consultants by undertaking some simple field work.

Whether the plan is to buy, build or lease a theatre, what factors regarding the community should be taken into consideration?

### AUDIENCE POTENTIAL ■

Statistical surveys have shown that somewhere between 1 and 3 percent of our population attend live theatre performances and that the ratio of theatregoers to nontheatregoers is higher in metropolitan areas. Excluding campus audiences, most theatregoers are drawn from white, middle and higher income categories, tend to be college graduates, hold professional or executive positions and are middle-aged or older. Although it is unquestionably a valid audience profile for commercial or "large" theatre, this description would not fit many theatre audiences in resort areas, those that attend experimental productions or those special-interest groups that attend theatres that consciously appeal to them. The profile is also radically altered when a theatre adopts a free-admission policy—a practice made increasingly more feasible by subsidization and more desirable by the alarmingly urgent need to attract a wider and younger segment of the population.

If, philosophically, a theatre wishes to attract a particular kind of audience it should be located as close to that audience as possible. It is well documented, for instance, that New York inner-city audiences do not attend Broadway theatres. Nor are they likely to attend college or institutionalized theatres, even in their own community—hence the idea for theatre-in-the-street and storefront theatre. Since almost any locale and almost any building will automatically determine the potential size and type of audience, both factors should be in keeping with the goals and desires of the theatre organization.

### PROXIMITY TO TRANSPORTATION ■

Is a theater easily accessible to public and private transportation? If located in a large metropolitan area, accessibility to public modes of transport—subways, buses, trains—will take precedence over private transportation routes. Can a majority of the potential audience reach the theatre easily, quickly and safely? If not, will authorities cooperate to improve transportation systems, especially during times of greatest need each day? Are parking facilities available or will costly provisions be required to handle a maximum number of automobiles? Can cars be accommodated equally well for both evening and matinee performances? Is the theatre located on a major highway or is it off the beaten path?

Generally, it has been found that theatregoers in the eastern states are not willing to drive as far to places of entertainment as those in the rest of the nation, but in any case the process of finding one's way to a theatre should not take on the mysterious characteristics of a treasure hunt. What are the federal and local regulations about placing directional signs on nearby roads and highways? As a public service and in order to facilitate a safe and orderly flow of traffic, most cities and townships are willing to cooperate with theatre managers by allowing at least a minimum number of signs, although signs for profit corporations are outlawed on federal highways and state and local governments are tightening regulations that deal with outdoor display advertising. Special permits are always required, unless a sign is located on private property by permission of the owner. Whether on private or public property there are likely to be limitations regarding size. When a theatre is located in a remote area, even road signs may not be sufficient to guide many patrons. In such cases, the local and state police as well as neighboring merchants and businessmen should be well informed about the location of the theatre in the event they are asked to give directions. Every attempt should be made to have the name of the theatre appear on as many road maps as possible—those distributed through official channels as well as smaller, more local maps such as those printed on restaurant place mats, on motel bath mats, in tourist guides and in chamber of commerce literature.

Modes of transportation may affect a theatre operation in a variety of ways. Large, professional operations find it necessary to transport everything from scenery to actors. Costs related to the transportation of materials and people will be smallest for professional theatres located in New York, Chicago, Los Angeles, San Francisco and Toronto simply because, aside from being supply centers for most theatrical materials, each of these cities also serves as a home or branch office for Actors' Equity Association as well as other theatrical unions, which means that professional theatres may (though they may also choose differently) hire performers locally and thereby avoid transporting them over long distances. On the other hand, metropolitan theatres are not necessarily free from high transportation costs. When scenery is constructed in studios away from the theatre, for example, trucking costs can be appreciable—especially for repertory theatres that lack adequate scene storage space. The problems of moving scenery in and out of the old New York Metropolitan Opera House on Fortieth Street and Broadway, where the sidewalks provided the only storage space, like the stories about getting the elephants in and out of the old Hippodrome for their performances, contribute to a legend that, however amusing, stands as a warning for contemporary producers. Blue laws that limit trucking on Sundays or after dark, freeways that restrict commercial traffic, interstate trucking laws and other such factors can easily upset both the schedule and the budget for theatres located in somewhat remote regions of the country. All bear close examination when plans for a theatre are being laid.

### THE COMPETITION ■

Contrary to general opinion, competition in the performing arts is a healthy thing provided, of course, that it does not involve an overly frequent duplication of similar entertainment or programming. Theatregoing is a habit. It can be cultivated by amateur or community theatres and applied to professional theatregoing. The opposite may also be true, although high quality entertainment tends to encourage audiences to demand more of the same high standards. But theatregoing is not a habit that people acquire quickly. Long and continuing availability of theatre in a given area is desirable. Without question, the new theatre that locates itself in a community already accustomed to playgoing has a more ready audience potential than others: it is easier to share an audience than to create a new one from scratch. But there is an obvious difference between sharing and dividing. If, for example, two Shakespearean repertory theatres are located within twenty or thirty miles of each other, one will doubtless hurt the other at the box office.

How large is the potential audience for a particular kind of entertainment? Can metropolitan areas that possess numerous performing groups of a similar type work more diligently to coordinate their programming? On a given night in New York, for instance, one might find twenty groups that are performing a Mozart recital and not one of them playing to a capacity audience. Even in a city the size of New York there are probably not eight or ten thousand people who would go out on a given evening to attend a Mozart recital. Yet, we criticize the television industry for *its* lack of programming diversity! Did the two New York musicals, *Canterbury Tales* and *Back to Canterbury*, presented simultaneously in 1969, help each other? While such duplication should be avoided, there are exceptions, among the most interesting being those times when two outstanding performers choose to appear at the same time and in the same role, as when both John Gielgud and Leslie Howard were playing *Hamlet* in 1936 or when the Metropolitan Opera and the New York City Opera present the same work during the same season next door to each other at Lincoln Center. But these are rare exceptions and not necessarily successful at the box office.

THE LOCAL MEDIA ■
    Finding a community with a good potential audience is one thing; reaching that audience with a message that stimulates it sufficiently to attend the theatre is something else. If audience potential is extremely high and people are in the habit of theatregoing, perhaps the job of selling tickets is as simple as disseminating minimal information about the play, the prices and the curtain times. But this is unusual. More often, people have to be enticed to attend a performance or, at least, strongly impressed about the existence of a theatre and the rewards of playgoing.
    The most efficient way of reaching an audience will differ with each community. Direct mail, the distribution of posters and handbills, newspaper advertising, radio coverage or some other channel of communication may prove successful at one theatre but unimportant at another. First, the size of the potential audience must be estimated and, second, its profile must be understood as intimately as possible. If the habits and living patterns of the average theatregoer are known, it will be easier to reach him. What newspapers does he read? What radio and television stations capture his attention? What stores does he patronize most frequently? Advertising is expensive and few theatres can afford nearly as much of it as they would like, so decisions about where and how to advertise are important.* Perhaps even more important is the amount of free space or time the local media are willing to provide. To secure such vital publicity, a theatre must establish and maintain a carefully nurtured relationship with the local media. Most editors and program directors recognize that a theatre is an asset to the community, to its economy and culture, and they are apt to welcome theatrical copy or programming material because it is usually more interesting and colorful than other copy they receive.
    Theatres located outside large metropolitan areas may find themselves in a community that has no local radio or television station and no local newspaper with a distribution reaching a majority of the potential audience. This situation requires a wider and more expensive advertising campaign and creates greater difficulty in determining the audience profile and communicating with it. And, of course, the further away a newspaper or radio station is from a theatre the less likely it is to provide free publicity space or time. Communicating with potential theatregoers in resort areas may also present special problems: the year-round residents follow the local newspapers while the tourists ignore these and continue subscribing to

*See chapter 13.

their home-city press. Fortunate indeed is the theatre that has an audience that can be reached in its entirety through one or two media outlets.

## LOCAL ORGANIZATIONS ▪

What groups exist within a given community that might offer assistance to a theatre? Helpful in the area of publicity and promotion, for example, are such organizations as chambers of commerce, tourist bureaus, information centers and travel agencies. Women's clubs, service clubs, senior citizen clubs and charity organizations can be a good potential source of personnel for volunteer ticket campaign committees. Their existence also indicates a public-spirited energy that can probably be tapped, at least by nonprofit theatre organizations. From the standpoint of financial assistance, what sort of philanthropic record is generally maintained by local businesses and industries? Is there a community arts council and what is the record of the state arts council?

## THE LOCAL ECONOMY ▪

Another yardstick for predicting the success of a theatre is to determine whether potential playgoers can easily afford the price of admission. What is the average income in the area? How much are people currently spending for live entertainment? How much can they afford to spend? Can group ticket sales be anticipated from large businesses, industries, schools and organizations? Has there been growth or decline in the general economy of the area over the past decade or so? Some communities can afford to support a theatre that charges comparatively high admission prices, others can afford no admission charges at all. The records in the local tax assessor's office will provide answers to some of these questions as will interviews with chamber of commerce officials, managers of local movie theatres and other businessmen. Long before a theatre opens its doors, the producers should take a hard look at the local economy and ask whether or not its planned ticket prices are within a range that the market can bear. Even though the answer may be positive, of course, it does not mean that a community *will* buy tickets. If the answer seems doubtful, can high-priced performances be alternated with low-priced or free admission performances? How much income is it reasonable to expect from nonadmission sources?

If the local economy can affect theatre business, then theatre business can also affect the local economy. This fact may provide a selling point and help to rally local support. For example, a successful eight-hundred-seat theatre that operates a five- or six-month repertory season in a small city could probably show that it stimulates the local economy each year roughly in the following manner:

| | |
|---|---:|
| Wages paid to city residents | $ 30,000 |
| Wages paid to resident acting company | 60,000 |
| Local property taxes | 2,800 |
| State and city sales taxes | 5,000 |
| Local advertising purchased | 20,000 |
| Lumber, paint and fabric purchased locally | 4,800 |
| Gasoline, auto repair and local travel | 3,000 |
| Utilities expenditures | 2,500 |
| Hotel and housing accommodations rented by the company | 15,000 |

| Hotel and motel trade: visiting playgoers | 28,000 |
| Restaurant food and beverage trade from company | 21,000 |
| Restaurant and bar trade from visiting playgoers | 75,000 |
| Total amount added to city's economy annually as a direct result of the theatre | $267,100 |

It is, of course, regrettable when theatre has to be justified in this way. But as a device for reminding people that theatre is a business that "gives as good as it gets," such information can prove helpful in establishing theatre as a valuable economic as well as a cultural asset. Variations on this theme are not difficult to concoct. For instance, theatres in resort areas are likely to attract tourists to the area and help to lengthen their stay. Many large corporations located away from the nation's so-called cultural centers are finding that it is less difficult to attract executives, scientists and other professionals when the community in which they are located can offer high quality leisure-time activities, such as theatres and museums. For these reasons it is sometimes possible for the arts to gain substantial support, morally and financially, from local businesses and institutions. Obviously, certain types of theatre are only appropriate in certain types of community, but more and more people believe that theatre of some kind should be available to everyone and that it is both a civic and private responsibility to make this possible.

## THE LOCAL CLIMATE ■

Weather conditions can seriously affect the business of theatre, especially in resort areas. How dependent is the tourist trade on climate fluctuations? What will general weather conditions mean in terms of heating or cooling an auditorium? Will weather make air conditioning a necessity? Will it necessitate large expenditures for fuel? Many a summer theatre has been purchased in the cool of winter when it is easy to forget or underestimate summer conditions. No theatre or building can be easily tested for comfort until it is in use.

Weather conditions are, of course, most important to tent and outdoor theatres. Numerous open-air amphitheatres are standing idle because it was discovered, too late, that the local climate was either too unpredictable or too uncomfortable to use them with any regularity. "Good ideas," such as theatre-under-the-stars, need careful scrutiny!

## LOCAL ATTITUDES ■

Even when all other conditions for theatre appear favorable, local attitudes toward the presence of a particular theatre may determine its success or failure. What, it must be asked, is the sum of all the information that has been gathered about a community? What is the general reaction to the idea for a theatre? Is it hot, luke-warm or cool? What is the history of previous theatre projects in the community and have these projects encouraged or discouraged local attitudes?

Communities comprised largely of well-educated and cosmopolitan people may be more ready to support a theatre than others; but it should be remembered that such communities may also have more deeply entrenched concepts of what theatre should be and how a theatre should be operated. That is all well and good for the more traditional or commercial types of theatre, but a decided liability for experimental groups. Taking theatre to the hinterlands is a noble gesture, but it is fraught with difficulties—largely those concerning local attitudes—that should be studied carefully. While a majority of the people in a community may possess negative attitudes toward theatre, strong community leaders (politicians, religious leaders and the like) may be able to turn the tide of local opinion. Once in the habit of theatregoing, the newly found audience may prove to be an extremely loyal and exciting one.

Finally, it is important for the people who will be associated with a theatre to ask themselves whether or not they will be comfortable and happy working in a particular community. If it is fair to ask that a community accept the theatre and its workers, it is equally fair to expect the theatre workers to accept the community. Many theatres, especially those with a resident company of actors and those located outside our largest cities, have been justly criticized for treating their community in a condescending or isolationist manner. Totally opposed to the humanistic mission of theatre, such attitudes only reinforce negativism within the community and obstruct the kind of empathy that should lie at the foundation of all theatre work.

## ▪ ACQUIRING THE THEATRE

### TO BUILD A THEATRE ▪

Before building a new theatre a number of questions should be asked, the most important ones pertaining to artistic needs. If the theatre is being designed to house a particular acting company, every effort should be made to provide that company with an ideal working plant. How can the architecture complement the working style and habits of the actors? It is usually preferable to aim for a good amount of structural flexibility that will facilitate various methods of staging and production. On the other hand, when this requires complicated machinery (such as stage lifts, an automated proscenium and the like), the machinery may dictate a style of its own.

What are the motivations for constructing a new theatre? Does the desire stem from artistic needs or merely from an urge to have a new building for the sake of newness? Have the alternatives been considered? Could the use of an existing building offer the same solutions as the construction of a new one? Can the anticipated income for a theatre comfortably support the costs of a new building? Will a new theatre complement the abilities of the acting company or does it run the risk of being more impressive than the actors? Will a new building inspire more local support and interest or, conversely, will it damage the loyalty and romantic associations that the community feels toward an existing theatre? However impractical and outdated an old building may be, it may have established a large following of its own and attract many customers to its box office regardless of the performance being offered. (Witness the hue and cry every time Carnegie Hall is threatened with destruction.)

After the decision to build a new theatre has been made, an architect must be found to translate artistic and economic needs into the permanent reality of a building. Unhappily, most architects are unfamiliar with theatrical structures, but a local chapter of the American Institute of Architects can be of assistance in locating one who is. When he is selected, a strong relationship should be established between the architect and the artistic directors of the theatre. Although artists in their own right, architects must not be allowed to design structural elements that impose unnecessary limitations on the artistic work of the theatre. The architect willing to collaborate with theatre artists, however, can be an enormous help in facilitating theatrical goals.

## TO BUY A THEATRE ▪

Any piece of property or real estate should be considered first for its general use. In terms of size, structure, location, age and history, and regardless of whether or not the building in question is used as a theatre, what is its fair market price? What is its potential resale value? Is it a sound structure or will major renovation and repair of heating, cooling, plumbing, electrical and physical support systems be necessary? Few buyers are sufficiently expert to judge these matters for themselves and a detailed report in writing from a professional building engineer is always wise. Among the things that are never what they appear to be, old buildings are high on the list. Too, every attempt should be made to discover the reasons why the building is for sale. The records of the business that previously operated the building should be carefully studied: past owners, managers and employees should be quizzed about it, as should neighboring businessmen and others in the community. Does the building have a reputation or image that will affect future business? The English director Joan Littlewood is fond of relating how her theatre at Stratford East, a London suburb, had acquired the epithet in the local community of "old blood tub," inspired by its less than reputable activities behind the scenes. One of Miss Littlewood's prouder moments occurred when, after operating the theatre for a number of years, the local butcher—scion of the area's middle-class morality—deigned to attend a performance. The restoration of a reputation may take longer than the mere restoration of a building!

Finally, of course, clear ownership of the property must be gained by commissioning a title search to legally establish the validity of the deed.

## TO LEASE A THEATRE ▪

Before signing a lease, one needs to consider the building in question from most of the same angles as if one planned to purchase it. Indeed, if the lessee hopes to operate for a long period of time, he should request that the lease include an option to buy the property at a stipulated maximum price and, if possible, with the rent serving as some type of concession in that price. The business of negotiating the lease for a theatre is a complicated matter which requires legal counsel, but everything in a lease will be related to one of two questions: what does the landlord provide and what must the tenant provide? As with all contracts and agreements, that which is not specifically withheld is given away.

Tradition dictates that most Broadway and Off Broadway theatre leases follow a basic format, although the specific terms vary greatly from theatre to theatre and from lease to lease. As a rule, New York landlords provide a theatre complete with a house staff (including house manager, box office treasurers, ushers, ticket takers, most maintenance employees and others), house insurance of certain types, utilities and an agreement to pay for a certain amount of advertising for the tenant production. Besides paying a minimum weekly rent, Broadway tenants also pay the landlord a percentage of the box office income.* As with other businessmen, theatrical producers and landlords are always concerned with the law of supply and demand. During poor theatre seasons, for example, when there are more theatre buildings available than productions to fill them, more favorable leasing terms may result.

*See chapter 5.

Or, when a production itself is highly successful, the landlord may be more favorably inclined toward it in anticipation of a long tenancy.

Theatre leases outside the New York commercial theatre are more open to negotiation but also subject to many pitfalls. The most favorable terms for a tenant would establish the rent as a percentage of the box office gross without a minimum guarantee. Some theatre groups have even obtained buildings merely in exchange for paying utility and maintenance bills although, depending upon the building, these can be very costly and unpredictable. The important thing is for the lease to state clearly what the landlord supplies and what the tenant supplies: what is the fine print, how easily can the lease be broken or extended?

ASSISTANCE IN ASSESSING AND ACQUIRING A BUILDING ▪

As one of four requirements for theatre, the *place* for the performances is a fundamental element and will deeply and unequivocably influence every other aspect of a theatre operation. Every precaution should be taken to guarantee the best possible theatre place. While producers and artistic directors should know the general architectural and physical requirements for their project, they are well advised to seek the advice and assistance of other professionals, at least in instances when a multiproduction, long-term project is the plan. Depending on whether the performance place is being constructed from the beginning, bought or leased, the following types of people may be contacted and utilized for the assistance they are trained to provide:

1. MARKET RESEARCH CONSULTANTS

Many market research companies, both small and large, local and national, experienced in theatre consultation and not, are available to conduct broad surveys in a community that result in a "feasibility study" dealing with such factors as audience potential, community attitudes and the local economy. Such studies may be helpful either before a theatre is opened or after it has been operating for some time.

2. MANAGEMENT AND ECONOMIC CONSULTANTS

A number of agencies are experienced in providing detailed analyses of feasibility studies or special problems regarding a theatre operation in order to determine what the operating costs will be, whether or not they can be covered by actual or anticipated revenue and how best to organize and control a given organization.

3. ARCHITECTS AND ENGINEERING CONSULTANTS

Theatre architects may be contacted directly, with the assistance of the local chapter of the American Institute of Architects, or a number of architects may be invited to submit designs or proposals for a new building. If the building is already in existence, professional building engineers or consultants of various kinds may be employed to analyze plant operations, make recommendations for changes or submit designs for renovation; these might include specialists in acoustics, plumbing, construction and the like. Consultants may be contracted either by the architect or by the landlord or producing organization.

### 4. ACTUARIES

In assessing a property for its real and special values an actuary may be requested to submit a report directly to the producing organization, to the insurance companies that are asked to provide coverage for the organization or to banks and financiers for the purpose of establishing a loan or mortgage value. Such reports are meant to be objective appraisals of the worth of a building in terms of the current market value.

### 5. REAL ESTATE BROKERS

When buying or leasing a building one usually prefers to avoid paying broker commissions, either directly or indirectly. But real estate brokers can be of great assistance in locating a desirable building in a particular area and are also likely to know a considerable amount about the history and reputation of buildings in their area.

### 6. LICENSING BOARDS AND INSPECTORS

All public buildings must be approved and licensed by certain agencies of the local and state governments. Theatres must be located on property zoned for business. Such zones are determined by public vote and then controlled by the local board of selectment or an office of the city government. Because zoning laws change and special permits pertaining to them are sometimes required, the proper officials should always be contacted before the site for a theatre is finally negotiated. Permits must also be obtained concerning public safety conditions, such as the accessibility of emergency exits, public elevators, fireproofing and the like. If not approved as safe and sanitary, a building may require extensive and costly work.

### 7. LABOR UNION INSPECTORS

Most unions concerned with employees who work in theatre buildings have a variety of rules and regulations pertaining to working conditions for their members. Actors' Equity Association, for example, requires minimum safe and sanitary conditions in dressing rooms, a certain temperature range during working hours, specific rest room and shower facilities, stage and rehearsal area flooring specifications and so forth. Union officials should be consulted about such building requirements before a theatre is designed or acquired.

### 8. LEGAL CONSULTANTS

Lawyers, preferably specialists in the type of contract or problem being negotiated, are both necessary and desirable. Their assistance may be for a specific purpose or they may be retained for a long period of time. In fact, one must now accept not two but three certainties in life: death, taxes and lawyers.

### RAISING THE BUILDING FUNDS ∎

Once an idea for theatre has been formulated and a place for that idea has been selected, efforts to raise capital must begin. If the enterprise is organized as a private corporation (profit or nonprofit), it may be financed entirely by a single person. Or, that individual may enter into partnership with others who will also put up a portion of the required capital and possess rights of ownership and control as specified in a partnership agreement. A corporation may offer shares to the public or adopt other methods of acquiring capital. The campaign to attract investors may be conducted in a comparatively exclusive manner (appealing only to acquaintances or some select group) or it may be done more publicly. For example, the Arena Stage in Washington once offered $100 bonds at 6 percent competitive interest rates and thereby raised nearly a quarter of a million dollars for its building fund—a good method of obtaining a loan from the public, in effect, without actually selling shares. British theatre director Bernard Miles sold bricks at the site of his proposed Mermaid Theatre at Puddle Dock in London in order to raise capital; the buyers then donated the bricks for the construction of the theatre. Philadelphia's Playhouse in the Park was given land by the city on a long-term lease for one dollar per year. Much of the land for the Tyrone Guthrie Theatre in Minneapolis-St. Paul was donated by a local industry. In other cases, building capital or land has been donated by individuals or financed by grants from private and public foundations, although most foundations favor grants for operating expenses rather than for capital expenditures.

A variety of tax advantages are available to corporations and individuals who donate or sell property to nonprofit organizations. For instance, if property is sold at the price for which it was acquired but for less than its current assessed value, the difference is tax deductible for the seller and no capital gains tax will be levied. If a potential donor of money or property or a potential seller of property is found, every effort should be made to explore methods of conducting the transaction so that both parties can benefit as much as possible. A degree of imagination together with sound legal and financial advice and up-to-date tax information can bring to light some attractive methods by which a theatre may raise capital and acquire property, especially if it is a nonprofit organization. Even in New York, building codes have been revised in recent years to facilitate theatre construction. Most city and government officials recognize that arts buildings are an asset to the community and this, together with a growing realization that the arts are dependent on a goodly amount of direct and indirect subsidization, is a point that greatly favors the growth of theatre in America. But raising capital, acquiring a desirable site and creating a favorable theatre facility are never simple or easy matters; in more cases than not a combination of funding techniques will be necessary. Organizations hopeful of building their own theatre are well-advised to study recently established theatres similar to their own planned operation and to benefit as much as possible from the experience of others. Hiring the services of a recognized fund-raising firm may also be a good idea.*

## ▪ THEATRE DESIGN AND ARCHITECTURE

### CENTRAL OPERATING SYSTEMS ▪

Among the most costly and essential aspects of operating any building are plumbing, heating, cooling and electric systems. The first consideration in regard to the

*See chapter 12.

engineering of these utilities is whether or not they should be centrally operated and how much flexibility of control they should permit. When speaking in terms of furnaces, water pumps, water towers, hot water tanks, compressor units, electrical generators and the like, it is usually less costly and more efficient to maintain and operate one large mechanical unit rather than numerous smaller ones. But this assumes that most of the plant is in operation most of the time. When large areas of a building are not used for long periods, utility systems that service them should possess the capability of controlling those areas separately from the ones in use. Is it necessary, for example, to provide heat and electricity for an entire theatre during its off-season periods when only one office or none at all may be required? Or, does the auditorium require heating in order to heat the rehearsal areas?

Most new buildings today, by virtue of construction methods and materials, provide built-in fire protection, but older buildings require fire-hose or sprinkler systems that are permanently operable. To avoid failure in the event of power losses, both the fire alarm and pumping equipment must be supplied with electrical power that is independent from outside power sources. Like all plumbing, sprinkler pipes that contain water must be kept at above-freezing temperatures (with a so-called dry system this as a rule only involves piping water to the source of the system where the generators and pumps are also located). Emergency power and light systems are also required by law in all public buildings and may receive their power either from a central generator or from individual, battery-operated units that are tied into the regular electrical system so they automatically cut in when normal power is interrupted.

Many problems arise when a theatre is part of a larger complex of buildings and its utilities are operated from a central system. Heat or air conditioning for a campus theatre, for instance, might be supplied from a heating plant as far as a mile distant, requiring troublesome and expensive arrangements at times when other campus facilities are not in use. Many architects and engineers, it seems, imagine that theatre rehearsals, performances and preparations all occur during a normal forty hour week, excluding weekends and holidays.

Central communications systems offer other problems and advantages. A telephone switchboard, for example, may provide communication efficiency within a building complex and control over the use of each unit, but it may not be fully operable at all times of the day and week. In order to obtain the greatest efficiency at the lowest cost, an organization should consult engineers from the public telephone company in its area and then carefully weigh the available systems against anticipated usage and needs.

## AUDIENCE SEATING CAPACITY ▪

The seating capacity and size of an auditorium will greatly influence both the business and artistic potentials of a theatre. Audience capacity will determine the total potential box office income (although this will vary depending on how tickets are priced) and therefore the total theatre budget, and it will dictate appropriate types of production and artistic goals. This does not mean, of course, that a great deal that is inappropriate is not attempted in certain theatre buildings or that the entire question of what is appropriate in a particular theatre is not a matter of opinion. Nonetheless, it would be generally agreed that to play *Hedda Gabler*, for example, in a twenty-five-hundred-seat theatre would be about as inappropriate as to perform *West Side Story* in a two-hundred-seat theatre. Unfortunately, circumstances often tempt producing organizations to make drastic compromises in suiting a particular production to a particular theatre. It is not always understood that the theatre itself, the performance place, is an integral element of the art. Change the place of performance and the performance itself also changes—a principle not far removed from Marshall McLuhan's theory that the medium rather than its message determines what is communicated.

As the result of considerable trial and error and as the outgrowth of long tradition, most theatre practitioners concede that each style of play production dictates an approximate ideal in terms of audience size. Laboratory or workshop theatres usually seat from one hundred to three hundred people, although the avant-garde theatre director Jerzy Grotowski prefers an audience of no more than forty. Theatres seating from five hundred to eight hundred people seem ideal for most non-musical presentations and about fifteen hundred seats is the norm for musical plays, tent theatres, commercial theatres and the like. Auditoriums that seat around twenty-five hundred people are acceptable for large musical plays, opera, symphony, dance and certain concert presentations. Naturally, such factors as acoustics, sight lines, decor and general comfort contribute substantially to the appropriateness and desirability of any performance place, and many dramatic works can be adapted successfully to theatres of vastly different sizes.

### TYPES OF STAGES ▪

Concepts of performer-audience relationships have varied greatly over the centuries, but forward-looking theatres today favor a more intimate relationship than the one offered by traditional, nineteenth century proscenium theatres. Partly because the cinema can accomplish these effects so much better than live theatre, fewer and fewer productions aim for lifelike illusions or the fish bowl look of a stage that is encased by a proscenium arch. Also, realistic styles of drama and theatre production are common only to a comparatively small portion of the total writing and staging output during twenty-five hundred years of theatrical history. More often than not, theatre has been admittedly theatrical. But it has not always attempted to achieve as intimate a performer-audience relationship as it frequently does today.

Briefly, what types of stages are commonly in use today and what kind of performer-audience relationship do they establish?

### 1. PROSCENIUM THEATRE

The stage is behind a picture-frame arch with the audience located directly in front of it.

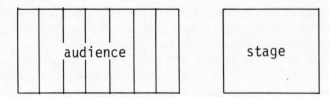

### 2. THRUST STAGE ■

An apron is projected into the audience area and may or may not extend out in front of a proscenium arch.

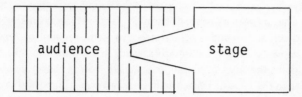

### 3. ARENA STAGE OR THEATRE-IN-THE-ROUND

The stage is surrounded on all sides by audience areas.

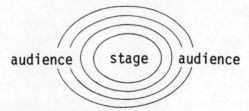

### 4. CENTER STAGE OR TWO-SIDED ARENA

The audience is placed in two sections, facing each other, on opposite sides of the performance area. (The least common type of staging.)

### 5. OPEN STAGE OR THREE-QUARTER-ROUND

The audience is arranged around three sides of the stage.

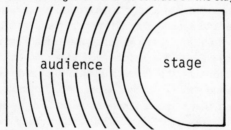

### 6. FLEXIBLE STAGE

A theatre designed and often automated in such a manner that a combination of several different types of stages may be used either simultaneously or at different times.

Any play or presentation can be adapted to any type of stage, although many plays intrinsically dictate an appropriate method of staging. Each type of stage, therefore, will suggest a certain repertory of dramatic literature and certain styles of production, just as it will suggest certain scenic and technical embellishments, certain staff positions to create and operate these embellishments and certain budget lines to pay for them all. For instance, a fully staged production of a musical like *Oklahoma!* will require a greater bulk of scenery when produced in a large proscenium theatre than when produced in a theatre-in-the-round seating the same number of people. However, a theatre-in-the-round might require twice as many stagehands to get its limited scenery on and off the stage in the same amount of time as fewer stagehands can move twice that amount of scenery in a proscenium theatre. From a budgetary viewpoint the size of the building and the seating capacity will have a much greater impact than the type of stage it contains. However simple and uncluttered a production may *appear*, it is a mistake to jump to the conclusion that it is less costly than a heavier-looking production.

### THE AUDIENCE AREAS ∎

"Going to the theatre" is an experience that begins when the playgoer leaves his home and ends when he has returned to it. In this sense, every place along the way during the evening is part of the audience area. Theatre managers and publicity directors cannot overestimate this fact. Ease and comfort of theatregoing are not only major factors in encouraging habitual theatregoing, they are also major factors in determining how the audience will respond to the performers. A primary goal of audience engineering and house management and of theatre planning is to organize things in a way that enables the audience to give its full attention to the performance. Theatregoers are strongly influenced not only by such factors as convenience in getting to the theatre and securing tickets and being greeted by the house staff but by the physical setting in which they find themselves while attending a performance.

Although Broadway theatres are notorious for their limited lobby space, their small rest rooms and their narrow aisles, there is a psychological point to be made in favor of crowding people in order to create an emotional and intellectual togetherness, ordinarily a desirable audience characteristic. (The "crowding effect" can also be accomplished by means of architecture and decor, without physical crowding.) The other extreme, that of arranging the performance place so that each member of the audience always has an abundance of empty space around him, polarizes audience members from each other and impedes the performer-audience relationship, making communication difficult if not impossible. Open-air theatres are especially susceptible to this problem. The focal point in any performance place must be the performer himself and he, in turn, should be able to feel a unanimity of audience response, which depends upon the audience feeling and responding as a whole.

The general atmosphere that a theatre generates by virtue of its lighting and decor can strongly affect audience reaction. Since warmth and intimacy are complementary to most live theatre experiences, an effort should be made to promote these feelings. The use of warm colors, surfaces and textures that are soft in appearance, a limited amount of empty space and architecture that focuses attention toward the stage are usually desirable. The bland, impersonal, cool and sterile look common to many public or institutional buildings should be assiduously avoided. (This is exactly the look for which the Kennedy Center for the Performing Arts in Washington is most criticized.) The emphasis in live performing arts should, after all, be on the living performer. If his surroundings dwarf his humanity, either physically or psychologically, by stressing a larger-than-life or other-than-human atmosphere, the entire perspective of live performance can be distorted. There are, of course, experimental theatre companies that, in pursuing their aim of creating "total theatre," have unusual requirements for theatre decoration and audience engineering. In most cases, however, theatre directors are desirous of an audience that is prepared to give its full attention to the performance, that is ready to respond as a whole and whose surroundings are in all ways sympathetic to the encouragement of these responses.

The following checklist contains items related to the audience areas of typical theatre buildings. Each item, of course, suggests that its condition, its presence or its absence and its arrangement in a given theatre will contribute to the value of the building, either as an asset or as a liability, and to the success or failure of artistic objectives.

## 1. THE THEATRE EXTERIOR

Proximity to public transportation
Automobile parking facilities
Access to streets and highways
Visibility from public highways and byways
Identification on the building
Marquee and display advertising provisions
Exterior lighting on and in front of building
Street and highway lighting
General security risks and provisions
Proximity to fire hydrants

## 2. THE THEATRE LOBBIES

Location and size of entrance-ways
Door bars and emergency exits
General appearance and decor
Ability to isolate when not in use
General lighting
Flooring and carpeting
Ease and economy of temperature control
Security provisions
Emergency lighting
Size
Potential for multipurpose usage
Box office in relation to audience traffic flow
Coat-checking facilities
Concession spaces (bar, shops, restaurant, etc.)
Space and provisions for display advertising
House-to-lobby speaker or television systems
Curtain-signaling devices
Elevators to upper levels
Gallery areas
Patrons' lounge areas

### 3. THE PUBLIC REST ROOMS

Accessibility from audience areas
General appearance and decor
Ability to isolate when not in use
General lighting
Flooring
Ease and economy of temperature control
Ventilation
Emergency lighting
Size
Sanitary conditions in relation to public health laws
Plumbing conditions
Number of toilet units (both men's and ladies' rest rooms should contain at
     least one unit per hundred of potential audience capacity)
Public water fountains
Disposal provisions
Vending machines for sanitary napkins
Soap vending units
Paper towel and water cup vending units
Automatic hand-drying devices
Number of sinks and mirrored areas

### 4. THE AUDITORIUM

Accessibility from street and lobby areas
General appearance and decor
Ability to isolate when not in use
General lighting
Flooring and carpeting
Ease and economy of temperature control
Emergency lighting
Emergency exits, fire escapes, etc.
Size and number of doors
Acoustics
Air conditioning and heating systems
Security provisions
Number of seats
Potential for increasing or decreasing seat capacity
Space for standing room
Comfort of seats
Condition of seats
Sightlines from house to stage
Elevation of floor and seats
Potential for altering audience-stage relationship
Aisle, row and door lights
Stairway lights and railings
Seating and aisle arrangement in terms of traffic flow, ticket-taking, ushering,
     etc.

Seat, row and aisle numbering system
Ease and economy of cleaning, maintaining, replacing light bulbs or fixtures, etc.
Provisions or space for house-to-stage lighting and projectors
Access to backstage
Ability to separate audience from performer areas
Potential for multipurpose usage

## THE PERFORMERS' AREAS ■

It is probably safe to say that a majority of existing theatre buildings contain backstage and dressing room facilities that range from inadequate to deplorable. Even when the audience areas are outstandingly lush and attractive, it often seems that the architects ran out of space, money, imagination and all respect for creature comfort when it came to constructing facilities for the performers. Dressing rooms are frequently several flights up and a good jog from the stage, contain inadequate heating, plumbing and ventilation systems, have an insufficient amount of space and totally lack anything aesthetically appealing. On the other hand, certain new theatres (especially, it seems, those associated with educational institutions) contain dressing rooms with an atmosphere of sterility reminiscent of surgical scrub rooms. A pleasing medium between these two extremes would seem desirable.

When a building that was not originally intended as a theatre is converted, some unfortunate compromises will probably be necessary when it comes to designing the backstage area. In locations such as Broadway, where every foot of space is a precious commodity, conditions can never be ideal. Examples of buildings poorly converted into theatres are numerous and sometimes almost unbelievable. The Players' Theatre in New York has a stairwell located stage center around which all scenery and action must revolve. The absence of a fire escape makes the balcony section of New York's Equity Library Theatre completely unusable. The tiny doors leading into many Off Broadway theatres render it impossible to carry in preconstructed scenery and set pieces. But much more unforgivable are the glaring errors built into new theatres because an architect was unfamiliar with theatre operations and failed to inform himself about basic production requirements. One new theatre in the Midwest was constructed with permanently installed stage lighting instruments that were wired into the circuits and dimmers, thereby necessitating the same lighting scheme for a big musical production as for a one-man concert. An expensive new dinner theatre in the South provided only one set of rest rooms which had to be shared by audience and performers. A new campus theatre in Texas offers less than a 55 percent view of the stage from a majority of seats in the auditorium. Architects, engineers and administrators should do their homework early and thoroughly.

The amount and type of backstage area required is determined by the type of presentation a particular theatre is designed to accommodate. Is the stage too large and costly to operate in relation to potential box office income? Are rehearsal rooms necessary or will the theatre seldom house a resident group of performers who will need them? Does the same rehearsal and dressing room space have to service more than one performance or production at a time? Can rehearsal areas be utilized during performance hours? Can the stage itself be used for rehearsals during nonperformance hours and can it be heated, cooled and lighted independently from the auditorium?

What are the most desirable and efficient types of stage machinery for the types of productions a theatre is designed to accommodate? Larger and more sophisticated facilities are required when the plan is to perform in repertory style or to produce numerous different productions in rapid succession. The Mark Taper Forum in Los Angeles (which has accommodated a busy resident production schedule since it opened) was built with virtually no rehearsal space and no administrative office space. The Vivian Beaumont Theatre at Lincoln Center, on the other hand, was designed to accommodate a repertory company which, it was expected, would rotate its productions each season. For this reason, an enormous amount of space was provided behind the acting area so that the scenery for two or three productions could be stored intact and simply moved into place when required. But a repertory policy was not practiced at the Beaumont. The large amount of unused space in the building prompted calls for the installation of a cinema theatre and a film library, among other things.

Most of the space in most theatre buildings sits idle most of the time—a startling fact that explains why theatrical real estate is such a costly and impractical holding. While there are disadvantages to multipurpose theatres, every reasonable attempt should be made to utilize theatre buildings as fully as possible and thereby to decrease the horrible necessity of having to support a twenty-four hour plant operation with a mere two hours of income-producing usage. When multipurpose usage can be accomplished without detriment to the operation of the theatre, the supplementary income accrued can comprise the best and most reliable kind of subsidization.

Whether building, buying or leasing a theatre, what is the essential checklist to ponder in regard to the performers' facilities? The following points include many that are required or regulated under Actors' Equity Association rules pertaining to safe and sanitary employment conditions, and these will be inspected periodically by an Equity representative whose approval is prerequisite to the employment of Equity actors.

1. STAGE

Size (depth, width, height, flexibility)
Ability to isolate when not in use
General lighting
Ease and economy of temperature control
Security provisions
Emergency lighting and emergency exits
Potential for multipurpose usage
Accessibility from dressing rooms
Accessibility from scenic loading areas
Asbestos or other fire curtain
Act curtain
Teasers, pipes, lines, rigging systems
Fly space, catwalks, etc.
Automated versus manually operated equipment
Wing space (preferably as large as stage on both sides and/or behind stage)
Quick-change dressing areas in wings

Cross-over wing space (minimum of three feet)
Wall-marked and lighted steps to stage
Stage flooring (must be of wood)
Floor traps
Stage revolves
Apron space
Footlights
Stage wiring and lighting systems
Back-of-house projection and control booth
Facilities for motion picture projection
Space and facilities for rear projection
Cyclorama
Upstage wall
Ability to isolate from street noise, etc.
Ability to seal from daylight and other light sources
Stage manager's control booth and area
Stage manager's communication systems (with front of house, dressing rooms
    and stage hands)
Stage-to-dressing room amplifiers
Sound systems
Orchestra pit (size, flexibility, etc.)
Orchestra pit entrances (below stage level, etc.)
Orchestra lift or elevator

2. THE DRESSING ROOMS:
Size (minimum of four feet of dressing table space per actor)
Number of
Ability to isolate when not in use
General lighting
Ease and economy of temperature control
Ventilation
Security provisions
Accessibility from stage and stage door
Space for doorman near stage door
Call-board and mailbox facilities
Flooring
Corridors and stairs to stage (wide enough for passing actors in large costumes)
General appearance and decor
Communication systems with stage and front of house
Water fountains
Elevators to stage (if more than two stories above or below stage level)
Chorus dressing rooms (for approximately fifteen actors)
Musicians' dressing rooms (for approximately thirty people)
Ballet dressing rooms (for approximately thirty people)
Star dressing rooms (with private rest room, for one actor each)
Conductor's dressing room (with private rest room, for one person each)
Makeup lighting

Mirrors

Overhead shelving and wig racks

Clothing racks in well-ventilated areas

Stage-to-dressing room sound systems

Dressing room sinks

Showers (required for all musical productions)

Rest-room facilities (distance from dressing rooms, number of; should be for
exclusive use by performers, etc.)

Safe and sanitary conditions in relation to public health laws and union regulations)

Green room facilities

Wardrobe room (preferably with washers, sinks, driers and ironing equipment)

Wig and makeup storage facilities

## 3. THE REHEARSAL AREAS

Stage-size rooms available for rehearsal

Flooring (preferably same as stage)

Other space available for rehearsal

Ability to isolate from rest of building

General appearance and decor

Ease and economy of temperature control

General lighting

Ability to adapt to multipurpose usage

Access to stage, orchestra pit, dressing rooms

Musicians' warm-up rooms

Ballet warm-up rooms

Dance barres, mirrors, etc.

Security provisions

Rest-room and shower facilities

Locker facilities

## THE SCENIC PRODUCTION AREAS ▪

Space and facilities for the construction of scenery, costumes and props is a
decided asset in any theatre building intended to support resident productions. Commercial theatres in New York and on the road do not require such space because the
physical production is usually a temporary tenant. But in cases where the landlord
(whether an individual or an organization) is also a producer who originates productions from the beginning, facilities for the construction and rehearsal of productions
will be necessary either in the theatre building or elsewhere. If located away from
the theatre, scenic construction areas may be more costly due to scenery transportation requirements and more difficult to control from the administrative point of
view. The operation that is centralized under one roof is always the most desirable
one.

Like the auditorium itself, adequate scenic production facilities require an enormous amount of space and a large capital investment in machinery and supplies,
which makes such facilities impractical for organizations that do not offer a number

of different productions on a regular basis. Scenic construction areas are also difficult to utilize for nontheatrical purposes. In cases where the theatre building does
not contain such facilities, it is possible to rent lofts, bowling alleys, warehouses
and other low-cost spaces. Some amateur and stock theatres find it necessary to
construct most scenery out-of-doors or in neighboring barns and garages. Some educational theatres utilize the industrial arts workshop in their school or college.
Whatever solutions are found, the place and the cost for scenic construction should
be studied carefully when plans to build or utilize a theatre are being formulated.
The following list should serve as a working guide:

### 1. THE SCENIC CONSTRUCTION SHOP

Size
Accessibility to stage
Space available exclusively for construction
Ability to isolate when not in use
General lighting and electric power facilities
Ease and economy of temperature control
Humidity problems (in relation to the drying of painted flats, drops, etc.)
Flooring
Fireproofing (and adequate space to fireproof set pieces)
Ability to use during performance hours
Lumber storage provisions
Scenery storage and dock areas
Loading docks and ramps
Scene-painting docks and convenient slop sinks
Scene-construction areas
Work tables
Tool storage cabinets
Paint and brush-cleaning and storage facilities
Tool inventory: hand and power tools
Stock scenery and platform inventory
Muslin and fabric inventory
Security provisions
Office space for designer and technical directors
Public and interoffice communication systems

### 2. STAGE ELECTRICS SHOP

Lighting designer's office space
Stage electrician's office and work space
Size
Security provisions
Accessibility to theatre and stage
Inventory of stage lighting instruments
Inventory of gels
Inventory of light projectors and special-effects equipment
Inventory of tools
Inventory of lamps, bulbs, etc.

Inventory of electrical cable, plugs, etc.

Storage space

Fireproofing

### 3. THE PROPERTIES SHOP

Size

Accessibility to theatre and stage

Security provisions

General lighting

Office and work space for properties supervisors

Storage space for hand props

Storage space for furniture and large props

Provisions near stage for storage and preparation of perishable props, food, etc.

Inventory of properties

Inventory of fabrics and supplies

### 4. THE COSTUME SHOP

Size

Accessibility to theatre and stage

Security provisions

General lighting

Office space for costume designer

Work space, cutting tables, etc.

Inventory of sewing machines, irons, etc.

Inventory of supplies

Inventory of fabrics

Inventory of costumes (clothing, hats, wigs, shoes, jewelry, etc.)

Storage cabinets

Storerooms for costume collection

Fitting rooms

Library of resource books

Fireproofing

Laundry and dyeing facilities

### THE ADMINISTRATION AREAS ■

As with the space and facilities provided for performers, many theatres also fall short when it comes to the areas in which its administrators must work. The members of a management staff in a fairly active theatre are usually required to work long hours in places that often resemble the cells of a maximum-security prison rather than places designed to encourage efficient work and pleasant attitudes. What, then, is an appropriate checklist of items and factors to consider when it comes to planning office space for an executive staff?

### 1. THE MANAGEMENT OFFICES

Size

Number of separate offices available
Physical relationship of offices to each other
Accessibility to theatre and rest of operation
Need for branch offices away from theatre
Ability to isolate when not in use
Security provisions
General appearance and decor
Ease and economy of temperature control
Flooring
Soundproofing
General lighting
Inventory of furniture, equipment, supplies
Storage space for records and supplies
Communication systems (with public, with other departments in theatre,
    between offices)
Reception space
Secretarial space
Executive space
Board room or conference room space
Library and archive space
Press office space and facilities
Reasonable privacy for executives

## 2. THE BOX OFFICE
Size
Security provisions
General appearance and decor
Ease and economy of temperature control (ability to isolate from exterior
    weather conditions)
Fireproofing
Soundproofing
General lighting
Proximity to business offices
Number of customer windows or spaces
Number of treasurers that can be accommodated
Communications systems (with public and offices)
Ticket storage space
Storage space for equipment and supplies
Inventory of equipment and supplies
Need for theatre-operated agencies away from building
Accessibility to general public
Safe
Work space away from public view
Convenience of telephone to the ticket window

Each item on the preceeding checklists can be translated into a considerable
amount of money when purchase or alteration of it is necessary. Its condition and

how close it comes to what is ideal and serviceable will contribute to the value of a theatre both as a physical asset and as a factor that contributes to or detracts from operational efficiency. While no theatre is perfect, most theatres could come much closer to achieving optimum conditions if more time were spent on detail in the planning and organizing stages of construction or renovation.

From the time an idea to build or acquire a theatre is conceived until opening night and throughout the life of the organization, it must be kept in mind that the performer is central to everything else. We build theatres primarily for actors to act in, not primarily to display scenery, to exhibit architecture or to memorialize an individual. Throughout every phase of planning and producing a play, the acting company, its repertory and its artistic objectives must be the dominating influence in all decision-making. Of all the raw materials available to the theatre today, perhaps the most important one, as British director Peter Brook has pointed out, is empty or open space. It is space, pure and simple, that the actor can best mold according to the unlimited dimensions of the imagination.

When contracting for a theatre, then, every precaution should be taken to insure that artistic policy will be established by the theatre personnel and not by the architecture and the physical surroundings or, at least, that these elements—the human and the physical—complement each other. A strong sales resistance must be developed against architects, designers, consultants and technologists who are more interested in form than in function, in methods as opposed to results, in efficiency as opposed to effect, in machinery as opposed to people. A newfangled stage lighting system, for example, may be a wonderful thing for a large professional theatre but a foolish luxury in a high school theatre where no one has the knowledge or ability to operate it. Traditional methods of doing things must always be weighed against those that are new and revolutionary. The methods finally adopted should be the ones best suited to the needs and objectives of a particular producing organization. Many people want the "newest and the best" while others merely want "a theatre that looks like a theatre." It is up to those who will work in a theatre building to exert their influence in securing what they believe comes closest to being ideal for them.

# CHAPTER FOUR

# The Staff for the Theatre

■ FINDING AND HIRING THE STAFF

### THE GOAL OF PERSONNEL MANAGEMENT ■

The artistic personnel in a theatre—actors, designers and directors—are assembled to breathe life into the thoughts and feelings of a script, the selection of which is, in itself, the foremost declaration of a producing organization's philosophy and objectives. The stage presentation and the artists who make it possible are the most obvious and important elements in the project. If they fail to demonstrate the desired image of a theatre, the efforts of others in the operation are fruitless. But the administrative staff is also a reflection of overall aims and policies. Supportive personnel, including administrators, stagehands, ushers and doormen, are not hired simply to follow orders. They are, like the artists, hired to support an idea.

In an open letter to the New York City Board of Estimate (reprinted in *The New York Times*, 10 March 1971), the famous drama critic, Brooks Atkinson, joined in an appeal to save the Public Theatre by providing a statement that illustrates how clearly and thoroughly a performing group can project its philosophy and aims to the public through its stage productions as well as through its administrative staff:

March 4, 1971
*Dear Members of the Board of Estimate:*

There is so much that is admirable about Joseph Papp's New York Shake-speare Festival that I will confine myself to one item—the new play *Subject to Fits*, based on Dostoevsky's *The Idiot*; it is a remarkable theatre event.

Since the play is a fluid succession of images and impressions it must have been very difficult to perceive in script form—but it was. It is certainly most difficult to stage. But the production of *Subject to Fits* is tangible and practi-cal, and the performance is brilliant. A difficult script has been understood and is expressed with great force and clarity by an excellent cast. New York is lucky to have a creative production center where original plays can be acted with en-thusiasm and professional skill for the pleasure and instruction of the public.

Mind you, *Subject to Fits* is only one of five productions currently on view in the Public Theatre. I wonder if anywhere in the United States—or the world —there is a theatrical institution of such scope and validity that has so much faith in the public without having a political program. The existence of a free festival of Shakespeare in Central Park is remarkable enough. But a free Shake-speare Festival that has developed an acting style of high caliber is almost in-credible. There is nothing second-rate about the free Shakespeare or the mod-estly priced productions in the Public Theatre.

One thing more and, I think, most significant. The young people in the box office, the young ushers, the young men who receive the public at the door are civil, have excellent manners and are personally attractive. The morale of the staff is conspicuously high. There is a reason for that. They know that the Public Theatre is on the level and that it does not serve the personal ambitions of any person or the interests of any group but the public. It is a public service organization with the highest motivation.

I hope the city treats it with honor and respect as a vital part of the rich civilization and culture of New York.
Respectfully yours,
*Brooks Atkinson*

Mr. Atkinson's letter is not only a testimony to the Public Theatre, it is also, by im-plication, a sad comment on how infrequently other theatre groups project a clear and unselfish image of their work and how rarely this is illustrated by administrative as well as artistic personnel. When the idea is a good one, it is worth carrying out to the last syllable.

FINDING APPLICANTS ▪

Knowing the goals and policies of an organization means knowing the type of people most suited to carry them out. Such basic differences as those between pro-fessional and amateur, profit and nonprofit, long-range and short-range, educational and noneducational, immediately dictate a great deal about the type of person most suited for the operation as well as where to find him.

In commercial theatre a majority of personnel—artistic, technical, administrative, maintenance—are derived from the membership of labor unions and other collective bargaining organizations, which specify minimum salaries and working conditions as well as the minimum number of union employees required for a particular job or department. This is not to say that management cannot hire outside such labor groups, although this may be difficult either because of pressures applied by labor groups or because virtually all the qualified people for a job belong to a labor organization. Nonetheless, it is important to remember that labor groups are voluntary both in terms of the employees who belong to them and the management groups that hire from them and agree to their terms. Unions are founded and subscribed to in belief that they can provide the best employment protection and bargaining power for a particular classification of worker. When most specialists in a field belong to and uphold the authority of a union, management is forced to bargain with that union. Periodic contracts are negotiated between representatives of the union on behalf of its membership and representatives of management.

These contracts establish minimum wages, benefits and working conditions. But contracts and agreements are not to be confused with state and federal employment laws (which also provide broad protection of workers' rights and minimum wage requirements). Federal law (namely, the Taft-Hartley Act) does not require management to hire from union ranks, if one excludes civil service positions. Management may hire nonunion people for any position (actor, designer, stagehand, etc.). The appropriate union must then offer that person union membership, which he is obliged to accept within two weeks. Serving apprenticeships and taking examinations are not, contrary to common opinion, the only ways to gain membership in certain unions. One merely needs to be offered a job in a unionized theatre or shop. Of course, some labor groups would doubtless protest this policy in order to protect jobs for current members. The term "brotherhood" is more than a euphemism in the jargon of unionized labor, and management is seldom allowed to forget this fact for very long. Examples of successful contract-breaking with unions are unusual in theatre as in other industries, although there have certainly been many contests and strikes between the two factions. Many arguments and imbalances exist that make theatrical unions difficult for managers to love. But, after all is said, the case in favor of unions remains a strong one.

Few labor unions serve as employment agencies for their members. They do provide prospective employees when requested to do so and most performers' unions and professional bargaining associations also provide helpful directories listing their membership. Too, they may distribute newsletters or maintain bulletin boards or catalogs of employment opportunities at their various offices and thus serve as a . helpful channel of communication between management and labor.

Large nonprofit performing organizations and commercial theatre companies usually seek artistic talent through the offices of established theatrical agents or by means of auditions and technical employees through union offices. Administrative employees may be hired through professional organizations or as a result of a personal acquaintance or recommendation. Nonprofit professional, educational and community theatres may avail themselves of placement services such as those operated by the Theatre Communications Group, Opportunity Resources for the Performing Arts and the American Theatre Association, among others. Even the nonspecialized employment bureaus, such as those operated by state unemployment offices or private agencies, may sometimes be useful in locating qualified applicants for certain jobs.

There are several summer employment guides, published annually, that are particularly helpful as a source for personnel in stock theatres and other groups that utilize
students and apprentices. A simple listing with agencies like the Advancement Placement Institute (Brooklyn, New York), the National Directory Service (Cincinnati,
Ohio), the American Theatre Association's "Summer Theatre Directory" (Washington, D.C.) or the American Collegiate Employment Institute (Los Angeles, California), which costs only a few dollars each year, may attract hundreds of applicants.
Hundreds more can be found if an organization lists its job openings with a few
dozen appropriate schools and colleges around the country, most of which maintain
placement services that make available listings of seasonal and year-round job opportunities for students and provide dossiers about their graduates when requested to
do so by potential employers. Various trade publications, including *Backstage* and
Leo Shull's *Summer Theatres*, also offer free or low-cost listings of theatres and job
opportunities which may be useful to both employers and applicants, although the
accuracy of such listings may be unreliable.

When the employing organization submits job listings for publication, it should
provide job descriptions that are clear, concise and accurate to avoid attracting unqualified or inappropriate applicants. The listing or statement should include the
name of the theatre organization, a brief description of its aims, the location of the
theatre, job openings listed by title, the salary range and other benefits (such as free
room and board), the approximate number of openings, whether it is a professional
or nonprofessional group and how to apply and to whom. For example:

STAR PLAYHOUSE: Located near Tanglewood, Mass., Star Playhouse is a
nonprofit summer theatre producing an annual season of six plays performed
by non-Equity actors and offering college credit through the University of
Massachusetts summer school. Auditions held each spring for 5 resident actors
($50.00 per week) and 10 apprentice actors (nonsalaried). Other openings for
technical and administrative positions (salary range: $50.00 to $100.00 per
week). Send pictures and resumes to: Mr. Jack Smith, 000 Broadway, Rm.
507, NYC.

Listings should never serve as an exclusive source of potential employees. Nothing,
after all, can replace an employer's personal acquaintance with a wide number of
people in the field, from whom he can either request recommendations for job openings or request applications directly. The active and thoughtful manager makes it a
habit to collect the names and adresses of people whose work he sees and admires.
Even though he may not have roles or positions available in the near future, he
knows that qualified and talented people are uncommon, that his memory is shorter
and more unreliable than a written notation and that being able to come up with the
right person for the right job is a priceless advantage that may eventually determine
the success of his endeavors.

Acquaintances that last a lifetime are likely to be formed while a person is still
a college student or budding professional. Being in early company with promising
and energetic people of one's own age can be a tremendous boon in later years
when life tends to offer fewer new friends and less time for the casual observation
of other people's qualities and abilities. The administrator should learn early to keep

two separate address books: one for social addresses and one for professional addresses. While it is foolhardy to believe that business cannot be mixed with pleasure, it is equally foolhardy to think that personal fondness or dislike for another person makes that person any more or less qualified for a given position. If there is any truth to the saying that "the surest way to lose a friend is to lend him money," it is even surer to claim "if you hire a friend, you lose a buddy." Indebtedness and subservience seldom breed friendship, especially if they stem from "noble" and "well-meant" intentions. Nor, obviously, should a person's ability to perform a certain job ever be confused with such things as the color of his skin, the manner of his dress or the company he keeps. When an employer surrounds himself with personnel who merely flatter his ego and confirm his prejudices, the enterprise is likely to resemble an adopted family rather than a serious business and the results will be more in the nature of personal testimony than honest labor.

The names of promising potential employees, then, can be systematically filed on index cards, informally entered in an address book or noted on scraps of paper and thrown into a shoe box. If one is active in hiring or recommending people for positions, a meaningful collection of names quickly becomes indispensable.

### PROCESSING THE JOB APPLICATIONS ▪

When an organization invites resumes and applications from potential employees, it should be prepared to answer each and every response it receives. It is both unethical and inconsiderate to invite applications and then to ignore them.

If there is an appropriate opening for an applicant and if the size of the theatre operation warrants it, he should be requested to complete a detailed information form that is geared to the special needs and problems of the job and organization. It should be clearly composed, with sufficient space for the applicant to write all answers on the form itself. The following standard items should be included on most applications:

Applicant's name
Present address and zip—if temporary, until what date
Permanent address and zip
Present telephone number
Answering service or other telephone
Education:
  High school and year completed
  College and degrees completed with dates
  Professional training, workshops attended, etc.
Housing needs
Driver's license?
Owner of automobile?
Date available for employment·(if seasonal operation)
Date when applicant must terminate employment (if seasonal)
Statement of career goals
Listing of theatre experience and positions held with dates
Names and addresses of at least three people who may be requested to provide statements about applicant
List of hometown and college newspapers (for the publicity department)

It should be noted that questions regarding age, sex and marital status are contrary to "fair employment" guidelines. The application form should be accompanied by a covering letter (a standard, dittoed letter may be used if applications are numerous) that describes the goals of the organization, the type of employees it is seeking, the nature of the employment and other details pertaining to the particular group. Every attempt should be made to disallow the applicant of false impressions he may have about the organization. For example, if apprentices are used but seldom given acting roles on stage, this should be clarified as soon as possible, as should the salary range, special housing or transportation problems that might be associated with the position and so forth. Too often, missing or misleading information causes both the applicant and the employer to waste a lot of time, money and energy.

If the applicant is not qualified, he should be so notified and his application placed on file for future reference. When the applicant appears to be promising, requests for letters of recommendation should be made, especially from people or groups familiar to the employer. The vast majority of letters written or comments made about an applicant by people he himself has provided as references are, of course, likely to sound more like eulogies than realistic appraisals. But any information and opinion may provide helpful clues concerning the applicant's personality and work habits.

Preferably before an applicant is interviewed in person and certainly before he begins employment, he should be given a packet of detailed information that includes such things as a brief history of the organization, short biographies of its artistic and administrative directors, an outline of typical production and work schedules, a table of organization listing the personnel and showing the chain of command, necessary details about housing and transportation and answers to whatever other questions applicants most frequently ask about the group and its theatre.

### INTERVIEWING THE APPLICANT ■

A person's first visit and personal contact with an organization and its directors creates an impression that, if he is hired, will last throughout his employment and serve as a positive, negative or fuzzy foundation for it. Few theatres are so large that every new employee cannot be given a personal tour of the building and an introduction to its directors. If the job opening is for a leading position, such as head of a department in the organization, the interview should be spread over several meetings and several days, thereby allowing the applicant to meet a number of people and to make himself better known to his potential colleagues. Before an applicant is hired, a conference should be held with appropriate people in the theatre who have met and talked with him. His qualifications should be discussed and the hiring agent should be able to discern from such a conference how well the applicant is likely to get along with others in the operation. When interviews and conferences go badly, it is generally because too little thought is given to seemingly minor details or because too little time is allowed.

### DETERMINING THE SALARY ■

When the fiscal organization of a theatre is determined by civil service laws and budget and salary lines are mandated by a parent institute (as with many educational and civic theatres), management may have little or no choice in determining salaries, raises, overtime payments, special bonuses and the like. While this may simplify the process of negotiating with job applicants, it also cancels out one of the strongest controls that management has over the employee. Employment situations that guarantee annual increments, provide tenure and rigidly stipulate how applicants are hired and from what sources, how they are promoted and where they may and may not work in an organization may present major personnel problems for the theatre administrator who is burdened with them. It is a situation common to many theatre departments in public colleges where as much as 90 percent of the non-student staff and faculty concerned with the theatre operation may have salaries, positions, hours and specific responsibilities that are nearly impossible to alter without something close to an act of Congress. While providing job security, such systems tend to encourage over-staffing, job duplication, apathy and inefficiency. They may also reward employees more for seniority than for ability and thus make it extremely difficult for management to maintain a consistently high quality of work. Security, such as that provided by tenure, tends to remove challenge, and without challenge the likelihood of meaningful human response is a greatly reduced.

In instances where the employer has a good latitude for setting and adjusting salaries, the person doing the hiring should bear in mind the following questions:

1. What are the current minimum wage requirements?
2. What is the minimum salary established by the applicant's union or collective bargaining association, if he belongs to one?
3. What are people in comparable positions and organizations currently earning?
4. What fringe benefits might be offered that should be figured as part of the salary (such as health and life insurance, pension and retirement plans, living allowances, travel and tax benefits, commissions or percentages, etc.)?
5. What is the current supply and demand for the job in question?
6. What opportunities for advancement and salary increases does the job offer?
7. Will the applicant bring more experience, training and ability to the organization than it will offer him?

Often, a starting salary may be negotiated downward from what the applicant first demands or expects because the job offers certain benefits and opportunities, financial and otherwise. Or, job applicants may accept lower salaries in order to work with a particular organization, in a particular location or during particular hours. In short, money is not the only kind of payment for labor. But terms of employment may also be overly compromised. For example, a part-time worker may cost the employer less than a full-time worker, but can reasonably be expected to accomplish the job in the time allotted. If "moonlighting" or outside employment is allowed, how will this affect the quality of work? How will the job title affect the worker? If, for instance, a person is given the title of "technical director," even though the job is that of stage carpenter, will he actually function as a carpenter or will he soon decide that he is primarily a supervisor in fact as well as in title?

Which salaries in a theatre, if any, should be computed on the basis of a percentage or commission? When the employee has a fair chance of realizing a meaningful gain from a percentage of some kind a commission can serve as a good incentive to the employee and a good efficiency investment for management. Positions concerned with publicity, group ticket sales, subscription sales and others fit easily into this category. Or, to encourage economy, management might offer purchasing agents of various kinds (the designer, the technical director, the properties master, the business manager) a percentage of any amount *below* a prestated budget for which they are able to accomplish certain projects.

Finally, the employer must scrutinize the hidden costs of hiring a particular person. Can the organization not only afford the person's salary but also support the manner in which he works? A low-budget operation might find it necessary to hire a stage electrician to maintain and improve the lighting equipment on stage. But can it afford a lighting designer who not only will contribute to more effective productions but also will require more instruments and better equipment, if not a supportive staff of his own? If the lighting designer is hired but there is no budget to support him, he cannot possibly do his job and his is therefore a wasted salary. Similarly, a highly qualified publicity director will require a budget and a staff to prove his value, as will other specialists. With experience and professionalism come higher efficiency *and* higher costs.

# ■ GENERAL PRINCIPLES OF PERSONNEL MANAGEMENT

### JOB ORIENTATION ■

Some managers believe in allowing people to learn their jobs simply by plunging them headlong into the work; others prefer to put the new employee through a period of special training and job orientation. Both methods may work well, but a person's real abilities can never be known until he has been tested in action. Also, some positions in a theatre allow more room for error and inefficiency than others. For example, a secretary who mistypes a letter can do it over without causing much damage, but a box office treasurer who gives a customer more tickets than he paid for cannot rectify his mistake as easily.

When an entire staff has been hired to begin work for the first time together, as in the case of a new theatre or at the beginning of a new season, a general orientation meeting involving virtually all personnel in the organization is essential to clarify and restate the goals and objectives of the enterprise, to establish a sense of unity, to introduce people to each other and to establish the general chain of authority. When only one or two new employees join a working organization, every effort should be made to help them become integral parts of the group as soon as possible.

Many positions in a theatre, and certainly all supervisory positions, should be clearly and specifically outlined in a work manual. Sometimes referred to as an "idiot book" (under the assumption that if the person who usually does the job is suddenly absent any idiot can pick up the manual and do the job), an effective manual describes all the responsibilities and peculiarities of a particular job or department. At the very least, every theatre should maintain updated manuals that cover general management, business management, press and publicity, box office operations, house management, stage management, company management, scene and prop construction, makeup, costumes and plant and tool maintenance and operations. Such manuals should include work hours, supervisory responsibilities, procedures to follow under both normal and emergency conditions, a list of vendors and service companies with their phone numbers, an inventory of supplies and equipment and a list of recommended improvements, submitted periodically by the department head. Work manuals should be reviewed and revised at least once each year and, collectively, should present a clear and objective picture of how the operation functions. Of course, no two people work in the same manner. A given system may work well for one person but not for another and there is always a better way of doing something. Procedural flexibility is desirable and a work manual should be used as a guide and history of operations, not as a bible.

## JOB COMBINING ■

Combining several jobs into one position may be frowned upon by large organizations and institutions or may be forbidden by labor unions, but job-combining is a practice common to many theatres because of limited finances or because it encourages greater efficiency. As a general rule, it is better to be slightly shorthanded than to be conspicuously over-staffed. No employee should be truly indispensable, but each person should feel and, indeed, *be* needed. As a person grows into a job, he should be able to assume more work and more responsibility. He will doubtless respond better if the increased work load brings with it not simply a greater volume of work but new types of chores and greater challenges. Even big industries have finally recognized this truism and are reassigning the one-task assemblyline worker to multi-task, beginning-to-end production work.

It is wise, however, to avoid combining a backstage with a front-of-house position, a leading acting job with any other job, any two jobs that involve similar hours or require being in two different places at the same time or any two jobs that require full-time work. Depending on the type of theatre organization and its size, what are some of the most frequent and successful job combinations?

Producer and Director
Producer and General Manager
Producer and Business Manager
Producer and Publicity Director
Director and Designer
Stage Manager and Lighting Designer
Assistant Stage Manager and Properties Master
Scenic Designer and Costume and Properties Designer
Scenic Designer and Lighting, Costume and Props Designer
Lighting Designer and Electrician
Designer and Technical Director
Publicity Director and House Manager
Publicity Director and Assistant Box Office Treasurer
Publicity Director and Assistant to the Producer
Publicity Director and Assistant Manager
Business Manager and Box Office Treasurer
Business Manager and Secretary
Business Manager and House Manager
Business Manager and Associate Producer
Business Manager and Assistant Manager

Job-combining is frequently a good device for offering a person the highest possible salary, providing him with the greatest set of challenges and making maximum
use of his abilities. Successful job combinations, however, always depend upon the
interests and qualifications of the individual doing the jobs. Because one person may
perform several jobs simultaneously in a superb manner does not mean that a replacement with the same ability can ever be found or, necessarily, even should be
sought. Jobs must be suited to people, not people to jobs.

### ALLOCATING RESPONSIBILITY ▪

There is a major difference between supervising people and, in effect, doing their
jobs for them. A competent employee will function best if he knows his responsibilities and knows, too, that no one else is going to carry them out. If his superiors continually subvert his authority by decision-making and acting in his stead without his
consent and consultation or deal directly with his supportive staff or crew members,
he is justified in adopting a careless attitude toward his work. Any problem or policy
should be forced either up or down a ladder of responsibility, one step at a time.
This procedure not only respects the authority of each staff member, it also insures
the most thorough examination and treatment of the matter at hand.

A table of organization will provide a helpful reminder of lines of responsibilities.
Especially for amateur and educational theatres, it should be displayed where everyone can see it often.  Knowing the right person to go to for a particular reason is
always a mark of professionalism. But this obviously cannot be accomplished unless
that person's name and position are known. The manner in which a person is approached is usually as important as the reason for approaching him. When people
take pride in their work they appreciate it when both the work and the worker are
given due recognition. For instance, the manager of a large restaurant that employs
a first-rate master chef is well-advised to ask that chef's permission when he wishes
to enter the kitchen. Similarly, a theatre manager should speak with the production
stage manager before entering the backstage or dressing-room areas during performance hours. It is not that the manager cannot go where he pleases and speak with
whomever he likes. It is a matter of observing certain courtesies and formalities and
thereby showing trust and allegiance to an office or position. Professional respect
should be paid from the highest to the lowest position on the ladder of authority.
When the lowest man on that ladder is approached, the man with no executive
title or supervisory responsibility to honor, he too deserves treatment that acknowledges the same amount of dignity that is accorded to his professional superiors.

### JOB MOBILITY ▪

Whether or not workers in a hierarchy tend to rise to their highest level of in-
competence, as Laurence Peter and Raymond Hull suggest in their book *The Peter
Principle*, is a matter of opinion. It does seem true that few people today are satisfied to remain very long in the first job they find. Job mobility is a fact of contemporary life and no employer can reasonably expect to hold on to a staff in-
definitely. Change-over of personnel, however, should never be so voluminous that
it resembles a game of musical chairs. If that is the case, it almost certainly indicates
an absence of leadership. When a theatre group lacks purpose and its leaders fail
to demonstrate fairness, willingness to allocate responsibility and praise for jobs

well done, its employees are bound to feel dissatisfaction. Nonunionized and low-salaried workers, especially, seldom remain very long with an organization that fails to provide psychic remuneration. The first step in retaining a staff is to treat it well. The second is to recognize individual talents and·abilities and to adjust these continually to the work at hand. The third is to recognize when a person has outgrown the organization and then to encourage and assist him to secure another position with challenges more commensurate with his abilities.

The creation of a reasonably permanent staff depends primarily upon finding people who can make a meaningful and needed contribution to an organization while at the same time receiving a sense of accomplishment from it. When the element of give-and-take is absent, it is time for the ambitious employee to move on. The organization that fails to encourage a certain amount of personnel change-over runs a serious risk of becoming overly staid and ingrown for lack of new blood. When this is carried to an extreme and a group becomes, in effect, a club that is closed to most newcomers and hence to the vitality of new ideas, it is insuring its own doom.

VOLUNTEER WORKERS ▪

The major disadvantage of employing nonsalaried, volunteer workers is the difficulty in holding them responsible for their work, since that work is really done as a favor to the organization. Volunteer workers are also likely to have other, perhaps more important things to do and, rightfully, feel only a secondary allegiance to their volunteer work. Yet, they are a necessity to most amateur, community, educational and stock theatres.

Whenever possible, volunteer help should be give tangible rewards and also be made aware of the intangible benefits and rewards of their labor. When work can be exchanged for such things as college credit, credit toward union membership and the like, greater control can be extended over work quality and output. Volunteer workers also may be rewarded with special privileges, such as parties, free tickets and the use of special rooms. In any event, their work should be officially recognized by the theatre's director, who should endeavor to give them credit at every opportunity (in speeches, in the program, in newspaper publicity) and who should aggressively avoid taking credit himself. Nobody turns green with envy when a director's name is not mentioned and, in fact, the opposite reaction will more probably result. Personal publicity and self-aggrandizement are never satisfying to anyone except the person seeking them. Supervisory personnel should attempt to strike a happy medium between false modesty and compulsive boastfulness. Giving credit to volunteers and supportive workers is a good way to begin. On the other hand, volunteer workers should also be treated as if they had the same obligations to the quality of their work as salaried or professional personnel. Frequently, the more that is expected of a person the more he will give, although it is also a supervisor's job to determine a worker's maximum capabilities and then to aim his demands at that level, neither higher nor lower. Management should not hesitate to dismiss volunteer personnel when it proves useless or frivolous or fails to complete assigned tasks. It is often easy to attract volunteers, but initial enthusiasm frequently wanes and work goes unfinished.

A number of states have special laws that may prohibit the use of volunteer workers in certain jobs, such as ushering or administrative work. Other laws restrict the number of nonsalaried apprentices an organization may utilize, and all states observe child labor laws. Good volunteer help may be drawn from local educational, religious, charity and women's organizations. Or it may be drawn from among the people who merely walk through the door and volunteer their services. As with good salaried employees, it may come from a personal acquaintance with individuals who, for example, are retired and feel flattered to have their knowledge and experience placed in harness again (several cities have organized groups of retired executives who offer their services, free of charge, to small or new businesses).

### WORK SUPERVISION ▪

Creating and maintaining good relationships between labor and management and within each department of a theatre is a delicate and time-consuming process not unlike that of being the parent of a large family. A supervisor of personnel, whether director of the entire operation or merely a part of it, may adopt a strong disciplinary attitude, a paternal and permissive one or something in between. The appropriate degree of supervisory formality is mandated by the size and type of operation in question. Few would argue, however, that an unhappy and dissatisfied staff functions as well as a happy and satisfied one. This does not mean that the supervisor should court the loyalties of workers by overindulging them with gifts, parties, small talk and the like. Professional honesty and fairness win loyalty and efficiency much sooner.

Once employees are hired and settled in their jobs, what are some of the measures that can be taken to encourage teamwork and efficiency?

The most skillful supervisor is the one who can prevent trouble before it begins. Early and minor corrections of some problem, especially where personalities are concerned, are always easier and less disruptive than trying to correct problems that have festered and grown into major crises. To recognize a problem in its early stages, the supervisor must be sensitive to what is going on among his staff members. He must establish and maintain lines of communication with them, which involves keeping his door open at least to key personnel, listening to different, representative viewpoints within a group and actively seeking more opinion and information whenever he is in doubt about some situation. He must be cognizant of the power structures within a group: who are the instigators, how are loyalties being divided? He must be able to guide the more dominant, aggressive employees in such a manner that their energies will be channeled in a positive way and the weaker so that their opinions and abilities are more fully utilized.

Perhaps the most corrosive attitude that can develop within a group is that of negativism. Every measure should be taken to prevent it even if it necessitates the dismissal of certain workers. A second factor that can quickly corrode the morale and efficiency of a group is that of factionalism or the formation of cliques. It is a malignant disease that affects the psychology of a group and should be dealt with severely.

Whatever the problem or situation, staff supervisors must attempt to analyze everything with a cool and objective eye, avoiding both over-reaction and a do-nothing policy. A supervisor must strive to establish himself as a fair arbitrator. He should be very cautious in stating his own opinions about the personalities and factions within a group and he must never appear to take sides except concerning artistic and professional standards, about which his opinions should be made completely clear. It should be clear, also, that no amount of favor-seeking, gossip or other personal appeal can influence or compromise his professional demands. The surest way to abdicate a position of leadership is to practice hypocrisy. Conversely, people will always respect steadiness and a good degree of predictability from their superiors. These are factors that can provide no small amount of employee security.

Criticism is constructive only when it helps the person to whom it applies to work more happily and efficiently. If there is a problem within an operation, it is the supervisor's responsibility to analyze and pinpoint the cause *in order to correct it*—not merely in order to place blame, pass the buck or "gripe."

The main purpose of this chapter is to discuss administrative and technical personnel in theatre. But more remains to be said on the subject of artists as employees. Although often protected by labor unions, performing artists are the most uncharacteristic of all unionized workers. In theatrical circles one frequently hears the expression "actors are children." Taken at face value, this is absurd and patronizing. It does, however, perhaps indicate that performers are not always as thoroughly indoctrinated as other laborers with a nine-to-five mentality and that the special nature of their work cannot ultimately or fully be regulated by union contracts and rule books. Actors provide a unique service in society, as dependent upon their innate abilities and God-given gifts as upon their training. Management has an obligation to nurture and protect meritorious talent in the theatre no less than society as a whole has an obligation to protect the resources of nature. Yet, too often, the performer has been regarded as servant rather than master in his own house. Only when performers are placed at the top of all other priorities in terms of theatre personnel can they be true masters of their art and only then can theatre stand comfortably beside the best in all types of artistic achievement. The theatre manager must recognize this priority and guard against any compromise that might, for example, allow the playwright, the designer, the technician, the publicity director or somebody else to convince himself that *he* is the *raison d'être* for the whole enterprise. He is not. Everyone and everything in a theatre is there to support the performer. When this perspective is lost, much else is lost along with it.

### MINIMUM STAFFING REQUIREMENTS ■

What size and type of administrative and technical staff does a theatre need in order to function efficiently according to its stated goals and its fiscal resources? The following chart demonstrates that typical minimum staffing requirements for a community, stock or Broadway theatre of the same size doing the same type of entertainment may not vary a great deal. Staffing differences, rather, are determined by whether or not a theatre employs professionals and whether or not these professionals are unionized. Professional salaried personnel are able to accomplish a job more efficiently than a nonprofessional volunteer staff, so the former *should* have fewer staff requirements. But this may not be the case. A fully unionized theatre must comply with union demands for the employment of a minimum number of people whether or not they are actually needed. From this point of view, the greatest flexibility in staffing and the optimum in employee efficiency may occur in a professional theatre that employs salaried but largely nonunionized personnel.

## AN 800 SEAT, NON-MUSICAL THEATRE   TYPICAL MINIMUM STAFF REQUIREMENTS

| Nonprofessional community theatre (multi-production season) | | Stock theatre using AEA company (multi-production season) | | Broadway theatre (one production) | |
|---|---|---|---|---|---|
| Full-time operating staff (nonsalaried) | Part-time or on fee, royalty or optional | Full-time operating staff (nonunion) | Part-time or on fee, royalty or optional | Full-time operating staff (union) | Part-time or on fee, royalty or optional |
| Artistic Director<br>House Manager<br>Box Office Treasurer<br>Stage Manager<br>Master Electrician<br>Properties Master<br>Stage crew<br>Makeup crew | Board of Directors<br>Committees<br>Executive Secretary<br>Business Secretary<br>Publicity Chairman<br>Ticket Sales committees<br>Legal Counsel<br>Director<br>Author*<br>Scenic, Lighting and Costume Designer<br>Scene and Costume construction crews<br>Ushers<br>Ticket-takers<br>Prompters<br>Maintenance crew | Producer or Artistic Director<br>General Manager<br>Business Manager<br>House Manager<br>Secretary<br>Box Office Treasurer<br>Assistant Treasurer<br>Publicity Director<br>Janitor(s)<br>Production Stage Manager*<br>Scenic Designer<br>Lighting Designer<br>Costume Designer<br>Properties Master<br>Technical Director<br>Carpenter<br>Seamstress and Wardrobe Mistress<br>Master Electrician<br>5-15 technicians or apprentices | Board of Directors (if nonprofit)<br>Attorney<br>Accountant<br>Director*<br>Author*<br>Group Sales Manager<br>Ushers<br>Ticket-takers<br>Doorman<br>Poster boys, etc.<br>Security Guard<br>Hairdresser and wig specialist<br>House Physician<br>Matrons | (*Producer's Staff*)<br>General Manager<br>Company Manager*<br>Stage Manager*<br>Assistant Stage Manager*<br>Stagehands*<br>Fly men*<br>Light men*<br>Makeup artist*<br>Hairdresser*<br>Wardrobe Mistress*<br>Press Agent*<br>Dressers*<br>(*Landlord's Staff*)<br>House Manager*<br>Treasurers*<br>Ushers*<br>Directresses*<br>Doormen*<br>Carpenter*<br>Electrician*<br>Property Master*<br>Cleaners*<br>Matrons*<br>Heat, air-conditioning and other maintenance<br>Fireman*<br>Watchman*<br>Porter* | Director*<br>Author*<br>Scenic Designer*<br>Costume Designer*<br>Lighting Designer*<br>Scene builders*<br>Scene painters*<br>Costume builders*<br>Wig makers*<br>Prop builders*<br>Scene transporters*<br>Attorney<br>Accountant(s)<br>House Physician |

*Working under union or other collective bargaining association contract.

A theatrical performance is the result of a great deal of work by many people. Who those people are and how their talents and abilities are utilized determines the quality of the performance. More important than the management of money or buildings or tickets for the theatre is the management of people.

Theatre personnel, unlike many other employees, have an uncommonly strong love for and dedication to their work. Hardly anyone is forced by parents, counselors or social pressure to select theatre as a profession. The reverse is likely to be true: people are usually advised *not* to attempt a theatrical career. Because of this, people in the theatre are especially apt to work hard, to make personal sacrifices and to adopt a strong commitment to an idea or concept. The value of their work very often depends upon the value of the concept they adopt.

# Part II

# Methods of Theatrical Producing

# CHAPTER FIVE

# Commercial
# New York Theatre

The term "commercial theatre" is anathema to some people while others use it to assert pride in the rather dubious ability of professional theatre to function without subsidy. It remains, however, the best term to indicate one of several economic systems of theatrical producing. Commercial theatre is centered in New York—on Broadway and Off Broadway—and its behavior in terms of economics, management and production profoundly influences all other theatre activity. Before discussing how Broadway and Off Broadway function, it might be useful to review the historical background of commercial theatre in America. How did the system evolve, who have been its leaders, how has the power and control been distributed and what have been the overall results?

■ BACKGROUND

THE BEGINNINGS: 1752 TO 1792 ■

One of the earliest-known professional theatre companies in the Western Hemisphere was headed by Francisco Perez de Robles and arrived in Peru in 1599. The first professional company of any consequence to reach North America was headed by Lewis Hallam and arrived in Williamsburg, Virginia, in 1752. Both were organized

77

as profit-sharing (or share-holding) ventures. A common means of financing theatrical companies during the Elizabethan period and earlier, the share-holding system provided that each actor own a specific percentage of the company which entitled him to a proportionate share of the profits. The organizer of the company, usually its leading actor and general manager as well, held the greatest number of shares either because he provided the largest initial investment or because of his extra duties as manager. The number of shares allotted to an actor might also be determined by the number of costumes he could provide, by his ability to play leading as opposed to supporting roles or by some family or romantic tie with the head of the company. Occasionally, playwrights and musicians were also shareholders.

Despite the large number of companies organized on a share-holding basis, the system posed several disadvantages and was never widely favored by either American actors or managers. Actors disliked it because it meant an uncertain income, when it provided any at all, and managers disliked it because it created a situation that deprived them of absolute authority and control. Of course theatre managers at that time were also actors. The roles of actor, manager, director and producer did not emerge as clearly separate positions in the theatre until the present century. Until then, both administrative and artistic control usually rested with the leading actor in a company, the so-called actor-manager.

Despite Puritan and Quaker resistance to stage plays and despite the fact that public theatres were officially closed by Congress from 1774 until 1783, professional theatre established a strong foothold in America by the close of the eighteenth century. A three- or four-hundred-seat playhouse, admittedly a rather flimsy structure, could be built for a cost of less than two thousand dollars, which investment could be recovered from the box office receipts of four performances. Nor did other expenses approach what they are today: actors were required to provide their own costumes, the scenery and properties were meager and there were no royalties, fees or commissions to pay. During the first forty years of professional theatre in America, theatrical real estate was regarded as no more important than scenery and other normal production costs, actors shared both the profits and the losses of their company and very few attempts were made to conduct the business of a theatre in a businesslike way.

## THE ERA OF THE INDEPENDENT STOCK COMPANIES: 1792-1860 ▪

By 1792 the share-holding system appears to have died a natural death. Until after the Civil War, the actor-managers and their investors took full administrative and financial responsibility for the theatre company, while other actors received set wages (ranging from ten to fifty dollars per week) together with the proceeds from occasional benefit performances. The heyday of the independent stock company, with its relatively permanent membership of actors, stock supply of scenery and repertory of classical plays mixed with current hits, occurred during the first half of the nineteenth century. Some companies wandered from town to town playing short engagements; others remained stationary in one city and operated in their own theatre. Like the scenery, the character portrayals were, in a sense, drawn from stock. Most actors specialized in certain character types, or "lines," which varied but slightly during their entire career. The actor today may regard this period as one that offered both security and the opportunity to develop one's acting ability.

In fact, it offered little of either. Describing the nineteenth century stock system in England, which largely parallels the American system, Bernard Shaw observed:

> To begin with, the playgoers of their towns grew so desperately tired of them, and so hopelessly unable to imagine them to be any but their too familiar selves, that they performed in an atmosphere of hatred and derision that very few of their members had talent or charm enough to conciliate. The modern practice of selecting for the performances actors and actresses suited to the parts they had to play was impossible: the stock company was a readymade cast that had to fit all plays, from *Hamlet* down to the latest burlesque; and as it never fitted any of them completely, and seldom fitted them at all, the casts were more or less grotesque misfits. This system did not develop versatility; it destroyed it. Every member of the company except the utilities, as they called the worst actors who got parts that did not matter, had his or her specialty or "line." Thus there were leading juveniles with an age limit of fifty. There were walking gentlemen, first and second light comedians, first and second low comedians, first and second old men, heavies who played all the villains, and, as aforesaid, utilities. There were leading ladies and walking ladies, singing chambermaids (soubrettes), and heavies to whom Lady Macbeth was all in the night's work, a pair of old women of whom one played the great ladies and the other the comic landladies, and, of course, female utilities. Each claimed as of right the part which came nearest to his or her specialty; and each played all his or her parts in exactly the same way.*

To breathe more life into the local stock company and to increase business, managers began to engage individual touring stars. From approximately 1820 until 1860 American stock companies were visited by a veritable parade of highly acclaimed English actors: Edmund and Charles Kean, Charles Mathews, Charles and Fanny Kemble, Junius Brutus Booth, William Charles Macready and many others crossed the ocean to seek the considerable profits that awaited them in the New World. They were greeted by popularity and success largely because they had so little competition from native luminaries. Edwin Forrest, the first American actor to achieve stardom, did not make his debut until 1820. If the stock system was less than ideal for either actor or audience, the advent of visiting stars only made matters worse. Stars became so numerous that their appearance with a company was almost essential for drawing an audience. The public was encouraged to ask "who's in it?" rather than, simply, "shall we go to the theatre?"

Because the salaries and percentages demanded by stars were so high, the salaries granted to resident actors had to be lowered to meet expenses, much less to show a profit. In short, the appearance of stars, however more skillful they may have been than native talent, did not do much to improve the overall integrity of theatrical production. Imagine a performance of *Hamlet* in preparation for which the star, in the leading role of course, met his supporting players only hours or minutes before and spent less time rehearsing than instructing them to stay away from cen-

---

*Christopher St. John, ed., *Ellen Terry and Bernard Shaw, A Correspondence* (New York: G. P. Putnam's Sons, 1932), p. xv.

ter stage! It must be assumed, however, that Hamlet did not enjoy the incongruities and foibles of a provincial American Gertrude any more than she could have enjoyed having her theatrical territory invaded by a foreigner who was fast making her professional life untenable.

### THE ERA OF THE COMBINATION COMPANIES: 1860 TO 1896 ▪

The unlikely development that changed the individual, traveling star system and virtually killed resident stock companies was the sudden growth of the American railway system, not the first time nor the last when the economics of theatre would be affected by the growth of another industry. In the decades immediately following the 1848 Gold Rush, thousands of miles of rail track were laid, thereby connecting the major cities of the nation and presaging an era of previously undreamed mobility. During the first half of the century, it would have been impractical for a star to travel with a complete supporting company plus all the necessary costumes and scenic appurtenances, but by the 1880s the "combination company" dominated the industry. Some historians credit actor-manager-playwright Dion Boucicault with having organized the first combination company sometime around 1860. In any case, the idea caught on quickly and soon undermined the century-old stock system. For the first time actors were not tied to a particular resident company, had no control or interest in the theatres they played and performed for long periods in a single play. Similar to stock "packages" that tour the summer and winter circuits today, the combination company usually featured a star and left little profit or glory for anyone else, whether actor or manager.

As American frontiers were cluttered by more and more towns and cities, the demand for entertainment became larger and covered more territory. It has been estimated that there were only about forty theatres of a permanent type at the time of the Gold Rush, but that the nation possessed over five thousand theatres by the end of the century! About one-fourth of these were primarily vaudeville houses, while the others played host to resident companies, to touring combination troupes and to touring stars playing with resident companies. Theatres along the frontier sometimes doubled as saloons and brothels, while the larger western cities anxiously sought to establish their respectability by constructing elaborate opera houses and engaging some of the world's most celebrated performing artists. It was a period of wild and woolly extremes in the American theatre and of phenomenal expansion. Until the 1880s, major control of the theatre continued to rest in the hands of actor-managers, whether they were stars in their own touring companies or less celebrated actors in residence at the local playhouse. How did it happen that these actor-managers so quickly and absolutely lost control over their companies, their theatres and their profession?

### THE CENTRALIZATION OF POWER: 1896 TO 1914 ▪

In both England and America the nineteenth-century actor-managers who were also stars were mostly impractical businessmen whose personal egos fostered such traditions as the long-running engagement, an emphasis on contemporary comedies and melodramas, productions that were blinding for their tasteless extravagance and a financial structure that usually teetered on the threshold of bankruptcy. The most common method used for averting the debtors prison was the revival of a particular

tour de force that had become the star's trademark and that audiences always
turned out to see.

If famous stars were ill-equipped to cope with the new demands of "the modern
age," so were the small-town actor-managers. The growth of touring combination
companies, the continuation of the star system, the advent of vaudeville and the
striking proliferation of playhouses during the closing decades of the nineteenth
century necessitated more than haphazard planning and management. With the
dismissal of local resident companies, theatre buildings fell under the ownership of
local bankers and investors whose primary concern was to utilize the property in a
profitable way. This situation placed a local manager, usually a non-actor, in charge
of selecting and booking touring performers and productions. It also made play-
producing clearly separate from theatre managing.

Because of complexities in routing companies from one city to another, local
managers welcomed the appearance of centralized booking offices, which began to
spring up in New York City around 1880. More or less invisible and unaffiliated
tour circuits were soon created due to the whims of the booking offices combined
with the realities of railway routing. Obviously, the more performances a company
could present in the shortest time the more profitable it would be for everyone
concerned. Before long, the booking agents were also selecting and producing the
plays—long the prerogative of the actor—as well as serving as the actors' agents. In
this three-sided position, agents could extract a booking fee from the local manager
plus a production fee, and from the actor a job-finding fee. Despite signed contracts
and agreements, booking agents were notoriously unscrupulous. Companies were
rerouted at the last minute, leaving the local theatre manager without an engagement; tours were canceled midway, leaving the actors stranded without return fare
to New York. (The famous story about the lost company of *Blossom Time* is no
myth!) Actors never received a salary for rehearsal time and were required to furnish their own wigs and costumes—which sometimes cost more than they could expect to earn during their engagement. In this lamentable fashion New York City became the nation's theatre capital; theatrical booking, producing and casting became
highly centralized and profits were taken by a middleman rather than by the actors
and playwrights. The era of the business tycoon in the theatre had begun.

In 1896 three of New York's booking offices merged into one and thereby
created the infamous Theatrical Syndicate, a partnership comprised of Sam Nixon,
Fred Zimmerman, Al Hayman, Charles Frohman, Marc Klaw and Abraham Erlanger.
Less interested in standards of production than in making large profits, these gentlemen set out to gain absolute booking control over the nation's theatres and, within a few years, succeeded. Such extreme centralization naturally fostered numerous
evils and the monopoly was bound to meet opposition. In 1902 the well-known
actress Minnie Maddern Fiske and her husband, Harrison Grey Fiske, established the
Independent Booking Agency, which attempted to break Syndicate control. Comparatively few actors of note were willing to join the Fiskes, who were frequently
forced to perform in barns and skating rinks because the Syndicate controlled most
of the theatres. David Belasco also waged a valorous campaign against the monopoly,
but the people who finally *did* manage to topple the Syndicate were the Shubert
Brothers. Beginning modestly in upstate New York and following the untimely
death of Sam in 1905, Lee and J. J. Shubert proclaimed themselves the liberators

of the AmericanTheatre, demanding an "open-door" booking and casting policy. Enough people in the industry swallowed the propaganda to make the Shuberts successful. But everyone soon woke up to the fact that the Shuberts has simply replaced the Syndicate partners as the ruling tyrants of the American theatre. There was, however, one difference. The Shuberts amassed an empire in theatrical real estate, thus making their power more complete.

Today, the founding brothers are dead and Shubert-owned theatres that have not been demolished to provide space for more lucrative ventures are mostly leased to independent producers of the type that came into power when commercial theatre ceased to be "big business." It should be added that, while the Syndicate and the Shuberts certainly took advantage of a business opportunity and milked it for every penny it was worth, they did not create the opportunity. They did not engineer the westward movement of America's population or encourage the demand for entertainment and the initial growth in theatre construction. Nor did they invent or encourage the star system and the combination companies. They did not destroy the independence of resident and repertory companies and they did not build the railway system. They simply grasped an opportunity that few actor-managers saw or cared about.

Rather than fighting for independence and economic control over their profession, actors embroiled themselves in a more fatalistic battle for "rights." By so doing they sealed their own status as mere laborers and simultaneously established the "right" of businessmen to control the theatre and its artists. Thus began the labor-management syndrome that haunts the theatre to this day. It is interesting to wonder what the industry might be like had George M. Cohan and others succeeded in their efforts to prevent theatrical unionism. After several abortive attempts, such as the Actors' Society of America, and following a conflict of interest with the White Rats (a union of vaudeville performers that had already been chartered by the American Federation of Labor), Actors' Equity Association was begun in 1913. After a famous three-month actors' strike in 1919, the union won its first meaningful contract with producers. This, ironically, at a time when the writing on the wall augured ill for the American theatre.

### THE DECLINE OF COMMERCIAL THEATRE: 1914 TO 1950 ▪

The phenomenal growth of electronic entertainment got substantially under way in 1915 with D. W. Griffith's film *Birth of a Nation*. By that time there were approximately ten-thousand movie theatres scattered across the country, a figure that doubled by 1920, and the average price of admission was fifty cents compared to the two dollar cost of the average theatre ticket. The advent of network radio shows around 1925 and of talking pictures beginning in 1927 greatly increased the competition that threatened live theatre. Furthermore, during World War I America mobilized its railroads for the war effort and, while shipping a can of film was an easy matter, rail travel for theatrical companies was frequently impossible.

Statistics vary greatly, but it seems feasible to claim that between 1900 and 1932 the number of theatres presenting live entertainment decreased from about five thousand to as few as one hundred, thirty-two of which were located in New York City. And only six of *those* were operating at one point in 1932! The stock market crash in 1929 and the subsequent depression also contributed to the near demise of commercial theatre in America. Fortunately, there were several encouraging developments outside the commercial arena during this period: the growth of the "little theatre movement," the first federal assistance to theatre, the growth of college theatre and other factors that will be considered in later chapters did much to revitalize both our theatre and our written drama. Beginning as noncommercial and largely experimental ventures, such groups as the Provincetown Playhouse, the Theatre Guild and the Group Theatre uncovered an impressive amount of talent as well as a new audience to support it, much of which was soon fed into the mainstream of commercial, Broadway theatre.

While Greenwich Village had long provided the space for experimental theatre, the history of the Off Broadway movement is usually traced from Jose Quintero's 1952 production of *Summer and Smoke*, which starred Geraldine Page at the Circle in the Square. Originally offering a showcase where producers could operate without union employees and at low cost, in less than two decades most Off Broadway productions, both in content and economic structure, belonged to the commercial genre. Nonetheless, the comparative economy and freedom offered by Off Broadway brought new blood to commercial theatre and encouraged a new generation of producers and playwrights.

### RETRENCHMENT: 1960 TO THE PRESENT ■

During its first hundred years, the professional theatre in America was dominated and controlled by actor-managers, by men of the theatre. During its second hundred years, professional theatre in America was largely controlled by businessmen and speculators, men with only a secondary interest in the art of theatre. In the final analysis it must be concluded that neither group managed very well to solve the fundamental economic problems of theatrical producing or to create a viable national drama. Both merely exploited a situation as they found it, doing little to improve that situation and less to prevent its disintegration. Actor-managers in the 1800s were no more aggressive in protesting the take-over of their theatres by traveling combination companies than producer-landlords of the 1900s were in avoiding turning their theatres over to the movie industry.

Bread and butter for theatrical employees of both eras were provided by the proceeds from meaningless farces, melodramas and operettas, although both eras were equally quick to produce the best of the contemporary companies and playwrights—as long as these had a pretested commercial value. Ironically, the most productive and important period of American drama occurred during the thirties when the American theatre was at its lowest ebb economically. But the promise symbolized by a generation of playwrights including O'Neill, Anderson, Hellman, Behrman, Sherwood and Rice was, unhappily, not fulfilled in subsequent generations, though such dramatists as Miller, Williams, Inge and Albee kept the hope alive—while, it should be added, commercial theatre people were mostly kept alive by comedies and musicals.

In the area of serious, non-musical theatre, the decades following 1950 were interesting chiefly for the foreign (mainly British) plays, actors and directors imported by Broadway and dramas of progressively diminishing quality by the aforementioned Miller, Williams, Inge and Albee. No new American playwright of comparable quality, seriousness and promise appeared on the scene for over a decade.

What had gone wrong? Had the business tycoons left commercial theatre destitute because of their profiteering tactics? Certainly not. Inflation and taxes had reduced the probability of easy profit-taking in the theatre, but there were numerous investors willing to take the gamble. Had a few generations of serious drama taken the joy out of theatregoing? On the contrary. It restored the faith of many people in the integrity of theatre and, besides, there was never a shortage of light entertainment. Centralization, electronic media, inflation and socio-political circumstances beyond the control of theatre managers and producers were among the leading factors responsible for writing the history of commercial theatre, although it may be said that our theatre has often allowed circumstance a very free hand in writing its history. After the 1950s, at least a few theatre people began to believe that they could meaningfully influence the industry by joining the activities of the world at large. In recent years both commercial and noncommercial theatre people appear to have increased their involvement in politics, society, economics and government precisely to seek solutions that could improve the health of the theatre. In addition, and at long last, much of the factionalism that previously kept each branch of the industry in its own isolation booth began disappearing so that, for example, it became common for a performer or director to alternate from live to electronic media, from commercial to noncommercial theatre, from musical to non-musical performances and so forth, a healthy practice both financially and artistically. Tired of merely listening to its own complaints, the Broadway theatre began to experiment with new policies and ideas, albeit rather sheepishly if compared with the resolute manner in which other manufacturers retool and revitalize themselves. New York preview performances instead of out-of-town tryouts, departure from the traditional 8:30 curtain time, flirtation with flexible ticket-pricing, computerized ticket sales at selected agencies, a foundation that subsidizes productions by purchasing large blocks of tickets and reselling these at low rates to special groups and other such ideas proved of little if any assistance in bolstering the Broadway economy. But they *did* prove the willingness of producers and landlords to take positive action to correct their problems, and they show signs that seeds of change are being sown in and around the New York theatre district. Perhaps commercial theatre is once again in the process of being restructured. Perhaps very little will actually change. As it begins its third century, however, commercial theatre is still alive and still waiting for solutions to its problems, but keeping its ear a little closer to the ground than it has in the past.

Theatrical novelty, sensationalism and shoddiness will remain in evidence as long as there is a commercial theatre, but it is heartening that a number of people still believe in the value of producing worthwhile projects and of going to considerable efforts to do so. The business of producing artistically salient productions in New York today requires a person of broad-based interests and abilities. The producer who sits in his Broadway office summoning the world to him is a creature of the past. Today's producer must go wherever he himself is summoned.

## ▪ THE PRODUCER AND HIS PLAY

### SELECTING THE PLAY ▪

Anyone, given the desire, can be a theatrical producer provided he has one thing, a play to produce. He may or may not use his own money, he may work alone or in partnership with others, he may work at producing full or part time, he may or may not have previous experience in the theatre. But he must have a play or dramatic manuscript of some kind together with the legal right to produce it. From the performer's point of view, a script is a "vehicle," a medium that allows him to display his talents. From the commercial producer's point of view, a script is a "property," a piece of theatrical-literary real estate that may enable him to make money. It is curious and perhaps indicative of how deeply commercialism has pervaded the theatre to note that in no other branch of the live performing arts (or the visual arts) is the work of a writer, composer or artist referred to as a "property." The term is a striking reminder to playwrights and producers that a script has financial as well as artistic potential.

The business of selecting a play for production is the producer's first and most important responsibility. He may be fortunate enough to find a script that is ready for production, as with a finished and polished original play or the revival of a previously produced play. More often, extensive work is required before rehearsals can even be contemplated: the author might be required by the producer to alter the manuscript; the producer might commission an author to translate a play from another language, to adapt a story or cartoon or idea into play form, to revise an earlier or classical work or to collaborate with other writers and composers—always at the risk of being disappointed with the final result or, indeed, of never seeing a finalized script because something happened to prevent its completion.

Some commercial producers begin their careers because they have specific property that they wish to produce. Others begin merely with a general desire to produce and then search for properties. In the latter case the world is their marketplace and they may spend as much time, effort and money as they have available to hunt for a play that appeals to them. They may solicit manuscripts from literary agents, by placing advertisements in theatrical periodicals or writers' magazines and by attending performances in community, repertory and college theatres both here and abroad. They may scour libraries for works in other media upon which to commission an adaptation. The possibilities are endless. The goal is to decide upon the right script or idea at the right time, written or adapted in a theatrically viable manner.

## BUYING THE PLAY ■

From the profit-generating point of view, one may speak in terms of "live" and "dead" literary property. In other words, it may have the potential to make money for somebody or it may have fallen into public domain and ceased to be the personal property of any person or estate. Once the producer has decided that he wants to present a script or commission a script to be translated, adapted or based upon somebody else's work or idea, he must take legal action to secure his rights of ownership. If he is dealing with the author of an original play (one that is not based on another work or idea), he must buy an option that, for a stated length of time, gives him the right to produce that play. This is done by negotiating an agreement with the playwright, using the device of a Dramatists Guild Minimum Basic Production Contract. Affiliated with the Authors League of America, the Dramatists Guild is a professional society open to anyone who wishes to join but comprised of two classes of members, active and associate, determined by whether or not the member has ever had a work professionally produced on the legitimate stage. In exchange for 2 percent of the author's weekly royalties (3 percent if these exceed three thousand per week) the Dramatists Guild negotiates or approves the terms of the playwright's contract with the producer, insuring certain minimum terms. It then continues to act as the playwright's protector in other ways. For example, the Guild mediates differences that the producer and the playwright cannot resolve between themselves, checks box office grosses to insure that the playwright receives the correct royalty and negotiates any sale of the play to a motion picture company, for which it receives 2 percent of that sale price. Its offices are located over Sardi's restaurant in the heart of the Broadway theatre district, and most playwrights agree that the Guild is a helpful and necessary organization of considerable benefit in guaranteeing their professional rights and security.

If the play a producer wishes to purchase is not original but a translation, adapted or based on some other work, he must initiate a copyright search to determine who owns the basic work and then negotiate with that party to buy the dramatic rights. In some cases this is done by the playwright, but in all cases it should be done as soon as possible. It is no less illogical to adapt somebody else's work without legal permission than it would be to build a house on somebody else's land without legal ownership.

Finally, a producer may decide to present a play that is in the public domain. Unless he causes that work to be rewritten in some way, he cannot secure the exclusive rights to produce it. In other words, he cannot prevent another producer from putting on the same play in competition with him. Copyright laws are among the most specialized and complex in the entire legal field, and an attorney should always be consulted when one is attempting to purchase or protect literary rights. Both producers and authors, however, might find it helpful to bear in mind the following elementary points:

1. All literary rights are extinguishable and cannot be owned by anyone in perpetuity.
2. A copyright is not divisible: one may own, sell or give away all of it or none at all.
3. The owner of a copyright may, however, grant or sell licenses giving another person the right to use the copyrighted material in a particular way, as in the case of granting the dramatization and attendant performance rights for a novel.
4. Subsidiary rights are related to the special licenses granted by the owner of a copyright and give the licensee permission to share in income generated from specific uses of a basic work, such as the production of a play on television, in the films or on a recording.
5. Copyrights cannot protect the title of a work nor may one copyright an idea.
6. Only the *expression* of an idea may be copyrighted.
7. The copyright office in Washington merely files copyright applications and copies of the work when these are submitted to it; any copyright dispute, therefore, must be settled in a court of law.

8. A statutory copyright means the "publication" of a work "with notice." "Publication" supposes an unlimited distribution of the work and "notice" means that the work is labeled with © plus the author's name and the date. This can be done by anyone without filing a copyright application in Washington.
9. The owner of a copyright must renew or republish his copyright within a specific amount of time or the work falls into public domain.
10. When obtaining any license, agreement or permit it should always be remembered that *anything not specifically withheld is given away*. (For example, if the license does not state that the producer controls the television rights to his play, he has probably forfeited by default all rights and control over that play as far as television production of it is concerned.)

Since ownership and rights related to literary property last only for a limited period of time, it behooves the owner to capitalize on his property as soon as possible. Buying a play (or writing one) is not like buying precious gems; it is a comparatively short-term investment. When a producer buys an option to produce a play, he wants to produce it as soon as possible in order that it may earn money for as long as possible—unless, that is, there is some unusual motive involved, such as buying an option on a work in order to prevent someone else from producing it.

SUBSIDIARY RIGHTS ▪
The New York production of a play may fail to show a profit but, due to the phenomenon of subsidiary rights, the production company may eventually recoup its losses by profits earned from other uses of the property. The Dramatists Guild Minimum Basic Production Contract stipulates that a Broadway or Off Broadway show must run for twenty-one consecutive performances in order for the production company to share in subsidiary rights (these performances exclude out-of-town engagements but may include New York preview performances). Subsidiary rights concern all purposes for which the basic property may be used and for which the author, the production company and others as required by contract must be compensated: that is, everything from the sale of the script for film production to the sale of the amateur performance rights. If the New York production runs for less than twenty-one performances all rights become the exclusive property of the author, although for a certain time he must give the original producer the opportunity to revive the New York production. The most common types of subsidiary rights related to New York productions are the following:

1. CAST RECORDINGS
The majority of musical productions contract with a recording company to produce an original cast recording of the show. This customarily takes place one week after the show opens, frequently on a Sunday. The Broadway cast and musicians must be reimbursed to the extent of one week's salary for this session. Off Broadway casts and other Equity companies negotiate the amount they get paid with the producer in the event that an original cast recording is

made. The director, star and others may also share in the royalties accrued from the sale of the recording if it is so stipulated in their contract. Some shows are recorded prior to their New York opening in order to create advance publicity. It is also fairly common for a recording company to provide a major portion of a show's capitalization in exchange for obtaining the rights to record it or the right of first refusal.

## 2. MUSIC PERFORMANCE RIGHTS

Music composers and lyricists retain the general rights to their creations in all cases when their music is performed outside the context of the show. Frequently individual songs from a show are recorded by pop singers, by instrumentalists and other groups and then sold as single discs or as part of a record album. They may not, however, publish the music, lyrics or script prior to the New York opening without special permission from the producer. The composer and lyricist must receive royalties for the sale of such recordings and further royalties when these recordings are played by radio or television stations, used in juke boxes, used in shows other than the one for which they were originally written and so forth. For the purpose of having an agency collect all such royalties and monitor the use of their property, a majority of composers and lyricists belong to ASCAP (the American Society of Composers and Publishers).

## 3. FILM RIGHTS

As previously mentioned, the Dramatists Guild negotiates the sale of all New York commercial productions to film companies. The director, authors, stars and others, as specified in their contracts, together with the producing company, may share in the money earned by this sale, as well as sharing in the box office profits accrued from all showings of the film and, when stipulated, in the sale of the film to television or other media. As with recording companies, it is not unusual for a film company to invest a large amount of capital in a production in exchange for the rights to film it. By negotiating such rights prior to the New York opening of a show, the film or recording company may be able to purchase rights at a lower price than if it waits for the show to become a hit.

## 4. TELEVISION RIGHTS

A television network may also invest in a show in order to present a special television showing of the stage version, the sale of which rights again are divided among the authors, the producing company and any others who may share in such revenue according to their contracts.

## 5. TOURING RIGHTS

Ordinarily, the original producing company arranges the national tours of a New York show. The union rules by which these are governed are covered in the Standard Production Contract of Actors' Equity and similar production contracts with other unions. The producing company shares in all profits. Another producing company, however, may purchase all touring rights for a show or specific touring rights, such as those for a bus-and-truck (short-stand engagement) tour. All such tours generally follow within a year or two of the closing of the New York production or are produced simultaneously with that production.

## 6. FOREIGN RIGHTS

The first-run showings of New York plays in foreign capitals are usually negotiated by the original producing company and profits are shared as in the above categories, with special guarantees provided the producer in regard to the first-run performances in the British Isles.

## 7. STOCK AND AMATEUR RIGHTS

Usually the same company purchases both the stock and amateur rights to a production. After paying the initial purchase price for such rights, it alone has the authority to release the play for production in stock, educational and amateur theatres throughout the world in exchange for which it charges a royalty fee to each producing organization, keeps a percentage of that fee and distributes the rest either to the original producing company or to the Dramatists Guild for further distribution to the authors of the property. Samuel French, Inc. and the Dramatist's Play Service, Inc. are the two leading play publishing houses that control most stock and amateur rights for non-musical properties. Tams Witmark, Inc., the Rodgers and Hammerstein Music Library and Music Library International control stock and amateur rights for most Broadway musicals. These companies also sell or rent the acting versions and scores of the plays they own.

## 8. PUBLICATION RIGHTS

While the house that controls the amateur and stock rights for a production usually has the exclusive right to publish and sell the acting scripts for that property, other publishing houses may wish to purchase the hard-cover or paperback edition rights, for which the author is reimbursed with a sale fee and subsequent royalty payments that result from the sale of copies.

It should be obvious from a quick glance at the above list that, if a play is successful in New York, it can earn considerable profits for its author and for the original producing company. It may even accomplish this feat when the New York run is not very successful, though the producing company may only share in the profits if the play runs for the specified "rights acquisition time." In short, a basic work is like a hen; it may hatch many, many golden eggs—providing, that is, that the first one isn't rotten!

## ▪ FORMING A PRODUCTION COMPANY

### THE LIMITED PARTNERSHIP AGREEMENT ▪

A producer or organization may form a corporation to embrace many diverse activities, but most commercial productions are structured on a special type of partnership that only controls a single play. If a producer is wealthy enough to provide full funding for a production or series of productions, as in the case of institutional theatre groups and as was often the practice in commercial theatre until the 1930s, there is no reason to form a separate company for each new production. But if a producer needs or wants to attract investors (as opposed to donors) in order to raise capital, then he will form a company specifically to produce that play. This both limits and simplifies the purpose for which invested capital may be used and limits the type and amount of profits that the investors are entitled to share—rather as if General Motors offered shares related to the manufacture of a particular automobile instead of shares covering all its operations. The more an investment is limited to a specific project, the greater the risk to the investor. Commercial producers have considered the implementation of less risky investment methods (a mutual fund that would invest in a number of productions on behalf of its members is one idea that has gained recent attention). But the single production company remains the most common type for producing on Broadway, and the play or literary property itself is the nucleus, the one necessary asset, for the formation of such a company.

Virtually all commercial productions are organized around a Limited Partnership Agreement, the terms of which differ from agreement to agreement but all have basic similarities that appear to offer the best legal and tax advantages for both producers and investors. The Agreement creates two types of partners: General Partners and Limited Partners. The former assume all control over the affairs of the partnership and all the legal liabilities and risks. The Limited Partners are liable only for the dollar amount of their investment plus, in most cases, an additional amount or "overcall" (usually 10 to 20 percent of their initial investment). Ordinarily, the Limited Partners collectively provide the total capital required to finance the production but share only 50 percent of the profits, with the other 50 percent going to the General Partners. In practice, this means that if a production is capitalized at $100,000 and a Limited Partner has invested $10,000, or 10 percent of the total cost, he will share in only 5 percent of the profits. The producers (General Partners) of the company start out with 50 percent ownership but seldom retain that amount because they usually deem it advisable or necessary to sell or otherwise forfeit a portion of it. If, for example, a higher capitalization is required than originally stated in the Limited Partnership Agreement, the General Partners may have to sell part of their share in the company because they are not allowed to issue more limited shares and thereby decrease the value of the original Limited Partners' shares. Or, portions of the General Partners' percentage may be given away in order to obtain a certain star, director or theatre. The Limited Partner's chief obligations and benefits are as follows:

1. To contribute a specified amount of money to the production.
2. To contribute a further specified amount if requested to do so and provided this is stated in the investment agreement.
3. To have no other financial or legal obligation or liability in connection with the production company.
4. To share 50 percent of any profits with the other Limited Partners according to the amount of his investment (these profits usually include money earned from the sale of subsidiary rights though, again, all such profit-sharing must be specifically defined in the Agreement).

The General Partners' chief obligations to the Limited Partners in the company are:

1. To guarantee that they have the legal right to produce the play in question.
2. To guarantee that they actually intend to produce that play, provided they can raise the required capital.
3. To guarantee the safekeeping and legitimate expenditure of all invested capital.
4. To return all invested capital in full if the amount specified in the Agreement is not raised within a stated length of time.
5. To desist from spending any invested capital until the full amount required has been raised, unless otherwise stated in the signed Agreement with the investor.
6. To guarantee that the total capitalization stated in the Agreement is sufficient to finance the production and that, for the purpose of determining the value of each share, shall not be changed.
7. To repay the Limited Partners' investments before they, the General Partners, begin to share in any profits.
8. To assume all legal and financial responsibility for the proper conduct of the partnership and the company.

Because they possess full control over the company, the General Partners may dissolve it at any time provided they can show reasonable cause for doing so. It may appear at first glance that a 50 percent share in a company is excessive for a man who doesn't invest a penny in it. While he is entitled to be reimbursed by the company for option money he has advanced to the playwright, for office expenses and other such costs, however, the General Partner is never repaid directly for all the time, travel and entertaining required to obtain his play in the first place. Nor may he receive any fee or salary as a producer or General Partner or, unless stated in the Agreement, for any other service or job he may perform in connection with the production. Nor is he entitled to reimbursement for any expenses incurred for purposes of fund-raising. An average of one to three years elapses from the time a play is optioned until it opens in New York and it may take another year of capacity business before it begins to realize a profit.* Whatever money a producer may finally earn is, indeed, well-earned.

### RAISING THE CAPITAL ■

A few producers are sufficiently successful and well-established to have a coterie of "angels" or backers who are always ready and willing to put money into their productions. Other producers may have affluent friends or acquaintances who, without too much prodding, can be convinced to invest in a production. But most often the process of raising capital requires time and special attention. After obtaining a property, financing the venture is the producer's most important function.

Law requires that a prospectus of the production company, together with a copy of the Limited Partnership Agreement and other documents, be filed with the office of the Attorney General of the State of New York and with the Securities and Exchange Commission. After the total capitalization for the production has been raised, the General Partners of the Agreement must file a Certificate of Limited Partnership

*See chapter 9.

in the County Clerk's office in the county in which the company is operating. Then notice of the partnership must be published in two different newspapers or periodicals consecutively for a period of six weeks. The cost of such publication can be as high as one thousand dollars, depending upon the length of the Agreement that is published and the number of investors it lists (there are methods that make it possible to limit or omit the names of the Limited Partners, but investors are best protected when their names and addresses are published). As a result of such publication, it is not difficult to gather a list of active angels (all Limited Partnership Agreements are published in the *New York Law Journal*) and, indeed, such lists are compiled and sold on a regular basis. Considering the personal or eccentric reasons why most investors back a show, however, the value of such lists is dubious.

The prospectus or offering circular distributed to potential investors provides a synopsis of the play and short biographies of the producer and authors and of leading artists who have committed themselves to the project. It must also describe in detail the financial and legal organization of the company and contain a statement about the risks of theatrical investing, giving the percentage of shows that failed in New York during the previous season.* Many such legalities were originally intended to protect investors from unknowingly taking extraordinary risks by investing in highly speculative ventures, like gold prospecting, or from phony ventures. Producers are fond of pointing out that the law seems to do everything in its power to discourage theatrical investors, producers and ticket buyers, and one must admit that there are numerous regulations of a kind that plague few other industries. However, it cannot be denied that theatre *is* a highly speculative business which, without legally imposed regulations, offers an uncomfortable amount of opportunity for dishonesty and fraud.

As part of the offering circular the producer may include a promissory letter for the investor to sign and return, the contents of which might be as follows:

---

Hy Hope Productions, Inc.
000 Broadway
New York, New York

RE:  *Romeo and Juliet*
by William Shakespeare
an Off Broadway production

Dear Sirs:

I hereby state that I would like to be an investor and Limited Partner in the "R & J" Company, which will produce William Shakespeare's *Romeo and Juliet* Off Broadway. Accordingly, I hereby invest a total amount of $
which shall entitle me to        units of 50 percent of any net profits based upon a total capitalization of $60,000.

$1,200 shall represent one unit or percentile.† I enclose my investment check in the above amount (or, upon demand, I shall deliver my check

---

*A sample offering circular is provided in Appendix 1-A.
†Traditionally, fifty limited partner shares are offered, each representing 1 percent of the capitalization and .5 percent of the profits, though, of course, an investor may buy part of a share or more than one.

to you). You shall hold my funds in trust in a special account until such time as $50,000 is raised, after which you may utilize the funds for production purposes.

In the event that capital contributions total at least $50,000 and you believe that the production can commence, then the capitalization of the Limited Partnership shall be reduced to the amount determined and the Limited Partners' proportional shall be increased accordingly.*

You shall hereafter forward to me the Limited Partnership Agreement for this production, which has been filed in the office of the Attorney General of the State of New York. I shall promptly sign and return it to you.

In the event that the Limited Partnership is not formed within twelve months from the date of this letter then the money advanced shall be returned to me in full. There shall be no overcall.

Sincerely,

_____     INITIAL ONE:

(Signature)

_____     My investment may _____
                                     may not _____
(Name, printed in full)              be used as front money

_____

(Full legal address)

It is important to emphasize that the above letter merely precedes or accompanies a Limited Partnership Agreement and is not a substitute for it; nor should it be used until the Agreement has been filed with the Attorney General. The extreme caution that a producer must observe when attempting to comply with the numerous laws and regulations related to establishing a theatrical producing company cannot be overstated. A few books, such as Donald Farber's *Producing on Broadway*, describe these regulations in greater detail than is appropriate here, but the producer is best advised to retain an attorney of impeccable credentials and experience in the field of theatrical law.

Perhaps the method most frequently employed to sell shares for commercial productions in New York is the so-called backers' audition. This entails inviting potential investors to a rented hall or private home to witness the informal presentation of scenes read from the manuscript by professional actors (not necessarily the ones who will appear in the actual production). The producer, author and others are present to answer questions and help promote the venture. Scenic design models or sketches may be displayed and generous amounts of food and drink are usually served. Most investors are incapable of judging the commercial value and theatrical effectiveness of a play by reading the script, and a backers' audition gives them only a slightly better picture of what the final production will be like. Nonetheless, backers' auditions are a good means of increasing enthusiasm for a project to the level

*This is the usual procedure when a production comes in under the stated capitalization: it is safest to overestimate the required capitalization and then to increase the value of each share.

where interested people will commit themselves and, more to the point, their
money.

## ▪ NEGOTIATING FOR A THEATRE

One of the most crucial and sensitive decisions a producer must make concerns
fitting his production to a theatre that is appropriate. The selection should be based
first upon artistic considerations and only second upon economic reasons. Many
plans automatically dictate an ideal audience size or arrangement, but others do not.
The annals of theatre are filled with examples of intimate plays that got lost in huge
theatres and of more flamboyant plays that were stifled in small houses.

New York commercial theatre is divided into two categories—Broadway and Off
Broadway—each determined by the seating capacity of the theatre and usually by
its location. As defined by Actors' Equity Association and other unions for the purpose of establishing minimum salaries and other requirements, an Off Broadway theatre may seat up to two hundred ninety-nine people, anything over which number is
classified as a Broadway theatre. Equity has also granted a "limited gross" contract
and thereby created a third category between the traditional Broadway and Off
Broadway types, determined not by the number of seats but rather by the total potential weekly gross at the box office.

Before going too far with contractual commitments to actors and others, the producer or his general manager must begin negotiating to rent a theatre (the rental
agreement is actually a license rather than a lease). The Off Broadway producer has
the advantage of being able to choose from a large number and variety of theatres
and of having considerable bargaining flexibility in the type of license he concludes
with the landlord. Many Off Broadway theatres are rented according to a "four-wall"
agreement. It simply provides the building, with no personnel services paid by the
landlord, and simply demands a fixed weekly rental fee. Broadway theatre licenses
are a more complicated matter. Although there is no standard license for renting
Broadway theatres, the League of New York Theatres (to which all Broadway theatre owners or licensers and most Broadway producers belong) serves as the negotiating agent with several unions on behalf of theatre owners. In some cases, including
negotiating the Standard Production Contract with Actors' Equity, it is also the
official representative of most Broadway producers—the only group of Broadway
professionals without their own, exclusive, bargaining organization. The League of
New York theatres, then, creates certain minimum terms that will be a part of all
theatre rental licenses. The League of Off Broadway Theatres and Producers negotiates the minimum Off Broadway contracts with Actors' Equity.

The Broadway theatre owner and the tenant-producer are both interested in the
same goal: a successful, long-running production. The terms included in a license
will depend a great deal on the potential success that the landlord ascribes to a particular show and, equally important, upon how many different shows are seeking to
use his theatre. During the busy fall season there are often more productions than
theatres to accommodate them or, at least, theatres of the type that producers consider desirable. Factors such as size, location and licensing terms contribute to the
desirability of a theatre and may render some theatres completely unfeasible for
certain productions. Contracts negotiated by the League of New York Theatres re-

quire all operating Broadway theatres to employ a minimum number of union
workers, such as a press agent and a house manager. Each theatre may also have
separate contracts with unions that require them to employ an additional number
of union men, such as musicians, whether the tenant production needs their services
or not.

The Broadway theatre owner and the tenant-producer are partners in a very real
sense. No Broadway theatre is licensed on a "four-wall" basis. Among other things,
the landlord and tenant share in carefully stipulated advertising costs, house maintenance costs, box office profits, employee salaries and revenue from concessions
such as the sale of souvenir booklets. Most Broadway theatre licenses provide that
the tenant shall pay a guaranteed weekly fee against the box office receipts and a
percentage of all income over that guaranteed amount. The weekly amount guaranteed to the owner ranges from $5000 to $15,000, against something between 20
percent and 30 percent of the gross receipts up to a specified amount. After that
amount has been earned, the landlord may receive 30 percent of the receipts up to
$20,000, 25 percent of the next $30,000 and 20 percent of all receipts over $50,000.
Any combination is possible.

Another crucial factor in Broadway theatre licenses is the so-called stop clause,
a weekly box office gross amount that is agreed to in the license. If the show fails
to realize this amount (usually for a period of two consecutive weeks) the landlord
has the right to evict it and the tenant may vacate without cost or penalty. The producer cannot logically arrive at a figure for the stop clause, however, until he has
first determined both the total capitalization and the weekly operating expenses for
his production. Theoretically, deciding upon a stop clause figure is a simple matter:
the producer merely determines the weekly operating cost for his show. Then he
knows how much box office revenue he must take in to "break even."* Why not
use that break-even figure in the lease for the stop clause? Because business can be
temporarily poor due to a number of possibilities: extended periods of bad weather,
a national emergency, adverse publicity, illness of the star. While such factors may
result in box office income below the break-even point, the producer may feel that
a temporary loss of business can be covered by renewed profits when the situation
returns to normal. For this reason the stop clause figure is usually less than the
break-even figure. If it is set too low, the producer risks operating for many weeks
at a loss with no easy or inexpensive way to terminate the lease.

Producers with an established record of success or those who own a property
written by a very "hot" playwright or one that features artists of known commercial value are in the strongest bargaining position. The star or lack of one is a primary factor in negotiating with landlords, and a license frequently requires the producer to use a certain star whom he has selected and promised to employ. The
landlord in many cases has the right to terminate the license if a particular star fails
to appear or leaves the production for any reason; or he may have the right to veto
the engagement or replacement of the star and certain featured players. For reasons
such as these the producer cannot effectively begin negotiating for a theatre until
his production plans are well under way and he has contracted the leading artists.
But, he also does not wish to sign too many contracts until he is assured of having

*See chapter 9.

a New York theatre. In other words, the producer must play both ends against the middle, and elements of time, luck and shrewd judgement are critical, to say the least.

## ▪ PRODUCTION CONTRACTS AND LEASES

Before discussing the jurisdiction and regulations of Actors' Equity Association (which generally pertain to all Equity companies both in and out of New York), a descriptive listing of all theatrical unions and collective bargaining associations related to Broadway productions might be helpful.

The only one allowed to sign contracts with union employees is the person who has posted a bond with the union or his authorized representative. Questions regarding union jurisdiction, contracts and regulations should be addressed directly to the appropriate union office, since many contractual terms involving salaries, benefits and working conditions change each year and special concessions frequently can be negotiated by direct contact with a union. Producers and managers are well-advised to make quick friends and acquaintances in union offices.

### CONTRACTS MADE BY THE PRODUCER ▪

1. *Dramatists Guild, Inc.* (234 West 44th Street, New York, N.Y.). Not a union but a professional association for the protection of authors of dramatic and dramatico-musical works. Virtually all scripts presented on the New York legitimate stage, except for those held in the public domain, must be contracted for by the producer on the Dramatists Guild, Inc. Minimum Basic Production Contract, negotiated separately between each producer and author under Guild supervision.
2. *Actors' Equity Association* (165 West 46th Street, New York, N.Y.). Equity derives its charter from the Associated Actors and Artists of America (known as the 4 As) which, in turn, is chartered by the American Federation of Labor-Congress of Industrial Organizations (AFL-CIO). Its jurisdiction covers all professional actors (principals, chorus members and extras as well as stage managers and assistant stage managers).
3. *Society of Stage Directors and Choreographers* (1350 Broadway, New York, N.Y.). Not a union but a society to which virtually all directors and choreographers active in New York legitimate theatre belong. It has a minimum contract, although each case is negotiated individually between the producer and the Society member.
4. *United Scenic Artists of America (USA) Local 829B* (268 West 47th Street, New York, N.Y.). Most scenic, costume and lighting designers working in New York legitimate theatre belong to this union. It requires all members to pass a lengthy and difficult examination before gaining membership, although there are instances when producers hire nonmembers who subsequently join the union.
5. *Wardrobe Supervisors and Dressers, Local 764* (250 West 57th Street, New York, N.Y.). Although producers or stars may hire whomever they wish as dressers and wardrobe workers, such personnel must immediately become members of this union, the minimum conditions of which are negotiated by the League of New York Theatres.

CONTRACTS MADE BY THE THEATRE ▪
1. *International Alliance of Theatrical Stage Employees (IATSE) Local 1* (254 West 54th Street, New York, N.Y.). Representing all carpenters, stagehands, electricians, sound technicians and property crewmen, this union is contracted to the theatre. The number of employees required is determined by the type of production in residence and the theatre's agreement with the union.
2. *Treasurers and Ticketsellers, Local 751* (235 West 46th Street, New York, N.Y.). This union is also contracted by the theatre, and the number of employees required depends upon the size of the theatre (seating capacity).
3. *Porters and Cleaners—Service Employees in Amusement and Cultural Buildings, Local 54* (826 Seventh Avenue, New York, N.Y.). Includes all cleaners, matrons, elevator operators and porters. All contracts are with the theatre.
4. *International Union of Operating Engineers, Local 30* (132 West 57th Street, New York, N.Y.). Includes all heavy-equipment maintenance personnel, such as heating and air conditioning engineers. All contracts are with the theatre.
5. *Ushers and Doormen—Legitimate Theatre Employees Union, Local B-183* (112 West 42nd Street, New York, N.Y.). Includes jurisdiction over all ushers, directors of ushers and front and back doormen. All contracts are with the theatre.

CONTRACTS MADE BY BOTH THE PRODUCER AND THE THEATRE ▪
1. *Association of Theatrical Press Agents and Managers* (ATPAM) Union No. 18032 (268 West 47th Street, New York, N.Y.). The producer contracts with the company manager and the press agent (both of whom must be employed in conjunction with every production during the length of its New York engagement and also while it is on tour), and the theatre contracts with the house managers. The number of employees and salary will depend upon whether the production is a musical or a non-musical and whether it is playing in New York or on tour.
2. *American Federation of Musicians, Local 802* (261 West 52nd Street, New York, N.Y.). Some theatres have agreed to employ a certain number of musicians whenever they have a production in residence, whether or not it is a musical. The other musicians used for a production, if any, will be determined by the production and contracted by the producer.

## ▪ THE ACTORS AND THEIR UNION

ACTORS' EQUITY ASSOCIATION JURISDICTION AND MEMBERSHIP ▪
    Equity is an open union. No one can be denied membership provided that a bona fide producer has offered him a job. Other theatrical unions, such as ATPAM, require a formal apprenticeship at reduced salary for several years as a condition of membership. Nonetheless, it is difficult for an aspiring actor to obtain the services of a good agent, attend auditions for Equity productions and win the confidence

of producers and casting directors unless he is first a member of Equity. A person may gain union membership in one of several ways. He may be given a contract as an actor with an Equity company; he may be given a contract as a stage manager, an assistant stage manager (also, in resident and stock theatres, as a choreographer, director or advance director) or he may automatically join Equity if he belongs to another performers' union (AGVA, AFTRA, SAG) for at least six months. Once a member of the union, a person may be employed as an actor (principal or chorus) or as a stage manager or assistant stage manager regardless of the type of position for which he was given his first contract. Directors and choreographers for Broadway, Off Broadway and LORT (League of Resident Theatres) productions work under contracts devised by the Society of Stage Directors and Choreographers, although in stock theatres they are employed under an Equity contract.

## TABLE OF ORGANIZATION    TYPICAL BROADWAY MUSICAL

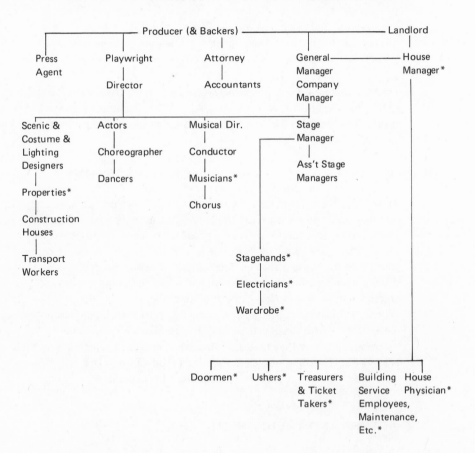

*Contracted by the Landlord or in some cases by both Landlord and Producer.

From its beginning in 1919 until 1956, chorus performers were represented by their own union, The Chorus Equity Association of America, generally independent from Actors' Equity Association. The two organizations merged in 1956 under the single banner of Actors' Equity, which now represents both principal and chorus performers. Both enjoy the same protection and benefits, although there are differences between the "principal actor" contract and the "chorus" contract. One area of Equity jurisdiction that is sometimes challenged concerns vaudeville-like performers, for example, burlesque shows or revues where both Equity and The American Guild of Variety Artists might claim jurisdiction. Equity, therefore, enjoys jurisdiction only over live and so-called legitimate stage productions. The other American performers' unions are:

*AGVA* (The American Guild of Variety Artists, covering performers in night-clubs, vaudeville, special acts, burlesque, etc.)
*SAG* (The Screen Actors' Guild, covering cinema and certain television performers)
*SEG* (The Screen Extras' Guild, covering cinema performers who do not have speaking roles)
*AFTRA* (The American Federation of Television and Radio Artists, covering most performers, newscasters and participants on the television screen or in front of a radio microphone)

Geographically, Equity's jurisdiction extends throughout the United States and Canada. There is no reciprocal agreement with British Equity or actors' associations in other foreign countries, so American Equity cannot guarantee or assist its members in gaining employment abroad. Indeed, work permits are difficult for American actors to obtain abroad. Foreign performers have a somewhat easier time obtaining permission to work in the United States, although the American union and its members often protest their employment here on the grounds that it denies work to native actors. It is unfortunate that regulations and attitudes exist to make an international exchange of performers such difficult business. Ideally, of course, it should be an easy matter for artists to work wherever they wish and, indeed, for a large-scale, international exchange of artists to be commonplace.

To state how many people belong to a given performers' union is meaningless for the following reasons: many members hold a union card more as a matter of prestige than to gain employment (teachers, students), many performers continue their membership in a union although they are almost never active in that field (screen actors, variety performers) and many performers join a union with little intention of working again (such as all the local, home-town kids who were cast in Equity touring productions of the musical *Hair*). Because of such factors it would not be surprising to find a majority of Equity members unemployed as performers on the live stage. Similarly, one cannot arrive at meaningful statistics that denote the average income earned by Equity actors. A majority of members earn most of their income in other fields, whether as performers or otherwise. For example, performers, such as Jack Benny or Bob Hope may belong to Equity and yet earn nothing in a given year from legitimate theatre appearances. Statistically, then, they would go down as "unemployed," which is clearly ridiculous.

### COMMON AEA TERMINOLOGY ▪

The following is a brief glossary of the terms most commonly used in relation to Equity contracts and rulebooks. Each term is defined according to union jargon and, therefore, may have a somewhat different meaning than it would in ordinary usage.

*Actor.* Any member of Actors' Equity Association.

*Principal Actor.* Any member of AEA signed to a contract, excluding those signed to a chorus or extra contract.

*Chorus.* Any member of AEA signed to a chorus contract or one who performs chorus work, as determined by the union.

*Extra.* Signed to a Standard Form contract furnished by Equity, an extra usually receives one half the minimum salary for principal actors. An extra must be employed for at least one week, may not perform any role that is defined in the script as a character but only those that are meant solely to provide atmosphere and background, may not make a makeup change and is allowed only one costume change, may not be rehearsed more than two weeks, may not sing, dance or understudy (except with union consent), may not go on tour except for a maximum of eight weeks for a pre-Broadway tryout tour and must receive at least a one-week termination notice.

*Supernumerary.* A performer who may not be rehearsed except on the day of his first performance, may not tour with a production and may not speak, even in omnes, on stage.

*"As Cast."* A principal actor whose contract assigns him "as cast" rather than to a specific character role. The role(s) he subsequently performs may be determined after the contract is signed, but may not be changed after his first public performance under that contract. The rule applies only to actors performing in revues and under LORT and CORST contracts.

*Understudy.* An understudy is usually, though not always, a member of the performing company who receives additional compensation for his preparedness to assume another role or roles in the production, in the event of which he is further compensated. The specific role(s) an actor understudies must be determined no later than two weeks after the New York City opening of the play or four weeks after the out-of-town opening, whichever is sooner. The rule does not apply to actors performing in revues.

*Nonprofessional.* Anyone not a member of AEA or other performers' union.

*Alien.* An alien is a nonresident, noncitizen of the United States. To employ an alien, the manager must make special application to Equity. The procedure for hiring aliens is complicated and, of course, must conform to laws established by the U. S. Immigration and Nationality Act and others. It must be shown that the alien has special merit or ability to perform a role which could not be performed by a U.S. citizen. There are, however, several exceptions when a performing company of recognized artistic status, performing as a unit, such as the Comédie Française and the Royal Shakespeare Company, may be more easily granted limited permission to perform in the United States. Intimate revues and other companies of special character may also be deemed exceptional for the purposes of securing permission to perform.

*Stage Manager.* Both stage managers and assistant stage managers work under Equity contracts. The union allows that assistant stage managers assume acting roles in a production for additional compensation. Equity also outlines their general employment duties and limitations, stipulates their minimum salaries and entitles them to all benefits and rights as provided for actors.

*Manager.* For the purpose of most contracts, the "manager" is the person who has posted bond with Equity and who is ultimately responsible for complying with the union rules. A few contracts use the term "producer" rather than "manager."

*Arbitration.* For the purpose of settling disputes between the manager and an actor of the union, all Equity contracts establish arbitration procedures. An arbitration board or panel, comprised of members approved both by Equity and the appropriate management organization, renders decisions upon request which both parties have agreed in advance to accept. The costs related to arbitrating a dispute are shared equally by Equity and the manager. In some cases, disputes are settled by a panel selected by the American Arbitration Association. In still other cases a dispute may eventually be heard before a civil court of law.

*Deputy.* A member of the performing company, elected by vote of the company, to serve as representative on its behalf in certain areas related to both management and the union.

*Council.* The Council of Actors' Equity is its governing body which has the power, among other things, to settle certain disputes between actors and managers, to define or redefine terms and to render interpretations of Equity rules and regulations.

## TYPES OF EQUITY CONTRACTS AND AGREEMENTS FOR COMMERCIAL PRODUCTIONS ▪

There are approximately a dozen different Equity rulebooks, each one pertaining to a different type of theatre management (Broadway, stock, resident theatre, etc.). There are also a number of different standard contract forms which pertain to different types of productions (cafe theatres, showcase productions, etc.). And there are a multitude of cases for which Equity has designed special concessions to oblige some unusual production or set of circumstances. All Equity rules and contracts are subject to the Constitution and By-Laws of Equity. Most union rules and regulations are essentially the same, regardless of the specific contract that is issued. The areas that vary most from contract to contract are those concerning salaries and benefits and those concerning the use of nonprofessionals, journeymen and apprentices. Producers and managers for all types of productions that utilize union actors are best advised to contact the Equity office closest to them to obtain the appropriate rulebooks, contracts and information and, in many instances, to negotiate special terms with Equity in regard to their organization or production. Excluding agreements that relate to stock, resident and educational theatre productions (which are discussed in the next two chapters), the following pages list the eight most commonly used types of Equity contract. Most though not all are related to commercial theatre productions. (Union rules do not recognize a difference between profit and nonprofit organizations.)

### THE BROADWAY PRODUCTION AGREEMENT •

The Basic Production Contract or, simply, The Production Agreement, is negotiated every three years by the League of New York Theatres on behalf of commercial producers. It dictates the terms of the Standard Production Contract and Run-of-the-Play Contract to which principal and chorus actors are signed for productions on Broadway, first-class and bus-and-truck tours or full-run productions in any of the Equity office cities. It is the basic agreement from which all other Equity contracts and agreements are derived. Familiarity with the Production Contract, its terminology and types of regulations, greatly assists in the comprehension of any type of Equity contract.

The League of New York Theatres was founded in 1930. Its membership includes a representative of each Broadway theatre. Everyone who produces on Broadway is also invited to join, though some Broadway producers are not members of the League. While the theatre owners negotiate contracts with labor unions that represent treasurers, building service employees and others, the producer members of the League negotiate the contracts with Equity. League membership approximates one hundred people each year. About one-third represent theatre owners and the others are active Broadway producers.

### THE OFF-BROADWAY AGREEMENT •

The 1970 Agreement between Equity and the League of Off-Broadway Theatres and Producers provides minimum salaries based on eight different sets of potential box office grosses. The more money a production can earn at the box office the more its actors must be paid until a certain maximum gross is reached.

Minimum salaries for Equity members are, of course, lower Off Broadway than on Broadway. Nonprofessionals, excluding supernumeraries, may not be used in Broadway productions, but Off Broadway shows may employ one nonprofessional in casts totaling from ten to twelve (excluding stage managers and understudies).

### THE CHILDREN'S THEATRE AGREEMENT •

Equity defines children's theatre productions as those presenting material expressly prepared or adapted for children up to and including the eighth grade level (excluding Shakespearean adaptations), with performance time not exceeding an hour and a half, including intermissions. Some Equity companies that perform expressly for high school audiences also work under the children's theatre contract. Actors may be signed to weekly contracts or they may work by the performance. In both cases the minimum salaries are low. The 1972 Agreement provided two categories of minimum salaries based upon the seating capacity of the theatre in which performances are held: (1) theatres seating less than 299 people and (2) theatres seating more than 299 people.

Additional compensation is required when the actor must sleep away from home or when he must travel to more than one theatre in the home city on a given day. Auditions open to all Equity members must be held at the beginning of each season and prior to rehearsals for each new production. A number of other regulations deal with special problems that relate to children's theatre. The use of nonprofessionals in such productions is left unclear and should be negotiated with Equity in each specific case.

Equity salaries for children's theatre performers are comparatively low, but before the first agreement was negotiated with the union in 1953, most actors in children's theatre companies fared far worse than they do now. Equity had long kept its eyes closed to children's theatres because, for the most part, few were profitable. But when more or less permanent children's theatre companies comprised of adult actors were formed and their producers began to realize sizable profits, Equity felt the time had come to guarantee the basic rights and wages which most actors were being denied. The Children's Theatre Agreement allows considerable flexibility for producers. The Producers' Association of Children's Theatre (PACT) negotiates the Agreement with Equity. There are, of course, a great number of nonprofessional children's companies and organizations that continue to operate outside union jurisdiction.

INDUSTRIAL SHOWS ■

An industrial show is a device dreamed up by Madison Avenue to promote or demonstrate the products or ideas of a particular industry. "Industrials" have grown in popularity at conventions sponsored by manufacturers at which franchised managers and salesmen gather to learn about "the new line" or new sales techniques. They have also been used at public conventions of an industrial nature, at world's fairs and at political conventions. An industrial show is a theatrical gimmick for increasing an audience's excitement about a particular product, person or idea. In essence, it is an expanded television commercial and it costs a very pretty penny to produce. But it stands to reason that the latest model car will look better if it is surrounded by beautiful dancing girls, demonstrated by costumed bunnies and described in mellifluous tones by the voice of a Shakespearean actor.

The Equity agreement covering industrial shows generally follows the Standard Production Contract. There are no provisions for the use of nonprofessionals, actors must receive additional compensation for overtime and travel and the minimum salaries are rather handsome as, perhaps, they should be. Industrials represent an extreme commercialization of theatre. They are produced by companies that specialize in that chore, by talent agencies and by advertising and public relations firms. Equity members are permitted to perform only in industrial shows produced by those organizations that are signators to the Industrial Shows Basic Agreement and must, of course, work under an Equity contract.

DINNER THEATRES ■

A dinner theatre is defined by Equity as one that presents productions for no less than two weeks each, on a year-round basis, in a room where both the dinner and the show occur and the price of admission includes both. Such theatres are not usually permitted in Equity office cities. No formal dinner theatre agreement has yet been negotiated, so each producer for this type of theatre must negotiate individually with Equity, which applies the Non-Resident Stock rules to dinner theatres, though there are usually modifications. Dinner theatres may utilize a limited number of nonprofessionals in casts numbering from seven to ten Equity members. If eleven actors are signed to Equity principal actor contracts, nonprofessionals may comprise 50 percent of the cast. An unlimited use of nonprofessionals is permitted once every six months for a production running no more than four weeks, if seven actors are maintained on principal contracts during such productions.

Dinner theatre managers must provide rest room facilities for actors that are not also used by the public or the kitchen crew—a fact some theatres have ignored when in the planning stages. Directors and choreographers, as well as actors and stage managers, are signed to Equity contracts in dinner theatres. Actors may be employed on weekly jobbing contracts or contracts that guarantee twenty-four weeks of employment, with minimum salaries being lower for the latter. The largest management organization for dinner theatres at present is the American Dinner Theatre Institute, which represents several dozen theatres (primarily those located in the South and Southwest). Many dinner theatres located in the eastern states belong to the National Association of Dinner Theatres.

### CAFE THEATRES ■

Although there is no official management organization representing cafe theatres, Equity has devised a special contract to oblige such operations. A cafe theatre may seat no more than three hundred people and must present its shows in the same room where beverages are served, often charging a cover or minimum instead of an admission price as such. If a production is transferred to a Broadway or other type of legitimate theatre, the manager must offer actors in the original production the opportunity to re-create their roles in such theatres or else compensate them with special payments. Similar arrangements must be made if motion picture rights are negotiated for the cafe production. A week's work includes, unlike other contracts, ten performances on six consecutive days. Unlike dinner theatres, cafe theatres are common in Equity office cities.

### SHOW CASE CODE ■

There are a number of instances in which a production may be presented for an invited audience at no admission charge or "suggested contribution" (although envelopes may be distributed for audience members to make donations of any amount they wish). When the purpose of the production is beneficial to the actor (who may gain experience, employment or an unusual opportunity as a result of it), then Equity may permit its members to work without compensation of any kind, although other regulations must be observed. Each showcase production must be individually approved by Equity and then translated into a written agreement between the producer and the union.

### SPECIAL CONTRACTS AND AGREEMENTS ■

While the previous pages have provided a brief description of Equity contracts and agreements in common use (excluding stock and resident theatre contracts), dozens more have been devised to accommodate special or unusual productions. Included among these are contracts for outdoor symphonic drama and a Special Production Contract. A producer should contact the Equity office nearest him whenever he is planning a new production or theatre organization. Such contact invariably eliminates difficulties or misunderstandings that would otherwise arise, regardless of how experienced the producer in question may be. Up-to-date membership lists for each of the management organizations discussed in the preceding pages may be obtained from Actors' Equity Association.

# ■ GENERAL ASPECTS OF EMPLOYMENT REGULATED BY AEA

The regulations discussed on the following pages, with minor exceptions, apply to all Equity productions whether in New York or not, whether produced by profit or nonprofit organizations and regardless of the size of the organization or its potential box office gross.

### AUDITIONS ■

Once a play has been optioned for production, the producer ordinarily negotiates to hire a director and the director ordinarily has the right to approve the selection of other artistic personnel, including the star, cast, scenic designer, costume designer and choreographer. It is the director's job to imprint his interpretation of the script upon the staged production. Consequently, he should have the right to hire or approve other artists who are to be associated with the production so he may engage people whose ideas and abilities are consonant with his own. Should the director's work appear to falter, the producer of course may replace him, although this usually involves considerable expense and there is always the risk that a new director will only compound the difficulties.

Most theatrical unions forbid or advise their members against doing any substantial amount of work on speculation. A producer may request performers to audition for him (indeed, Equity requires screening interviews or auditions for all productions, open to all its members), but he may not require actors to spend a great deal of effort polishing a role without compensation unless they wish. He may request directors or designers to show him their portfolios and to discuss their concepts of the script, but they are never encouraged by their respective unions to produce actual designs or staging plans until they are under contract. Speculative work cannot, of course, be regulated by union rules nor should it be. On the other hand, guide lines do exist to protect artists from unscrupulous practices.

Actors' auditions for commercial New York productions are usually initiated under the supervision of the producer's general manager. Some producers also hire a casting director or consultant. After auditioning or screening a number of actors, the most promising candidates are called back to audition for the producer, playwright and director, all three of whom usually have the right to veto the selection of any performer. Separate auditions are held for chorus and principal actors. An actor may audition for a chorus role only on two days and for a principal role only on four days, after which the producer must pay him for his time. Liability insurance must be taken by the producer to cover all performers at auditions and an Equity representative must be present at auditions.

The producer or director may approach specific stars or principal players directly or through their agents, inviting them to read the script and indicate whether or not they are interested and available to play a role. (A listing of franchised agents may be obtained from any of the performers' unions.) Rarely, however, is an entire production cast in this manner. Scripts or role requirements are sent to actors' agencies in hope that the agents will provide clients who fill the bill. Other roles are cast as a result of open auditions or producers may contact performers as a result of thumbing through the annual Players' Guide (available from Players' Guide Publications in New York and listing most Equity members together with their picture and agent's name). Actors also may be auditioned at the suggestion of the star, the choreographer, the musical director or someone else. Casting, especially for large productions, can be extremely difficult and time-consuming because the opinions of so many people are involved and human beings—a species that includes most actors—simply cannot be ordered according to exact specifications. Consequently, as actors are auditioned for a role, the director's original concept of that role is likely to change since the actor almost invariably brings unanticipated dimensions to it, which, after all, it is his business to do.

Auditions for Equity productions in theatres outside New York are ordinarily held in the city closest to the theatre that maintains an Equity branch office (Chicago, Los Angeles, San Francisco and Toronto). Despite the inconvenience and the fact that it may cost more to transport actors to a theatre far removed from New York, many producers prefer holding auditions in New York, as opposed to a closer Equity office city, because they believe the quality and variety of actors living in New York is greater. It is dangerous to generalize about "Chicago actors," or "L.A. actors" as opposed to "New York actors," but many producers and managers swear by such generalizations.

### REHEARSALS ▪

If they are signed to a Standard Minimum Contract, the rehearsal period may serve as a probationary trial for performers, in which case they may be replaced (given proper notice and severance pay). Or the actor may be given a Standard Run-of-the-Play Contract, which carries a higher minimum salary but perhaps not as high as the actor will demand if he senses that he has proved himself of value to the production and signs it after rehearsals have begun or the play has opened. Stars are usually signed to a long-term contract from the outset, making it more expensive to replace them before the termination date. Before the advent of Actors' Equity, actors were frequently rehearsed for many weeks without salary and then the production was likely to close after a mere performance or two. Today, rehearsals for New York productions usually last four weeks for non-musicals and five weeks for musicals. All the performers receive rehearsal salary, although it is a low salary allotted to star and minor player alike.

Most rehearsals are conducted in rented studios and only a few days are set aside for dress and technical rehearsals in the theatre where the show will open, though Off Broadway productions are apt to get more time than Broadway shows in the theatre itself. When a play is trying out in a stock or college theatre, it is generally found less expensive to rehearse at the tryout theatre. Actors may object to this practice because of the low rehearsal salaries they are receiving, but they cannot refuse if the producer so dictates. Equity rules carefully regulate the conditions under which rehearsals may occur as well as the number of rehearsals and rest periods. Nonetheless, it is impossible to prevent actors and directors from getting together for informal discussions or line readings. The stage manager is charged with the day-to-day responsibility of enforcing Equity rules during both rehearsal and performance periods.

**SALARIES AND BENEFITS** ▪

The minimum salaries that producers are required to pay Equity members in various job categories are negotiated approximately every three years by the management organization of a particular branch of the industry. Automatic salary increments are granted each year. In addition to these, salaries may be increased annually to cover rises in the cost of living based on the Cost of Living Index compiled by the U.S. Bureau of Labor Statistics's revised Consumers' Price Index.

Numerous provisions stipulate that actors and stage managers must receive extra compensation or insurance coverage for the performance of special tasks or feats, such as being responsible for the transportation of costumes, performing a risky feat on stage or playing a second role. Equity members also receive overtime payment when specified time limits are exceeded for rehearsals, picture calls, performances and travel. Nearly all contracts require the actor to work six days per week and to give eight performances during that time. The producer pays the actor for these performances whether or not they are given. If more than eight performances per week are required, the actor must be paid one-eighth of his weekly salary for each additional performance. This is also the case when a performance begins before 2:00 P.M. or after 11:00 P.M. on any day, when more than two performances are given on the same day or when the actor is required to work seven days out of seven.

All Equity contracts provide that the union member shall receive illness and hospitalization insurance as well as coverage by Workmen's Compensation. The (Broadway) Production Contract also provides life insurance. The manager must make a contribution to the Equity Pension and Welfare Fund for each Equity member he employs and, of course, match the employee's social security payroll deductions for payment to the federal government. At stipulated intervals, every actor under a Production Contract is required to perform without salary in a benefit performance, the profits from which are donated to The Actors' Fund of America, a nonprofit organization that assists aging and infirm union members.

**COSTUMES AND MAKEUP** ▪

Generally speaking, the actor making over $500 per week furnishes his own stage clothing, footwear and wigs provided these are things that he might normally own. Any such item that is associated with a particular profession or a noncontemporary period is classified as a "costume" and must be furnished and paid for by the manager and approved by Equity. Actors making less than $500 per week may not be required to provide their own clothing or footwear, though in many cases they do. Management is also responsible for cleaning and maintaining all clothing, footwear and wigs on a regular basis and for paying all expenses involved when an actor is required to change his hair color or style.

**TRANSPORTATION AND TRAVEL** (See chapter 6).

**PUBLICITY, PHOTOGRAPHS AND BILLING.** (See chapter 14).

SAFE AND SANITARY WORKING CONDITIONS (See chapter 3).

## ■ THE PLAY IN PERFORMANCE

### TRYOUTS ■

Unhappily for producers, few contracts with leading artists permit the employee to be dismissed without being compensated for the full amount of his contract, including run-of-the-play wages and percentages when these are stipulated. Despite this fact, it is not unusual for a producer to "buy out" a contract during the tryout period in the belief that a replacement will be worth the expense. When a production is "in trouble" and showing obvious signs of weakness, the most difficult job is to analyze exactly where the trouble lies—with the script, the direction, the performances, the staging? In some cases, a "play doctor" will be brought in to make script and/or staging changes and contractual provisions are generally made with the playwright and director that allow the producer to hire a "doctor" if he wishes.

Few Off Broadway productions go out of town for pre-opening engagements either because of the expense involved or because it is difficult to find audiences outside New York City for experimental or unusual productions. But the Broadway producer is always faced with the decision of whether or not to take his production out of town before opening in the City. During the nineteenth century, nearly all shows opened first in New York, if only for one or two performances, and were then sent on the road so they could use the then-magical phrase "direct from New York!" in their advertisements. Later, the situation was reversed and nearly every show began outside New York. It now seems safe to say that neither "prior to Broadway" nor "direct from New York" are slogans that, in and of themselves, attract much of an audience. Because of this, but primarily due to economic reasons, a less frenzied method of trying out a show became popular during the 1960s, that of the New York "preview." Eliminating the pre-Broadway, out-of-town engagement, of course, meant that many shows would never be seen outside New York and that "the road" would be diminished to a noticeable degree. But lower operating costs and the belief that preview audiences in New York are more representative of post-opening Broadway audiences soon made the preview system popular among producers.

Out-of-town tryouts seldom earn enough revenue at the box office to pay for the expenses of the tour. Costs include not only normal operating expenditures but also the transportation of actors and everyone else associated with the production as well as the scenery and costumes and the expense of setting up and disassembling the physical production in every theatre it visits. They also involve licenses with out-of-town theatres, out-of-town advertising that little benefits the New York engagement and contracts with out-of-town union employees.

In recent years it has become increasingly common for a producer to offer his play for pre-Broadway production in a college or summer stock theatre. This gives him the opportunity to see it in performance without any appreciable cost or commitment on his part except for the option money advanced to the playwright. The college or stock theatre pays all transportation, scenery and production expenses as well as all cast and musician salaries and it may also pay the producer and author certain fees and royalties. The disadvantages of this system are that productions are likely to be less than professional, audiences not at all representative of Broadway audiences. The producer and playwright also may be reducing the amount of time during which the copyrighted property can earn money for them. Nevertheless, if the producer is skeptical about a script or if it needs extensive work, a college or stock production may prove extremely helpful as well as inexpensive. Its most attractive advantage is that no commitments beyond the tryout need be made either to the performers or to a New York theatre which removes the terrible deadline that haunts most rehearsals and tryouts: the New York opening.

THE NEW YORK OPENING ■

The opening night of a production in New York is likely to be, as anyone who has ever attended one knows, the least typical night a show will ever enjoy or regret. The house is generally packed with well-wishers, celebrity hounds, critics, nervous backers and others whose purpose for being there is not primarily to be entertained. Little wonder that "opening night jitters" have become part of the tradition. Under such conditions, the performance may easily suffer. But it always goes on to the happy or bitter end, as the case may be, and it is usually followed by parties that merely serve to reinforce earlier reactions and pass the time while everyone waits for the newspaper and television reviews to come out.

During the long newspaper strikes that hit New York in the 1960s, radio and television news programs began reviewing theatre productions and they have since become yet another important factor in the business of "making" or "breaking" a show. With fewer and fewer New York newspapers of major importance being published, this redistribution of critical power can only be welcomed. Nonetheless, *The New York Times* review continues to wield the greatest influence. If one studies all the New York openings over the past five or ten years, comparing critics' reactions to the longevity of productions, several observations are possible: (1) almost no production has survived unanimously poor reviews, (2) comedies are more likely to survive mixed reviews than musicals and serious plays and (3) even favorable reviews together with follow-up rave articles and awards often cannot save a serious play. Unquestionably, a larger percentage of the New York audience prefers comedies to serious plays and there are, it seems, certain plays that, by virtue of their title or subject matter or off-putting advertising campaign, audiences simply stay away from "in droves."

MAINTAINING A HIT AND DISSOLVING A FLOP ■

Once the reviews are known, the producer must decide almost immediately whether to continue the production or not. If the reaction is unfavorable, he might post a closing notice after opening night (or before) in order to terminate all contracts and other financial obligations as quickly and inexpensively as possible. But when critical reaction is mixed, when there is a large advance sale of tickets or when audience reaction appears to indicate the possibility of a limited run, he may decide to risk further loss and keep the show open. In the event of rave notices, of course, the producer's decision is both obvious and easy.

If the show continues, the producer must first meet all weekly operating costs, then pay back the capitalization and, finally, begin splitting profits between himself and his investors. He must also do everything possible to keep his production alive and fresh. The producer, director and company manager should attend performances frequently and keep an eye open for "tired performances" or harmful liberties that performers may be taking with the script. New interest in a production can sometimes be generated by the engagement of new stars and leading performers, by moving the show from one theatre to another, by imaginative publicity gimmicks or striking advertising methods. Operating a New York production is like operating any other business that depends upon selling something to the public.

When closing a show and dissolving the Limited Partnership Agreement, the producer must dispatch all obligations as quickly as possible and render a final accounting of the enterprise to his limited partners. Nowhere is the sad business of closing a show more accurately or goodheartedly recorded than in Moss Hart's classic comedy about show business, *Light Up the Sky*. Something similar to the following dialogue probably takes place after every Broadway fiasco. In this instance it is between the star's mother, Stella, and the producer's wife:

STELLA. This the first show you put money into, Frances?

FRANCES. Yes.

STELLA. Well, I'll tell you about the scenery first. You can't sell it—get *that* out of your mind right now—and what's more, you can't even walk away and leave it here.

FRANCES. All that scenery?

STELLA. All that scenery! You can't even make believe you forgot about it. No, dear. First you have to pay somebody to have it carted away from the theatre—and then you have to pay somebody to burn it.

FRANCES. Pay somebody to burn it?

STELLA. Pay somebody to burn it. You and Sidney want to run about the city dump lighting matches? You have to *pay* someone to burn it. Regular union rates, and it's my impression this scenery is going to burn real slow.

FRANCES. Listen, Stella—don't rib me about this. My stomach just turned over.

STELLA. I'm just telling you what happens, Frances. You might as well know it.

FRANCES. Yeah. I can tell Sidney. I'll tell him nice and slow—for about two years. Go on, Stella. What happens with the costumes?

STELLA. Well, in an ordinary show, Frances, a costume that cost two hundred dollars they buy back for about two dollars but this is an allegory, dear. The costumes in this show are mostly rags, the survivors of the world are walking around in. Right?

FRANCES. Right! So we get about a dollar apiece for 'em.

STELLA. Oh, no! I wouldn't think so, Frances. What are they going to do with 'em? Can't even cover chairs with 'em!

FRANCES. Can't leave 'em here, either.

STELLA. That's right.

FRANCES. Cart 'em away. Burn 'em. Union rates. Pray for a windy day on the dump so they'll burn fast. Do people who put money into shows know about this, Stella?

STELLA. Well, usually a backer gets at least some kind of a souvenir for his dough, Frances. Say, he puts up five thousand dollars—he gets a lamp to take home, or his wife gets a pocketbook. But you're dealing with an allegory here, Frances. You see anything in this show you can take home?

FRANCES. I got no use for a wind machine. That I know right away.

STELLA. You got any place in your house for the mountain with the faces of Washington, Jefferson and Lincoln carved on it? Or the rain effects?

FRANCES. Sidney's bedroom. He should wake up every morning and look at it, and the rain should pour down on him. So, actually, Stella, it's going to cost more money, even to close it.

STELLA. Oh, sure. It would be wonderful if you could just stick up a sign saying "gone to lunch" or "if not called for in thirty days, forget it"—but it just doesn't work that way.

FRANCES. How did you figure my interest was worth eleven dollars, Stella? That's pretty high, isn't it?

STELLA. Well, I wanted to slip it to you easy. This is your first show.

FRANCES. Yeah. Boy, I can't wait now to run into Irving Berlin. "There's no business like show business." He ought to be arrested.

©Copyright by Moss Hart 1948, 1949.

The commercial theatre in America has always been a speculative business. In some periods it has just managed to provide a living for the people who work in it. At other times the commercial theatre has made large profits, most of which have been distributed to people other than its performers and artists. Ostensibly, it has continued to exist without the benefit of subsidy, but a closer look will reveal that it is ever dependent upon the noncompensatory time and energies invested by nearly everyone before he had "made it" and by many fortunes in private capital invested and lost, which represent a kind of subsidy or, at least, philanthropy. The strongest force working in favor of the commercial theatre is the autonomy it offers producers and artistic directors, allowing them to function without the invariably harmful interference of board directors, institutional bureaucracies and other extraneous powers. While the majority of its productions possess less than universal significance, commercial theatre continues to function as a primary marketplace of entertainment, both for audiences and for other branches of the industry.

# CHAPTER SIX

# Stock and
# Resident Theatre

Although there are many differences between stock theatres and resident theatres, the two share a common historical lineage and many of the same management features. Both are related to the stock company system of the nineteenth century, both were rekindled by exclusively amateur efforts during the first two decades of the twentieth century, both developed a sizable number of professional theatres that fell under the jurisdiction of Actors' Equity Association, both began outside New York City and have generally remained there. Stock and resident theatres also resemble each other in their budgetary, staffing and operational requirements. Excluding the national touring companies of Broadway shows, stock and resident theatres today comprise all but a minuscule amount of professional, regional theatre in America. There is, however, a difference between the two systems as they are currently structured: stock theatre is a largely commercial purveyor of "popular entertainment" (if, indeed, there is such a thing in live theatre today), while resident theatre tends to be noncommercial, nonprofit and more interested in serious or experimental work. A third type of theatre that also falls into the stock category because of its commercialism is the dinner theatre.*

*See chapter 5.

## ▪ BACKGROUND

### THE FALLOW YEARS: 1900 TO 1914 ▪

While Broadway enjoyed prosperity and a rash of activity through the 1920s, the road began to decline at the turn of the century and professional theatre outside New York virtually disappeared by the end of World War I. The advent of combination companies eliminated the nineteenth-century stock companies, just as the growth of motion pictures and other factors eliminated the combination companies. If regional theatre was to be reborn it could only result from the work of amateurs since the road was no longer capable of supporting paid professionals and no independent resident companies had survived the new century and the tentacles of power that stretched out from New York.

As empty or unprosperous playhouses were rapidly converted into movie palaces, many Americans were having second thoughts about "the good old days" of commercial theatre. Hastily assembled productions, unrewarding plays, companies that displayed no degree of ensemble acting and stars who often failed to measure up to their reputation had made audiences less than satisfied with commercial theatre and less than anxious to salvage it or to build a new theatre according to the old and familiar model. The belief that a more vital theatre could be created was reinforced from abroad by the example of the Free Theatre Movement and the work of innovators like Antoine, Stanislavsky, Meyerhold, Ibsen and Shaw. Some Americans, including Kenneth Macgowan, Robert Edmund Jones, Joshua Logan and Elia Kazan, traveled abroad and observed the work of such men at firsthand and returned to the States to put the new European theories of theatre into practice. Several native Europeans, including Lee Strasberg and Herbert Bergof, who had been exposed to the Free Theatre Movement abroad, migrated to America and also became its proponents. A sense of action and a sense of promise eventually came to fruition and transformed the American theatre. In both play-writing and play-staging two essentially new styles were developed, realism and expressionism, which by the forties gave the theatre an altogether new look. The copyright acts of 1889 and 1919 made it possible for a man to earn his living as a playwright, and the new emphasis given to the staging of productions elevated stage directors and designers to an important professional status separate from other theatrical artists.

### REBIRTH OF INDEPENDENT THEATRE COMPANIES: 1914 TO 1930 ▪

The first important, nonprofessional resident theatre companies sprang into existence just prior to 1920. The Washington Square Players was started in 1914. The Provincetown Playhouse produced O'Neill's *Bound East for Cardiff* during its first season in 1916 on Cape Cod at the Wharf Theatre and soon set up permanent headquarters in New York City. The Theatre Guild was established in 1919. These organizations became venerated prototypes of numerous resident groups that were established in the ensuing decades. They seemed to prove that nonprofessional, serious theatre could survive—even in the capital of theatrical commercialism—and, more important, that they could offer major contributions to the art and craft of theatre.

During the 1920s the noncommercial movement (including resident, community and college theatres) grew at the encouraging rate of roughly one hundred new theatres or groups per year, the vast majority outside New York. Many, of course, were seasonal operations and nearly all were funded more by optimism than by cash. It is important, however, to stress the independence of these early resident companies—from each other and from New York control—rather than to dwell on their amateurism. Nearly every movement and innovation in theatre begins on an amateur level, where the air is less intoxicating and the company more free than in the heady confines of a commercial or institutionalized establishment.

Eva Le Gallienne attempted to revive the repertory system with her Civic Repertory Theatre, founded in 1926, and the Group Theatre was established in 1929 by several defectors from the Theatre Guild. At the same time, dozens of lesser-known and less ambitious theatre companies were being created in the hinterlands. Of those theatres that now fall into the category of "summer stock" the first to open that is still operating was the Lakewood Playhouse in Skowhegan, Maine. Established in 1901 as part of a summer resort, Lakewood utilized a resident company of actors under a resident director and staff, operated on a seasonal basis and produced a different play every week or two in a humble, wooden playhouse that could easily pass for a converted barn.

During the twenties, men like Richard Aldrich, Milton Stiefel and Guy Palmerton, who later became the scions of a summer theatre establishment, were casting around the small resort communities of New England for hospitable places to establish amateur, resident companies. Aldrich founded the Cape Playhouse on Cape Cod in 1926 (later he also operated the Falmouth Playhouse and the Cape Cod Melody Tent). The Ivoryton Playhouse in Connecticut opened in 1930, the Westport Playhouse (founded by Lawrence Langner as an informal laboratory for Theatre Guild activities) in 1931, the Ogunquit Playhouse in Maine in 1932.

Many summer activities, then as today, opened with loud beating of local drums but failed to survive for many seasons. Most were organized and staffed by enthusiastic youngsters just out of college or by teachers and professors not *quite* out of college. One of the earliest and most famous of such theatres was the University Players Guild that operated for five summers in Falmouth, Massachusetts, and later transferred to Baltimore for several seasons. Members of its young company who later achieved considerable success included Joshua Logan, Margaret Sullivan, Henry Fonda, James Stewart, Kent Smith, Mildred Natwick, Myron McCormick and Norris Houghton—not a bad graduating class for an amateur group on Cape Cod. Until recent times it is probable that a majority of Broadway and Hollywood actors began their careers in a summer or winter stock playhouse. By 1930 there were hundreds of stock theatres, and the movement had spread from its New England beginnings to the South and Middle West. Some lasted only a few years, others continued as amateur resident theatres and the remainder followed a more commercial course. The winter stock movement, concentrated in Florida and the southern Atlantic states, began a bit later than the summer movement but was also comprised of amateur and resident companies and star-package houses. Some, like the elegant Royal Poinciana Playhouse in Palm Beach, little resemble the barn-like summer theatres in outward appearance but are in all other ways similar.

## HISTORY REPEATS ITSELF: 1930 TO 1950 ▪

Most of the better-known summer theatres that still are in operation were started

during the late twenties and the thirties and followed the same pattern of development. They progressed from amateur-resident companies to Equity-resident companies, to Equity-resident companies with visiting stars, to roadhouses for Equity-
nonresident-touring-package productions—exactly the same pattern as that followed
by the independent stock theatres of the nineteenth century!

When the Stock Managers' Association negotiated its first contract with Actors'
Equity in the early thirties, only about a dozen summer theatres were under the
jurisdiction of the union. By 1950 that number had increased to approximately 130
and continued to grow. Minimum salaries were at first comparatively low and Equity
required that each stock company employ only a half-dozen union actors. The remainder of the company was comprised of apprentice actors who, after several seasons, were required to join the union if they wished to continue working in an Equity house.

It appears that the first "star" in this century hired to perform with a resident
stock company was Jane Cowl, whom Richard Aldrich paid $1,000 in 1935 to
appear for a week in *Romance* with his company at the Cape Playhouse. Many
stock managers were horrified by this extravagance but, since the experiment appeared to pay off at the box office, the idea soon caught on and, once again, audiences were asking "who's in it?" And, once again, the shady townships of rural
America were brightened by the seasonal visitation of theatrical luminaries—Zasu
Pitts, Billie Burke, Bea Lillie, Gertrude Lawrence, Cedric Hardwicke, Helen Hayes,
Lillian Gish and the perennial Tallulah Bankhead were among the atypical tourists.
Star salaries climbed as high as $5,000 per week, forcing managers to pinch pennies
in every way possible. Providing somewhat of a vacation for the star, if no one else,
the system usually required the star to spend several weeks rehearsing with the resident company before the performance week. Soon, however, stars began traveling
with several feature players, and by the 1950s they generally carried their entire
company, directed, costumed and rehearsed in New York and spending only the
performance week itself at each theatre. The "package system" had begun. As a
result, the professional-resident stock system virtually ceased to exist.

Other theatrical unions, such as the Association of Theatrical Press Agents and
Managers and the International Alliance of Theatrical Stage Employees, also attempted to organize stock houses. They succeeded, however, only in those theatres
near New York City and a few others located in large cities where their jurisdiction
was already established. Nonetheless, the weekly operating cost for a typical 600-
seat summer theatre employing Equity actors rose from about $2,500 in 1930 to
about $10,000 in 1950. Today, the same theatre is likely to have average weekly
costs that exceed $15,000.

**THE COMMERCIALIZATION OF STOCK THEATRES: 1950 TO PRESENT** ▪

While stock theatres never fell under the control of a syndicate (although some
producers have operated several theatres simultaneously), stock managers lost most
artistic control over their productions when they adopted the package system. Only
a limited number of top attractions, that is, big-name stars making their first appearance on the summer circuit or hit shows fresh from Broadway, are available each
season. Most managers want the same attractions, and consequently they book nearly
identical production schedules. The Stock Managers' Association was replaced during

the fifties by a similar organization of summer and winter theatre managers and producers, the Council of Stock Theatres (COST), which each spring serves that branch of the industry as a central booking exchange. Stock companies that maintain a resident company also formed an organization, the Council of Resident Stock Theatres (CORST), mainly to negotiate with Actors' Equity. Although the resident stock theatres individually control their own casting and production standards, they are, like COST theatres, highly dependent upon what Broadway offers them each season in the way of hit plays.

Despite commercialization, stock theatre still serves the industry as a whole in two important areas. It provides more job opportunities for actors, apprentices and technicians than any other branch of the professional theatre and it often provides a testing ground for new plays. In some cases the stock manager himself serves as the originating producer for productions that he later brings into New York. Michael Ellis, operating from the Bucks County Playhouse in Pennsylvania, and Zev Bufman, operating from the Coconut Grove Playhouse in Florida, are leading examples from the fifties and sixties of such managing producers. In other cases a New York producer who has no affiliation with a stock theatre may offer a stock tour of his production before it opens in New York. Among many dozens of plays that have traveled through stock on their way to becoming hits are *Life with Father, The Fourposter, A View from the Bridge* and *Barefoot in the Park*.

Because of the apparent success and rapid growth of stock theatre during the forties, it was inevitable that some people would attempt to convert it into big business. The attempt took the form of musical tent theatre. Beginning in the fifties, a number of tent theatres seating from one thousand to two thousand people were put up from Boston Harbor to San Francisco Bay, and another stock managers' organization was formed to deal with Equity, the Musical Theatre Association (MTA). Initially, the tents presented popular musicals and operettas with a largely resident company, chorus and orchestra, and aimed at pleasing the entire family at low admission prices. The prototype of all tent theatres is the Music Circus in Lambertville, New Jersey, founded by St. John Terrell. The largest and most successful operations involved the simultaneous management of several tent theatres, such as John Price Junior's Musicarnival (begun in 1954) which controlled a summer theatre in Cleveland and a winter theatre in Palm Beach. Messrs. Guber, Gross and Ford operated five theatres just south of New York City during this period.

But the popular appeal of such attractions as *The Student Prince, Carousel* and *My Fair Lady* began to dwindle as they were revived for the third or fourth time, and Broadway simply wasn't keeping up with the demand for new hit musicals. Not surprisingly, tents began to engage stars in their productions and to supplement their seasons with special performances by rock groups and nightclub personalities. Ticket prices went up and tent theatres soon found themselves ensnared in the star system and all its attendant problems. Furthermore, because of the large potential grosses of the tent theatres, many stars adjusted their salary demands upward and thereby became unavailable to the smaller, proscenium stock theatres. By 1970, for example, it was not unusual for a personality like Victor Borge or Liberace to receive $10,000 per week plus a percentage of the gross. A few stars, like Lana Turner, received even more. The weekly operating costs for a fifteen-hundred-seat tent theatre rose from around $8,000 in 1950 to as high as $30,000 in 1970. As with the growth of commercialization in most theatre movements, higher costs and higher ticket prices were not accompanied by a proportionate rise in the quality of production. But there *was* an important difference between 1910 and 1970. In 1910 regional American theatre consisted largely of New York-controlled commercial endeavors. In 1970 there were numerous locally controlled theatre organizations, both professional and amateur, to counterbalance the commercial structure.

## THE GROWTH OF RESIDENT NONPROFIT THEATRES ▪

A large number of young, twentieth-century producers organized theatres that sooner or later fell into the commercial genre, but other pioneering producers began groups outside New York that remained closer to the example of Provincetown. More ambitious and intellectually aware, these theatres include the Cleveland Play House (1917), Jasper Deeter's Hedgerow Theatre (1923), the Pittsburgh Playhouse (1933) and the late Robert Porterfield's Barter Theatre (1933). Though largely comprised of amateurs, such groups kept alive the idea and the dream of a serious, regional theatre. In 1947 two theatres that serve as prototypes for numerous others that followed and that now comprise what we regard as "resident theatre" came into existence. Neither Margo Jones's Theatre '47 in Dallas nor Nina Vance's Alley Theatre in Houston originally maintained a resident company of professional actors, but they were serious, ongoing organizations which established a sense of permanence in all other ways.

The 1950s saw a steady growth of resident groups, including Zelda Fichhandler's Arena Stage in Washington (1950) and the Actor's Workshop in San Francisco (1952). Festival theatres, generally offering Shakespearean productions, such as those in Stratford, Connecticut, and in Oregon, also increased in popularity during the fifties. Initially encouraged by substantial grants from the Ford and Rockefeller foundations and later by subsidization from state and federal arts councils, the resident theatre movement grew rapidly during the sixties. Toward the end of the decade there were about forty resident theatres operating with Equity companies. The movement embraced nearly half the states in the union and thereby signified a big step toward the decentralization of professional theatre.

Operating under a special Resident Theatre Agreement with Actors' Equity, the managements of these theatres are represented by the League of Resident Theatres (LORT), not to be confused with the Council of Resident Stock Theatres (CORST), which represents stock theatres that have resident companies. It seems certain that the rapid growth of nonprofit resident theatres would never have occurred without the rather sudden financial assistance provided by foundations and the government. Nor is it surprising that a number of the resident groups formed during the sixties have since collapsed—in most instances because they lacked sufficient support apart from foundation and government help or lacked adequate administrative talent or because their work did not result from careful artistic development.

Most of the successful resident theatres grew from very modest beginnings and had time to resolve fundamental artistic difficulties and to build local support before plunging into a fully professional and high-budget status. It is important to note that every significant resident theatre was founded and operated by a single if not singular personality who could easily qualify as "dynamic." One question that resident theatre must answer is this: How can an organization survive the death or departure of its founding producer? Some, like the Guthrie Theatre, have outlived such a development and others, like Theatre '47 in Dallas, have not, which suggests that safeguards *do* exist to insure that a "permanent" theatre company can be truly permanent. The next question that nonprofit, resident theatres must eventually face is: How can such an organization survive with greatly reduced or nonexistent subsidization? No American arts manager should be so optimistic as to believe that private and public subsidy for the arts is inevitable.

## ▪ TYPES OF COMMERCIAL, STOCK THEATRE

### NONRESIDENT DRAMATIC STOCK ▪
Stock theatres in the nonresident dramatic stock category typify the older and better-known commercial operations, most of which have proscenium stages and seat under a thousand people. They are located throughout the nation, concentrated in the eastern states, include both summer and winter seasons and operate under the "Stock Nonresident Dramatic" Agreement with Actors' Equity. The management organization that negotiates this agreement is the Council of Stock Theatres (COST), which meets each spring in New York City to consider available stars and packages and to book the most commercially promising of these. COST theatres "buy" package productions almost exclusively, though occasionally they may book a national touring company or a pre-Broadway tryout company.

All COST theatres hire their own resident stage manager and, because the scenery is usually constructed at each theatre, each has a resident scenic designer and technical staff. They also employ a resident front-of-house staff to handle publicity, box office, business and house management responsibilities. Most COST theatres also hire about a dozen nonsalaried apprentices. Under the package system, however, apprentices rarely gain an opportunity to act but, rather, spend most of their long hours each day in the scene shop or engaged in front-of-house chores. Apprentices also may constitute the stage crew during performance hours, running lights, sound, props and wardrobe. A few COST theatres, such as Westport, maintain a unionized stage and scenic construction crew, but, generally, nonprofessionals in COST theatres have ample opportunity to learn their craft through direct job experience. Because the shows usually change each week, with only one "dark" day between productions, the work and the learning experience can be intensive.

### RESIDENT DRAMATIC STOCK ▪
Those stock theatres that do not present package productions but maintain a resident company of actors (at least seven people signed to an Equity Minimum Contract for Stock are required) and present a season of plays (not in repertory rotating style) are represented by the Council of Resident Stock Theatres (CORST). Most of these are commercial in that they produce Broadway hits and seek to earn profits for a private corporation. Salary minimums are somewhat lower than in COST theatres and a further distinction is made in that, as of 1973, Equity recognized three categories of CORST theatres, determined by the potential weekly gross:

"X" Companies: $13,500 weekly gross or over

"Y" Companies: $7,500 to $13,500 weekly gross

"Z" Companies: $7,500 weekly gross or less

Separate salary schedules are negotiated for each category, adjusted downward from "X" to "Z." CORST theatres are also allowed to make a greater use of nonprofessionals than COST theatres. As of their 1969 agreement with Equity, CORST could employ a ratio of 75 percent Equity actors to 25 percent nonprofessionals in casts of fifteen or more, including the director, stage manager and assistant stage manager, who must be signed to Equity contracts. Equity allows this rule to be waived for one week each season (permitting an entirely nonprofessional company to perform at the theatre) provided that the minimum of seven Equity contracts is maintained during that week.

The COST theatre, then, need only employ the number of performers required by the script each week, plus a stage manager. The director of a package production is paid a salary during the rehearsal period and then a royalty starting with the third performance week of the package or when it moves into its second booking, whichever occurs first. The CORST theatre, on the other hand, must maintain seven people on minimum salaries, regardless of whether they are required by the script or not. But because the salary minimums are higher in COST theatres and, more significant, because the average costs of all actors' salaries in package productions are well above minimum, the total weekly Equity payroll is invariably lower in the CORST theatre. Also, few plays call for less than five actors. Assuming that the director and stage manager are counted among the minimum number of seven, there is little risk of having to carry actors who are not performing each week in a CORST company.

### INDOOR MUSICAL STOCK ∎

The organizations represented by the Musical Theatre Association (MTA) are mostly theatres-in-the-round, some operating under canvas tents and others within a permanent structure. Their seating capacity ranges from about twelve hundred to two thousand and most are profit-taking ventures. They are comparable to COST theatres in that the minimum salary range for principal players is about the same level and they present package productions almost exclusively, although the number of weeks a show performs at each theatre is likely to be longer, and each theatre is likely to package some if not all of its own productions. Most MTA theatres have become very active in booking children's theatre productions, pop musical groups and nightclub personalities, mostly on a one-performance basis, to supplement the revenue from regular weekly attractions. Their bill of fare is even known to include cooking lessons and Sunday church services!

Nonprofessionals may be employed under the MTA Agreement only in companies with eleven Equity principal actors, in which case three nonprofessionals may be used. If the company is comprised of fourteen or more Equity principal performers, however, there is no limitation on the number of nonprofessionals that may be used. Directors, advance directors, choreographers, stage managers and assistant stage managers must also work under Equity contracts. Chorus members are employed under special chorus contracts which carry complex rules requiring chorus members to receive additional compensation when they perform particular feats on stage, when they have dialogue, perform solo bits and so forth. Most principal performers in MTA theatres are employed under Stock (weekly) Jobbing Contracts, although

Minimum Contracts for Stock (which guarantee a longer period of employment) may be used. Like COST theatres, most MTA theatres employ apprentices for largely nonperforming duties. Their work in theatres-in-the-round, however, is likely to be more arduous and less rewarding than in the smaller proscenium houses. Running props up and down the aisles, cleaning the house after each performance and serving as dressers for the performers are among the most common apprentice assignments in MTA operations.

#### OUTDOOR MUSICAL STOCK ▪

The most uncommon type of stock theatre is that which presents its productions out-of-doors. Comprised of only three member organizations at the time of its 1969 agreement with Equity, the Association of Civic Musical Theatres (ACMT) represents the St. Louis Municipal Theatre Association in St. Louis, Missouri, Starlight Musicals in Indianapolis, Indiana, and the Starlight Theatre in Kansas City, Missouri. While salary minimums are close to those for the MTA theatres, as are the other Equity requirements, ACMT theatres are allowed a greater use of nonprofessionals. Rather amusingly, nonprofessionals who may be used in ACMT productions are defined by Equity as:

1. Persons prominent in civic and community affairs
2. Pre-established local organized groups
3. Groups of children
4. Individual children under fourteen years of age who are recruited from the local community and perform other than a principal part

As with nonprofessionals performing in any kind of Equity company, management must submit an affidavit to the union stating that the performer is not and never has been a member of any branch of the 4 As (AEA, AGVA, AFTRA, SAG, AGMA) or the Hebrew or Italian actors' unions.*

## ▪ NONPROFIT, RESIDENT THEATRE (LORT)

While a few nonprofit stock theatres operate under COST and MTA Equity agreements, such cases are exceptional (the Cape Playhouse in Dennis, Massachusetts, for example, is operated by the nonprofit Raymond Moore Foundation, the Corning Summer Theatre in New York is owned by a local glass company and Philadelphia's Playhouse-in-the-Park is owned by a local bank and run on a nonprofit basis). Professional theatres in the seasonal stock category are usually operated to make money for private corporations and, consequently, they present moneymaking plays and stars, allowing the smallest margin of financial risk possible. When theatres outside New York and cities with Equity branch offices wish to produce serious, ambitious or "noncommercial" productions, they generally form a nonprofit corporation and operate longer seasons than the typical ten-week stock season. This allows room for greater artistic growth as well as time for longer-running productions.

The management organization that represents resident theatre groups, whether they perform in repertory-rotation style or not, is the League of Resident Theatres

---

*The "4 As," as defined earlier, is a term standing for "The Actors and Artists of America," which is chartered by the AFL-CIO and is the parent organization for all the performers' unions.

(LORT). If a touring production from a LORT theatre performs in New York or away from its home theatre, it is governed by the Equity rules for the type of theatre that it visits (Broadway, Off Broadway, touring company, etc.) or by special Equity regulations that cover touring LORT productions. The member theatres of LORT vary greatly in terms of seating capacity. Equity recognizes four company categories, determined according to potential weekly gross receipts:

"A" Company: $32,000 weekly potential gross and above

"B" Company: $16,000 to $32,000 weekly potential gross

"C" Company: $ 8,000 to $16,000 weekly potential gross

"D" Company: $ 8,000 weekly potential gross and under

Salary scales covering actors, journeymen, stage managers and assistant stage managers—all of whom must be signed to Equity contracts—are adjusted downward from the "A" to the "D" category. While actors' minimum salaries remain the same whether they are performing in a repertory theatre or not, stage managers' and assistant stage managers' salaries are generally higher for repertory than for nonrepertory operations. Some nonsalaried apprentices or students may be used in "B," "C" and "D" companies, except in New York and Los Angeles theatres, according to limitations dictated by Equity. On the other hand, Equity does permit a limited use of "journeymen" in LORT companies who, as will be discussed later in this chapter, are signed to Equity contracts and paid no less than one half the applicable minimum salary. Special rules and types of compensation exist to cover LORT companies (such as the Trinity Square Repertory Company in Providence, Rhode Island) which operate two theatres simultaneously in the same city.

Actors in resident Equity theatres may be signed either to a Standard Contract or to a Seasonal Contract. A Seasonal Contract requires the manager to guarantee the actor from twenty-four to fifty-two weeks of employment. The contract must specify at least 50 percent of the roles that the actor will be required to perform if the theatre plans more than six productions. When six productions or less are involved, the contract must name at least two of the actor's roles. Neither of these stipulations, however, are enforced too strenuously by Equity.

The Equity rulebook governing employment in resident theatres does not, perhaps wisely, define the term "resident theatre." There is no stated ratio of standard vs. seasonal contracts for resident theatres. This means that a theatre can qualify as "resident" without in fact maintaining a resident company of actors for twenty-four weeks or more each year. Some LORT theatres do exactly that. The current resident and repertory theatre movement in America is comparatively new and delicate, not having begun until the 1950s, and needs as much flexibility and growing space as it can find if its young roots are to become firmly implanted.

## ▪ COMMERCIAL "PACKAGE" PRODUCTIONS

### BOOKING THE PACKAGE PRODUCTION ▪

As we have seen, all theatres belonging to COST book primarily package productions, as do many of the theatres belonging to MTA. How do packages originate? A packager is a producer, a person who initiates a production and then sells it to a number of theatres from which he collects a packaging fee. Because this fee is a nominal one (usually $300 from each theatre that books the production), a packager is likely to supplement his income by serving in some other capacity, such as that of advance director, director or actor in the production he is packaging. Also, the packager is entitled to be reimbursed for legitimate preproduction expenses incurred in connection with his package. By wearing several hats it is possible for a packager to earn from $500 to $1,000 per week during the busy summer season. The owner or operator of a stock theatre often packages a production he wants for his own theatre and then sells it to other theatres. Since the theatre operator already has a staff, as well as rehearsal space, preproduction costs are likely to be lower than when a non-theatre-owner packages a show. Theatre-packaged productions insure the theatre manager greater control over the type and quality of shows produced. Finally, a package may be originated as an inexpensive kind of pre-Broadway tryout.

Most packages originate because the stock performance rights for a New York hit have just been released or because the packager knows a star who is seeking a vehicle. In the case of a hit show—only one or two of which ordinarily become available to stock in a given season—a number of different packages of the same play may be organized, each using different stars. If the hit is big enough and has gained sufficient national publicity, it may be packaged without a star, in which case the cost will be considerably lower. *Who's Afraid of Virginia Woolf?* and *The Boys in the Band* are two examples of plays from the sixties that enjoyed successful tours in stock without the benefit of expensive star casts. Except for musicals, however, it is rare that the title of a play alone is enough to attract large audiences.

The stock rights for a Broadway play are usually not released until the play has completed its New York engagement (or, if it is late spring, unless the producers anticipate an imminent closing and wish to capitalize on New York publicity before the summer goes by). If the production is sufficiently successful to warrant a national tour, the stock rights are usually not released until after that tour. The New York producers may limit the areas in which their play is released to stock because they anticipate another tour in that area or believe that it will hurt business for the New York production. Stock rights generally precede amateur rights—giving the professional theatres first crack at a production—and they generally precede the release of a film version of the play. Broadway musicals are released first to large tent and proscenium (MTA) stock theatres, and not until the following season are the smaller theatres allowed to produce them. Any stock manager, however, is free to negotiate directly with the New York producers of a show to obtain exclusive permission to present a show, to engage a national touring or bus-and-truck company at his theatre or to insure that the play will not be released to other theatres within a certain radius of his own.

One reason that a syndicate of stock theatres has rarely worked is because, aside from what are likely to be major differences between physical plants, each theatre is likely to have a different type of audience. The most conservative audiences—those most easily shocked by four-letter words and unusual subject matter—are those in the southern and "Bible belt" states, where producers and theatre owners assiduously comb each script for potentially offensive material and either demand cuts or refuse to book the play into their theatres. Other communities, especially resort areas for tourists from the metropolis, prefer plays that are mildly if not wildly titillating and risqué. In some theatres the "tired" movie star constitutes the biggest draw, in others it is the star of television soap operas. In still others the legitimate,

Broadway star is easiest to sell. The star who does sell-out business in Ohio may do poor business in Connecticut. The manager of a stock theatre must know his audience and book his season accordingly. Yet, an unbelievable number of stock bookings are made by managers who have never seen or read the play they are buying and base their decision solely on the star who is in it.

It cannot be disputed that the star's name is often responsible for getting people into the theatre, but it is unreasonable to expect an audience to return to a theatre if it is disappointed by the play or the production as a whole. A manager's ignorance about a production may also be regretted for other reasons, among them the fact that more expensive sets than anticipated are required or that particular properties or special effects cannot be locally obtained. Naturally, a manager may simply "guess wrong" about what will be well-received at his theatre. Perhaps the most disastrous opening night in the history of stock occurred when Bert Lahr and Tom Ewell performed the American premier of Samuel Beckett's *Waiting for Godot* at the Coconut Grove Playhouse in Miami—hardly an ideal community for avant-garde European drama. It should be added, however, that nobody at first associated with that production seemed to understand what it was all about. It was advertised as "the laugh sensation of two continents"!

From March to June of each spring, COST and MTA meet regularly in New York City to interview hopeful packagers and to consider the stars and plays that are being offered. Packagers who do not belong to the organization to which they are offering a production must be sponsored by one of its members. Usually, the packager simply tells COST or MTA members the name of the play he is offering, the star and the approximate cost of the package. Until he is assured a satisfactory number of bookings, he does not officially begin to cast the production. He merely has a verbal agreement with the star and knows that the stock rights for the play can be obtained.

Theatre owners vie with each other for the most promising bookings and trade engagement weeks in order to accommodate themselves and each other. Although the cost of transporting a company of actors from one theatre to another is a major expense for most theatres, transportation routing actually receives little serious thought when productions are being booked. This is due to conflicting engagement weeks, difficulties in coordinating the schedules of numerous theatres and the distance separating various theatres. Consequently, it is not unusual for a company to play weekly engagements according to something like the following routing: Skowhegan, Maine-Westport, Connecticut-Denver, Colorado-Falmouth, Massachusetts-Poconos, Pennsylvania-Ogunquit, Maine. Obviously, the most sensible routing would be from Skowhegan to Ogunquit to Falmouth to Westport to Poconos to Denver, traveling steadily in one direction. But probably the two theatres in Maine did not wish to play the same show back-to-back and probably the others had already committed a number of their weeks when they booked the show, so they were unable to arrange for the company to travel the shorter distance to their theatre.

### THE PACKAGE AGREEMENT ▪

Once the packager knows that enough theatres are willing to book his production to make it worthwhile, he enters into a Package Agreement with each of those theatres. This agreement follows a standard format provided by COST and MTA. It requires the packager to provide the following items to the theatre several weeks in ad-

vance of the date when the production is scheduled to open:
1. Contracts and biographies for each member of the cast
2. Photographs of each cast member
3. A property list and plot
4. A scenery floor plan and elevations when necessary
5. A lighting plot and cue sheet
6. A costume plot
7. A master script with all cue sheets
8. All necessary tape recordings and a list of sound equipment
9. An itemized list of preproduction expenses
10. The transportation routing for the production
11. Housing requirements

At a specified date in advance of the show's opening, the theatre must pay the packager's fee ($300), as well as its share of the preproduction expenses, which are divided equally among all the theatres that book the package. The more bookings a package gets, the lower its cost will be for each theatre. Few if any theatres seating less than nine hundred people can afford to originate and produce a full season of productions with stars unless the preproduction costs are shared with other theatres. Hence, the *raison d'être* for the touring star-package system.

Perhaps the most curious aspect about a packager's role is that he has almost no liability in relation to his production, because the theatre and not the packager signs all actors' and musicians' contracts and is responsible for obtaining the performance rights for the play and for paying royalties. The theatre and not the packager pays royalty advances that may be required and puts up the bond with Actors' Equity (an amount of money usually equivalent to two weeks' cast salaries), which is why the union does not recognize the packager as a bona fide producer. AEA stipulates that the first theatre in which a package show performs will be responsible for paying all rehearsal salaries and the related taxes and benefits. The actor, therefore, has not *one* contract for the entire tour, as he would if he were performing in a Broadway show or in a national touring company, but, rather, a stock jobbing contract with *each* theatre where the production is booked.

Because stars can and do change their minds about appearing in a stock tour or at one of the theatres where it is booked, it behooves the manager to secure the star's signed contract before signing the other actors. Regardless of any circumstances that might cause a star not to appear in the production, the theatre must still honor all other contracts it has signed. It is also curious that, while the packager negotiates the contracts, it is the theatre that must sign and uphold them. Each theatre may attempt to change contractual provisions that have been made by the packager, but such changes are usually minor.

### THE UNIT PACKAGE ■

The one instance in which contracts are signed by the packager is that of a so-called unit production. This type of show travels with its own stage manager (ordinarily, stage managers in stock are contracted by the theatre and remain at the same theatre throughout its season) and the theatre merely signs a single agreement with the packager and pays him a single fee for the unit production. Although this may appear to be a more simple and efficient method of organizing a package, it is fraught with potential problems for the packager. A unit production renders the packager liable for all contractual provisions with the actors and the royalty house and requires him to make up and distribute the weekly payrolls, to post bond with Actors' Equity and to pay all the necessary state and federal payroll taxes. In short, unit packages make the packager responsible for what happens at each theatre. One packager of a unit production, for example, got involved in a serious and expensive law suit because the publicity department at a theatre where the package played made a mistake in the way the play director's name appeared in the playbill. Had the contracts been between the director and the theatre, rather than between the director and the packager, the theatre would have been liable for the mistake. Needless to say, a packager is not anxious to take responsibility for everything that might happen in connection with his production at theatres where he has no real control.

### THE ADVANCE DIRECTOR ▪

Most package productions are preceded at each theatre by an advance director or coordinator. Working under an Equity contract (which doesn't make sense since an advance director is primarily an administrative and technical adviser, not a stage manager or director, except during a brief rehearsal period), the advance director spends the week prior to the opening of a package advising the resident staff about the production so that its arrival and opening can be as efficient and pleasant as possible. Because the advance director is frequently the theatre's only tangible link with the star and the production, his knowledge about the production and his efficiency are crucial in assuring a happy and successful transfer of the play from theatre to theatre.

While packages travel complete with costumes and often with difficult-to-obtain properties, each theatre employs a resident scenic designer and a staff to build the sets. (On some occasions the scenery also travels with the actors.) Set plans are sent to the resident designer of each theatre and he follows a ground plan and color scheme determined in advance by the director. But productions have a way of being altered during a tour, the sets always have to be adapted to fit the particular dimensions and limitations of each stage and the resident designer may wish to employ certain ideas and solutions of his own. The advance director is the only person to advise the designer about such matters. Similarly, the advance director advises the theatre manager about the actors' housing preferences and about publicity matters and also can provide personal information about actor's personalities and habits that may greatly assist the manager in avoiding trouble and enjoying a reasonably pleasant week.

If the manager treasures his own peace of mind, he will attempt to follow the bits of advice he receives about the touring company. For example, if the star expects the theatre to provide a gallon of mineral water in her dressing room every night, it is worth winning her appreciation by spending a few dollars to provide the balm. If a company has been complaining at previous theatres about unclean dressing rooms, it would pay to provide them with exceptionally clean ones. Anticipating trouble before it arrives, correcting a situation or even overcompensating in areas of special difficulty can bring amazingly happy results. If the advance director is truly concerned about the well-being of his production and his company, the manager need only follow his advice. Unfortunately, many advance directors are hired by the packager because they are an old friend, an out-of-work actor or a last-minute decision. An incompetent advance director is easy to spot, in which case the theatre manager is best advised to contact the packager, the director or, best of all, the star of the production and request information directly from them. Because neither the director nor the packager usually travels with the show, the star rather automatically takes control once the tour begins and is the person most important to please if a satisfactory production week is to be realized.

## ■ AEA REGULATIONS PERTAINING TO STOCK, RESIDENT AND TOURING COMPANIES

Actors' Equity Association rules and regulations discussed in chapter 6 apply to the actor wherever he may work. But when an actor works outside New York City (or one of the other four cities that has an Equity office, provided he was hired through that office) the theatre manager has further contractual obligations. The following AEA regulations pertain to the actor in all types of stock, resident and touring companies.

### TRANSPORTATION FOR THE ACTOR ■

Management is always responsible for arranging and paying the actor's transportation from the doorstep of the actor's home to the doorstep of the theatre or place of lodging. During the regular run of a play in an Equity office city or when, away from home, if his place of lodging is within a half mile from the theatre, the actor must get back and forth to rehearsals and performances at his own expense. The business of transporting the actor to a theatre where he will remain in residence for the duration of the production or for a season is usually a simple matter because time is seldom pressing. Rail transportation is the mode recommended and covered by Equity for most travel, though bus service is permitted if trains are unavailable. If travel exceeds ten hours, a Pullman sleeping accommodation must be provided for the actor or, if it is not available, the actor must be reimbursed for the equivalent cost of such. When first-class rail transportation is not used, it is good practice for the manager to check carefully the appropriate Equity rulebook or to apply directly to Equity for special dispensation to use some other type of transportation.

Actors may not be required to travel by air against their wishes and, when such travel is necessary to meet a time schedule, the manager should protect himself by entering such an obligation in the actor's contract. Whenever actors are required to travel, the manager must notify the actor in advance of departure time, telling him management's prescribed routing. In most instances, management must provide actual travel tickets at least three days in advance of departure. If the actor elects some other mode of transportation, he may redeem his ticket for cash and assume any additional travel costs himself (unless the manager has given him written permission to travel in another way, in which case management pays all the expenses). If travel is by chartered bus, plane or private limousine, any of which may require special permission from Equity, then management is not required to reimburse actors who travel in other ways. When public or chartered buses are used, they must be first-class, air-conditioned vehicles.

Most touring companies are contracted to a single producer who is responsible for all travel costs and arrangements. In the case of package shows, when the actor is working under a jobbing contract with each theatre he visits on a tour, the particular theatre to which he is traveling is responsible. If, however, there is a period of three days or more between contracted performance dates, the actor is entitled to be reimbursed for travel back to his home city. Suppose that a package opens in Westport and is scheduled to play Ivoryton the following week. The Westport management must get the company from New York to Westport. Ivoryton is responsible for moving the company from Westport to Ivoryton. If the tour ends at Ivoryton, the management must then get the company back to New York. In other words, the first theatre that has booked a show must get the company from New York and the last theatre on the tour must get it back to New York. (This means that the last theatre on any tour will usually pay the highest travel costs.) In between, it is always the upcoming theatre that is responsible for travel costs and arrangements. A perfectly simple system—except for one complication: When the distance between two consecutive theatres on a package tour is greater than the distance from New York City to the theatre to which the company is traveling, the theatre *from* which it is departing must pay the difference. For example, if a company is going from the Poconos Playhouse in Pennsylvania to Ivoryton, Connecticut, Poconos must pay the fare from there to New York, where Ivoryton's obligation begins. But that's a simple case: one can clearly see on a map that Poconos is on the other side of New York City and public transportation routes form a pretty direct course from Poconos to Ivoryton via New York. But what if a company is required to travel from Buffalo to Cape Cod? If it travels via New York City then, of course, each theatre pays the full fare from the City to its theatre. But what if there is a shorter route going directly from Buffalo to Cape Cod? The Cape Cod theatre must determine (1) the Buffalo-New York rail fare and (2) the New York-Cape Cod rail fare. If the fare is greater from Buffalo to Cape Cod than from New York to Cape Cod, Buffalo must pay the difference. The cost breakdown might be as follows:

**First Class Rail Transportation**

| | |
|---|---|
| A. Direct Buffalo-Cape Cod fare | $25.00 |
| B. Buffalo-New York City | 23.50 |
| C. New York City-Cape Cod | 18.75 |
| D. Buffalo pays (difference between A and C) | 6.25 per actor |
| Cape Cod pays (C) | 18.75 per actor |

In this way no theatre ever pays more than the travel costs from New York City. It follows that when the distance from "Theatre A" to "Theatre B" is shorter than from "Theatre B" to New York City, "Theatre B" gets a bargain—provided that its manager knows his algebra! Unfortunately, transportation problems are made even more complex because rail travel is frequently nonexistent between two given theatres or other modes of public transportation are very limited and require a ridiculous number of change-overs and waiting periods. It should be evident, then, that the theatre that frequently books package productions should at the beginning of each season make a point of collecting a full set of rail, air and bus schedules or, better still, find a patient and clever travel agent who is willing to do all the necessary work.

When travel exceeds time limits dictated by Equity rules or when specified rest and day-off periods are not observed, the actors must be compensated with special payments over and above the cost of their fare. Management must also reimburse the actor for taxi fees from his home to the transportation terminal or departure point, for porter fees and, in the case of air travel, for flight insurance. At no time may a theatre take advantage of round-trip fares. Upon arrival at the place of engagement, the actor is entitled to submit an itemized breakdown of his transportation expenses (if these have not been prepaid) for immediate reimbursement. When the manager fails to notify the actor of his prescribed routing three days in advance of departure, the actor makes his own arrangements for getting to the theatre and must be reimbursed in full.

It should be evident that the cost of transporting a company to theatres outside New York and other Equity cities can be a major item in any production budget. For instance, if a single bus fare from New York to Cape Cod is $18.75 and the average taxi and porter cost from the actor's home to the bus station is $3.50 and the theatre must transport a company of nine actors both to and from New York, the company transportation cost will total $400.50. Such costs should be estimated early so the theatre can arrange for a chartered bus or for driving the company in private cars when such means of transport are less expensive than public transport.

The business of transporting large or numerous wardrobe trunks, boxes of stage properties and scenery is often more expensive and complicated than that of transporting actors. For extra compensation, an actor in a company may agree to be responsible for the transportation of certain trunks and props. But when these are large or numerous, special arrangements will have to be made. If time is not a factor (which it usually is) then the arrangements may be simple. Before booking any touring show, a manager should be aware of the items that are traveling with the company and what kind of problems and expenses will be involved in transporting them. Ignorance of such matters has caused some theatres to cancel performances because it was physically impossible to transfer a production in time from its last place of engagement.

Once a company is in residence at a theatre, management must see to it that the actors are transported back and forth via well-lighted byways from their place of lodging if it is more than a half mile from the theatre. Specific pickup and departure times may be set and any properly insured theatre car, taxi or limousine may be used. To simplify such matters, the actors should be housed either in one place or in close proximity. If the theatre is lucky, the actors' hotel or guest house will agree to transport them to and from their performances. Ideally, lodging will be sufficiently close to the theatre, or accessible by inexpensive public transportation, so that the actor is able to get back and forth on his own.

## HOUSING FOR THE ACTOR ▪

When the actor is living away from home, Equity forbids that his housing expenses reduce his salary below a specified minimum. This minimum, of course, varies according to the type of theatre and the contract under which the actor is working. The 1972 MTA and COST agreements, however, specify that if an actor's weekly salary is less than $1000, his rent may not exceed 20 percent of his earnings.

When living costs exceed the amounts dictated by the union, management must reimburse the actor for the difference. Obviously, company living expenses can cost the manager dearly unless he can provide room and board very inexpensively. In the nation's larger cities, it is not difficult for the manager to make reasonably low, discount deals with local hotels, guest houses and restaurants, especially if he can guarantee a goodly volume of such discount customers. But in resort areas and out-of-the-way places, local businessmen are loath to discount their prices when it might mean forfeiting business at full price. In these cases it may be cheaper in the long run for a theatre to operate its own housing and dining facilities. Of course, such operations require considerable amounts of extra, nontheatrical time, money and energy. A special staff will be necessary to operate them, special laws will have to be complied with, special licenses obtained and so forth. But theatre-operated housing and dining facilities may reduce costs and create a more efficient organization. They are especially desirable when the theatre employs a large technical and administrative staff on a seasonal basis. Although staff members in regional theatre are seldom protected by unions, not many such employees will be willing to work at a theatre where most if not all of their earnings must be spent on room and board. So the theatre must either pay high salaries or provide inexpensive room and board—it is merely a question of which is least expensive and most efficient.

When management provides housing for Equity actors, it must offer a choice of accommodations. (If there are six actors to house and the manager offers seven rooms for this purpose, he has fulfilled this obligation. All the rooms may be located in the same building.) The housing choices must be made available to the actor in advance of his arrival at the theatre and he must state his preference. Having done so, he becomes responsible for one night's room cost. Actors may not be required to share a room against their wishes. As with transportation, when the actor elects to make his own housing arrangements he thereby cancels all management obligations regarding room cost and transportation to and from the theatre. A manager may refuse to take any responsibility in regard to the housing, feeding and transportation of anything on two or more legs that has not signed a contract with him.

### MEALS FOR THE ACTOR ■

Equity requires that actors have at least one hour to rest between performances on the same day, exclusive of half-hour call. When the time between two performances is less than one and a half hours, management must provide each actor and stage manager with a hot meal at the expense of the theatre. This rule applies most often to theatres that offer "twilight" performances (usually a 6:00 P.M. curtain followed by a 9:30 performance on the same evening).

In most cases there are restaurants or cooking facilities in or near the actors' place of lodging. When this is not true, the theatre is responsible for transporting the actor to and from eating places for every meal. Other Equity rules regulate the number and frequency of meal stops actors are entitled to receive while traveling.

## ■ APPRENTICE SYSTEMS IN COMMERCIAL STOCK THEATRE

### DEFINITION OF "APPRENTICE" ■

A theatre apprentice is a nonprofessional, nonunion worker. Most often, apprentices are associated with a theatre for a full season or a consecutive number of weeks. If they receive any salary at all, it is likely to be a very small weekly allowance. Their job responsibilities are likely to be limited. Any type of stock or resident theatre may employ as many apprentices as it wishes so long as it does not overstep the rules and regulations pertaining to nonprofessionals as prescribed by the theatrical unions contracted by the theatre in question. Apprentices may observe and assist unionized workers, but they may not perform the actual duties of unionized workers. Apprentices are, in fact, students of a particular art or craft which, it is assumed, they wish eventually to master. The apprentice system in stock and resident theatre provides young actors an opportunity to earn Equity membership in a fairly easy, though time-consuming manner. If the theatre formally registers an apprentice with the union, the apprentice may play an unlimited number of roles during his first season and up to three roles during his second season. As of his next role (whether during the second or third season as an apprentice) he must be signed to an Equity contract. This system was designed to protect actors against unscrupulous stock managers who demanded high apprentice "tuition fees" in exchange for "giving" the apprentice an Equity card—in short, from selling Equity memberships.

When the apprentice system was first regulated by Equity, package productions that traveled with complete casts had not yet come into existence. Each stock theatre therefore needed a corps of apprentice actors to play roles not filled by union actors. Such roles were numerous and apprentices thus could gain considerable acting experience. Today, most stock package productions are fully cast with union members in New York so apprentices, when they are employed at all, are generally relegated to technical and administrative areas. Resident stock companies, dinner theatres and resident theatres under the LORT Agreement, however, can still provide numerous roles for nonprofessionals. Progressively more stock theatres are abandoning the term "apprentice" and, instead, hiring a number of "technicians" who receive a small salary and are primarily interested in technical theatre rather than acting.

### THE ECONOMICS OF APPRENTICE SYSTEMS ▪

Laymen are surprised to hear that summer theatre apprentices work for very little if any salary and parents of would-be apprentices often question this point, preferring their children to take summer jobs that offer a decent salary. From the apprentice's point of view, is an apprenticeship worth the sacrifice? If the theatre is a reputable one and apprentices are given meaningful jobs and not required to do extensive maintenance work and there are not too many apprentices working at a given theatre, the answer is yes. Non-Equity stock theatres are the most likely to offer the apprentice experience as an actor. Equity stock and resident theatres, however, offer affiliation with a professional operation and contact with people who may be important to the apprentice's career later on. If an apprentice spends most of his time for several months constructing scenery and working on stage crews, he should gain the equivalent in knowledge that he would get from five or six college courses in stagecraft and production. In fact, many college theatre departments now give credit for such work experience. A good apprenticeship is likely to be a major factor in helping a person to decide whether or not he wishes to pursue a career in the theatre. After one season as an apprentice, the competent person should qualify for salaried positions in stock and resident theatres and should certainly be ahead of others in his school or college theatre activities and classes. In short, ten or twelve weeks without salary is a small sacrifice for what the apprentice should learn from a good theatre operation.

From the theatre's point of view apprentices are, at first glance, a source of cheap labor. But managers should not let this factor blind them to the hidden costs of apprentice labor. The theatre may have to absorb some or all of the apprentices' room and board expenses. It may have to hire a salaried person to supervise apprentices. It may find that the salaried staff members are spending the majority of their time teaching and supervising apprentices rather than doing their own work. Apprentices may cost the theatre dearly because of mistakes they make and this cost may accrue both in the financial sense and in terms of the theatre's reputation. For example, apprentices may be responsible for breaking and ruining stage properties or they may fail to return borrowed properties. They may also be more accident prone than professional workers, another source of grief and expense. A manager must weigh all such liabilities against the potential advantages of an apprentice program. He may decide to employ a completely salaried staff unless he is dedicated to altruistic, educational or some special set of goals or programs.

### APPRENTICE SCHOOLS AND PROGRAMS ▪

Some seasonal theatres, both Equity and non-Equity, operate an apprentice school in conjunction with their play season. As many as one hundred apprentices may be accepted each year and charged a tuition of as much as $1,000, plus room and board expenses. In virtually all such cases the apprentices tend to be of high school and junior high school age and the program serves as little more than a slight step up from summer camp—a place where parents may send their children when they've outgrown the kiddie camps and are not yet ready for their first summer job. The experience apprentices gain in such programs is likely to be minimal. On the other hand, some stock theatres are affiliated with a school or college and provide apprentices formal class work resulting in a stage production or two. These programs usually possess some educational value.

The majority of stock and resident theatres that accept apprentices have no formally organized program or classes. Rather, each apprentice is rotated on a weekly basis so that, by season's end, he has served in every area of theatre production. Regardless of the type of theatre to which he is applying, the apprentice today has a right to expect positive answers to at least 80 percent of the following questions:

1. Is maintenance work for apprentices kept at a minimum?
2. Do apprentices gain experience in all areas of theatrical production?
3. Are apprentices guaranteed at least one free day each week, exclusive of performance hours?
4. Is room and board available within walking distance of the theatre?
5. Are apprentices reimbursed for their expenses when their cars are used for the theatre business?
6. Does the theatre absorb any of the apprentices' room and board expenses?
7. Does the theatre offer any apprentice stipends or salaries?
8. Are apprentices given first opportunity to be cast in roles not filled by Equity actors?

9. Do apprentices always work under the supervision of a salaried staff member?
10. Is the theatre willing to submit documentation about apprentices seeking to earn college credit for their work?

Good apprentice programs in professional theatres should probably accept college-age applicants only, young people who have demonstrated a serious interest in theatre but who have not amassed sufficient experience to be capable of supervisory work. Apprentices should be responsible adults and treated as such—not, under any circumstances, as slave labor. Up to a point, it is generally true that the more responsibility a person is given the more responsible he will be. The reverse also tends to hold true. When a dozen or so apprentices are hired and there is no formal apprentice program or director of apprentices, the manager must hire staff members who are willing and able to work with and teach nonprofessionals. This requires patience and a rather generous desire to share knowledge and experience with beginners. It does not, however, require that staff members overly indulge apprentices.

Perhaps the most valuable lesson an apprentice in stock can learn is the need for professional discipline in theatre, which involves the realization that excuses and mistakes are never acceptable. When a theatre employs Equity actors it makes a commitment to professionalism that should be upheld in every aspect of its operation, including the behavior and performance of its apprentices. Equity actors, by virtue of their own hard-won professionalism, have the right to expect professionalism from others working in the theatres they visit. Audiences that come to see professional actors, by virtue of the ticket prices they pay, also have the right to expect an entirely professional organization. If a manager wishes to operate a training school for amateurs, this should be a stated policy reflected in all areas of the theatre. If he wishes to operate a commercial venture in order to make a profit, he should not expect either his audience or his employees to judge his operation on anything except a professional level.

## ■ JOURNEYMEN IN RESIDENT (LORT) THEATRES

### DEFINITION OF JOURNEYMAN ■

A major factor that sets the resident LORT theatre apart from other types of Equity operation is the existence of a special type of employee known as a "journeyman." In effect, a journeyman is a student actor or stage manager signed to a special Equity contract. He is, therefore, a member of Actors' Equity Association and protected by all its rules and regulations. The purpose of serving as a journeyman is either to gain professional acting experience for the first time or, in the case of a professional who has been an Equity member prior to serving as a journeyman, to retrain and revitalize his craft by working with a resident company. The journeyman system is a good and fairly flexible solution to the problem of providing professional training for actors, although the union forbids its practice in all but a few theatres.

### EQUITY REGULATIONS GOVERNING JOURNEYMEN ■

As with nonprofessionals, Equity has established a ratio of journeymen vs. professional contracts for certain theatres that operate under the LORT Agreement.

The ratio of journeymen and nonprofessionals combined may not exceed 30 percent of a given company, but is only allowed in "A" companies (those operating in theatres with a weekly potential box office gross that exceeds $32,000). LORT theatres in the "B," "C" and "D" categories, however, are permitted to use a limited number of nonprofessionals, dependent on the number of Equity actors they employ.

Journeymen may not be used in theatres that have a season of less than sixteen weeks or in touring companies that do not operate from a resident or home theatre. A journeyman's contract, which generally pays a salary of more than one-half the minimum actors' salary established for a particular category of theatre, may at any time be converted into a standard seasonal contract at full minimum salary or more. That process cannot, however, be reversed. Actors who are already members of Equity may accept journeyman contracts only if they have not previously worked under a standard LORT contract. To prove it, the actor must sign an affidavit for submission to the union together with his professional biography or listing of credits. A journeyman contract must guarantee at least sixteen weeks of employment, not to exceed two seasons or two years (whichever is shorter), but provisions may be made so that the manager can terminate the contract at the end of twelve weeks.

Journeymen are usually required to attend classes in conjunction with their work (the class requirements must be stated on the journeyman's contract) and some journeyman programs are affiliated with college theatre departments. Unlike the case of resident actors on standard seasonal contracts, the manager does not have to stipulate or name any of the acting roles which the journeyman will be required to play. The journeyman may be cast in a principal role or serve as an understudy as the manager or director requires him to do throughout the season. Finally, a journeyman contract must state whether the employee is a journeyman actor or a journeyman assistant stage manager. Each position carries certain limitations regarding the permissible type and amount of employment.

As an alternative to the conservatory approach of training performers and to the apprentice system of earlier decades, the journeyman system is a logical method for training professional actors.

## ▪ SPECIAL PROBLEMS OF STOCK AND RESIDENT THEATRE MANAGEMENT

Everyone in theatre works for the audience. It is the final and indispensable ingredient that must be added to consummate the theatrical experience. The stock or resident theatre manager will also find it helpful to establish a set of priorities in relation to theatrical employees. These priorities should assist the manager in daily decision-making and in the business of budgeting time and money. One standard that may be used is to establish employee "importance" according to the length of time that particular employee will be associated with the theatre. In stock theatres that produce a series of weekly, package productions, this means that the resident technical and administrative staff—which remain at the theatre throughout the season—should receive highest priority in terms of working conditions, housing and other such matters. The logic of this is that it's better to have problems of dissatisfied employees who will only be around a week or so than ones who will be around for the entire season. In the same vein, a theatre generally caters more to its season ticket-holders than to its one-time customers.

Naturally, such priorities do not mean that actors who work at the theatre for only a week or one-time ticket-buyers should be treated in any way that is intentionally shoddy or condescending. But long-term staff and audience support are crucial factors in most successful operations and there is nothing unethical about favored treatment for people who provide it. Yet, there are many theatre operations in which, for example, visiting actors are provided scrumptuous living accommodations compared with the lodging places allocated to resident staff members. Or, a considerable budget may be used to entertain visiting actors but nary a penny for such amenities as "strike night" food for the technical crew, occasional parties for nonsalaried apprentices or similar gestures that could go a long way in creating a happy, loyal and efficient resident staff. Indeed, some managers appear to regard their season-long employees—upon whom they must heavily rely—as little more than indentured servants. Somehow, a reasonable and gracious balance must be found so that a kind of "family" attitude is adopted toward the people who are most faithful to and longest associated with a given theatre.

### WHICH COMES FIRST, PLAY OR PLAYER? ▪

High on the list of decisions that determine the ultimate success of a performance is the decision of whether to select the play before the players or the players before the play. As we have seen, commercial productions almost always originate with the dramatic property and are then cast. The same is true in most stock theatres, where plays are determined by available New York hits or by the preference of a star. Educational and amateur theatre groups, on the whole, tend to select the play before actors are auditioned, although sometimes the director may have pre-cast one or two of the leading roles. But when the goal is to create a close-knit company from which a repertory or season of plays can be developed in response to the artistic development of the actors, either as individuals or as a company, the problem is a difficult one. How can a director know the potential of an actor until he has observed his work? How can the ability of actors to work as an ensemble be known when each is auditioned individually? When well-known performers are hired to join a resident company—as Hume Cronyn and Jessica Tandy were hired by the Guthrie, for example—their range of talent is familiar to the director. But such cases are exceptional. Most resident companies are comprised of actors whose talents are unknown to the director when he hires them. Consequently, the director may cast according to stereotype or, as in the eighteenth- and nineteenth-century stock companies, according to "acting lines."

Although acting companies will be partially determined by the type of plays that a theatre plans to produce, a full season of typically diverse plays would tend to require a company comprised of the following "types": leading man, leading woman, second man, second woman, character man, character woman, ingenue and juvenile. It is a casting system as old as the commedia dell 'arte and as new as the television soap opera. It is also a system that tends to result in productions that are never ideally cast; and sometimes badly cast. It necessitates one artistic compromise after another unless the theatre "jobs in" numerous actors for each of its productions while continuing to pay other actors who are on seasonal contracts whether they are performing or not. As a result of such difficulties, expenses and frustrations, more and more so-called resident companies are, paradoxically, operating without a company in residence. Instead, each production is cast separately, although in most cases the manager and director cast from an unofficial pool of performers who have worked with them in the past.

How is it possible, then, to develop a professional company of actors who can achieve true artistic teamwork, or what is called "ensemble acting"? When working within the organizational structure of a producing Equity theatre, such a company may be difficult to create. It is, however, feasible that ensemble acting can be developed by professional schools or workshops, as the Actors' Studio, the Herbert Bergof Studio and the Julliard School have sometimes managed to do. But most such workshops are usually neither intended nor equipped to present public performances, unless one counts occasional showcase performances given for limited audiences. The English director Peter Brook was able to develop a company of actors over many months by establishing a school (and Equity actors are perfectly free to join any school or workshop they wish) and then casting a production from the students who had been working and developing as a team over a long time. Conceivably, such a casting policy could be challenged as legally prejudicial since it is fundamentally in opposition to union rules for open auditioning and casting. An American example, similar to the Brook technique, is the manner in which Elia Kazan cast a number of his New York productions from the talent he had been working with at the Actors' Studio. Theatre companies that are organized in commune-like fashion, such as the Living Theatre company or Grotowski's Polish Theatre Laboratory company, are likely to run into difficulty in complying with union regulations, although the managers of such groups are always free to seek special dispensations from the unions, or, indeed, to ignore the unions entirely (although this could cause difficulty for the theatre landlord if he wishes to lease his theatre to union shows in the future).

### PLANNING THE SEASON OF PRODUCTIONS ■

Stock theatres that present package productions, as discussed earlier in this chapter, book their seasons on a somewhat catch-as-catch-can basis. They are always limited by which New York hits are available and by which stars are willing to go on tour. Resident theatres, however, are not locked into the star system and generally have audience support for noncommercial plays. Nearly every resident theatre manager has once dreamed up an ideal season of productions, his personal formula for a season of capacity business. Maybe the formula calls for a splashy musical to open the season, followed by several light comedies and ending with a mystery-melodrama. Perhaps it calls for a series of plays related to some central theme (a festival of international drama, a series of plays by a single dramatist, a series of plays all in the same historical period or production style). The organizer of any season of plays, however, must take the following factors into account:

1. The primary goal of the producing organization
2. The physical plant
3. The resident company
4. The budget
5. Potential audience support

Some organizations feel that the time of year when a play is produced is also a major factor (summer means light comedies, fall means mysteries and melodramas, winter means serious dramas and spring means musicals). Some educational and amateur theatres follow this "seasonal formula" with amazing religiosity, although its validity is highly dubious, to say the least. Professional resident theatres, however, appear to rely less and less on any type of formula for planning a series of plays, and even places as established as Shakespearean festival theatres are producing non-Shakespearean plays on a regular basis. One is tempted to conclude that the nature of theatrical production largely defies most attempts at formularization. As with furnishing a house, if each piece is of high quality, uniformity of period and style is unimportant.

## DEALING WITH THE STAR SYSTEM ▪

Because stars command high salaries which, outside commercial New York theatre, leave only a small margin of profit for the theatre, and because everyone working for a star theatre feels the economic pinch created by star salaries, it is always tempting to berate the star system if not the star himself. If one deeply disapproves of the commercialization engendered by the use of stars, one should obviously work in a theatre where the only stars to appear are on painted backdrops. In most serious branches of the performing arts, it is only possible for an artist to command an exceptionally high salary when the quality of his work is also exceptionally high. In the field of popular entertainment (meaning entertainment that is transmitted by means of the electronic media and thus available to an audience of millions), it is easier for a performer to gain great popularity on the basis of some physical quirk or personality trait rather than that of artistic talent. Nonetheless, one must recognize that pop stars fulfill a need felt by their audiences. They provide satisfaction as no one else can and this unique ability makes them worthy of stardom.

Other epochs and societies have recognized and rewarded their leading performers in a number of ways. In America stars are frequently recognized with almost cultistic worship and rewarded with large sums of money. The point is this: a star is a person who has struck a human response in the heart of the public and he deserves professional respect because of this alone. Sometimes respect is difficult to give because of one's personal opinions about the star's work or personality. In that case, it should be given on faith. More often than not, such faith will be supplanted by respect that comes from observing or working with the star over a period of time. It is important for theatre managers to encourage their resident staff members to adopt such attitudes of respect toward stars and leading theatre artists. In summer stock, for example, apprentices often will be too young to remember the accomplishments of some visiting diva. They should be taught to take the diva's reputation on faith. If they are serious students of theatre, they will make a point of informing themselves about the star's career. A few words on that subject from a professional staff member in advance of the star's arrival can be helpful.

Because of the star's high salary, it is tempting for staff members to assume a "why don't you do it or buy it for yourself?" attitude. Again, this behavior is inappropriate and simply a sign of amateurism or sour grapes. When the economics of an entire theatre operation is based on star reputations, the theatre should obviously treat the star in a manner that reflects his importance to it.

Several other points also should be made in regard to star performers. Invariably, the theatre that plays host to performers who are making their first tour outside New York or Hollywood will experience the greatest difficulties. Performers are likely to expect the same treatment and facilities to which they have been accustomed and, of course, this will be impossible in regional theatres. The first theatre they play must be prepared to register and absorb the "star shock." Also, of course, the first theatre on any tour is likely to have the greatest technical and scenic difficulties and the least-polished performances—all good reasons for a manager to avoid booking a tour's first performance week.

There is usually a considerable difference between performers who have worked exclusively in television and films and those who have worked mostly on the legitimate stage. The former may be nervous about facing live audiences, may be used to having lots of "yes men" around and will almost certainly be unprepared for the rigors of touring. The legitimate theatre performer, on the other hand, has probably done many tours in theatres both lavish and humble, been stuck in dilapidated rooming houses in God-forsaken towns and worked with many beginners and under many less than ideal circumstances. In short, the "legit" performer is almost invariably easier to get along with than the film or TV performer.

While a star is certainly capable and often entitled to make many demands on the theatre staff, it often happens that a theatre experiences even greater difficulty with supporting players. This is usually the result of jealousy toward the star, a competitive sense or a defensiveness that the player feels is necessary in order to "make it." Generally, however, the entire company of actors will reflect the personality and moods of the star. If the star is unhappy and always complaining, the other actors are likely to follow suit. If the star is gracious and professional, others will respond in that vein. At the risk of sounding like a male chauvinist, it may be added that male stars generally seem to command the respect of their company more easily and frequently than female stars.

Whatever problems may arise between a star and other performers or theatre staff members, it should be remembered that the star is a leader in every sense of that term. When his leadership is undermined, it follows that the entire production and organization will suffer.

---

Stock theatre in America has enjoyed two lives that bear remarkable similarities. Stock has always been the commercial theatre's provincial representative. Serious, professional regional theatre is represented by the nonprofit resident groups that began to thrive in the early fifties but are still young and still experimenting with different types of organizational structures. Together, stock and resident theatres form the largest segment of the live theatre industry in terms of actors employed and professional productions mounted. While stock has become tied to the star system and the hit show economy of New York theatre, the resident movement has thus far remained reasonably independent from New York and from self-styled centralization. Reliance upon central casting and staffing agencies, development of a system of exchanging or touring productions from one resident theatre to another, extensive dependence upon subsidization, the use of stars or total reliance upon a single founder or artistic director are factors that, if not kept in check, could spell doom for the resident theatre movement. While unionism has brought professionalism to stock and resident theatre, it has also forced greater commercialism and helped discourage the growth of truly resident, ensemble acting companies. Unions have made some attempts at flexibility in regional theatre, but there is obviously a need for more.

Finally, stock and resident theatres, by means of apprentice and journeymen systems as well as the numerous staff positions that are available, provide the largest professional training ground for theatre students and beginners. As New York feeds plays and performers into stock and resident theatre, so stock and resident theatre feed a considerable amount of fresh talent into New York. Each, then, is vitally dependent upon the other. It stands to reason that, on the whole, one cannot be much better than the other. Thus, the leaders in stock and resident theatre have an obligation that commands them to recognize, educate and provide professional experience to the best people they can find. Such is the nature of their contribution to the profession.

# CHAPTER SEVEN

## College Theatre

Educational theatre is, in the broadest sense, any theatre sponsored by an educational institution. Chapter 1 points to a difference between educational and educative theatre. The former indicates educational sponsorship of a production and the latter dramatic content or purpose of a special nature (to propagandize, to demonstrate, to provide therapy). Remembering that the word "educate" is derived from the Latin *educere*, meaning "to lead out," one realizes that all theatre is educational in its effect upon the audience. Educative theatre, paradoxically, tends to enforce thoughts and feelings *upon* its audiences. A third category might be called theatre *in* education, indicating professional groups that visit the campus and the classroom. This chapter is concerned primarily with educational theatre on the college campus.

Poets, philosophers and educators since Plato and Aristotle have been concerned about the educational and moral values of theatre. Does the drama have an obligation to teach and enlighten its audiences? How deeply and in what ways can the living theatre influence its audiences? Questions such as these have pragmatic as well as academic relevance. Until the present century, schools and colleges in the Western world were concerned with theatre almost exclusively as an instrument for teaching, especially in connection with classical subjects. In other words, educational theatre for the participant and not for the audience. The first plays written and

141

performed in English were the products of schools like Oxford and St. Paul's. In the eighteenth and nineteenth centuries theatre was accepted as an extracurricular school activity and as an appropriate addition to commencement and assembly programs. Not until the twentieth century were theatre courses as such included in college curricula and not until recently have educational theatre programs begun to recognize an obligation to campus and community audiences as well as to student participants. The history of educational theatre, therefore, is largely modern history.

## ▪ BACKGROUND

### EARLY THEATRE SCHOOLS: 1871 TO 1914 ▪

Nearly forty-five years elapsed between the establishment of the first schools to train professional actors in America and the introduction of the first four-year theatre program in an American college. Among those who had an early impact upon the growth of professional schools was Steele MacKaye, one of the most inventive and innovative men the American theatre has ever known. Influenced by Francois Delsarte and the Paris Conservatorie, MacKaye established a school of acting at the St. James Theatre in New York in 1871. Although it failed after several months, he founded the School of Expression on Union Square in 1877, the declared purpose of which was "to instruct and elevate society beyond merely entertaining it." MacKaye was the school's only teacher and again the venture collapsed. But in 1884 he was the major force behind the establishment of the Lyceum Theatre School, an institution that evolved into the present American Academy of Dramatic Arts. Early management of the Lyceum School was assumed by Franklin Sargent, with Charles Frohman as business manager and a faculty that included David Belasco.

During the 1870s other schools offered classes in acting, such as the New York Conservatory of Music and James E. Frobisher's College of Oratory and Acting. Subsequently, many more acting schools opened, especially in the eastern part of the nation. Most were privately sponsored and a few were affiliated with a producing theatre, such as the Lyceum, the Empire and the Madison Square schools.

Early theatre schools were founded to provide students an alternative to the traditional method of learning theatre by joining a stock or repertory company. As stock companies disappeared early in the twentieth century, formal school programs became increasingly accepted and influential. At first, curricula included such courses as body movement, mime, vocal expression and, later, diction, stage effect, makeup, elementary dance, ballet and fencing. Many schools adopted the Delsartian "Life Study" approach to acting, which advised the student to look to life and nature as a basis for dramatic characterization—a method well-suited to the contemporaneous plays of Ibsen, Chekhov and Shaw. Little if any attention was paid, academically, to technical aspects of theatre, and schools of elocution that emphasized the verbal and oral elements of interpretation continued to be popular.

As the little theatre movement increased its activity, the new European drama became known to Americans and people grew more dissatisfied with commercial theatre, the nation's colleges slowly began to pay lip service to the dramatic arts. The Wisconsin Players was founded in 1911, though it was only unofficially identified with the state university. George Pierce Baker bagan his '47 Workshop at Harvard University in 1912 and in 1914 the first four-year program in theatre, leading to a baccalaureate degree, was inaugurated at the Carnegie Institute of Technology in Pittsburgh.

**THE GROWTH OF THEATRE PROGRAMS ON THE CAMPUS: 1914 TO 1950** ■
Theatre courses and performances on the campus increased tremendously after World War I and again after World War II. Part of this increase—like so many other changes in American life—can be attributed to the liberalizing effect that foreign military duty had upon young Americans. This is not to imply, however, that college theatre programs in America are designed after European models. The performing arts are still treated either in an extracurricular or in a highly academic manner in the majority of European colleges and universities. The business of training performers abroad is done in a conservatory or a special school or through apprenticeships with professional performance organizations. College degree programs in theatre are uniquely American.

At the outbreak of World War I and in the following two decades, American theatre schools could be divided into four categories: (1) professional training schools, (2) schools of expression, (3) community and art theatre-affiliated schools and (4) college theatre programs. The first type, similar to the Lyceum School, was often affiliated with a professional theatre or designed to offer specialized training in some aspect or method of theatre. Examples include the National Dramatic Conservatory of New York, the American School of Playwriting, founded by William T. Price and Richard Boleslavsky's Laboratory Theatre School, founded in 1924 and modeled after the Moscow Arts Theatre School. Those affiliated with regularly operating theatres included the Henry Jewett School of Acting in Boston and the Detroit Civic Theatre. Both the Washington Square Players and the Theatre Guild operated schools for a brief period of time. Schools of expression, offering a slightly more refined and "respectable" approach to the drama, were, predictably, concentrated in Boston. Inspired by Professor L. B. Monroe of the Boston University School of Oratory, Charles Wesley Emerson founded the Boston College of Oratory (later Emerson College) in 1880; Anna and Samuel Currey founded Currey College and the Leland Powers School was founded in 1904. All were schools of expression which, nonetheless, reflected the influence of Delsarte and the Lyceum School.

Noncommercial community and art theatres that operated schools include the Pasadena Community Playhouse, founded by Gilmore Brown in 1917, the Cleveland Playhouse, organized in the late '20's under the guidance of Frederic McConnell, the Goodman Theatre, which was affiliated with the Chicago Art Institute, and the Neighborhood Playhouse in New York. Following upon the heels of the first college theatre department at the Carnegie Institute of Technology, other institutions of higher education began to offer special courses in theatre, among them, New York University, Iowa, Northwestern, Cornell and Yale. Often a department was inspired by the activities of a campus theatre club, such as the Carolina Playmakers, which started in 1918 at the University of North Carolina.

From the beginning the trend was to offer college courses that emphasized theatre practice as well as history and theory. The study of dramatic literature and playwriting, rather illogically, generally continued under the domain of English departments. Practical training required the use of actual theatres and the presentation of plays before an audience, a fact that took many notable professors many years to establish: Brander Matthews at Columbia, Alexander Drummond at Cornell, Edward Mabie at the University of Iowa and Frederick Koch at North Carolina, among others.

The first large campus playhouse opened in 1926 at Yale, which enticed George Pierce Baker to join its faculty. Like European colleges, Harvard refused to create a separate theatre department and, after a fire destroyed his laboratory theatre, it also refused to provide Baker with a new theatre for his '47 Workshop students. When Baker transferred his energies from Harvard to Yale, the headlines in the Harvard *Crimson* read "Yale 47, Harvard 0!" During the 1930s, large and well-equipped theatres were constructed on one campus after another: Iowa, Stanford, Amherst, Indiana. Also during the decade, theatre began to emerge as a separate academic discipline. Organizations such as the National Theatre Conference, the American National Theatre and Academy and the American Educational Theatre Association gave voice to the standards and goals of campus theatre and provided an important wedge that helped make theatre study distinct from other disciplines such as English and Speech. To this day, however, many theatre programs both in colleges and high schools remain tied to nontheatre departments, budgets and regulations.

### THE PROFESSIONALIZATION OF COLLEGE THEATRE: 1950 TO PRESENT ▪

Theatre came into higher education through the back door. A major justification for the study and practice of theatre was that it offered the best approach to drama appreciation and, under the guidance of college dons, a far more responsible approach than that of attending commercial theatre productions. Little wonder that the academic world long disassociated itself (rather snobbishly, at times) from the commercial and professional theatre. But as higher education in general came to recognize and use the knowledge of professionals, first in the sciences then in all disciplines, its attitude toward professional theatre began to change. Ivory-towerism faded as practice was mixed with theory, the practitioner was heard alongside the professor and the laboratory was used as well as the library. More and more theatre programs became vocationally oriented. More and more they replaced instruction that had previously occurred in independent schools and institutes. The professional became a frequent lecturer on the campus. Visiting artists, entire theatre companies and professionals-in-residence became almost commonplace.

In 1962 the Association of Producing Artists (APA), under the direction of Ellis Rabb, took up residence at the University of Michigan. With a large grant from the Rockefeller Foundation, New York University established a professional theatre training program and, with another Rockefeller grant, Stanford University hired nine professional actors to form a resident company to work with its students. The University of Minnesota offered credit-generating internships for its theatre students at the Tyrone Guthrie Theatre; Indiana University operated a showboat on the Ohio River; the University of Kansas established an exchange program with acting students from Yugoslavia; the University of Missouri (Southwest Missouri State campus) operated an annual summer tent theatre; the University of Missouri at Kansas City inaugurated a summer repertory program, as did many other colleges.

The list of professionally oriented theatre programs offered by colleges is impressive. Most were inaugurated during the sixties and many were accompanied by ambitious plans for the construction of new campus theatre facilities, of which the Krannert Center for the Performing Arts at the University of Illinois is among the largest and most elaborate. Many campus theatre programs were supported by sizable grants from government agencies and private foundations and many found it increasingly desirable to present professional attractions that would earn profits to help support them. Educational theatre today is big business. It is not yet, however, as active in booking professional artists and companies as is the college concert bureau, primarily, one assumes, because more professional music groups are available for tour than professional theatre groups and the one-man recital format is not easily adapted for the actor.

New theatre programs and facilities on the campus resulted from the dreams and labor of senior faculty members, long frustrated by inadequate theatres and budgets, and by theatre programs still tied to other departments. Once a new theatre became reality, however, it often required professional management of a kind that aging professors, however knowledgeable and well-intentioned, were unable to provide. Not unlike the manner in which businessmen took local control away from nineteenth-century actor-managers, many theatre departments lost considerable autonomy when they moved into shining new facilities. Centralization and bigness often create an identity crisis among constituents.

## ▪ TYPES OF CAMPUS THEATRE PROGRAMS

### EXTRACURRICULAR THEATRE ACTIVITIES ▪

Most high schools throughout the country have long-established theatre clubs that function independently from classroom work. Such clubs frequently offer the student his first exposure to live theatre, either as an audience member or as a participant in productions. Unfortunately, high school theatre clubs are often underfinanced and ill guided. In too many cases the faculty supervisor has no background in theatre and the activities of the club develop haphazardly. On the other hand, there are a number of outstanding high school theatre programs, notably in the states of Texas and California, where state education agencies have strongly encouraged arts education in the public schools.

Theatre production can serve the adolescent in a number of unique ways. Aside from offering a practical demonstration of the importance of teamwork and coordination (much as a sports team might do), theatre can provide insights into literature and the arts as well as into the student's own personality. When properly guided, theatre practice offers self-confidence, self-awareness and sensitivity. When ill guided, it becomes merely another channel for the extroverted student to show off and for others to develop an unrealistic assessment of their acting abilities and of the theatre as a profession. Drama clubs are comprised of students who have enthusiastically joined of their own volition. This offers the faculty supervisor a fine opportunity to guide and instruct the student and to encourage his creativity, craftsmanship and sense of value.

Extracurricular theatre clubs and productions are also common in higher education, especially in colleges that see a conflict between drama as an academic subject and theatre as a vocational practice. Such colleges do not perceive theatre as an appropriate field of study in the humanities or liberal arts, but generally approve extracurricular theatre activity. Some schools and colleges fail to offer theatre courses for reasons of size, finance or a dedication to some specialized curriculum.

Sometimes theatre activities receive faculty supervision, other times they are entirely directed by a student organization. It is disturbing that, while extracurricular sports teams traditionally receive official funding (from tuition income, student activities fees, or whatever) as well as the proceeds from gate admissions, high school and college theatre clubs are often funded exclusively by the proceeds from their performances. This practice bespeaks a serious prejudice against the arts and humanities, as well as against a majority of studen: who do not prefer to spend their extra time in the sports arena. It is, of course, dangerous to compare the arts with another field of study or activity. The arts are justifiable on their own grounds and should be regarded as valuable for their own sake. But glaring inequities found in educational funding, administration and traditions make such comparisons tempting and, sometimes, useful. Student government bodies that administer budget allocations for campus activities often respond more favorably to arts activities and recognize their value sooner than members of the college faculty or administration. Theatre clubs frequently exist alongside large, vocationally oriented instructional theatre departments. They may produce plays on their own and in competition with department-sponsored productions or they may serve the department as a source of volunteer labor and talent. Many are a substructure or miniature of the department itself, something that students can "call their own." A neat way for students to enjoy the illusion of power! But today's college student is interested in direct involvement and is quick to spot tokenistic involvement. Only if the voice of an extracurricular club is taken seriously by the theatre department and made part of its operation can serious confrontation be avoided in most cases.

## SELECTIVE THEATRE COURSES ■

While over 50 percent of the nation's accredited colleges offer a "major" in theatre arts, over 75 percent offer a limited number of elective courses in drama, theatre history, practice and criticism. Theatre production is usually extracurricular on campuses where there is no "major" and emphasis in the classroom is placed on scholarship, with little thought that the student may enter theatre as a profession or pursue graduate work in the field. Courses and productions on these campuses are designed to complement a liberal arts or humanities education or a concentration in some specialized field of study. Only one or two faculty members are required, but instructors should be hired who have a special background and experience in theatre. The theatre professor or specialist on campus, especially when he is the lone representative of the field, can provide a point of view as well as a pedagogy that will broaden curriculum and campus life in a manner most likely promised by the college catalog.

## LIBERAL ARTS THEATRE PROGRAMS ■

Similar in humanistic philosophy and emphasis on scholarship to colleges that offer a few selective courses in theatre, the liberal arts college that offers a theatre major is likely to discourage careers in professional theatre and, rather, prepare its students for careers in educational theatre. Productions may be extracurricular or cocurricular. Laboratory and workshop theatre activities may be extensive and two or more full-time instructors who also direct productions are usually required. Specialization in theatre is combined with course work in the liberal arts and humanities and theatre courses are structured so that the nonmajor may take them on an elective basis. Many such programs permit the student to matriculate either for a bachelor of arts or a bachelor of fine arts degree. Traditionally, the B.A. requires course work in foreign languages and/or mathematics that are not required for a B.F.A., although many degree requirements have been liberalized or eliminated in recent years.

The liberal arts theatre program emphasizes theory over practice but, by offering students a chance to specialize in theatre, it may create a fundamental contradiction of purpose—at least in the mind of the student. The administration and college curriculum committee in such colleges seldom permit courses that are practical in nature, such as those in stage movement, makeup, costume construction and even acting and directing. History, theory and content are stressed. But the theatre department itself frequently feels that practical courses are essential. Consequently, course titles and catalog descriptions may appear far more academic than they really are because this is the only manner in which the department can satisfy general college regulations. Obviously, this dichotomy of purpose can easily confuse and frustrate both the theatre student and the instructor. And the hypocrisy of it is a decided detriment to the college where it exists. But if the problem is fundamental, so is the cause of it. Too seldom does the college state, clarify and reiterate its educational philosophy. Too seldom are potential faculty members appraised of this philosophy before they are hired or reminded of it afterward. If faculty members clearly understood the philosophy to which they are asked to subscribe, subsequent problems and frustrations would be greatly diminished. Certainly, the avocational-humanistic approach to theatre is as justifiable as the vocational-pragmatic approach. One aims to provide appreciation; the other aims at preprofessional training.

These aims are often confused, because most theatre students and faculty today, regardless of the degree program, advocate greater and greater practical and vocational course content. With their familiar cry for "relevance" they are fast getting their way. The result is that the true liberal arts theatre program, in which theatre serves as a focal point for a broad-based education, is fast becoming a rarity. Hundreds are being graduated with B.A. degrees in theatre who have been led to believe that they are prepared for a career in theatre (either educational or professional) but who are, in fact, grossly lacking the practical knowledge and experience desirable for any theatre career. Such students, unless they pursue further training and experience, join the growing ranks of the quasi-professional in theatre, often becoming teachers and turning out more graduates like themselves. Aside from avocational work in amateur and community theatre, a career in education is the major one open to them. Characterized by a limited concept of the humanities, these students also possess a limited understanding and negative regard for the professional arts. Equipped neither as scholars nor as practitioners, quasi-professionals in educational theatre collectively represent a serious and influential threat to the development of high artistic achievement in America and the type of appreciation needed to support it. In short, unless it is carefully organized and administered, the liberal arts theatre program may be neither fish nor fowl.

## VOCATIONALLY ORIENTED UNDERGRADUATE THEATRE PROGRAMS •
A growing number of college theatre programs openly subscribe to a pragmatic

or vocational approach to education. The student continues to be judged in terms of scholarship, but it is assumed that he is seeking a career in educational theatre or, possibly, in the professional theatre. The program of study is performance-centered, offering considerable activity in campus theatres both large and small. The student is expected to participate in productions on a frequent basis, for which he receives credit, and nontheatre students are generally discouraged from such participation. There is a distinct departure from the use of theatre as an extracurricular activity. The campus playhouse serves the vocationally oriented program in much the same way as the chemistry laboratory serves the science department—not as a toy but as a training resource. Only when this attitude toward the college theatre is prevalent can a program be characterized as vocationally oriented.

The pragmatic approach to theatre education may be found in liberal or fine arts colleges where the theatre faculty is comprised of four or more full-time instructors and, often, guests and part-time lecturers from the professional theatre. There are sufficient courses to enable the student to concentrate in acting, directing, play-writing or designing. Other areas of specialization may include television, dance, cinema and opera. Professional guest artists may appear in student productions or the program may be affiliated with a professional theatre or operate its own full-time summer theatre. While no theatre student or educator should pretend that a four-year degree program will fully prepare the graduate for a career, the results will be more satisfactory for this purpose than those gained from a nonvocational, liberal arts theatre program. The student is given a broader education than he would receive in a professional theatre school, a longer and more deliberate opportunity to develop as a person and as a professional and a more intensive opportunity to test his commitment to a field than he would receive in the nonvocational liberal arts program.

### VOCATIONALLY ORIENTED GRADUATE THEATRE PROGRAMS ▪

A graduate school of theatre can offer a more concentrated and professionally oriented program than is possible or desirable on the undergraduate level. Depending upon the traditions and requirements of the university with which it is affiliated, a graduate theatre program may offer master of arts, master of fine arts, doctor of education, doctor of fine arts or doctor of philosophy degrees. At present, over two dozen institutions offer a Ph.D. in theatre. Both the degree and the requirements vary greatly among institutions. Some, such as the Yale School of Drama, require three years for a master's degree, while two years is the average and a one-year program is not unusual. More and more, the master's degree is regarded as terminal and not merely the stepping-stone to a doctorate.

Graduate theatre programs are frequently associated with a professional theatre organization and make frequent use of guest artists and lecturers from the profession. Or they may operate a repertory company of student actors, as does the Juilliard theatre program. Of course, graduate programs also offer a concentration in the academic aspects of theatre, such as history and criticism. Criteria for judging graduate as well as undergraduate theatre programs have been suggested by the *Directory of American College Theatres* and other such comprehensive studies, as well as by numerous articles in *The Educational Theatre Journal, The Drama Review* and other periodicals. Vocationally oriented programs are giving progressively greater emphasis to professional theatre practice, although they tend to encourage students toward educational, regional and repertory theatre. Commercial theatre continues to be downgraded in the classroom and hope for the future is placed with nonprofit, regional theatre. If graduates subscribe to this belief in their professional careers—and early evidence shows that they will—nonprofit, regional theatre should continue to grow at a healthy pace.

## ▪ MANAGEMENT OF THE COLLEGE THEATRE DEPARTMENT

### FACULTY VS. STUDENT CONTROL ▪

College graduates of ten or more years often register surprise regarding recent increases in student power and control in campus decision-making. Although this was an inevitable result of progressive and liberal philosophies of education from the kindergarten up, college faculties and administrators were among the last to reform themselves or, in many cases, to be reformed. The sudden explosion of campus riots, ethnically oriented demonstrations and forceful demands made by political, ethnic, feminist and student groups is having a measurable effect upon higher education. It is characterized by greater student involvement in such fundamental areas as curriculum-planning, faculty-hiring and promotion, budgeting, grading and admission procedures. During the late sixties and early seventies, there was a massive turnover of college presidents (many out the door and many others, doubtless, in their graves), a widespread restructuring in campus administration and a general shift toward community service. This was accompanied by a scurrying away from research and employment relationships with the so-called military-industrial complex. In some cases student involvement has a meaningful effect upon campus governance, in other cases it is tokenistic. In general, the college professor is no longer the autocrat of the classroom that he used to be; his credibility, his authority and his knowledge are no longer assumed automatically by his students.

Because of the collaborative nature of theatre production and, perhaps, the humanistic nature of the arts, the student-teacher relationship tends to be less rigid in the theatre department than in most others. Recent surveys show a decrease in degree candidates for such disciplines as classics, education and sociology and an increase in such "individual-oriented" subjects as psychology and the arts. While this trend bespeaks a reaction against the depersonalization of life brought on by advances in technology, it also presents a striking opportunity for arts educators, who are now challenged by a generation more responsive to the arts than any previous one in the history of American education. So long as the need for discipline in arts practice and scholarship is not confused with the need for cooperation, performing arts departments can take advantage of current trends to increase and intensify the personalized factors of their work without endangering educational values or faculty leadership.

There are few areas in which the informed and well-guided student cannot make meaningful and helpful contributions to decision-making. Specifically, in a department of theatre arts, these areas include play selection, curriculum-planning and production management. Today's college theatre student is not disposed merely to do the leg work involved in theatre production—distributing posters, ushering, taking tickets—unless he understands and believes in the project at hand. To promote such understanding and belief is as important in the management of college theatre as in any other and the best way to do it is through the involvement of all participants in the decision-making and planning stages of production. Theatre department chairmen and faculty members now find that involvement in decision-making is a primary student demand. When teachers misinterpret this as a demand for control, their reaction is likely to become defensive. Or they may be tempted to surrender their responsibilities of leadership and pedagogy. Student demands today are aggressive and challenging but, despite strong language and lack of patience, the majority of students are not yet so confident as to believe in their ability to teach themselves. But they soon will believe it unless teachers respond to them in a flexible yet positive manner.

### THE COMMITTEE APPROACH VS. THE AUTOCRATIC APPROACH ▪

Many large colleges and universities, especially tax-supported institutions, are governed according to the committee system. In fact, committees may so permeate the power structure that individual decision-making is impossible or is conveniently avoided to absolve everyone from personal blame. In the military one can always "pass the buck" and defer to a higher officer. In a bureaucratic system, one defers to a committee. On close examination, however, it will be found that numerous bureaucrats enjoy and exercise a considerable amount of individual power. The committee is a security blanket that creates the appearance of a democratic distribution of power when, in fact, very little democratic representation or government by consensus may be at work.

The department chairman in a large, tax-supported institution invariably inherits an administrative system that he is powerless to change and that he must work with and adapt to his own purposes. The administrator in a privately endowed or small institution has greater freedom to establish the system of his preference. The advantages of government by committee should include:
1. Decentralization of political power
2. Majority rule
3. Guarantee that minority opinions will be heard

The usual disadvantages include:
1. Time-consuming delays
2. Decisions that lack the personal commitment of the people who must carry them out
3. Compromise that negates both meaning and action

These factors hold true regardless of the student-faculty ratio of the committees that possess decision-making power. Both the committee approach and the autocratic approach, where all power rests in the hands of the chief administrator, can work well. It is entirely a matter of the people involved and how they accept their responsibilities, either as leaders or as committee members. Any system should, however, aim at clarity of purpose and leadership (autocracy) together with fair representation of its member-participants (democracy). In practice, this means that the department chairman with unlimited powers must work diligently to encourage and utilize the talents and ideas of everyone below him and the chairman whose powers are severely limited must fight hard to impose a single program and viewpoint upon his colleagues.

The sharing of information, knowledge, work and abilities is crucial to the success of any organization. The principles of personnel management discussed in chapter 4 are as applicable to college theatre as to any other, although the college administrator is burdened by extreme institutionalization and greater duality of purpose (education as well as entertainment) than theatre administrators in most other circumstances.

An eclectic approach to department management—one combining the advantages
of democracy and autocracy—is the most desirable. It also has the advantage of
sufficient flexibility to change according to changes in leadership and personnel,
priority and programming. The table of organization below suggests one set of appropriate student-faculty relationships and lines of authority for an active, vocationally oriented theatre department.

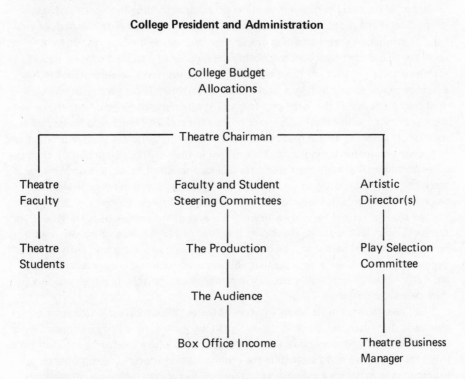

**College President and Administration**

College Budget
Allocations

Theatre Chairman

Theatre            Faculty and Student            Artistic
Faculty            Steering Committees            Director(s)

Theatre            The Production                 Play Selection
Students                                          Committee

                   The Audience

Box Office Income                                 Theatre Business
                                                  Manager

### THE INTEGRATED PERFORMING ARTS DEPARTMENT ▪

The trend toward housing several performing arts under one roof, professionally
and academically, is an important move both in and of itself and because it symbolizes a newly independent status for the arts, separate at last from gymnasia, town
meeting halls, dance palaces, English departments, Speech departments and other
strange bedfellows. In terms of college curricula and administration there are reasons both for and against the formation of an integrated performing arts department
as opposed to separate departments of theatre, music and dance. At smaller colleges
that are primarily dedicated to one of the performing arts, such as Emerson College,
Oberlin and the Manhattan School of Music, an integrated arts department would
weaken the value of existing programs. Schools like Juilliard or the Center for the
Performing and Visual Arts at the new Purchase campus of the State University of
New York (where the entire school is dedicated to arts education) logically maintain separate departments with cooperative course programming and activities that
form, in effect, a monolithic performing arts department. These may serve as models
for the formation of smaller departments that operate within a liberal or fine arts
college.

Curriculum planning, course programming and faculty utilization may all be easier and more sensible when the performing arts are administered as a single large unit. Much depends upon the administrative and budgetary flexibility of the college in question. Regulations often exist, for example, that make it impossible for a faculty member in the theatre department to teach a course in the music department or for a dance student to gain credit toward his major for a course in mime that is offered by the theatre department.

Budget allocations in higher education are made according to a variety of standards. One of the most common methods of allocating money is on the basis of paying a department a specified dollar amount for each student who registers for a course in that department and computing the number of "student contact hours" each instructor generates in the classroom. This means that if an instructor teaches a lecture course to one hundred students the department is credited with one hundred contact hours. If the instructor is teaching a seminar of five students the department is credited with only five contact hours and receives a much smaller budget allocation. If students do not gain course credit for participation in theatre productions, in the costume construction shop or elsewhere in their production activities, then the department receives no budget credit for a large portion of its work. Furthermore, if the faculty director, designer or supervisor receives a reduced number of classroom teaching assignments in exchange for his work in the college theatre, the department's teacher-student ratio is further reduced in the eyes of the college budget office. Clearly, this is ridiculous, because it assumes that the teacher is not teaching when, in fact, he may be working harder and teaching in a more penetrating manner than he would be in the classroom. Arts faculties that are burdened with such systems—and there are many—must launch highly persuasive campaigns to gain the budgetary support they deserve and require.

The "classroom contact hours" system of budget allocation establishes educational criteria that favor the quantity of students taught over the quality of education. It is a method that severely endangers arts departments, where the teacher-student ratio might be as low as one to six—while the economics and education departments, for example, may maintain a ratio of one to twenty-five or more. When a college faces financial difficulty and a cost analyst looks at expenditures, he quickly sees that arts departments are the most expensive to operate on a "cost per student" basis. Sometimes, as was the case at Columbia, the college decides to eliminate a theatre or arts department. For reasons such as these, it may be advantageous for a theatre department to join others and form a larger performing arts department. (It also explains why a theatre division may be hesitant to break away from a large speech or English department.) The trouble is that music and dance departments, or departments of the visual arts, are no better off in terms of the student-teacher ratio. But it may be that television and cinema departments maintain large enrollments with comparatively few teachers. This suggests an administrative marriage between the live and electronic performing arts departments, the advisability of which is often debated.

From the academic viewpoint, an integrated performing arts department can make a wide variety of courses easily available to students. It also can design unusual and individually tailored course programs for students and easily pool faculty, student and physical resources. If the current trend continues, and professional artists and arts workers more and more divide their careers between live and electronic media, between professional and educational arts organizations, between one performing art and another, then exposure to all the arts when one is a student appears highly desirable. Whether a degree program is vocationally or avocationally oriented, it should provide the student with a concept of how the arts are interrelated. A student of voice who may someday perform in the opera house or on the concert stage should, for instance, take courses in acting. The student actor should certainly have courses in period movement and dance, in television production, in musical theatre. Students interested in theatre administration, especially on the graduate level, should learn something about concert and broadcast management.

One reason why the television, film and theatre industries took so long in developing any meaningful cooperation and exchange among themselves is that, on the educational level, each area was approached and studied independently. The television executive with a degree in broadcasting knew little if anything about theatre history and production. A theatre student could graduate without taking a single course in broadcasting or cinema even though, eventually, his livelihood might depend on those media. To further illustrate the breach between these three performing arts industries, one need only glance at the usually disastrous attempts to adapt theatre productions to television or film. Yet, many of the most active and successful artists and producers of this century move comfortably from one media to another primarily because, one may assume, they possess a well-rounded overview of the arts together with the knowledge and imagination to enable them to adapt their ideas to a variety of art forms.

Just as one cannot have a liberal arts education by taking courses only in the history department, for example, one cannot ignore the arts as a whole and pretend to understand theatre art. Whether or not there is a unified departmental or administrative relationship among the performing arts on a campus, students who specialize in one area should not be encouraged or allowed to ignore the others. The table of organization on page 154 suggests titles and lines of authority that might be suitable for a performing arts department on a sizable campus. The same organization could also include television and cinema or, with a few changes in job titles, could be utilized for a performing arts school or college within a university system.

## A CENTRALIZED PERFORMING ARTS MANAGEMENT OFFICE ▪

Not all colleges may find it possible or desirable to create a single performing arts (teaching) department, but any college can quite easily create a central performance management office that supervises and carries out all performance-related activities and facilities without having jurisdiction over the teaching programs. On the other hand, a central office should work in close relationship or partnership with instructional programs and personnel in the performing arts. Performance facilities that are located in and managed by a student union or student center facility may already constitute a good central management office, as is the case with the Wisconsin Union at the Madison campus of the University of Wisconsin. Or an office of this type may form the basis for a reorganized performing arts office that is designed to work closely with instructional programs. Some campus performance facilities are operated by a student activities office, a buildings and grounds office or another administrative unit that functions on behalf of the college as a whole and awards numerous priorities unrelated to classroom-oriented student performance programs.

Too frequently, different departments duplicate each other's work in such areas

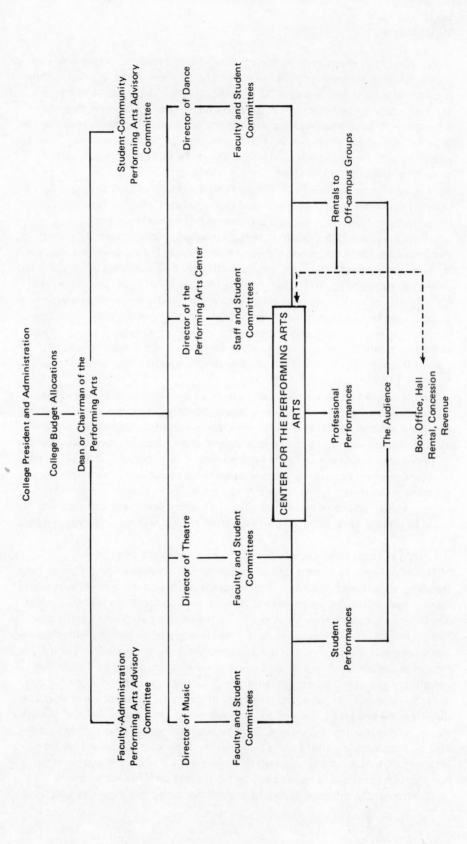

College President and Administration

College Budget Allocations

Dean or Chairman of the Performing Arts

Faculty-Administration Performing Arts Advisory Committee

Student-Community Performing Arts Advisory Committee

Director of Music

Director of Theatre

Director of the Performing Arts Center

Director of Dance

Faculty and Student Committees

Faculty and Student Committees

Staff and Student Committees

Faculty and Student Committees

CENTER FOR THE PERFORMING ARTS

Student Performances

Professional Performances

Rentals to Off-campus Groups

The Audience

Box Office, Hall Rental, Concession Revenue

as publicity, bookkeeping, scheduling and general management. The college administration is forced to deal with three or four department heads instead of one, a unified publicity or advertising image is impossible and in many ways the performing arts programs are in competition with each other for space, for audience, for budgets and for grant monies. By centralizing all such matters into one office, as practiced at Brooklyn College of the City University of New York and several others, a great deal of efficiency, economy and strength of purpose can be gained. The central office should be funded primarily by college allocations. If the office is being created from scratch, much of its money and personnel may be drawn back from individual departments and reassigned to it, thereby requiring little additional cost to the college. Box office, rental, concession and other revenues should be poured back into the office budget either for production purposes or for the operation and maintenance of performing arts facilities. Because the expenditure of money from official college allocations may be fraught with red tape and lengthy payment systems, box office revenue may constitute a cash account extremely important to the payment flexibility required in most performing arts operations. As one educator put it: "Getting money from a university comptroller's office to a departmental project is roughly like shipping lettuce by rabbit!" Additional flexibility of budgeting is gained by the availability of a central office to spread "profits" and deficits among various performance programs as needed for the greatest benefit to the whole.

A central performing arts office is easiest to create when the main theatres, concert halls and rehearsal areas are all located in the same building complex, forming (in effect if not in name) a performing arts center. When these facilities are scattered over a large campus, a central management office may be even more useful for its ability to coordinate space utilization and other factors. The central office should handle all advertising, publicity, budgeting, accounting, banking, scheduling, fundraising, house management, house personnel, security and maintenance responsibilities related to performance facilities and activities. If there is a concert bureau or policy of booking professional, touring groups on campus, it also should fall under the supervision of the office.

In essence, the director of the central office is also the general manager of the campus theatre or performing arts center. To safeguard student programs and interests and to assure educational priorities, the director should be a faculty member with specialized training or experience in arts administration. In fact, he and his staff (business manager, publicist, etc.) could serve as the faculty for a graduate program in arts management. He should be accountable to a head or dean of the performing arts or to a faculty-student policy-making council comprised of the appropriate chairmen of the teaching departments, faculty artistic directors and conductors and selected student leaders. When performing arts facilities on a campus are managed by professional administrators or others not involved in curricula programs, there is a serious possibility that facilities will be utilized to the disadvantage of teaching programs, that they will become too dependent upon large box office revenues from a professional concert series or the like or that space will be assigned so often to community, campus and class groups that performing arts groups and classes are squeezed out much of the time. While multi-purpose usage and goals are desirable for maximum productivity in a performing arts facility, the campus that offers a performing arts instructional program of any size should allow that program first priority in terms of facility usage.

If a college offers courses or degree programs in performing arts administration, the central office should be used as a teaching laboratory, partially staffed by students with scholarships or assistantships in administration and partially serviced by volunteer student workers and by students assigned to management field studies by their classroom instructors. In short, the central performing arts office and the facilities it manages should be used as fully as possible as an educational resource.

The table of organization on page 157 for a central performance management office is a detailed expansion from the previous table (page 154) for the area indicated as "Director of the Performing Arts Center." Depending upon the size of the college and the facilities involved, various jobs can be combined or expanded, increasing or decreasing the size of the staff, and student workers can be more or less active. Directors and supervisors in such an operation should be faculty members who teach at least one course in their area of specialization and use students as part of their support staff. This policy insures that facilities will be used as an educational laboratory and that they will be controlled by faculty and not by a group of bureaucrats or technicians who have little interest in educational programs and values.

# ▪ PLAY PRODUCTION IN COLLEGE THEATRE

### PLAY SELECTION ▪

Chapter 6 defines certain criteria that may be applied to play selection and the business of planning a season of productions. Decision-making in this area for many theatres is surprisingly casual, or it is guided largely by what plays the artistic directors wish to direct at the moment. When college theatres engage in quick and haphazard methods of play selection, it is especially unfortunate. In no other type of theatre do the people involved enjoy such job security and leisure for planning. Most students are in residence for four years and most faculty members are likely to have tenure or long-term contracts. The problem of paying the rent on the theatre is seldom as urgent on the campus as elsewhere. Campus theatre leaders, before all others, should feel obligated to know the answers to the following questions: Where are we now? What is our potential? Where will we be four years from now? In commercial, stock, resident and community theatre four years usually seems like an eternity, four months is a long season and four days can make or break the entire operation.

If a campus theatre program is primarily extracurricular or avocational, its major obligation is to the audience. If it is vocational in purpose, the student participants must receive high priority in terms of play selection. In either case, four years is a natural cycle due to the length of most undergraduate residencies and all programming should take this into consideration. What will be the total accumulation of productions and activities over four years? What will the graduate walk away with in terms of his experiences and opportunities both as a theatre spectator and as a theatre participant?

Traditionally, college theatres favored the classics—Sophocles, Shakespeare, Congreve, Wilde, Ibsen, Shaw, Strindberg and, of the American dramatists, O'Neill, Miller and Williams. Recently, however, there has been a trend toward producing more contemporary playwrights on the campus, of doing new plays, less-well-known classical works or recent New York productions. The contemporary, experimental or unusual play series may, of course, be well justified. But it may also stem from a reaction by

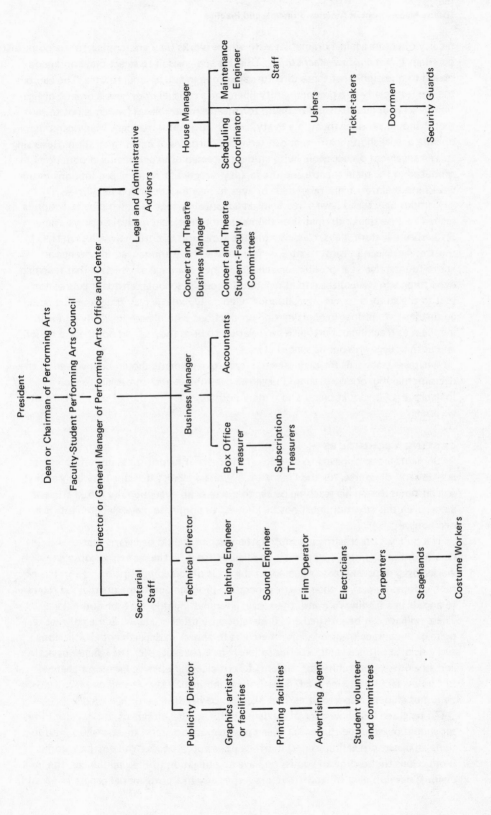

faculty directors against dramatists with whose works they are familiar to the point of boredom ("Not *another Macbeth!*"). This is a poor reason to select plays and good reason to question what those directors are doing in educational theatre. The campus theatre (especially at a predominantly liberal arts college) *does* have a unique obligation to serve as guardian and museum for theatre masterpieces (which is not to say that it should produce them in a dusty, overly worshipful manner). Many campuses operate a workshop theatre that can serve the purposes of experimentation. Reversing this arrangement on occasion—with student-directed or experimental productions produced in the main theatre and the faculty-directed or classical productions in the workshop theatre—might open a lot of eyes to new insights and possibilities.

Campus play series have often favored a festival format in which play selection is related to a particular dramatist or theme: an international festival of plays, the Shakespeare history plays, classics from the American theatre, new voices in the theatre, American musical theatre. A few colleges have announced in advance an entire four-or five-year production schedule, one advantage of which is that teaching departments in the college and in neighboring public schools can adapt course content to the study of plays in production. Generally, college play programming could go further than it does in coordinating productions with classroom study and utilizing them as teaching opportunities in relation to both theatre and nontheatre majors and both college and public school classes.

Whatever standards for play selection are used, students should be involved in the decision-making, priorities should never be overlooked and immediate as well as long-range goals should be set and understood: what are we doing? why? where are we going?

### CASTING TECHNIQUES ▪

Students are as opposed to casting on the basis of favoritism as any other actors are—except, of course, for the "favorites." While a faculty director may be gratified several times during his teaching career to discover an exceptionally gifted student actor, even this situation must not be allowed to dominate play selection and casting decisions.

If a policy of precasting is adopted, the method should be clearly stated and understood. For example, actors may be selected from particular acting courses or workshop groups and plays selected on the basis of the composition and abilities of such groups. As part of their credit-generating program acting majors may be required to appear in a leading role and, therefore, given casting priority over nonmajors. These policies can be justified and understood by other students. Some colleges require or encourage theatre faculty members to appear in department productions every so often. It is a valid experience (perhaps a necessity) for the teacher of acting and a healthy opportunity for students to criticize and observe *him* for a change. But unless faculty casting is a regular policy, shouts of "favoritism" or "faculty usurpation of student opportunities" are likely to be heard.

To heighten his knowledge of student ability and development, the faculty director should observe the student at every possible opportunity: in workshop productions, in classroom acting scenes, in off-campus appearances. While major campus productions that charge an admission have an obligation to their audiences, the individual development of student actors (especially in a professional program) should always be considered. College theatre is in the best position of all to avoid type-casting and, indeed, has a primary obligation to provide student actors with roles and experiences they might not gain elsewhere.

A card catalog indexing the theatre students in a department and all previous student production workers and actors still on campus can be an indispensable casting and "crewing" device. It can be consulted before play selections are made, not for precasting but as an indication of talent resources. It can serve as a record of student activities and accomplishments (the director should be required to up-date it following each production, adding his comments about the student's work and additional cards for new participants). It can be used as a basis for grading, for written recommendations, for awarding scholarships and other honors, for counsel-ing and for periodic checks to assess the frequency and variety of the student's theatre activities.

Double or alternate casting can substantially increase the number of learning ex-periences for students. Directing two or three casts for the same production is, of course, difficult and time-consuming for the director. Students may vie for the privilege of appearing in the opening night or Saturday night performances. Cos-tuming and publicity will be more expensive and complicated. But many educators feel that the advantages of alternate casts, performing on alternate nights, far out-weigh the disadvantages. And, of course, it is much less expensive and more eco-nomical in terms of time than mounting two different productions. Another good educational technique is that of switching the roles that actors in the same cast are to perform, thereby giving them experience in different roles on different nights. Such practices create performance inconsistencies, but these may not be sufficiently detrimental to affect audience appreciation seriously. They are good examples of how a college theatre may simultaneously honor its priorities in terms of the stu-dent and audience.

## TECHNICAL PRODUCTION FACILITIES AND PERSONNEL ▪

The formation of a central, technical production shop or department is as de-sirable for the active college theatre as the formation of a central management office, though the former may fall under the jurisdiction of the latter. Large campus thea-tres may employ a considerable staff of professional, unionized technical workers. Their work is required to service nonstudent productions, special meetings or events held in the theatre facility and for general maintenance and plant operation. None-theless, if the college offers instructional programs in theatre, every effort should be made to prevent full-time, professional technicians from usurping student learn-ing experiences or otherwise establishing a superstructure of authority and organiza-tion that ignores or preempts educational goals. Technicians should be ultimately responsible to a faculty director, not to an administration or union director. Their work should be closely coordinated with educational programs and student workers and crews.

Small campus theatres are often staffed entirely by faculty and student techni-cians, in which case opposing power structures and goals are less likely to exist and the theatre can be utilized more easily as a teaching laboratory. In either instance, operational efficiency and economy require that technical resources (personnel and equipment) be pooled for the availability of all performance programs, be they music, theatre, dance, visiting productions or special events. They should be organized under one supervisor, assigned according to predetermined priorities and aimed at uniformly high production standards. Surprisingly, many colleges support different departments that duplicate each other's work, space and costs in such areas as costume construction, design, scene construction and storage, properties and makeup. This practice stems from the administrative and curricula separation of music, dance and theatre departments, each of which may slowly establish and jealously guard its own production resources, resulting in great inefficiency and cost duplication.

There is a school of thought among theatre designers and technicians in academia that advocates that each production should be built from scratch and then discarded when it is over. This, it is argued, provides maximum learning experience for student technicians and frees them from limitations imposed by the necessity to use stock scenic and costume items. It is similar to the system in New York commercial theatre, where, due to union regulations, costumes and scenery are new for each production. It is seldom the system in stock, resident or community theatre and, except for dubious pedagogical reasons, there is little justification for it in college theatre. Naturally, one would not wish to impose the severely limited budgets and results of stock theatre upon the campus theatre. But neither should academic theatre be adverse to a reasonable degree of economy nor forget that many of its graduates will eventually work in stock or other theatres where success depends more upon imagination than upon money and fancy equipment.

Without the educational theatre market, many manufacturers and wholesalers of theatrical hardware, lighting equipment and stage machinery would doubtless go out of business. This is not because of the size of the educational theatre market but because of its compulsiveness to buy "the latest and greatest." Technical theatre expenditures have been allowed to grow unchecked, along with other matters, because campus theatre has so consistently lacked business managers with a theatrical background. Perhaps there has also been an excessive pride among educators in technically outstripping the professional theatre or a not-very-academic value placed on the *visible* assets of the educational institution. After all, an impressive new theatre and spectacular stage effects are things that college administrators, trustees and alumni can *see*. Learning and artistic achievement are not as obvious. The same factor dominates much of the philanthropy that benefits college arts programs, with large donations earmarked for the purchase and construction of material assets rather than for the support of productions, programs and scholarships.

This is not to say that the American college theater has not made substantial contributions to the standards and techniques of theatrical production. But when production budgets begin to rob money from teaching programs, the physical production begins to hide the values and aims of the script and the actor or productions are selected primarily because of technical assets *or* liabilities, the validity of the theatre program needs to be cross-examined. Beware the ghost of Inigo Jones!

## ▪ THE PROFESSIONAL ON THE CAMPUS

### VISITING LECTURERS ▪

Classroom teaching can be complemented by the inclusion of appropriate guest speakers who offer students a fresh point of view, a professional's perspective on some subject or special knowledge. Instructors on a large campus may invite other teachers to address their classes or, especially if they are located in a major city or there is college money available for guest lecturers, they may easily invite off-campus professionals to participate in lecture seminars and class discussions. As long as the practice is not used merely to "pad" instruction and the guests are knowledgeable about their subject and able to communicate with students, many colleges could encourage an increased dialogue between the classroom and the profession.

When a college program wishes to offer certain courses but lacks the faculty to teach them, it should consider hiring a guest lecturer for the entire term, on a part-time basis, to serve as instructor. This device may attract leading if not celebrated professionals from a special field who may add considerable depth to a degree program. On the other hand, some colleges have made the mistake of staffing their classrooms almost exclusively with such part-time, visiting lecturers. The inevitable result is that the program lacks resident leadership, the student has difficulty in obtaining counseling outside class and the student-faculty relationship is virtually nonexistent. No matter how brilliant and famous the instructors may be, an instructional program will lack teeth unless it is reinforced outside the classroom through counseling, supervised field work and projects and faculty-directed activities in the campus theatre.

Perhaps surprisingly, those professionals most anxious to accept a limited amount of teaching (often for a very modest fee) may be the busiest or most celebrated people in their field. Once a person has achieved status and financial success, he is apt to find that his activities give him less and less personal satisfaction. The "psychic rewards" derived from sharing knowledge with others and helping others to learn may be highly valued by the prominent professional. Too, he may feel an obligation to contribute something to the future of the field that has been so good to him. College administrators, then, should not be shy about sending lectureship invitations to prominent professionals. They should also remember, however, that the visiting lecturer is not a professional teacher. His loyalties are not primarily toward the student or the teaching institution and so he should not be used to the exclusion of resident faculty members.

## ARTISTS-IN-RESIDENCE ▪

Actors' Equity Association has devised two agreements that pertain to its members when they are employed on the campus: the Guest-Artist Agreement (for professional actors who are assigned exclusively to performance duties) and the University Actor-Teacher Contract (for actors who are assigned both teaching and performance duties). Both contracts are available at Equity offices along with related information that may facilitate the use of professional actors on the campus.

The University Actor-Teacher Contract is a simple form which, briefly, guarantees the actor the following terms of employment:

1. Preknowledge of the productions and courses he will be assigned
2. All rights and privileges accorded to the college faculty and accorded to him as a member of Equity
3. Agreement to length of employment (no week to exceed an average of forty hours of work and to include at least one full day of rest)
4. Agreement on salary (no less than the minimum salary for faculty members

of comparable status)

5. Agreement on pension, medical and insurance coverage (the actor is covered by Equity provisions in these areas until such time as he becomes eligible for coverage through the college)

If an Equity member wishes to accept a teaching position that does *not* involve him in any public performances he is not obliged to negotiate through the union.

If many prominent professionals accept teaching positions primarily for "psychic reward," so do many celebrated artists. Almost any actor, director or designer of status and ability has a particular project or two he would like to undertake but knows he is unlikely to be given the opportunity in commercial theatre or in the normal course of events. If he is approached by a college that is willing to produce what *he* wants to do, his services may be acquired at surprisingly low cost. However, the cost of the production itself may be considerable, especially if the guest artist is a designer or director. Nonetheless, when educational institutions have the resources, they can make singular contributions to the arts by supporting outstanding professional artists in this manner.

The Guest-Artist Agreement is issued on a quadruplicate contract form similar to other Equity contracts. It is used for professional actors who appear with student companies or who work in residence on a campus with other professional actors. The Guest-Artist Agreement may also be employed by amateur and community theatres or by summer theatres affiliated with educational institutions. The list of amateur, community and college theatres that have used the Guest-Artist Agreement is a long one, numbering more than two hundred organizations located in over forty different states.

### RESIDENT PERFORMING COMPANIES ▪

If a campus wishes to maintain an entirely professional resident company, as is the case at the Yale School of Drama, at the University of Texas (Fort Worth) and at the University of Michigan (Ann Arbor), it may employ actors on the Guest-Artist Agreement or, more likely, it may operate under the League of Resident Theatres (LORT) Agreement.* A national organization that represents college resident theatre companies, both professional and nonprofessional, is the University Resident Theatre Association (affiliated with the American Theatre Association).

Whether their purpose is to offer students the opportunity to observe and work with professionals or to provide a laboratory for long-term student development, the number of resident college companies has grown considerably in the past decade. Most offer preprofessional training and experience that was previously available only with summer stock companies, amateur groups and, to a lesser extent, Off Broadway. They also serve as a tangible means for reinforcing a general faith in the future of resident, regional theatre groups as opposed to commercial New York and stock theatres. Should resident companies of high professional quality firmly establish themselves on the college campus, it may eventually become possible for a student of theatre to secure his general education, his graduate and preprofessional training, his professional apprenticeship and his very career all on the college campus. This, of course, parallels the conservatory approach to performing arts training and indicates many promising developments for the future.

*See chapter 6.

During the sixty years that have elapsed since the establishment of the first theatre programs on the college campus, the study of theatre has become an accepted
part of higher education, vocationally oriented theatre programs have increased tremendously, colleges have allocated many millions of dollars for performing arts
facilities and many campuses have become important centers for the professional
arts. There has been increased dialogue and understanding between educational and
professional branches of the theatre, an encouraging trend away from theatre merely
as an extracurricular plaything and a massive increase in the number and variety of
productions to which campus and community audiences are exposed. At the same
time, a great deal of confusion and inequity still exists in regard to campus theatre
programs. While literature students are required to take writing courses and most
B.A. programs require laboratory courses in a science, academicians still have difficulty in comprehending the need for laboratory work in theatre, music and dance
programs that lead to a B.A. or B.F.A. degree. Arts departments frequently fare
badly when college budget allocations are made, because the per capita cost of arts
education is high and student and faculty work outside the classroom is not usually
recognized by the budget office—much less the educational services that a campus
theatre is providing for the thousands of students and community members who
attend its performances.

The struggle to make political and fiscal officers, as well as the general public,
understand the value of the arts and their need for subsidization is as difficult on
the campus as off. But, as attested by the fact that both public and private agencies
subsidize professional arts organizations much faster than educational arts organizations, arts educators will have to fight more vigorously than they have in the past to
gain support. The battle should become easier as the campus more obviously becomes a cultural center with a broadening commitment to the entire community
and offers more diversified avocational as well as vocational programs for its students.

# CHAPTER EIGHT

# Community Theatre

There is considerable justification for discussing community and amateur theatre before other systems of producing. All theatre from ancient times to the present has been rooted in amateur activities which reflect man's urge to imitate and his eagerness to watch others engage in this deeply human impulse.

The amateur in theatre is a person who does not receive financial remuneration for his endeavors. He is not necessarily ignorant, untalented or inexperienced in theatre art. In fact, the amateur may be highly knowledgeable and gifted. He has simply not chosen to earn his living in the theatre. "Community theatre" connotes an organizational structure largely or exclusively comprised of nonsalaried amateurs who represent a cross section of the citizenry in a given area, whose theatrical activities are restricted to that area and whose audiences are derived from it.

## ▪ BACKGROUND

Amateur theatricals unrelated to a distinct theatre organization have long been common in America. Judge Samuel Sewall, the Pepys of New England puritanism, wrote in his diary in 1687 that a maypole had been set up in Charlestown, Massachusetts, that public dancing was seen and a stage-fight occurred in the streets. During the same year, Increase Mather noted "much discourse of beginning Stage-Plays in New England." By the early 1700s amateur theatricals were being offered in the southern colonies and one Tony Ashton, the first professional actor to perform in the colonies, was paving the way for the arrival of Lewis Hallam's company in 1752. When public theatres were inactive during the Revolution, the spirit of theatre was kept alive by amateur theatricals performed in military camps and organized by such eminent "producers" as Generals Howe, Burgoyne and Clinton. So began the nation's tradition of amateur theatre. The purpose of this chapter, however, is to consider organized community theatres which, like today's college theatres, did not really evolve until the present century.

Both community and educational theatre sprang from the same urges and sources of inspiration. Both began at about the same time, in the years immediately before and after World War I, and both had considerable influence upon the development of resident and Off Broadway theatre which, in turn, influenced the commercial theatre. The little theatre movement (also referred to as the "tributary theatre" or "nationwide theatre" or, simply, "community theatre") was a reaction against the quality of the flagging commercial theatre, a vote in favor of the European Free Theatre movement and, not insignificantly, an indication that as average Americans gained leisure time they lost certain puritanical standards for using it.

Inspired by the genius of men like Reinhardt, Stanislavsky and Craig, by the example of the Abbey Theatre in Dublin and American tours of the Irish Players, countless little theatres began to organize in communities throughout the nation. Initially, their resources were slight, their leadership was lacking and their activities were primarily aimed to please participants rather than audiences. By the mid-twenties, however, many community groups could boast a salaried, year-round director and, perhaps, several other salaried workers. Many had acquired or constructed a permanent home for their productions and achieved sizable membership and audience support. Unfortunately, the growth of community theatre was curtailed by the depression that followed the stock market crash of 1929 and by the diversion of energies into World War II.

To provide employment for professional theatre people during the depression and to help reinforce nationwide theatre, the Federal Theatre Project was inaugurated under congressional sponsorship in 1935. During its short, four-year history it gave employment to tens of thousands, operated theatres in forty states, published nationally distributed theatre periodicals, premiered many new American plays, invented the "Living Newspaper" style of production, developed a Negro theatre, earned over $2,000,000 in box office receipts and played to millions of people, perhaps a majority of whom had never seen live professional theatre before. One dollar was the highest price charged for tickets and, in fact, most of its productions were admission-free. In purpose and in dramatic content, the Federal Theatre was a people's theatre. Its outspokenness on political and economic issues of the day eventually brought congressional investigation and liquidation. However, its influence on the growth of community theatre was considerable. If nothing else, it established the idea and the feasibility of local theatre.

As community theatre found its own voice through the meetings and publications of organizations like The Drama League and The National Theatre Conference, its standards and goals became more ambitious and well-defined. Although there are many ill-guided and selfishly oriented community theatres, there can be little question that many maintain standards and resources that are the highest in the world for amateur activity.

The fundamental principles that should govern community theatre organizations are discussed in Part I. Later sections deal with specific factors of administration. This chapter is concerned only with areas unique to community theatre or those that need special emphasis and attention.

## ■ CENTRAL ELEMENTS OF A COMMUNITY THEATRE

### LEADERSHIP ■

A successful community theatre depends no less on strong, imaginative leadership than a commercial theatre production, a resident theatre or a college theatre. Theatrical productions simply don't spring out of the ground, nor do they result merely from good intentions. They result from the hard work of many people under the guidance of a clear-minded leader. Because an energetic, knowledgeable theatre director is not always available to a community, there may be frequent gaps in local leadership. This is especially true when the organization does not employ a salaried director. To avoid the problem, every attempt should be made to groom directors before some crisis necessitates a change-over. When events conspire to leave a group without effective leadership (a situation, when it occurs, that is readily obvious to everyone), the organization should consider a temporary suspension of major productions. This might dampen membership enthusiasm and weaken audience loyalties, but it is a more honest and ultimately more rewarding policy than that of presenting productions that are inferior to established standards. The membership, during such times, can remain active in other areas or can present less ambitious productions. And meanwhile, of course, it should search for a new artistic director who is able and willing to assume leadership.

### MEMBERSHIP ■

When there is talk about forming a new community theatre or about reactivating one that has been dormant, the leading organizers should question their motivations to be certain that they wish to establish a long-term venture. Perhaps they are merely enthused about producing a particular script for a particular cause, in which case they should limit their sights accordingly. Or, they might produce a play as a trial venture *preceding* the formation of a community theatre group in order to test local support, attract potential leaders and participants or serve as a rallying point. A trial production uncovers problems and factors that, subsequently, can be dealt with intelligently when writing the constitution and bylaws for a new organization.

Most community theatres provide for several types of membership. Full members usually pay annual dues, serve on committees, work on the productions and are eligible to serve as officers and directors. Associate members may be comprised of all those who buy a season ticket or a block of tickets but are not eligible to vote in the organization unless they also pay dues and thereby change their membership status. Patrons or sponsors may constitute a third class of membership, comprised of people or businesses who donate money or materials to the group or who purchase program advertising.

The important thing is to maintain a large nucleus of enthusiastic and active members. To do this, the organization must offer a range of activities sufficient to satisfy the diverse abilities and desires of its membership. Not everyone will want to perform on stage, and those who do should not be regarded as so "special" that other workers and activities are made to seem unimportant or unnecessary. It must become known throughout the community that the organization can serve the interests of many individuals and that it welcomes the nonactor as readily as the actor.

### CAPITAL ▪

Before writing bylaws and planning productions, the organizers of a community theatre should estimate how much their activities will cost. Where will the money come from? Ticket sales, patrons, donations, membership dues, advertising revenue? How much money can be reasonably expected from each source? Does the anticipated revenue indicate that the proposed activities of the group are too costly for it to support? Should ticket prices and dues be increased? How much money will be required before any ticket income is seen? What provisions can be made for a reserve fund? Whatever the answers to these questions, they will determine the early activities and plans of the organization. To realize the best legal and financial advantages, a community theatre should be formed as a nonprofit organization.

### THEATRE FACILITIES ▪

Like the availability of capital, the availability of physical plant facilities will dictate a great deal about what a community theatre can produce, how frequently and at what cost. Often, the organization may negotiate for free or low-cost usage of a school or civic auditorium. Or it may use a professional theatre during its off-season or nonperformance periods. The owners of such theatres may welcome off-season usage for several reasons: the rental income, the fact that it may introduce new audiences to the theatre building, the fact that it may reduce the landlord's maintenance and security problems. Some community theatres are sufficiently established and resourceful to own a theatre. Chapter 3 is especially pertinent in regard to the plant facilities operated by community theatre organizations.

### CONSTITUTION AND BYLAWS ▪

After stating the goals and objectives of the organization, the constitution and bylaws of a community theatre should spell out carefully determined specifics. Legal counsel should be obtained before the document is finalized. While basic operating rules and organizational structure should be defined, enough flexibility should be provided to accommodate changes and future developments. The bylaws for a typical community theatre should probably include details related to the following:

1. General:
   Name and location
   Preamble
   Legal counsel
   Bookkeeping and audit procedures
   Corporate status
   Amendment and repeal procedures
   Rules of procedure

2. Officers and Board of Directors:
    Election procedures
    Terms of office
    Powers
    Duties
    Replacement during absences and vacancies

3. Members:
    Definitions
    Types of
    Dues
    Obligations
    Powers
    Privileges

4. Meetings:
    Annual
    Special
    Purposes of
    Quorum requirements
    Advance notice for
    Order of business
    Time and place requirements, if any

5. Committees:
    Standing committees
    Types and purposes of
    Membership of
    Quorum requirements
    Chairmanship of
    Membership change in committees
    Appointment or election to
    Duties of
    Powers of

The revised edition of *Roberts' Rules of Order* is generally recognized as the authoritative guide for parliamentary procedure, a system of discussion that is highly efficient and democratic, especially for large meetings or those that are meant to result in formal, important actions.

It is possible to conduct an organization without any official constitution or bylaws simply letting things develop casually and using the precedent of past actions as the basis for governance, and this kind of common law technique may be suitable for some organizations. But when the goals, objectives and nature of the organization assume a different character each year these matters should be discussed by the membership frequently so they are understood by everyone.

## ▪ ADMINISTRATIVE ORGANIZATION

### THE BOARD, THE OFFICERS AND THE COMMITTEES ▪

When a nonprofit corporation is established as the legal base of an organization, there must be a board of directors (or trustees) and a set of officers to control it. If the board is a large one, it may appoint an executive committee comprised of a few of its members together with the president of the group and its leading managers. An executive committee can help to facilitate the rapid transaction of routine business. The fundamental responsibilities of a board of directors in a civic or community theatre should include the following:

1. To set long-range goals and objectives
2. To safeguard and improve physical and financial assets
3. To insure the legality of the organization's activities
4. To approve annual budgets
5. To receive annual reports from all leading officers and standing committees
6. To ratify the appointment of salaried personnel, especially the artistic director

A board of directors should not officially concern itself with selecting productions or with any of the routine, day-to-day business of the organization. If a salaried artistic director is employed, he should be given a great amount of power and flexibility in all areas of artistic decision-making. If the board is unhappy with the results, it may decide not to renew his contract at the end of the year.

While the following tables of organization show typical structures for community theatre groups, many different schemes are possible. The number of standing and special committees will be determined by the number of active members and, of course, by their interests. Sizable groups should attempt to operate a publications program which, among other projects, should write and distribute frequent newsletters to keep the membership informed about activities and, more important, maintain a high level of membership support and enthusiasm.

When a production is being prepared, the artistic director must organize workers under his immediate supervision as shown in the second chart. Some of these workers may come from standing committees, if the group is sufficiently active. For example, there might be a standing "design" committee that studies problems and techniques in scene and costume design and then applies its knowledge to the organization's productions. The same could hold true in the areas of publicity, makeup and house management. When there are groups of people permanently working in such areas, it is much easier to organize a production staff and it guarantees more knowledgeable and better-prepared workers. Following each production, the appropriate committees and workers should analyze the results to learn as much as possible from their experiences. Suggestions and written reports should then be submitted for the benefit of future production workers. Too many community groups virtually disband between productions. Unless there is loyalty to and participation in the organization itself and not merely in its productions, little growth and development will be possible. Each production will have to be staffed anew, each will make the same mistakes as the last, each will face the same ponderous difficulties.

## ▪ AFFILIATION WITH OTHER ORGANIZATIONS

To strengthen theatre activities and standards on the community and amateur level, local organizations should devise both informal and official methods of working together. Sometimes a community arts council or some other umbrella group

**Table of Executive Organization**

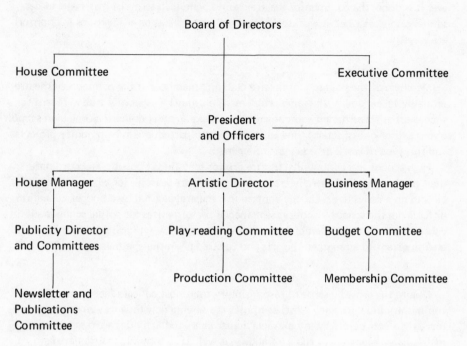

Board of Directors

House Committee

Executive Committee

President
and Officers

House Manager

Artistic Director

Business Manager

Publicity Director
and Committees

Play-reading Committee

Budget Committee

Production Committee

Membership Committee

Newsletter and
Publications
Committee

**Table of Production Organization**

Artistic Director

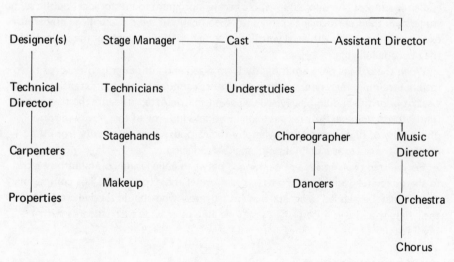

Designer(s)

Stage Manager ———— Cast ———————— Assistant Director

Technical
Director

Technicians

Understudies

Carpenters

Stagehands

Choreographer

Music
Director

Properties

Makeup

Dancers

Orchestra

Chorus

can serve to coordinate, sponsor or fund broad-based community programs. However it is done, the community theatre should benefit in terms of material and personnel resources when it works with local school, college or civic groups in appropriate ways.

PUBLIC SCHOOLS •

Members of the high school theatre club and members of the community theatre probably face many of the same problems. This may be especially true in regard to such areas as scene design and construction, makeup and publicity. Some high schools give credit or out-of-school time to students who participate in community projects and this type of work deserves encouragement.

High school and community theatre groups may find it possible to coordinate their productions and thereby create a local "theatre season" for which tickets can be sold on a series basis. Or, the community theatre, assisted by a budget allocation or fee from the school, might present special performances for public school audiences. Whatever the affiliation, cooperative efforts between local arts organizations are important to strengthen the arts and to strengthen the community itself.

COLLEGES •

Due to the growing sense of responsibility that most colleges feel toward the community in which they exist, campuses are serving nonstudents alongside students more than ever before. Many extracurricular clubs and activities are open to non-matriculated members of the community as well as to formally matriculated students. This makes many campus groups true community organizations, although they are funded and supervised by the college. Sometimes community members are encouraged to participate in performance programs in the hope that they will eventually matriculate as students; or, the policy may be adopted to increase community audience support. A college may also operate a program to attract local public school students in their performance programs, specifically to serve as a college preparatory experience with a view toward enrolling the high school students in the college when they become eligible.

When the college program is highly formalized and aims at preprofessional or vocational training, then nonstudent participants cannot be used too extensively. Also, a set of priorities should be devised to permit matriculated students the first opportunity to participate. But there is a lot to be said in favor of the "revolving door" philosophy of higher education whereby the campus serves practically from the cradle to the grave as a pivotal point in a person's life.

Formalized programs may be arranged between college and community theatres to share facilities, audiences, materials, personnel and experiences. The community theatre may be pleased to accept student workers (who should receive credit for their field work) and in some cases may be able to provide such students with a small fee or salary.

CIVIC ORGANIZATIONS •

Many community theatres are forced into an affiliation with a civic agency or organization in order to secure their theatre facilities. When a town or city operates a recreation center, this may include a theatre, auditorium or some other space suitable for stage productions which the local theatre club can use at a low cost. By working under the umbrella of a city agency, the theatre may be able to benefit by utilizing the agency's personnel, fiscal resources, mailing lists, public information services and space facilities. Conversely, such a marriage may also detract from the desired image and independence of the theatre group, force many compromises in regard to space usage and, if the town fathers are especially conservative, may force compromises in regard to the plays selected for production.

A community theatre may affiliate itself with a local service club, business or charity organization that offers it some kind of sustaining support. But, although security of this kind is always tempting, it is likely to be accompanied by compromises in the theatre's policies and attempts by outsiders to impose their vested interests upon the theatre organization.

## ■ RELATIONSHIP OF COMMUNITY TO PROFESSIONAL THEATRE

The quality of work produced by community theatres reflects the quality of interest its members have toward professional theatre and, indeed, toward life itself. If the membership of a group is comprised largely of people who are seeking mere ego satisfaction, the productions are unlikely to satisfy the audiences. Nor, in the long run, are they apt to provide much personal satisfaction for participants. It is not contradictory for nonprofessional groups to aim at professionalism. People who join ongoing community theatres should have an ongoing interest in the arts as well as a desire to develop as individuals. There is a big difference between the dedicated amateur and the dabbling dilettante. To keep the standards and goals of professionalism ever before it, a community theatre may establish varying types of relationships with professional artists and organizations.

A standing or special committee should be formed within the community theatre organization to assist and encourage its members to attend professional plays and events. This committee should negotiate with professional theatres for group rates, arrange for backstage tours and lectures and invite professionals to speak at membership meetings. When the community theatre is located many miles from professional theatres, it should arrange annual trips to visit distinguished professional theatres. Most professional managements are extremely gracious about providing backstage tours, will frequently arrange for groups to be addressed by leading artists or craftsmen and willingly make other special arrangements when requested to do so. The same may be said of college theatres, which also stand ready to receive touring groups and provide special lectures.

When members of a community theatre attend outside productions and activities in groups, follow-up discussions should analyze and evaluate the productions seen and the experiences gained. Also, thank you letters should be sent to the host theatre—a matter that is often overlooked.

### SPONSORSHIP OF PROFESSIONAL EVENTS ■
There is no reason why a community theatre should not sponsor a professional series of public events together with its own productions. This may take the form of a lecture series featuring well-known speakers, a poetry and play-reading series or a series of seminars. If there is strong membership and local support, events like these

can be self-supporting and, if they are tied in with the sale of tickets for the organization's regular productions, may increase general ticket sales. Guest speakers and individual guest performers may be engaged through direct negotiation or, more simply, through agencies like the American Program Bureau (Boston) or the International Platform Association (Cleveland), which offer nationwide bookings.

An ambitious community theatre might also sponsor, co-sponsor or arrange for local productions of touring professional companies.

### EMPLOYMENT OF PROFESSIONAL GUEST-ARTISTS ■

While a civic theatre organization can hire professional stage directors, designers, conductors, choreographers and others without necessarily negotiating a union contract (though some type of formal agreement should always be employed), professional actors who work with community groups must be contracted according to the terms of the Actors' Equity Association Guest-Artist Agreement. This is designed for use by individual actors who appear with an otherwise amateur company. If an entire professional company is hired to work in a community theatre, it should be employed on a resident theatre contract.* The Guest-Artist Agreement carries the standard AEA stipulations regarding work conditions, travel, living accommodations and the like. The salary minimum and other information can be obtained through an Equity office.

The Guest-Artist Agreement permits the actor to work only as a performer and his role(s) must be specified in his contract. A professional's association with an amateur group will afford considerable opportunity for its members to learn about professional attitudes and techniques. Not all actors are anxious or suited to engage in this type of association and effort should be made to avoid the employment of guests who are interested only in the salary they will receive. The community theatre group should know why it wants or needs the services and talents of a professional and the professional should have good reason for working with a community organization. Prehaps it offers the artist a role that he might not play elsewhere, an opportunity to experiment in some way or the gratification of teaching and assisting nonprofessionals.

The Guest-Artist Agreement has been used by a large number of colleges and nonprofessional stock theatres. Among the civic or community theatres that have employed Equity guest artists, the following is a representative list:

Arizona Civic Theatre, Tucson, Arizona
East/West Players, Burbank, California
Long Beach Community Playhouse, Long Beach, California
Los Angeles County Parks, Los Angeles, California
Tampa Community Theatre, Tampa, Florida
Columbus Little Theatre, Columbus, Georgia
Macon Little Theatre, Macon, Georgia
Savannah Little Theatre, Savannah, Georgia
Honolulu Community Theatre, Honolulu, Hawaii
Fort Wayne Civic Theatre, Fort Wayne, Indiana
Wichita Community Theatre, Inc., Wichita, Kansas
Grand Rapids Civic Theatre, Grand Rapids, Michigan

*See chapter 6.

Springfield Little Theatre, Rogersville, Montana
Albuquerque Little Theatre, Albuquerque, New Mexico
Little-Theatre of Greenville, Greenville, North Carolina
Fargo Morehead Community Theatre, Fargo, North Dakota
Oklahoma City Lyric Theatre, Oklahoma City, Oklahoma
Tulsa Little Theatre, Tulsa, Oklahoma
Erie Civic Theatre Association, Erie, Pennsylvania
Williamsport Recreation Committee, Williamsport, Pennsylvania
San Antonio Little Theatre, San Antonio, Texas
The Virginia Museum Theatre, Richmond, Virginia

## COOPERATION WITH PROFESSIONAL COMPETITORS ■

As mentioned earlier, theatregoing is a habit and, generally speaking, the more
theatre that is available to a public the more theatregoing will take place. Provided
that good sense is applied to performance scheduling, play selection and related
matters, a number of different theatres and performing organizations can live comfortably together in the same community and, furthermore, contribute substantially to
each other's success.

Obvious areas for desirable cooperation between theatre groups include the sharing
of mailing lists, fund-raising campaigns, plant facilities, material resources and personnel resources. Mutual endeavors can be organized without loss of image or independence to any of the participating groups. On the other hand, no group should merely
"use" another for its own self-centered purposes. By keeping lines of communication
open between various arts organizations in a community, many opportunities for
joint endeavors and benefits will be discovered. An energetic community arts council
can be especially helpful in promoting such activities and increasing audience support.

## ■ STREET THEATRE AND OTHER "OPEN" ORGANIZATIONS

While this book is primarily concerned with types of theatre that are organized
along traditional lines, there is, perhaps, justification for a companion book that deals
with the administration of what might be called the "unorganized theatre." Not a de-
rogatory, but rather a promising term for a newly exploding movement in amateur
theatre, the "unorganized theatre" includes street theatre and outdoor theatre of
other kinds as well as activities that are organized merely for the joy of sharing the ex-
ploration of artistic discovery. What other explanation can describe the mime who
performs in the city park, the musicians who play on the street corner, the sidewalk
dance groups and the larger groups that perform full productions in open, public
spaces? Some of these entertainers, as they progress, specialize in productions for inner-
city, prison or hospital audiences and the like. In fact, this kind of theatre has become
so established in recent years that it seems only a matter of time before Actors' Equity
attempts to unionize the performers. The National Endowment for the Arts has already recognized it by establishing a separate department under the name of "The Expansion Arts."

Many amateur performing groups are established by professionals who feel their
creativity is not given full vent within institutionalized branches of the industry. It is,
perhaps, the same impulse that causes the professional visual artist voluntarily to paint

a mural on the side of a building: the desire to work and the desire to contribute to the society in which he lives. The theatre director or actor, too, wishes to contribute and to work. If traditional organizations are closed to him or somehow inaccessible, or if they fail to provide the artistic satisfaction he craves, he may well turn to the community, to the people. Somewhere, sometime, he must make a beginning. So he gathers together a group of interested volunteers. He begins holding classes or rehearsals. He finds a storefront, a barn, a recreation center, and he goes to work. If the work is stimulating for the participants—and it frequently is—then others begin to join the group and soon the project becomes community or people's theatre in the fullest sense. Soon, also, the director may find that support is available to assist his work—from the community, the city, local industry, the schools, even from the federal government. Increasingly, it is understood that the arts can provide a community service and, increasingly, the community is willing to pay for this service.

---

If all theatres, productions and organizations begin as one man's idea, there is no arena in which more beginnings can and should be made than in the community, among amateurs and dedicated laymen.

Community theatre is grass-roots theatre from which the nation's audiences and many of its professional artists are developed. The standards and goals of community theatre thereby serve as a basis for much professional work. The higher the quality of community theatre, the higher will be the demands of professional theatre audiences and, hence, of the professional theatre itself.

Due to often limited financial and personnel resources, the community theatre depends heavily upon what it can garner from educational and professional organizations. A primary responsibility of its leaders is to secure the best outside guidance and to follow the highest standards available. Do-it-yourself craftsmanship should not mean doing it from ignorance! The availability of professional and college theatre around the nation today, the availability of a sound library of books about theatre practice and present-day mobility make ignorance within and misdirection of amateur groups inadmissible.

While past and present national organizations have helped to encourage, represent and develop the community theatre, the vast majority of community groups do not belong to or participate in any outside theatre societies or associations. This, of course, is a detriment to the individual theatre as well as to the movement as a whole. Also, it makes meaningful assessment of the nation's community theatre very difficult, hinders much-needed communication between groups and prevents much assistance that might otherwise be forthcoming.

While community theatre in America has long passed the blushing vigor of youth, it has yet to reach full maturity. Since patterns of living have tended to deemphasize communal structuring and campus theatre has become more active in community relationships, civic theatre may, in fact, never reach a true maturity. Nonetheless, there are signs that the time is ripe for a revitalization of the arts at the grass-roots level: the formation of strong local and state arts councils, an increase in government and business support for the arts, an awakening realization that the arts are for Everyman or, as one slogan puts it, the arts *are* man. A wiser and better-educated nation is less censorious about artistic subject matter, although an alarming number of community spokesmen across the nation still regard the playhouse as "the devil's own drawing room," a phrase used to satirize such spokesmen nearly two hundred years ago in *The Contrast*, America's first professionally produced comedy. Hence, before any serious work can be accomplished, many community theatre leaders must do battle with the homespun fears that continue to dominate local mores and taboos: fear of the unusual, fear of the untested, fear of embarrassment, fear of exposure, fear of being publicly rebuked, ostracized or laughed at. Arts workers in communities where such attitudes exist—and there are many—have no greater task than to create a social atmosphere in which truth and courage can thrive in the arts as they should and —as they then will—in the lives of the audience.

# Part III

# Business Management in the Theatre

# CHAPTER NINE

# How Much Will it Cost and How Much Will it Earn?

How much will the organization earn? How much will it cost to operate? Carefully formulated answers to both questions constitute the basis for good business management. Answers should be arrived at soberly, conservatively and even pessimistically before serious work begins on the project at hand, before contracts are signed, before commitments are made.

An estimate is a knowledgeable guess and a budget is an estimation. It is also a plan of action. Its accuracy depends on the experience and expertise of the person who devises it, although accuracy can be shot to Kingdom Come by unexpected developments that even an expert cannot foresee. At certain times, an organization should think about catastrophic possibilities (fire, flood, embezzlement, etc.) and should plan for contingencies. But an organization must also put faith in the budget it adopts and proceed with the conviction that it will turn out to be a close approximation of actual income and expenditures.

## ▪ MAJOR VARIABLES IN COST-ESTIMATING

No two budgets are alike. The most common variables that influence theatrical production budgets are:

1. Whether it is a profit or nonprofit organization
2. Whether it is an independent organization or affiliated with some other group or institution
3. Whether it is professional (unionized) or nonprofessional
4. Whether it plans a single production or a series of productions
5. The frequency with which its productions are offered
6. General overhead and maintenance costs
7. Whether it operates in a single or multi-plant facility
8. The seating capacity of its theatre
9. The total potential income from all sources
10. The condition of the physical plant
11. The geographical location of the theatre
12. The nature of the production(s) being offered
13. The length of time the production(s) will or may run
14. The number of performances per day and per week

Theatre budgets also possess similarities. For instance, the percentage relationship of each item to the total budgeted cost may be the same from theatre to theatre. If one stock theatre has a total weekly operating budget of $15,000 and spends 10 percent of that, or $1,500, on advertising, a smaller theatre with a $5,000 weekly operating budget is probably spending about $500 for the same item. Of the variables in the preceding list, several warrant special attention.

### THE LARGER THE CAPACITY, THE HIGHER THE COST ■

The dollar amount of many budgetary items will be influenced by the volume of space contained within the physical plant. Larger buildings require more maintenance, more heat and air conditioning, greater repair and renovation, more powerful and extensive machinery and, of course, a larger staff and more complicated security provisions. As a general rule-of-thumb, the following people will be required on the house staff at performance time to service five hundred theatregoers:

House manager (1)
Parking attendants (2)
Box office treasurer (1)
Ticket taker (1)
Ushers (4)
Auditorium maintenance staff (1)
Ladies room matron (1)

Excluding the house manager, this portion of the staff should be doubled to serve an audience of one thousand, tripled for an audience of fifteen hundred and so forth. The larger audience also requires that more programs be printed, more tickets —more of nearly everything. Advertising costs usually increase proportionately with the seating capacity so that more seats will be sold.

### THE NEWER THE THEATRE, THE HIGHER THE COST ■

Old buildings invariably present operating problems that account for high costs, especially in the areas of maintenance and repair. Poor plumbing and wiring, leaking roofs and senile machinery that sometimes forgets to work often inspire the tenants of an old plant to lease or build a new one, believing that it will be less expensive to operate. A new building should offer greater operating efficiency than an old one, but only for a price. A new building will probably contain more telephones, more light bulbs, more rest room facilities and more machinery than an older building. As with a mimeograph machine and a photocopy machine, the newer and more efficient building may be a wonderful thing, but is it necessary to do the job at hand? A new building, like a new employee, must also be broken in. Perhaps it will be found that it is necessary to correct the acoustics in the auditorium, that the box office or some other space isn't large enough to service the operation properly, that Indian pole-climbers have to be brought in to change the light bulbs in the chandelier. Replacing the old with the new can sometimes amount to little more than swapping one set of frustrations and expenses for another.

The new or younger producing *organization* may be more costly to operate because it may spend more to advertise its existence, benefit less from various types of free or automatic public attention given to an established organization and spend more to build up a steady group of customers and to inform the public where it is located and what it is doing. A young organization will also make unavoidable and costly mistakes which must be written off as "growing pains." Mistakes in staffing, in the selection of productions, in where and how to purchase supplies: inexperience is an expensive item.

A new building or a newly established operation also brings down upon the shoulders of its operators a myriad of inspectors and officials who may ignore or go more softly with an established operation. Labor unions may demand that the organization employ more of its members or use its members where nonunion employees were engaged previously. Building, health, insurance and public safety inspectors will almost certainly make thorough investigations of the building which may result in unexpected costs. Building codes and operating regulations are usually more severe for new buildings or for extensively renovated ones than for existing operations.

## THE MORE GEOGRAPHICALLY REMOTE, THE HIGHER THE COST ▪

Theatres located off the beaten path must spend many dollars merely to call attention to their existence and to direct customers to their doors. They may also have high transportation costs for personnel and supplies, and it may be difficult to find housing for personnel. If located away from shopping centers, for example, a simple errand may become a time-consuming and expensive safari.

## THE MORE UNUSUAL OR ERUDITE THE FARE, THE HIGHER THE COST ▪

Because the general public is hesitant about the new or the unknown, extra advertising and public information are usually necessary to promote unusual types of entertainment or organizations. Generally speaking, opera is more difficult to sell than musical comedy, Shakespeare more difficult than Simon, the new play more difficult than the Broadway hit, the unknown actor more difficult than the star. Unusual productions require employees who possess special skills or training and who therefore command high salaries—operatic singers, musical instrumentalists, acrobats, technicians, designers, animal trainers, whatever. Novelty or sophistication may require special or additional equipment in terms of stage lighting and sound systems, costumes and properties, scenery and rigging systems. Novelty can pay off at the box office, but seldom without greater investment than would be required for the tried and true.

# ■ THREE IMPORTANT "DON'TS"

### DON'T SPEND YOUR INCOME BEFORE YOU EARN IT ■

Few producers or organizations make plans for a production unless they believe that it will do well at the box office. Optimism about ticket revenue, therefore, is likely to run high before opening night. Commercial New York producers determine the weekly box office income that will be necessary to pay the operating expenses for their production and, if this income is not realized, they almost always close the show immediately. Most other types of theatres, however, commit themselves to a minimum number of performances, regardless of box office income, and thereby incur considerable risk. Whether or not tickets are sold, the show goes on. If ticket revenue falls far below what was anticipated, the producing organization itself may be forced out of business. (One of the major advantages of a repertory theatre is its ability to increase performances of a popular production and decrease performances of productions that are doing poorly at the box office.)

Most ongoing theatres, whether they are profit or nonprofit, should be able to realize at least 50 percent to 60 percent of their total potential box office gross and, hopefully, more income will actually be earned. (Leading nonprofit theatres often pay as much as one-half of their total operating budget from grants and gifts and the remainder from box office receipts. But few foundations or grants agencies look favorably on a group that cannot pay at least 40 to 50 percent of its expenses from ticket receipts. Although subsidiary income may supplement box office receipts, caution should be used in estimating potential revenue from concessions (such as program advertising, packing lot, food and beverage concessions). Revenue from foundation and government grants or private donations (so long as it is promised in writing) is, of course, money in the bank.

There are some cases where producers are justified in counting on more than 60 percent of the potential gross. Once in a while a production or a star is virtually a "sure sell-out." Or the production may be largely sold out because of exceptionally high advance sales or season ticket orders. Then the producer may decide to spend as much as 90 percent of the potential box office income. If every ticket is sold at full price (and all the costs are fixed costs), the 10 percent profit may be greater than the profit on a lower-budgeted show that only fills 70 percent of the theatre. And the success of the show may generate more business for future productions or provide unusually high satisfaction for regular customers.

Theatres that offer a season or series of different productions should think in terms of *average* box office income and *average* costs so that the sell-out shows "carry" the less successful ones and expensive productions are balanced by inexpensive ones. Broadway producers do not have this flexibility because each show is a completely separate enterprise.

When a theatre organization has estimated its cost and sees that it must count on subsidiary income *plus* more than 60 percent of capacity business in order to break even, it is usually a sign that its costs should be reduced, its revenue increased or its plans abandoned.

**DON'T SPEND OR BUDGET THE SAME DOLLAR TWICE** ▪

There is always a need to "stretch" the dollar as far as possible, but there is a limit to how much this can be done. Optimism or inexperience sometimes leads people into the illusion that the same dollar can be spent twice. For example, theatre organizations often have to post bonds with unions before they can begin to operate. The bond may be in the form of cash, a savings account book or some other security. Although the person posting the bond is entitled to receive the interest it earns, the bond will not be returned until after the production or the season has concluded. And, if there is unfinished business or a dispute between the two parties involved, the bond will be held up until everything is settled. Bonds are returnable and represent a cash asset, but they do not represent readily available cash.

Most theatres generate income in advance of opening night through preopening or season ticket sales. Season tickets or subscriptions may be sold as much as a year in advance of the opening night (and the interest earned from such income before it is spent can be considerable). It should be remembered that each ticket sold represents a legal contract with the customer—a contract promising that the production will take place as advertised on the ticket. In effect, therefore, the producing organization holds advance ticket sales income in public trust. If for any reason the production does not occur as advertised, the ticket money may have to be returned to the customer. Because of this reality, ticket revenue (1) should be held when possible until the production takes place, (2) should thereafter be spent only for operating costs until all these have been paid and (3) should never be regarded as money earned until the production has occurred. In other words, ticket income should not be used for capital expenditures (until, of course, it represents profit actually earned). This practice is followed by commercial New York productions in a manner that is especially obvious. Law requires the producer and his backers (limited partners) to provide *all* the capital necessary for funding the production up to opening night. Advance ticket sales revenue—which may be considerable—may only be spent for weekly operating costs, after which it may be distributed as profit. The wisdom of this practice is not always clear to the producing organization that is mounting productions as well as operating its own theatre building. There have been a number of unfortunate cases in which ticket revenue has been exhausted before production and operating costs have been paid, forcing the organization into bankruptcy. One group used its advance season ticket income as the down payment on the purchase price of its theatre!

**DON'T GET INTO THE BOAT UNLESS YOU CAN AFFORD TO SINK** ▪

If a project is initiated and financial commitments made before there is good assurance that the necessary capital will be forthcoming, a lot of money is likely to be lost and a lot of reputations ruined. Because theatre is so highly speculative as a business and because so many unexpected things can happen to increase expenses or prevent productions from taking place as planned, producing organizations must always keep the possibility of financial disaster in the back of their minds and protect themselves, their investors and the ticket buyers accordingly. Of course, it is sometimes necessary to take calculated risks. The New York producer who spends his own time and money trying to secure the option on a play knows that he may never be compensated. The organization attempting to establish an acting company or construct a new playhouse should also know that its efforts may never pay off. The late Lawrence Langner liked to relate how he broke ground for the construction of the Shakespeare Festival Theatre in Stratford, Connecticut, without having the slightest idea of where the construction money would come from. Such risks are often necessary to attract attention to a project so that, in turn, investors may be found. But one must be able to afford to lose the seed money or initial investment in a project.

## ▪ CAPITAL EXPENSES

In theatrical financing the capitalization represents the money required to pay all expenses of maintaining and operating a building or a production. For the commercial producer, the capitalization only concerns production-related expenses. An ongoing producing organization, however, may be concerned with building, construction and renovation costs as part of its capital expenditure. Theatrical jargon refers to the capitalization as "the nut." How this term was coined nobody knows for sure, but one story claims that it originated in Medieval times when strolling troupes of players traveled from town to town in a wagon that could be converted into a stage for outdoor performances. To get permission to perform, the players were required to pay a tax or fee to the burgomaster of each town. Of course, then as now, actors were usually broke and couldn't pay the fee until after they had performed and collected donations from the audience. To insure that they wouldn't run off without paying the fee, local officials removed a nut from the actors' wagon wheel and returned it only upon payment of the fee—or so the story goes. Hence the phase "recouping the nut" means earning back the investment in a theatrical production or paying off the expenses.

### THE COST OF MAKING IT LEGAL ▪
Everyone is familiar with the phrase "It takes money to make money." From the time an idea for theatre is conceived until some type of legal structure has been formed to accommodate the idea, a certain amount of seed money will be necessary. For the Broadway producer, as mentioned, this will include the expenses involved in finding a play, in optioning that play, in setting up a limited partnership agreement and in finding investors. Other theatre groups may spend a considerable amount of time and money looking for a community and a building in which to establish a theatre and then spend more money merely securing estimates on how much their dreams will cost them. While initial costs such as these are unique with each producer and organization, both should know at the outset how much time and money they have available for such purposes and both should be prepared never to see any return on this type of "front" money. If the organizer manages to raise the full capitalization for his project, he will be repaid for some of his early expenses (such as the cost of optioning a play or novel), but not for all of them (such as entertainment costs involved in raising the capital). The danger is that all available resources may be spent merely to get a project under way, by which time nothing is left to proceed any further.

### BUILDING AND CONSTRUCTION FUNDS ▪
The resources and the budget related to building, renovation or construction costs should be separate from those related to production and operating expenses. The pro-

ducing organization that is already presenting plays should not endanger its productions by committing its operating capital to other uses. The acquisition of a new
building may entail a separate publicity and fund-raising campaign as well as many
workers and experts who are not directly related to the regular production schedule.
Eventually, of course, construction and renovation costs will appear in the operating
budget of the organization in the form of plant amortization. If a loan or mortgage
has been secured, the payments will constitute the organization's rent or "occupancy
cost." Campus and civic theatre groups may not be required to contribute directly to
capital expenditures, since these are often paid by their city or institution. When
financial responsibility for building costs *does* rest with the producing organization,
cost estimates should be double-checked before actual commitments are made. Then
it should be determined if and how the organization can pay for such costs. Using
hypothetical examples related to several branches of the industry, this chapter discusses two types of budget:

1. *Capital Budget* (an estimation of construction, renovation and other major,
   nonrecurring costs required to initiate a project, be it a building, a season
   of plays or an individual theatrical production)
2. *Operating Budget* (an estimation of all the costs required to keep the project going)

A third kind of budget, called a *cash budget*, could be designed for an organization
to estimate when, on one hand, payments will fall due and when, on the other, income
is expected to arrive. A cash budget is especially helpful to large organizations whose
complex financing includes careful management of loans, interest from bank accounts,
large advance ticket receipts, mortgage payments, large payrolls and the like.

Let's assume that a professional resident theatre decides to purchase and renovate
a building for use as a theatre. Its capital budget and funding sources might resemble
the following:

| | | |
|---|---|---|
| Building fund-raising campaign | $ 3,800 | |
| Purchase price of building | 43,000 | |
| Title search, legal fees, etc. | 4,000 | |
| Renovation costs (exterior) | 25,000 | |
| Renovation costs (interior) | 80,000 | |
| New, permanent equipment | 52,700 | |
| Permits, licenses, etc. | 1,500 | |
| Miscellaneous | 5,000 | |
| Total Capital Expenditure | | $215,000 |
| Proceeds from fund-raising | 55,000 | |
| Federal grant | 50,000 | |
| State grant | 10,000 | |
| Gifts from private industry | 50,000 | |
| Total Capital Assets | | $165,000 |
| Differential | | $ 50,000* |

*To be mortgaged over a ten-year period.

In other words, the mortgage payments impose an annual cash outlay of $5,000 plus interest for ten years, an amount that will appear as such in the annual cash-flow budget of the organization, prorated over the number of performances or productions it offers each year.

## ■ ANNUAL OPERATING COSTS (INFLEXIBLE BUDGET ITEMS)

Once the cash occupancy cost has been determined—whether it is in the form of mortgage or loan payments or direct payment to a landlord—then the organization must estimate its annual operating expenses. What salaried employees and what costs will be necessary for the theatre to operate the kind of season it wishes? The items in this phase of the budget should all be of an annual, one-time or nonrecurring nature. Most of them will be essentially the same whether the theatre presents five or eight performances each week, whether it presents eight or thirty-eight productions during the year. Like the rent or occupancy cost, the total of all inflexible or fixed operating expenses may later be amortized or averaged into each production's operating budget. An annual cash operating budget for a busy professional resident theatre operating a twenty-week season in its own building might appear as follows:

| | |
|---|---:|
| Mortgage payment | $ 5,000 |
| Interest | 675 |
| Auditions | 300 |
| Automobile expense | 1,500 |
| Board meetings and expense | 500 |
| Heat, light, power, water | 4,300 |
| Insurance | 3,100 |
| Legal and auditing | 3,000 |
| Licenses and permits | 425 |
| Maintenance and repair | 2,500 |
| Office supplies | 850 |
| Postage | 2,000 |
| Real estate taxes | 5,000 |
| Preseason advertising | 5,000 |
| Rental of equipment | 3,400 |
| Plant opening and closing | 1,500 |
| Salaries: | |
|    Administrative | 73,780 |
|    Maintenance | 18,950 |
|    Payroll taxes and benefits | 8,600 |
| Telephone and telegraph | 2,200 |
| Travel (administrative) | 1,800 |
| | |
| Total estimated annual operating expenditures | $144,380 |

## ▪ PRODUCTION OPERATING COSTS (FLEXIBLE BUDGET ITEMS)

Thus far, we have estimated the cost of acquiring a theatre building and the annual cost of administering a business in that building. Now a third category of costs must be estimated: those that directly relate to the stage performances. Using the same example of a professional resident theatre, how should production costs be estimated? A few standard facts serve as the basis for this budget: length of season, number of productions, number of performances, size of the resident company, technical and artistic staff required to operate the theatre, union employee minimum salaries and so forth. Based on knowledge of these facts, it is possible to devise a production operating budget. Better still, if the organization can decide on the specific plays it wishes to produce during the season, it can estimate the costs for each production and then arrive at a grand total. Naturally, the production that requires twenty professional actors will require higher salary costs than the production that calls for only six actors. Musicals and recent Broadway hits carry higher royalty costs than other shows, while noncontemporary plays are in the public domain and (excluding recent translations or revised versions) carry no royalty charges at all.

The manner in which an organization wishes to produce its productions, the quality and the desired results comprise the most flexible aspect of all. The use of highly accomplished and well-known actors, directors and designers requires high salaries and fees; an insistence upon detailed and elaborate scenery and costumes requires high expenditures. Nonetheless, one either may determine annual budget allotments for each item on the production budget and then divide these among the selected productions or one may work from individual production budgets and arrive at the annual allotments. In either case, the figures probably will have to be revised as plans are revised and clarified. An annual production operating budget for a professional resident theatre presenting six productions during a twenty-week season might resemble the following:

| | |
|---|---|
| AEA pension contributions | $ 3,600 |
| AEA health insurance | 600 |
| Box office (tickets, etc.) | 1,975 |
| Concession supplies, etc. | 3,500 |
| Costumes, makeup, wigs | 10,700 |
| Electrics and sound | 2,500 |
| Fees and commissions | 900 |
| Hospitalization insurance | 600 |
| Laundry and dry cleaning | 925 |
| Newspaper and media advertising | 9,000 |
| Piano | 200 |
| Program printing | 10,000 |
| Promotion and publicity | 7,000 |
| Rehearsal supplies, rentals, etc. | 800 |
| Royalties | 9,800 |
| Scenery and props | 18,600 |
| Salaries: | |
| Production (artistic) | 35,000 |
| Production (technical) | 47,400 |

| | |
|---|---:|
| Performers | 98,300 |
| Musicians | 16,000 |
| Scripts, duplicating, etc. | 375 |
| Social Security and Unemployment | 23,000 |
| Transportation (company) | 5,600 |
| Welfare (stagehands) | 1,800 |
| Trucking (scenery) | 1,200 |
| Total annual production operating expenditures | $309,375 |

Now that all the estimations are in, what is the total operating cost for our professional resident theatre according to the preceding budget proposals?

| | |
|---|---:|
| Annual operating costs (including building capitalization) | $144,380 |
| Annual production costs | 309,375 |
| Total annual budget | $453,755 |

This total figure is now set aside until the organization has estimated its annual revenue and can thereby decide whether or not it can afford its plans. Once again, it is possible to work in reverse and to estimate revenue first and then to budget that revenue.

Unlike the ongoing organization that produces a multi-production season each year, the commercial New York producer is only concerned with one production at a time, each one being a separate venture. The preopening expenses for a commercial New York production constitute the capitalization for the show (commonly funded by the investors in a limited partnership) and the operating expenses are comprised of the performance-related costs (funded by box office income). The following budget proposal for an Off Broadway production shows both the preopening and the weekly operating costs.

### SAMPLE EXPENSES: OFF BROADWAY PRODUCTION

| Item | | Capital Budget: Preopening Expenses | Operating Budget: Weekly Operating Expenses | |
|---|---|---:|---:|---|
| SALARIES | | | | |
| 6 Actors | $155 x 3 wks. | $2,790 | $1,800 | (6 x 300) |
| 1 Stage Manager | 175 x 4 " | 700 | 175 | |
| 1 Press Agent | 250 x 2 " | 500 | 250 | |
| 1 Production Assistant | 100 x 4 " | 400 | 100 | |
| 1 General Manager | 175 x 4 " | 700 | 175 | |
| 4 Crew | 100 x 4 " | 400 | 200 | (2 x 100) |
| | | 5,490 | 2,700 | |

**How Much Will It Cost and How Much Will It Earn?**

| Item | Capital Budget:<br>Preopening<br>Expenses | Operating Budget:<br>Weekly Operating<br>Expenses | |
|---|---|---|---|
| ROYALTIES AND FEES | | | |
| Author | _____ | $ 450 | (5% of $9,000) |
| Director | $2,000 | 180 | (2% of $9,000) |
| Designer | 1,000 | 50 | |
| | 3,000 | 680 | |
| | | | |
| PRODUCTION | | | |
| Scenery | 2,900 | 25 | |
| Costumes | 1,250 | 20 | |
| Electrics | 650 | 30 | |
| Props | 800 | — | |
| Sound | 100 | 15 | |
| | 5,700 | 90 | |
| | | | |
| PROMOTION | | | |
| Newspapers | 4,000 | 1,300 | |
| Photos | 350 | 25 | |
| Signs | 200 | 25 | |
| Public relations expenses | 300 | 150 | |
| | 4,850 | 1,500 | |
| | | | |
| REHEARSAL | | | |
| Scripts | 225 | | |
| Actors' expenses | 100 | | |
| Stage Manager's expenses | 200 | | |
| Theatre with staff | 3,600 | 1,000 | |
| | 4,125 | 1,000 | |
| | | | |
| OTHER EXPENSES | | | |
| Audition | 100 | — | |
| Legal expenses | 2,900 | — | |
| Insurance | 350 | 55 | |
| Blue Cross and | | | |
| Hospitalization | 175 | 45 | |
| Payroll tax | 290 | 185 | |
| Auditing | 550 | 50 | |
| Office expenses | | 150 | |
| Tickets | | 235 | |
| Maintenance | | 50 | |
| Miscellaneous | 500 | 50 | |
| | 4,865 | 820 | |
| | | | |
| ADVANCES | | | |
| Author guarantee | 1,500 | | |
| Theatre guarantee* | 6,000 | | |
| AEA bond (returnable) | 3,600 | | |
| ATPAM bond (returnable) | 500 | | |
| | 11,600 | | |

*After the rent quarantee is depleted a rental amount must be added to the weekly operating expense.

| Item | Capital Budget: Preopening Expenses | Operating Budget: Weekly Operating Expenses |
|---|---|---|
| CONTINGENCY | $5,670 | $ 300 |
| TOTAL (preopening) | $45,300 | |
| TOTAL (weekly operating expenses) | | $7,090 |

# ▪ GENERAL BUDGETARY CONSIDERATIONS

### THE CONTINGENCY ▪

All budget estimations should include both a "miscellaneous" fund and a "contingency" or "reserve" fund. The combined total of these two figures should probably represent no less than 10 percent of the total budget estimation. A miscellaneous fund is intended to provide money for minor but unexpected costs: overtime payments to workmen, increases in costs due to inflation, unanticipated supplies and other factors that are easy to underestimate. The contingency fund, on the other hand, is intended to provide financial insurance against costly emergencies that may and often do occur in the theatre: loss of performance, unexpectedly poor box office receipts, replacement of personnel. The absence of such reserve money often spells disaster. Unfortunately, most budget allocations from college, university, civic and public agencies will not recognize or provide contingency funds. Perhaps it is assumed that the organization or department has automatically overestimated its costs and thereby provided a "built-in" contingency. Once such allocations are received, the recipient must protect himself (if he has *not* purposely inflated his budget requests) by readjusting budget commitments to provide for miscellaneous and unexpected costs. When every dollar is closely and specifically budgeted, a deficit will almost certainly result.

### DEFICIT SPENDING ▪

While it usually "takes money to make money," it is a peculiarity of fund-raising and financing that it may take a deficit to gain more revenue. Many nonprofit organizations believe that if they maintain sizable cash assets and are therefore known as a "rich" organization, they will not easily be able to attract subsidization. After all, who gives charity to a rich man? Many nonprofit groups can build a goodly bank account, but how much will be lost in terms of artistic quality, how much compromising will be necessary and how much more will have to be charged at the box office? The line between solvency and bankruptcy is often a very thin one. The line between quality and mediocrity, however, is a very broad one. Deficits, consequently, are a fact of life for nearly all serious, noncommercial theatres. Most nonprofit organizations have the ability to carry a limited deficit all of the time and a large deficit some of the time. The seriousness of deficits is frequently exaggerated by the press, which may be encouraged in this practice by the deficit organization itself because it is seeking to dramatize its financial need and to attract donors and subsidization. One must prove a *need* for subsidy before one is going to *get* subsidy. On the other hand, if the organization cannot prove its value to society as well as its financial need, then fund-raising efforts will seldom be successful. Too, there is the old danger of crying "Wolf!" once too often.

## COST-AVERAGING ▪

In any type of multi-production or seasonal theatre operation it may be helpful to average the projected costs over the different productions, rather than attempt to assign exact amounts to each one. This system emphasizes the overall picture rather than each production. And it provides an average weekly or per-production operating cost figure that may serve as a break-even point for the purpose of granting royalties and percentages or for the purpose of estimating profits (also called "marginal revenue"). In many theatres, the star and others are granted a salary guarantee (let's say $2000 per week) against a percentage of, say, 25 percent over the break-even point. If the theatre determines its break-even (weekly average operating cost) at $18,000, this means that the star will earn a percentage of box office income only when it exceeds $18,000, but that a $2,000 salary is assured whatever the box office gross turns out to be.

The commercial New York production, because it is organized as a separate venture, has little need for cost-averaging. The basic unit of measurement for a Broadway show is one week (because nearly all contracts and theatre rental licenses are based on weekly periods). The college or community theatre offers only a few performances of each production, which makes their basic unit the single performance. Stock and resident theatres usually commit themselves to a certain number of weeks each season so the season may be regarded as their basic unit. To give a general picture of what is happening, the average of all costs may be spread over a series of units (performances, weeks or seasons) and the revenue may be averaged in the same manner.

## THE VARIABLE COST ▪

Since many items, such as salaries, are predetermined at fixed dollar amounts, a large portion of operating expenses can be estimated with considerable accuracy. But there may be a number of costs that cannot be determined until the exact box office income is known. This is especially true in commercial theatre where many costs are based on and derived from a given percentage of the box office income. While royalty charges for amateur and educational theatre productions are flat per-performance amounts, in most professional theatres there is a guaranteed minimum royalty charge against a percentage share of the box office revenue. Similarly, the commercial theatre usually pays its stars, directors, designers, playwrights, composers and choreographers according to the same plan: a minimum guaranteed fee or salary plus a percentage of the box office gross. Theatre rent itself may be determined largely by the box office gross. This means that there will be a difference between the fixed weekly operating cost and the actual weekly operating cost, a difference referred to as the "variable cost."

For example, it may appear according to the preceding Off Broadway production budget that, after the capitalization has been paid back, the production will begin to show a profit as soon as it earns more than $7,900 per week. But the higher the box office gross, the higher the royalties and percentage payments will be. So the estimated weekly operating cost is not a static figure. The fixed costs *plus* the variable costs at the actual box office gross are what finally tell the true story.

### THE MARGINAL COST ▪

An operating budget is always based on the assumption that the producing organization will present a certain number of productions and a certain number of performances per production and per week. When the costs of doing this are averaged out among all the performances, the resulting figure represents the "per-unit cost" of producing the product (in theatre the unit is either a single performance, a week or a season of performances). As any manufacturer knows, it is cheaper to produce one hundred units of the same product than to produce one hundred different products. Inability to do this in live theatre is the core of its economic dilemma. Hollywood can produce one hundred different prints of the same film for showing in one hundred different movie houses simultaneously, and all for about the same investment and the same number of man-hours it would take to produce a single print of the film. Live theatre, on the other hand, cannot even approach such mass production. Yet, there are several ways by which live theatre may be able to decrease its per unit cost. One of these, when business warrants it, is to increase the number of performances presented in a given week or the number of productions presented in a given season at the same theatre. Capital expenses and operating and production expenses remain essentially the same whether a theatre presents four or eight performances in a given week. If the budget is based on a schedule of eight performances per week and the show is a smash hit, the producing organization may wish to know how much extra cost would be involved to present a ninth performance during that week. The figure that answers that question is called the "marginal cost," as illustrated in the budget for a twelve-week musical theatre season on page 195, showing how the per-unit cost decreases as production of the unit increases.

## ▪ ESTIMATING THE INCOME

Theatrical revenue is derived from two general sources: the box office and subsidiary income. The commercial theatre depends almost entirely on box office revenue, while other types of theatre may depend heavily on grants and subsidiary income.

### THE FEE ADMISSION POLICY ▪

There has been a growing trend in recent years to regard free theatre productions with favor. If many libraries, parks and museums are free to the public, the argument goes, why shouldn't free theatre also be made available? Experiments with this policy, such as Joseph Papp's Shakespeare in the Park productions in New York, indicate that free theatre may attract large numbers of people who would not otherwise attend. On the other hand, there is a widespread belief that holds "if it's free it's bad" or "you get what you pay for." Whichever policy the producer may favor, he wants his productions to be performed before capacity audiences.

The commercial, nonsubsidized theatre must charge admission fees in order to survive. But the nonprofit, subsidized theatre may have a choice or, at least, wide flexibility in ticket-pricing. One guideline that may be followed is this: If a theatre is earning less than 50 percent of its total potential box office gross and if this is covering less than 25 percent of its total operating expenses, it should consider a free admission policy (or, most assuredly, some other drastic change of policy). Is it not preferable to reduce expenses (depending, let's say, more upon word-of-mouth publicity

# SAMPLE OPERATING COSTS (ASSUMING BASIC 12-WEEK SEASON, 7 REGULAR PERFORMANCES) MUSICAL PRODUCTION

| SALARIES: | 1st WEEK of 7 Perf. | 2nd WEEK OF SAME SHOW | Addl. Cost 8th PERF. IN WEEK | Addl. Cost 9th PERF. IN WEEK[5] | MARGINAL COST OF ADDITIONAL SAME SHOW | MARGINAL COST OF (13th) WEEK NEW SHOW |
|---|---|---|---|---|---|---|
| Cast (principals) | $ 2,200 | $ 2,200 | $ – | $ 275 | $ 2,200 | $ 2,200 |
| Cast (rehearsal) | 500 | – | – | – | – | 500 |
| Chorus ("Parts") | 1,300 | 1,300 | – | 165 | 1,300 | 1,300 |
| Performers (overtime) | – | – | 205 | 300 | – | – |
| Director and choreographer | 500 | 500 | – | – | – | 500 |
| Orchestra[1] | 1,400 | 1,400 | –[3] | 100 | 1,400 | 1,450 |
| Stage Manager and technical[2] | 650 | 650 | – | 20 | 370 | 650 |
| Box office and office | 700 | 700 | – | – | 700 | 700 |
| Parking and ushers | 300 | 300 | 40 | 40 | 300 | 300 |
| Maintenance | 175 | 175 | – | – | 175 | 175 |
| Press department | 225 | 225 | – | – | 225 | 225 |
| **TOTAL SALARIES** | $ 8,000 | $ 7,450 | $ 245 | $ 900 | $ 6,670 | $ 8,000 |
| Advertising and press expenses | 1,000 | 900 | 200 | 200 | 900 | 1,000 |
| Ground and equipment rental | 300 | 300 | –[4] | –[4] | 300 | 300 |
| Royalty and rental materials | 1,600 | 1,600 | –[4] | –[4] | 1,600 | 1,600 |
| Costume rental and shoes | 750 | 500 | – | – | 500 | 750 |
| Wardrobe costs and freight | 100 | 50 | – | – | 50 | 100 |
| Scenery, lighting and props | 150 | 20 | 10 | 10 | 20 | 150 |
| Cast (travel pay) | 100 | – | – | – | – | 100 |
| Office supplies and expenses | 700 | 650 | 10 | 20 | 650 | 700 |
| Box office tickets and supplies | 60 | 60 | 10 | 10 | 60 | 60 |
| Light, water and heat | 100 | 100 | 10 | 10 | 100 | 100 |
| Maintenance, repairs and auto expenses | 150 | 150 | 10 | 10 | 100 | 150 |
| Payroll taxes, HIP and W/C Insurance | 450 | 420 | 15 | 50 | 150 | 450 |
| Package deals and production expenses | 40 | – | – | – | 400 | 40 |
| **TOTAL OPERATING COSTS** | $ 13,500 | $ 12,200 | $ 500 | $ 1,200 | $ 11,400 | $ 13,500 |
| TOTAL OPENING/CLOSING COSTS AND CAPITAL COSTS AMORTIZED OVER 12 WEEKS | 3,500 | 3,500 | – | – | – | – |
| **BREAK-EVEN POINT** | $ 17,000 | $ 15,700 | $ 500 | $ 1,200 | $ 11,400 | $ 13,500 |

[1] Includes musical director, choral conductor, rehearsal pianist, union tax and contractor fee.
[2] Includes set designer, carpenter, scene shifters, props master.
[3] Assumes musicians contract calls for eight performances at no additional pay.
[4] Assumes no percentage rent or royalties based on gross receipts.
[5] Assumes ninth performance in week does not interfere with day off.

than upon costly advertising) and play to larger audiences than to continue absorb-
ing losses merely to attract small audiences? From a per capita standpoint, free
tickets may actually reduce losses (a good argument to use in applications for financial assistance). For example, if the weekly operating costs for a production are
$10,000 and one thousand people per week are paying $2.50 each to see that production (bringing $2,500 into the box office), then each person is being "subsidized"
in the amount of $7.50. But if no admission is charged and, as a result of this, the
production plays to five thousand people weekly, each person is subsidized in the
amount of only $2.00! This is a logical rationale, provided that the goal is not to
"make money." Furthermore, if box office income is small, an analysis of expenses
may show that the income is barely paying the costs of maintaining a reserved seat
admission policy (box office costs, ticket costs, ushering, house staff costs and so
forth). Many nonprofit theatre groups are doubtless able to afford a free admission
policy without realizing it and they might benefit enormously both in terms of public relations and public response if they revised their admission policy, especially in
cases where admission prices are almost tokenistic or box office income covers a
mere pittance of total operating costs.

## "SCALING THE HOUSE" AND TICKET-PRICING ▪

Ticket prices are often determined more from intuition than from logic. A producer may simply "feel" that certain prices are the best ones for his theatre and his
community. It is difficult to judge whether there will be price resistance until tickets
are actually on sale. Many people believe, for example, that there is a psychological
advantage in pricing a ticket at $4.95 rather than at $5.00, and that the five cents
lost will be more than compensated for by an increase in ticket sales at that price.
Recently, however, there appears to be a preference for round dollar figures ($2.00,
$4.00, $6.00). Advantages of this policy are that box office treasurers can make
change much more easily, there is a smaller chance for error and it's easier to compute the total cost of multiple-ticket orders. The second easiest method is to round
off ticket prices to the nearest quarter ($2.50, $3.75, $5.25) so that the only silver
necessary for making change will be quarters.

Differences in ticket prices should reflect differences in the auditorium seating
arrangement: one price for the orchestra, another for the mezzanine and another for
the balcony. But numerous theatres have a long stretch of uninterrupted rows of
seats, in which case it may be necessary to select an arbitrary point where the price
changes. If rows of orchestra seats proceed from A to Z, for instance, the producer
may decide to decrease ticket prices beginning at row N. To make such arbitrary
divisions obvious to customers and ushers, different colored seat covers or some
other indications may be used. No theatre, incidentally, should include a row "I" when
designating its row and seat numbers; the letter "I" is too easily confused with the
number "1." Many theatres label the first few rows of the orchestra by using double
letters (row AA, row BB, etc.) and commence anew with row A further back in the
orchestra. Or, the first ten rows may proceed from A to K and the next ten from
AA to KK. The psychology of this system is that ticket-buyers are less hesitant to
purchase a seat in row KK than in row U. But there is also an element of deceit involved here.

Pricing tickets for a theatre-in-the-round offers special problems. Since it is a comparatively unusual type of audience seating, the public is likely to be confused about which seats are the best ones. The answer given by producers and treasurers in such theatres is, invariably, "They're all good." And, indeed, a theatre-in-the-round production should be staged in such a manner that no section of the audience is favored over another. If there are less than five hundred seats, perhaps there should only be a single ticket price. Otherwise, prices should diminish as the rows of seats gets further from the stage. However, when sightlines are poor in certain sections of the house (often the case in arena theatres that have an elliptical stage), ticket prices should be adjusted accordingly.

Ordinarily, a theatre manager prefers a large number of seats to sell when he has a popular attraction. On the other hand, he is sorely embarrassed by a large expanse of empty seats when ticket sales are low. An intriguing strategy for obtaining the best of two worlds is to design the audience area so that it contains a large transverse aisle (an aisle that runs parallel to the stage and separates one price of seats from the price of the section behind it). The wide transverse aisle reduces the seating capacity of the house. But, when ticket sales are brisk, additional seats can be placed in such aisles to increase the capacity. Best of all, these additional seats can be priced much higher than if they had been placed at the back of the house or if standing room had been sold in lieu of actual seats.

Auditorium and ticket terminology varies from one theatre to another and creates confusion among ticket-buyers. How should the various sections of a theatre be labeled? Some terms are preferred because they sound more elegant than others: "terrace" instead of "first balcony," "family circle" instead of "second balcony." While this preference may be desirable for sophisticated, metropolitan audiences, more accurate-sounding terms are probably a better choice for audiences that are not habitual theatregoers. Almost any box office treasurer will tell you that a surprising number of ticket-buyers do not even understand the term "orchestra." Suffice it to say that theatregoing should be made as easy as possible. The following are the most commonly used seating terms:

| Front Auditorium | Middle Auditorium | Rear Auditorium |
|---|---|---|
| Orchestra | Mezzanine | Balcony |
| Stalls (England) | Dress Circle | Rear Orchestra |
| | Front Balcony | Family Circle |
| | First Balcony | Second Balcony |
| | Boxes | Rear Balcony |
| | Side Terrace | The Gods (England) |
| | Side Balcony | Second Tier |
| | Loge | Second Terrace |
| | Parterre | |
| | Galleries (England) | |
| | First Tier | |

When planning or renovating an auditorium, rows containing odd numbers of seats should be avoided because most theatregoers buy tickets in pairs. Continental seating (in which there is no center aisle running down the middle of the orchestra and, consequently, each row contains many seats) may require fewer ushers but also requires a wider distance between rows to allow people to get in and out (hence, the elimination of aisles may not mean a greater number of seats). Whatever the seating arrangement, a diagram of the auditorium should be displayed near the box office where ticket-buyers can study it and determine where they wish to sit. If a producing organization offers only a few performances of each production, it might consider adopting what the airlines use in regard to seating selection. In the lobby or within the customers' view inside the box office a seating board may be displayed on which a little tag is hung for each seat. When the seat is sold, the tag is removed so it is always clear which seats are still available. Of course, this gives a graphic picture of whether business is good or bad, but it is a workable idea for amateur and college theatres and it combines honesty and novelty that ticket-buyers may appreciate. When no seating chart is displayed, box office treasurers will constantly be faced with questions and long discussions about seat locations.

### ESTIMATING POTENTIAL BOX OFFICE INCOME ▪

Once the seating arrangement has been determined and the various sections have been labeled, then a price value may be affixed to each seat and the gross determined as follows:

| | | |
|---|---|---|
| Orchestra | 500 x $5.75 | $2,875.00 |
| Mezzanine | 200 x  4.50 | 900.00 |
| Balcony | 100 x  3.00 | 300.00 |
| Total potential gross for a single, evening performance | | $4,075.00 |

If matinee or "twilight" performances are offered, ticket prices are traditionally lowered. (While there is great precedent for this policy, it is not altogether justifiable. Most theatregoers who attend matinees do so for reasons other than the lower prices and would probably not resist paying evening prices if the tradition were changed.) To simplify the treasurer's job, matinee prices should simply drop the top evening price category and continue the other prices downward:

| | | |
|---|---|---|
| Orchestra | 500 x $4.50 | $2,250.00 |
| Mezzanine | 200 x  3.00 | 600.00 |
| Balcony | 100 x  2.50 | 250.00 |
| Total potential gross for a single, matinee performance | | $3,100.00 |

If the production is scheduled for a limited run of less than a week, the total potential gross for the entire run can be computed and then set aside for study once the estimated production costs have been determined. If the theatre operates on a regular basis, offering a set number of performances each week of the same production or different productions, then a total weekly potential gross should be determined as follows:

| | | |
|---|---|---|
| 6 evening performances x | $4,075.00 | $24,450.00 |
| 2 matinee performances x | 3,100.00 | 6,200.00 |
| | | |
| Total potential weekly gross | | $30,650.00 |

As well as having different price scales for evening and matinee performances, a theatre may also elect to increase its ticket prices for weekend performances (as is practiced on Broadway) or for special events, for musical productions or for those that feature an especially popular performer).

It must be kept in mind that the total potential gross will almost never be reached due to:

1. Complimentary tickets and press seats
2. Discounted tickets for theatre parties, etc.
3. Commissions paid to ticket agents
4. Unclaimed or canceled (unpaid) reservations
5. Difficulty in selling single, scattered seats

The only way to offset such revenue losses is to sell standing room or additional chairs that are not included in the potential gross estimations.

In 1966 the 10 percent federal entertainment tax was repealed and the traditional method of dividing estimated revenue between "net gross" and "tax revenue" was dropped. Recently, however, a number of states and localities have imposed local taxes on theatre tickets. When this is the case, a breakdown of the two figures should appear in all revenue estimates, on all box office statements,* on the tickets themselves and on the price scale displayed in the lobby. Royalties and percentages should never be paid on the tax portion of ticket prices. Meanwhile, performing arts leaders in communities that impose such taxes should work diligently to convince legislators to repeal taxation on income earned from cultural events, whether sponsored by profit or nonprofit organizations.

### ESTIMATING POTENTIAL SUBSIDIARY INCOME ▪

Subsidiary income, discussed in greater detail in chapter 12, may be included by an organization in its estimated revenue and applied to the regular operating budget, but it is safer not to count on such income when it is minimal. Again, estimated figures should be conservative and always based upon past records of income from such sources as:

| | |
|---|---|
| Coat room income | $ 100.00 |
| Souvenir program sales | 500.00 |
| Program advertising | 1,000.00 |
| | |
| Estimated total weekly subsidiary income | $1,600.00 |

*See Appendix C.

Unless subsidiary income is collected as a contracted fee from concessionaires, the organization will incur expenditures that relate to and decrease the profit on this revenue: the salary for the coat room attendant, the cost of printing souvenir programs and so forth. If these expenditures are not included in the operating budget and yet the organization *does* include the subsidiary income they generate in its total estimated revenue, then many dollars are being valued at twice their actual worth.

Most nonprofit theatres, both professional and nonprofessional, depend on revenue from grants or from budget allocations given to them by the parent institution to which they belong. For example, a campus theatre may receive from the general college budget an annual allotment of $22,000. This figure, it may be supposed, is like money in the bank once it is officially promised. It becomes part of the total estimated revenue which may be applied to operating expenses. In many cases, however, institutional budget allocations are broken down into "budget lines" that specify how the money must be spent. Perhaps the college or university budget office has assigned $22,000 to the theatre department in the following manner:

| | |
|---|---|
| $10,000 | Budget Code #201—Rentals, service charges, fees for services |
| 7,000 | Budget Code #300—Expendable or perishable supplies |
| 5,000 | Budget Code #450—Permanent equipment |
| | |
| $22,000 | Total annual allocation |

This system makes budgeting less flexible than it may appear at first, and this inflexibility will be a factor in establishing policy. For example, while an unencumbered allotment of $22,000 might make it possible for the theatre department to engage visiting professional actors at a cost of $12,000 in salaries, the fact that only $10,000 can be spent for such a purpose (Budget Code #201) will limit this policy unless, of course, another source of unencumbered revenue can be found. In a similar manner, most grant money given to an organization is earmarked for certain types of expenditures (capital as opposed to operating expenditures, research as opposed to production) or for application to a particular production. Both institutional budget allocations and grant allotments almost invariably specify that the money must be spent within a given fiscal year, so the recipient of such funds is seldom able to limit expenses one year in order to apply the savings to another year's budget. When annual allocations are not exhausted by the end of the fiscal year, the irresistible tendency is for the organization to rush out and spend the remaining funds in a burst of extravagance rather than permit the unexpended amount to return to its source. Because allocations governed in this manner are usually derived from tax-levied dollars, it is the taxpayer who is most victimized by the system, the abuse of which is so common and so wasteful that one cannot imagine why it has failed to ignite civil uprising!

## ▪ PROJECTING PROFITS AND DEFICITS

### INCOME VS. EXPENSES ▪

Money to cover the costs of an operation, as we have seen, may come from a variety of sources. In the case of our hypothetical resident theatre, the total estimated revenue might appear as follows:

| | |
|---|---|
| Estimated weekly box office gross (60% of capacity less discounts, etc.) | $ 16,800 |
| Estimated weekly concession revenue | 1,600 |
| Total estimated weekly revenue | $ 18,400 |
| Total estimated annual revenue ($18,400 x 20 operating weeks) | $368,000 |
| Total estimated annual expenses | 453,755 |
| Projected annual deficit | ($85,755) |

At this point it is obvious that the organization cannot afford to carry out its plans. What can be done to balance the budget so that revenue is at least equal to the expenditures?

1. Expenses can be lowered.
2. Ticket prices can be raised.
3. The number of performances can be increased (which will also increase the operating costs).
4. More subsidiary revenue can be sought, from grants or private donations, or more concessions or wherever.

Balancing a budget can be a tricky affair, largely because it is tempting to make so many false assumptions. For example, it is easy to assume that if ticket prices are raised the theatre will continue to draw 60 percent of its capacity. But perhaps the higher prices will discourage ticket-buyers and produce a lower actual gross. Perhaps the decision is made to produce five instead of six productions over the twenty-week season, thereby lowering production costs. But this makes the dangerous assumption that more ticket-buyers will be found to support the additional performances of the five productions and thereby maintain revenue at the same amount estimated from six productions. These assumptions concern the elasticity of demand for tickets as opposed to the fixed demand. What is the top price the consumer market will pay for theatre tickets? How many consumers will pay it? If the audience would willingly pay more than it is being charged for the tickets, then a lot of potential revenue is being lost. In other words, the producer must know his market. And he must often make his judgments—about ticket-pricing, about length of run and about play selection—not according to his own tastes but according to those of his consumer market.

Most budgeting involves a certain amount of "robbing Peter to pay Paul." Money for one item is reduced so that money for another item can be increased. Again, realism must be brought to bear upon decision-making. For instance, if it is decided to hire only two box office treasurers rather than three, can the box office still operate efficiently? (If hiring only two treasurers means reducing the hours when the box office is open to the public, the result could be a loss of ticket sales.) If the scene designer decides not to construct a revolving stage unit, can the production still work effectively? (Perhaps it will require long scene changes or require more stagehands to move the scenery manually.) Budgets are not devised merely to impress the investors or the board of directors. They are devised to tell a realistic story, to serve as a plan for action that will lead to specific results.

A budgetary surplus or deficit, especially for nonprofit organizations, can determine many things about future budget allocations. For example, if the Broadway producer underestimates the amount of capitalization for his show and, even after overcall investments are sent in, it exceeds his estimate, then he, personally, is usually liable for the difference. There are more than a few sad stories along Broadway about "hit" shows that never earned back their capitalization even after several years of capacity business. Why? Because cost-revenue estimations failed to take variable costs into account and so actual profits turned out to be only a tiny fraction of the total revenue. Investors in such shows are not likely to support the same producer again.

In the nonprofit organization, if there is a surplus at the end of the year the institution, the private foundations and the government agencies that supported it will most probably cut their support in the following year. If there is a large deficit, they may also cut their future allocations in the belief that the enterprise is badly managed. The horrifying truth about budget administration is that the administrator can be penalized just as severely for efficiency and economy as he can be for inefficiency and extravagance. What he does, then, is to make every attempt to arrive at a realistic budget that will lead to only a small surplus or deficit. More cryptically, budgets for commercial ventures should produce a little surplus and budgets for nonprofit ventures should produce a little deficit!

### THE BREAK-EVEN POINT ■

In England the break-even point is called the "get-out cost," perhaps a more graphic phrase. Both refer to the amount of money required to make the first penny of profit. As has been noted, there is a difference between fixed weekly operating cost and the variable costs; the latter account for percentages that are determined by the exact revenue earned. The point at which the fixed and variable costs equal the gross income is the break-even point. If revenue exceeds the break-even point, then expenses will increase due to percentage payments. If revenue is less than the break-even point, then the actual operating cost will be lower than the break-even point. How can a break-even point be determined without first knowing the potential or actual revenue? To illustrate this in the simplest manner, let's look at a Broadway musical weekly operating budget which assumes that all percentages are paid in addition to the weekly guarantees (usually, the guarantees are paid *against* percentages).

| Item | Fixed Cost (plus) | Variable Cost |
|------|------|------|
| Theatre rent | $ 4,000 | 25% |
| Star | 2,500 | 10% |
| Lyricist | 750 | 2% |
| Composer | 1,000 | 3% |
| Director | 500 | 2% |
| Author (book) | 1,000 | 5% |
| Total of all other weekly operating costs. | $40,250 | 0% |
| Total weekly operating costs | $50,000 (plus) | 47% (of the actual gross) |

This budget shows that the fixed weekly operating cost is $50,000. But the producing company must take in well over that amount in weekly revenue in order to show a profit, due to the 47 percent variable cost. The formula below provides a way to compute the actual operating cost (the break-even point). It divides the fixed cost by what may be called the marginal income ratio (meaning the margin of profit that can be gained after variable costs are paid. In this example the producer has given away 47 percent of every dollar that will be taken in at the box office, leaving a 53 percent marginal income).

$$\frac{\text{Fixed cost (\$50,000)}}{\text{Marginal Income Ratio (53\%)}} = \text{Break-even Point}$$

or: $50,000 ÷ .53 = $94,340

proof:

| | | |
|---|---|---|
| Gross Income | | $94,340 |
| Variable Cost (47%) | $44,340 | |
| Fixed Costs | 50,000 | |
| Total Costs | | 94,340 |
| Profit or loss | | 000 |

If the total potential weekly gross at the theatre where this musical is playing is $106,000, then at capacity business the show can earn a $6,180 weekly profit—but only after the capitalization, or preopening expenses, have been paid off. If the actual production cost (preopening expense) is $250,000, then the show must play at capacity gross for over forty weeks before any true profit can be realized. Notice that although the producer and his backers must wait until the capitalization is repaid before they earn a profit, the theatre landlord, the star and others begin to earn their percentages from the first ticket sold. Notice, again, that actual operating costs of a production vary according to the actual box office income. If the total weekly potential gross is $106,000 but the *actual* weekly gross is $95,000, then the actual cost for that week will be $94,650 (47 percent of $95,000, plus the $50,000 fixed cost) which leaves a fat $350 in weekly profit! If the show opens at and maintains this $95,000 weekly gross, it will take over 714 weeks merely to pay off a $250,000 capital investment. Once a weekly gross falls below the break-even gross of $94,340 the show is losing money. Is it any wonder that so few Broadway productions ever "recoup the nut"?

To reduce these figures in terms of profit dividends (assuming that the producer shares profits equally with his limited partners) at a $95,000 weekly gross the producer can earn no more than $175 per week after 714 weeks or 14 years of waiting (plus all the time he spent on the show before it opened). And the man who bought a 10 percent investment in that show (providing $2,500 of the total $250,000 capitalization) can earn no more than $17.50 per week (10 percent of $175). Let's hope they both share in a multi-million dollar sale of the show to a movie company!

The length of time it will take to pay back the capitalization for our Broadway musical at capacity business can be pictured more graphically. (See page 204).

A similar graph can be constructed to show the cost-revenue relationship for a college or community theatre production. Here the basic unit of measurement is the single performance valued at $1,000 in total potential revenue.

In other words, with $4,000 in production and operating costs, this production has the potential to break-even after four performances, after which all revenue will represent a profit.

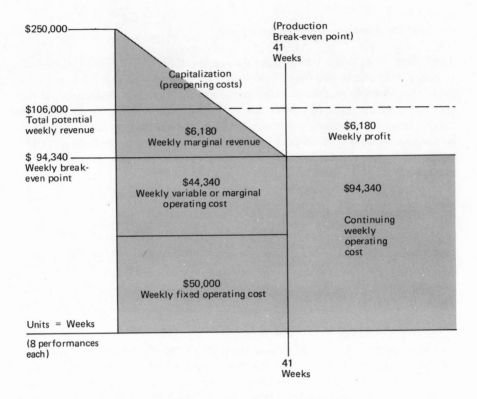

$250,000 ─

(Production
Break-even point)
41
Weeks

Capitalization
(preopening costs)

$106,000 ─
Total potential
weekly revenue

$6,180
Weekly marginal revenue

$6,180
Weekly profit

$ 94,340 ─
Weekly break-
even point

$44,340
Weekly variable or marginal
operating cost

$94,340

Continuing
weekly
operating
cost

$50,000
Weekly fixed operating cost

Units = Weeks

(8 performances
each)

41
Weeks

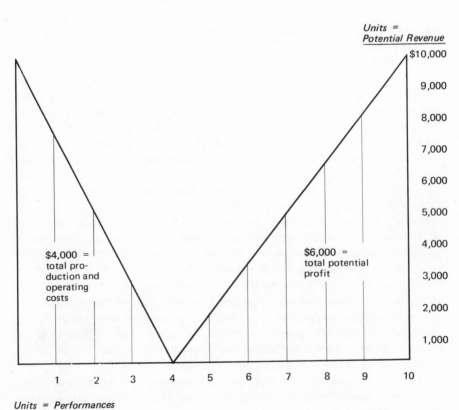

Units =
Potential Revenue

$10,000

9,000

8,000

7,000

6,000

5,000

4,000

$4,000 =
total pro-
duction and
operating
costs

$6,000 =
total potential
profit

3,000

2,000

1,000

1   2   3   4   5   6   7   8   9   10

Units = Performances

The previous graphs are based on the assumption that variable costs may be computed from the first dollar of revenue—in other words, the playwright and others all earn a flat percentage from the bottom dollar. In some circumstances, however, percentages are paid on a system of graduating revenue: 5 percent of the first $10,000 in revenue, then 7 percent of the next $15,000 and so forth. When this is the case, the marginal income ratio may be estimated by using the *average* of all the percentages that are involved.

### THE STOP CLAUSE ▪

Most tenants who rent a building negotiate a lease that allows occupancy for a specified length of time at a specified rental. Off Broadway leases usually require the tenant to guarantee rent payment for four to eight weeks. If the production closes after the first week, the tenant still pays that guaranteed amount. For this reason, the Off Broadway landlord may hope to rent his theatre to a number of different productions that flop in rapid succession. Ideally, he hopes to get six or eight weeks rent for every week of the season—an ideal that hardly favors the Off Broadway producer. The Broadway landlord, in marked contrast, is a participant in the gross income with the tenant-producer and has every hope that the tenant production will be a long-running hit.

In contrast to a conventional lease, a Broadway theatre license calls for a percentage of the box office take *against* a low minimum guaranteed rental fee. Rarely is there a specified date when the production must vacate the theatre. The date when the production *will* leave the theatre is usually determined by the so-called stop clause.

The stop clause is a provision in the Broadway theatre license stipulating that when weekly box office revenue falls below a certain figure (usually for two consecutive weeks) either the landlord or the producer may terminate the lease. Termination notice must be given within so many days after the gross has dropped below that predetermined figure. The question is, what box office figure should be used in the stop clause? If the weekly break-even point is projected at $94,340, perhaps that figure should be used, because the producer doesn't wish to lose money. On the other hand, what if bad weather or illness of the star or some other occurrence results in business that is only temporarily bad? The producer obviously doesn't wish to give the theatre-owner the right to close his production. In most cases, therefore, the Broadway producer selects a figure slightly below the break-even point. The reasoning is that, while he can sustain a loss for a few weeks, if business is going to be permanently bad, it will probably get worse quickly. If receipts fall to $80,000 one week they will probably fall much lower the following week and lower still the week after that. But if the producer must sustain a continuing weekly loss, he is in trouble. After the capitalization has been exhausted and previous profits spent, further losses probably must be paid by the producer himself. Hence, the importance of the stop clause.

---

People who can successfully project profits and losses do not depend on occult powers or magical formulas. They depend on experience, knowledge and a degree of intuition. An intelligent projection of costs together with a projection of revenue for a project should provide the basis for decision-making. Measured against this projection, a person is able to classify each decision he makes as (1) cautious, (2) reasonable or (3) risky. There is certainly no law against making risky decisions—and many success stories are based on such action—but it is stupid and needless not to know *how* risky a decision may be.

There are many factors, some obvious and some hidden, that influence costs and revenue. The best business manager for an organization is the one who is familiar not only with general business practices but, perhaps more important, with the art and the organization that he is managing and the community in which it is operating. Business managers and their financial projections frequently provide facts and opinions that nobody wants to hear. But, as with physicians, one is foolish to avoid or ignore their advice.

# CHAPTER TEN

# Controlling the Cost

Economists and accountants have devised cost control systems to suit the needs and peculiarities of every type of theatre organization. Of course, any system is only as good as the personnel who execute it. Most important of all is the comptroller or supervisor of the system. In the theatre this supervisor is usually called the business manager. Whether he works full time or part time, whether he is the same person as the producer or the director, whether or not he is a Johnnie-come-lately to the business of theatre, he is always a key figure in the producing organization.

## ▪ THE BUSINESS MANAGER

### QUALIFICATIONS ▪

A theatrical business manager is charged with the responsibility of organizing and supervising the income and outflow of money. Because his daily routine is keeping books, paying bills, making deposits or supervising such activities, the business manager usually has the most accurate picture of the organization's financial health, so his advice should be sought and heeded on many matters. A business manager should not merely be a bookkeeper, he should be regarded as a partner in the enterprise for which he is working. He should see it as his duty to facilitate the realization of the organization's goals. He should be able to make knowledgeable statements about what is and what is not possible from a financial viewpoint, never unnecessarily bothering others about detail. For example, if the producer or director asks if a certain actor can be paid by certified check, the answer should not include a discourse on the difficulties of doing this. To be certain of the statements he makes, the business manager must at all times have a clear idea of the current assets and liabilities of the organization and of the many factors that may affect them in the near term. Large operations require a full-time business manager, while smaller ones usually combine the position with that of producer or general manager. It is not wise to allocate business management functions to the stage director (although it is sometimes unavoidable, especially in educational and amateur theatres, where a single, full-time person must assume all leadership responsibilities). Good business management requires an overview and objectivity that the person intimately involved in directing a production is usually unable to assume. A good business manager is interested in his work, as well as the work of the theatre organization, and he is willing and able to pay attention to the myriad details that make things run smoothly, establish financial soundness and make everybody's job easier and more secure.

### DUTIES ■

Aside from being an assistant and adviser to the general manager, the producer, the artistic director or the board of directors (depending upon how the organization is structured), the business manager should be responsible for the following aspects of the operation:

1. The box office
2. Banking
3. Insurance
4. Budgeting
5. Purchasing
6. Taxes
7. Payroll
8. Accounting
9. Fulfilling contract and license obligations
10. Union negotiations and contracts

The business manager should be the direct supervisor of all staff members concerned with the above areas, with one exception. If an independent accountant or accounting firm is retained, it should conduct periodic audits and submit financial reports directly to the board of directors or head of the organization. This provides a check on the business manager; not only on his honesty, but upon his way of doing things and upon his judgment.

The business manager serves in many ways as a public relations representative. It is important to establish and maintain good will with unions, vendors, bankers, creditors, insurance companies, foundations, grants agencies and local authorities, just as it is to have the good will of the audience. In fact, the audience will include many people with whom the theatre conducts business. The business manager, more than anyone else in the organization, is the theatre's day-to-day spokesman to the local power structure upon which the theatre depends. If, for example, merchants and the banking element of the local community are angered and opposed to the local theatre, the life of that theatre will be an unhappy if not an impossible one. The business manager must, therefore, create an image of efficiency and responsibility on behalf of the theatre. Businessmen outside the arts tend to be skeptical about theatre organizations, about their seriousness as business enterprises, about their chances for success, about their very worth. It is probably true to say that a farm or a factory would automatically be given a higher credit rating by a bank or a vendor than a legitimate theatre would. So the business manager's job is not easy. If he can articulate the goals and values of the theatre for which he works and can demonstrate its sense of fiscal and legal responsibility, he is a priceless asset. Also, as a leading management spokesman to performing artists themselves the business manager has an obligation to demonstrate trust and goodwill in his dealings with them.

TOOLS ▪

The business office of a theatre should occupy a separate room that affords privacy, security and quiet. This is especially true if it is a room in which money is counted and stored or in which payroll checks are distributed (Actors' Equity, in fact, requires that its members be paid somewhere out of public view and not be required to stand in line at a box office window). If box office income is counted in this room, it should be directly next to the box office with a door connecting the two. People who are required to work with figures should, at very least, be located away from noise and interruption.

The equipment, tools and supplies required by a business office of a moderately active theatre are obvious to any person qualified to work in one. But such items can be expensive—a fact that should be kept in mind when the budget is being determined.

# ▪ METHODS OF BUDGET CONTROL

### BUDGET MEETINGS AND CONFERENCES ▪

Managers of ongoing theatres should hold a general business meeting at the beginning of each year or season at which the business manager instructs the entire staff about business, payroll, purchasing, payment, inventory and budgetary procedures. Who is authorized to make purchases? How will the payroll be distributed? What checks and balances have been devised to control purchases and supplies? Answers to these and other questions should be known by the entire staff.

Once an annual or seasonal budget has been determined, another set of budget meetings should be arranged in connection with each production. All such meetings should be held sufficiently in advance so that production plans can be changed, modified or abandoned according to budgetary realities. One of the most important factors in budget control is that of time. The less time allowed between the planning and the execution of a project, the less control there will be in relation to that project (this applies to controlling the quality, the personnel and the organization of the project as well as the expenditures related to them).

Budgets should not be composed in secret by a single person. They should result from the thoughts, suggestions and experiences of all key people, all people eventually responsible for accomplishing the project. If the supervisor of some department (which is to say of some part of the budget) believes from the outset that he cannot execute his responsibilities with the money allocated to him, this should be made known to the business manager, who must then reexamine both the budget and the supervisor's plans: one of the two is unrealistic. One of the two must be changed in some way. If a person does not believe he can work within the boundaries established for him, it is fairly certain that he will exceed those boundaries or do a poor job.

Different people have different idiosyncracies about the use of money. Some have little concept of thrift; others jeopardize the project to spare the penny. Some work best with clearly defined budget allocations; others do not. Some spend everything allocated to them, on general principle; others do not. Some consistently overestimate costs; others underestimate them. Hence, the business manager must analyze the working habits of each department head and establish a business relationship based on that person's outlook toward budgeting and spending. Different supervisors in an organization may be treated in different ways, some given more leeway and trust in financial matters than others.

In all cases, the business manager must maintain contact with the people responsible for spending budget allocations. When emergencies or unexpected expenses arise that change cost and revenue projections, then special business conferences must be arranged to discuss possible adjustments. The business manager must establish credibility among staff members so that his statements will be trusted and his advice followed.

### REQUISITIONS ■

Small organizations in which all financial control rests in the hands of a single person can dispense with many formalities that are necessary for larger businesses. Requisitions and purchase orders should not exist merely to frustrate people. They should serve as tools of record-keeping, planning and cost control. A requisition is a request for the purchase of something and should be submitted sufficiently in advance to allow time for the business manager to "shop around" and secure bids for the requested items. Meaningful cost control only exists up to the moment a commitment is made to purchase something. The business of haggling over payments once these payments have come due is unsavory and should also be unnecessary if goods and services are properly negotiated to begin with and, of course, if they are delivered as bargained.

In each department of a theatre operation only one person should be authorized to submit requisition forms to the business manager or the head of the organization. Standard requisition forms can be purchased in stationery stores or a theatre may design its own form to suit its particular purchasing and bookkeeping system. The form on page 211 is typical.

### PURCHASE ORDERS ■

While a requisition is a request, a purchase order is an offer to buy. The business manager probably should be the only person authorized to sign purchase orders, to insure that his office will know about all purchases as they are made and determine whether or not they fit budgetary goals. All vendors with whom the theatre does business on a "charge" basis should be informed in writing that no charges will be honored without a purchase order signed by an authorized agent of the theatre. After signing a purchase order, the business office should retain a copy of the order for eventual comparison with the vendor's bill. Purchase orders should be in triplicate,

# No. R 241766

## GENERAL REQUISITION

IMPORTANT - SEND COPIES OF ALL CORRESPONDENCE, SPECIFICATIONS AND QUOTATIONS WITH THIS REQUISITION.

FOR PURCHASING DEPT. USE ONLY

| VENDOR | * | STORES | | P.O. NO. |

FURNISH TO

DEPARTMENT

CHARGE TO

VENDOR

ADDRESS

CITY

SHIPPING - INSTRUCTIONS

WHEN REQUIRED

| DEPT. MUST ANSWER | |
|---|---|
| ORDERED | DELIVERED |
| NO | YES | NO | YES |
| | | | |

DATE

AUTHORIZED SIGNATURE

TERMS*

F.O.B.*

| QUANTITY | UNIT | STOCK NO. SUGGESTED VENDOR | DESCRIPTION OF ITEM | UNIT PRICE* | AMOUNT* |
|---|---|---|---|---|---|
| | | | | | |
| | | | | | |
| | | | | | |
| | | | | | |
| | | | | | |

PURCHASED BY                    DATE

BUDGET APPROVAL                 DATE

FILLED BY                       DATE

RECEIVED BY                     DATE

*REQUISITIONER TO FILL IN IF KNOWN

COPY NO. 1 - PURCHASE REQUISITION

GENERAL REQUISITION

allowing a copy for the purchaser to keep, one for the vendor to keep and a third for the vendor to mail along with his bill. The use of purchase orders tends to eliminate hasty purchasing. In the heat of dress rehearsal, for example, a designer, director or properties master may be tempted to rush out and buy items that are later discarded or left unused. While quick purchases are often necessary, a system that requires approval from the business office helps to make people think twice. Also, it gives the business office a chance to suggest the best or least expensive places to purchase an item or, in many cases, to discover that the item is already on hand or can be borrowed or substituted for with another item. A typical payment order form is shown on page 213.

### TAX-EXEMPT FORMS ∎

All public and many private nonprofit corporations are exempt from state and local sales taxes. To qualify for this exemption, however, the organization must be listed as nonprofit with the appropriate departments of taxation and in most jurisdictions it must present a tax-exempt form to each vendor with which it does business (so they, in turn, have proof for their own tax records). This tax-exempt form must show the name and address of the tax-free organization and must carry the signature of an authorized representative and show his title. The business managers of civic and educational theatres should instruct all personnel to obtain a signed tax-exempt form before they make cash purchases or charges. Inadvertent payment of sales tax can amount to a sizable sum.

### COMPARATIVE BUDGET ANALYSIS ∎

A budget should be examined and analyzed (1) before it is adopted, (2) during the period when it is in effect and (3) after all the actual costs are known. Once preliminary cost estimates are in, these estimates should be checked against current retail prices and services to be sure they are realistic. Department heads should be given an opportunity to think about their estimates and be certain they can work within those figures. If the budget in question applies to a theatrical production or season, at least once during the preproduction period or halfway through the season, a comparative budget should be drawn up, showing actual costs subtracted from budgeted costs and then showing the unexpended balance. Does this balance appear sufficient to cover the costs necessary to complete the project? Do the original estimations appear too high or too low? Can the organization anticipate a budget surplus or deficit? Is it necessary to take corrective measures? A comparative budget form, showing both estimated revenue and estimated costs for a seasonal theatre operation, might appear as on page 214. Two more columns could be included on this form to allow a final analysis at the completion of the project. Column (F) could show "Final Action for Project" and column (G) "Difference Between Original Estimation and Final Figures." Original, interim and final budget reports such as this are usually requested when a theatre receives foundation or government assistance or when it is tied to a larger institution that provides an annual budget allotment. Comparative budget sheets provide a clear and easy method by which an organization may examine its financial status and improve future budget-planning.

PURCHASE VOUCHER

N? 890

Date

FROM

TO: SUPPLIER

Name

Address

This voucher issued to

Furnish the following:

Your Invoice
Must Show
Our Order
Number

| Quantity | DESCRIPTION | TOTAL |
|----------|-------------|-------|

Show:

Account:

Approved by

### VARIANCE ANALYSIS ■

An effective management tool for evaluating the financial performance of a business organization and its component departments is to make a comparison between actual costs and budgeted costs. This comparative analysis is called a variance report. Its purpose is to compare budgetary projections with actual costs and revenue to determine a variance or differential and thereby to judge the accuracy or inaccuracy of earlier estimates. In large and complex business organizations management often decides where to focus its investigations by locating the greatest variances. For instance, a general variance report (estimated vs. actual costs) might show that overall costs for an operation are currently exceeding the overall estimates (see Chart A). One would then wish to see detailed variance reports for each area or department in the operation. Then it will become obvious exactly where the greatest variance occurs. Let's say that the cost for scenery was estimated at $1,000, but $1,800 was actually spent. Perhaps the scenery budget included funds for lumber, muslin, paints, hardware and lighting equipment. By examining the costs in each of these specified areas, it is seen that the overage occurred largely in regard to lumber, which cost much more than anticipated (see Chart B). The scene designer and technical director may then be asked why this happened. Perhaps it was because more scenery was required than originally planned, because lumber prices were misjudged, because lumber was stolen from the scenic shop or because costly mistakes were made in construction. Whatever the cause for the variance, it should be known to management and corrective procedures should be instituted as quickly as possible.

#### SAMPLE BUDGET ANALYSIS SHEET

| ITEMS | (A) Original Estimation | (B) Actual to Date | (C) Balance | (D) Estimate to Complete | (E) Difference |
|---|---|---|---|---|---|
| 1. Box Office Income | | | | | |
| 2. Concessions Income | | | | | |
| 3. Grants and Contributions | | | | | |
| TOTAL REVENUE | | | | | |
| 4. Less: Total Operating Expenses | | | | | |
| 5. Surplus or (Deficit) | | | | | |

### INVENTORIES ■

Everything that belongs to a theatrical organization should be listed in an inventory, and copies of all inventories should be kept in the business office as well as in a fireproof safe or vault. For insurance purposes it is helpful to send inventories of all insured items (together with the dollar value of each item) to the insurance company. As valuable equipment or items are added, the insurance company should be notified. Especially when the physical assets of a theatre are extensive or when items are stored in a variety of different places, appropriate inventories should be available to department heads who may then easily check to see what is on hand and what is not. The properties department, for example, should not have to rummage through five cluttered storage rooms to determine whether or not the theatre owns a seltzer bottle! Each department head should be responsible for keeping its inventory list up to date. At the beginning and end of each season the department head, together with a representative from the business office, should check the inventory. Then department heads should be made responsible for all items on the list, within the boundaries of common sense. A master carpenter, for instance, is more likely to worry about locking up shop tools and retrieving them at the end of each day if he knows that he will be penalized for missing tools. Even when no financial penalty is imposed for missing or broken items, it is good business practice to check the inventory list with the appropriate staff member before that person is given his final pay check or before he ends his employment.

## CHART A
## SAMPLE VARIANCE REPORT
### (College Theatre Production)

| ITEM | ESTIMATED COST | ACTUAL COST | DIFFERENTIAL |
|---|---|---|---|
| Tickets | $ 45.00 | $ 47.63 | $ 2.63 (over) |
| Publicity | 150.00 | 162.00 | 12.00 (over) |
| Programs | 200.00 | 150.00 | 50.00 under |
| Costumes | 350.00 | 164.32 | 185.68 under |
| Scenery and Props | 1,000.00 | 1,800.00 | 800.00 (over) |
| Trucking | 50.00 | 21.59 | 28.41 under |
| Lighting | 25.00 | 0 | 25.00 under |
| Royalty | 130.00 | 130.00 | 0 ( − ) |
| Makeup | 50.00 | 18.47 | 31.53 under |
| Scripts | 30.00 | 28.19 | 1.81 under |
| House Manager | 100.00 | 85.80 | 14.20 under |
| Sound | 2.00 | 0 | 2.00 under |
| Reserve Fund | 200.00 | 200.00 | 0 ( − ) |
| TOTALS | $2,332.00 | $2,808.00 | $476.00 (over)* |

*Note: While scenery costs were $800.00 higher than estimated, savings in other areas and the use of the $200.00 reserve fund brings the final differential to only $476.00.

## CHART B
## SAMPLE VARIANCE REPORT ON SCENERY EXPENSES
### (College Theatre Production, as per Chart A)

| VENDOR | ITEM | Est. Cost | Actual Cost | Differential |
|---|---|---|---|---|
| ABC Lumber Co. | lumber | $ 155.00 | $ 313.60 | (158.60) |
| ABC Lumber Co. | lumber | | 472.00 | (472.00) |
| Acme Color Co. | scene paint | 25.00 | 25.50 | ( .50) |
| J & J Rental Co. | prop rentals | 200.00 | 325.00 | (125.00) |
| Joe's Hardware | nails, braces, etc. | 58.70 | 61.20 | ( 2.50) |
| Lighting Associates | gels | 15.80 | 15.80 | − |
| Local Electrics Co. | projector rental | 200.00 | 200.00 | − |
| B & B Fabrics Co. | muslin | 75.50 | 75.50 | − |
| Transfer Assoc. | prop transport | 100.00 | 100.00 | − |
| Miscellaneous | | 170.00 | 211.40 | ( 41.40) |
| TOTALS | | $1,000.00 | $1,800.00 | $800.00 (over) |

Expendable and salable items must also be inventoried: the cash on hand in the box office, postage stamps, theatre tickets, candy and soda in concession booths operated by the theatre and so forth. Remaindered items (unsold tickets, unused money, unsold candy bars) should be checked periodically against cash receipts. Obviously, when the records do not balance, an investigation should be conducted. A method of auditing the box office (with an inventory control technique for theatre tickets) is provided in Appendix D. If a theatre operates a vending concession within the theatre building, it should utilize a concession sales form to be maintained and checked not by sales personnel but by the business office of the theatre. The form on page 217 may be used whether the theatre operates the concession directly or leases it for a rental fee determined by the volume of sales.

# ▪ METHODS OF PAYMENT

### WHEN AND HOW TO PURCHASE ▪

"Haste makes waste" is a proverb especially applicable to the business of purchasing. Although theatre production necessarily involves quick decisions and crises that are impossible to anticipate, when theatre is run in a hasty manner *most* of the time it is badly planned and badly managed. Purchasing and payment flexibility are necessary to cope with the inevitable emergencies and needs of a theatre, but this does not negate an equally important need for more deliberate methods of purchasing and payment. As any housewife knows, the longer one has to shop around for a particular item the better and less expensive the purchase is likely to be. Hence, the wisdom of requisitions and purchase orders. The most common means of securing goods for less than full retail prices include:

1. Bulk order purchases
2. "Off-season" purchases
3. Purchases under long-term contract
4. Purchases during sales, specials and auctions
5. Purchases as part of some type of reciprocal agreement

Once an item or service has been selected, there are often a choice of ways to pay for it. Delayed payment may involve interest or service charges that mount up to a considerable sum over a period of time. Prompt payment may be rewarded by special discounts taken off the purchase price (often the case with advertising bills).

### PROCESSING THE PAYMENT ▪

When the business office of the theatre receives a bill (original invoice), it should observe the following procedures:

1. Check the bill for mathematical accuracy
2. Check the bill against the purchase order. (Did the vendor supply what was ordered?)
3. Check the purchase order against the requisition. (Did the order request what was requisitioned?)
4. Check to be certain the merchandise or service was received in proper condition. (To accomplish this in a large operation, a "Receiver of Goods" form may be sent to the appropriate theatre supervisor who will then verify or disclaim that the merchandise or service was actually received. In effect, this is a "Lab Report.")
5. Issue a check in payment of the invoice

Concessionaire _____    Week Ending _____

| ITEM | MERCHANDISE RECEIVED | | | | | | | | Opening Inventory This Week | Less Closing Inventory | Allow-able Credits | Total Unit Sales | Unit Selling Price | AMOUNT OF SALES |
|---|---|---|---|---|---|---|---|---|---|---|---|---|---|---|
| | Mon | Tues | Wed | Thurs | Fri | Sat | Sun | Total | | | | | | |
| | | | | | | | | | | | | | | |
| | | | | | | | | | | | | | | |
| | | | | | | | | | | | | | | |
| TOTALS | | | | | | | | | | | | | | |

CONCESSIONS SALES SUMMARY

Payments should be made only from original invoices or bills, never from statements sent by the vendor. Payment by check allows more time than cash payment for the business office to study bills, to examine the service or merchandise, to compare bills with purchase orders and to correct mistakes or problems before final payment is made. Mistakes in billing are much more commonplace than might be thought. This is as true in regard to bills composed by computers for large utility companies as for bills composed by the scrawling pen of a Yankee merchant in the local drugstore. In fact, computerized billing systems are *more likely* to be incorrect and are much more difficult to remedy than those made by human hands.

### THE PETTY CASH FUND ▪

A petty cash fund is essential for all theatre operations. Small operations need only maintain a single petty cash fund, while more complex organizations must maintain petty cash funds for numerous departments. It is often a temptation to pay for certain items with box office money, placing a voucher or chit in the box office cash drawer whenever money is needed. This may work well in some instances, but it adds one more possibility for error in accounting for box office cash and should be avoided when possible. The better method is to keep a petty cash box in the business office, from which small amounts may be paid in exchange for signed and itemized vouchers. When the fund is almost depleted an overall accounting should be made (placing all the vouchers in a large envelope) and a check drawn in the total amount to replenish the fund. Institutional budgets refer to this as the "imprest fund," small allotments of money advanced to be accounted for later by the presentation of receipts. Instead of requiring each person in the theatre to come to the business office every time he needs a few dollars, each person involved in making frequent and small cash purchases should be allotted his own limited petty cash fund. (Or, of course, he may be asked to spend the limited amount from his own pocket and be reimbursed later upon presentation of the receipts.) The publicity director, the properties master and the stage director are the ones most likely to need their own petty cash fund. Periodically, at the end of a production or according to need, such people should submit all their accumulated vouchers and receipts, and only then should their petty cash fund be replenished.

### TYPES OF CHECKING ACCOUNTS ▪

At the very least, most theatres need two different checking accounts, each with its separate checkbook, account number and name. These are:

1. Box office account
2. General checking account

The box office account should begin each fiscal year with a balance of 0 dollars and thereafter receive only those deposits that represent ticket income. All ticket income should be deposited into this account, so that an exact record of paid ticket sales is maintained. In the case of a single production project, the final balance in the account should be exactly the same as the final total gross on the box office statement. For theatres that operate a multi-production season, the cleanest way to maintain records is to transfer (by check) the total weekly gross or individual production performance gross out of the box office account into the general account. At the end of the season the account should be back to exactly 0 (excluding bank service charges). Of course, management may take a "loan" from box office funds or extract money for a variety of reasons, but the less active the box office account, the less chance there will be of difficulties when it comes time to reconcile the box office statements with the actual income. One fundamental principle should always be observed, namely, that all box office income *must* be deposited into a separate box office account before it is disbursed for any reason at any time. Another principle of theatrical financing deserves reiteration at this point: Avoid spending money that represents income for advance ticket sales. (If money is not removed from the box office account until *after* the performance that ticket money generated is over, this temptation is greatly diminished.)

The general account should be that from which all financial obligations are paid. Large organizations may wish to divide this into several accounts for various purposes and may also maintain savings accounts. It may be helpful for some theatres to open a payroll bank account separate from the general account, or a separate checkbook may be used that draws payroll money from the general account.

As a matter of course, when a theatre maintains several checking and savings accounts, it is good practice to use several different banks. This is helpful in establishing credit ratings and good relations with the business community. Each checking account should use different colored checks to avoid mistakes and confusion in the business office. All checks should provide space on the left-hand side to itemize or describe the transaction. Payroll checks should provide a detachable stub with preprinted spaces where gross wages, taxes and other deductions may be itemized.

## ▪ PAYROLL PROCEDURES

It is good practice to enter into a written agreement with all employees. If the worker belongs to a union recognized by management, that worker will be required to sign a written contract. But this is not always the case by any means. Many employees, part-time workers and casual laborers have no employment protection. Still the employer-employee relationship is mutually dependent. A letter of agreement that specifies salary and other compensation, work hours and other employee obligations should be signed by both parties. For one thing, this will help either party to terminate the employment when this becomes necessary or desirable and, for another, it keeps the relationship on a businesslike rather than a personal level. Too many people have learned the hard way that an "unwritten" or "gentleman's" agreement is no agreement at all.

### CASH PAYROLLS ▪
When employees are paid in cash, a single check should be drawn from the general account for the total net amount of the cash payroll. The business office may then instruct the local bank (in writing) to divide the total into appropriate cash amounts. The bank may request the organization to fill out pay envelopes, showing each employee's name and the amount of his salary, but most banks are willing to insert cash into the individual envelopes. Upon receipt of the envelope, the employee should be

required to count the money and then sign a payroll sheet or receipt to indicate that he has received the correct amount.

### THE W-4 FORM ▪

The business office obtains basic payroll information from the W-4 form, required by the federal government, which each employee must fill out and submit to the business office. It requires the employee to state his name, permanent address, social security number and the number of exemptions he is claiming. This is a mandatory procedure and necessary in order for the employer to prepare payroll tax returns and W-2 forms (showing the gross annual amount earned by each employee) at the end of each year.

### THE INDEPENDENT CONTRACTOR ▪

An independent contractor is a person or group paid by fee from which no tax deductions are made. The responsibility for paying all income taxes, therefore, falls on the independent contractor and not upon the employer. The independent contractor must, nevertheless, fill out and submit a W-4 form and must sign a statement certifying that he is working as an independent contractor. The obvious advantage of this for the employer is that he need not pay the matching tax and social security contributions that are required in all other cases. Many stars and artists who earn large amounts of money work as independent contractors, forming their own corporation into which all their earnings are deposited. In such cases, the fee is made payable directly to the corporation and the corporation then becomes responsible for declaring its earnings and paying taxes at the end of each year. This system often provides an individual with a more advantageous tax situation than if he worked for a regular salary, but only when very large earnings are involved. The employer who pays independent contractor fees must indicate this on Form 1099 when filing his tax records with the government at the end of each year.

Strictly speaking, the Internal Revenue Service does not regard any individual as an independent contractor unless he is incorporated (such as an accounting firm or an architectural or consulting firm) and working for the corporation. This means that all people working under union contracts and *all* casual or part-time laborers are employees, subject to employee tax laws. If an unincorporated person who is not legally authorized to receive a fee as an independent contractor is discovered, and if that person fails to pay the appropriate taxes, the employer may be held liable both for the employee wage deductions and the employer's wage tax contribution. And this frequently happens because a nontaxed, ex-employee applies for unemployment benefits.

### DEPOSITORY RECEIPTS FOR WITHHELD TAXES ▪

A federal depository receipt, which is Treasury Department Form 450, is a record of payroll taxes turned over to the federal government by the employer. The total federal withheld taxes should be paid to the Federal Reserve Bank or to a depository bank at the end of each payroll week. The payment should be made by check, drawn from the general account, and sent to the bank with a completed Form 450, which will show the employer's name, address and registration number and the amount being paid.

**WITHHOLDING TAX AND SOCIAL SECURITY FORMS** ■

By the end of each month after the close of each calendar quarter, Form 941 must be filed. By January 31 of the following year, law requires that Form W-2 be filed for each employee. In order to facilitate this an individual payroll record should be kept for each employee. (See the form that follows.)

The business office and the accountant should obtain and make a permanent note of its (1) Employer's Registration Number, (2) Federal Insurance Contribution Identification Number and (3) State Unemployment Insurance Identification Number.

**UNEMPLOYMENT FORMS** ■

All states require that employees be furnished with a record of their employment upon termination of that employment. The form on which this information is given varies from state to state: they are obtained from the state Unemployment Insurance Commission. It is wise to attach this form to the employee's final paycheck as it will be necessary for the employee to show it in the event that he applies for unemployment compensation. When this occurs, the state in which he applies will send a notice to the employer requesting verification of the employment period and salary. This must be returned within a specified number of days, after which time a penalty is imposed upon the employer.

**FAILURE TO SUBMIT WITHHELD TAXES** ■

The Internal Revenue Code imposes a 100 percent penalty on a corporation that knowingly and intentionally fails to pay the government the taxes it has withheld from salaries, plus the employer's tax contributions. (The manager is held personally liable for such monies. Even bankruptcy does not discharge the liability he has in regard to employee tax payments.) At no time should a corporation attempt to use withheld tax money for operating expenses or any other purpose. The wisdom of transferring withheld tax money to a Federal Reserve Bank at the end of each week is that the employer will not then be tempted to budget that money for any other purpose. The Internal Revenue Service vigorously enforces the collection of taxes and is quick to impose a penalty upon defaulting corporations.

**PAYROLL SHEETS** ■

Any theatre that maintains a salaried staff and is responsible for administering the payroll should keep its payroll records on a payroll sheet that is devised to suit its specific needs. The entries on this sheet will vary, depending upon the state and city in which the theatre is located and the nature of the operation. In most cases, however, a separate column on the payroll sheet will be required for each of the following types of entry:

1. *Salary code number.* Large organizations may divide employees into various categories (i.e., artists, technicians, maintenance, etc.) for budgeting purposes.
2. *Home state, number of dependents, marital status.* This information is obtained from the W-4 form. If the employee claims his residence in another state he will be exempt from local city and state taxes. The entry in this column would be something as follows: NY-4-M.
3. *Name of employee.* Check W-4 forms to be certain that employee's name

| NAME OF EMPLOYEE | | | | | | | SOCIAL SECURITY NUMBER | | |
|---|---|---|---|---|---|---|---|---|---|
| ADDRESS | | | | | | | CITY OR TOWN | | |
| DATE OF BIRTH | | MARRIED ☐ OR SINGLE ☐ | | NUMBER OF EXEMPTIONS | | | PHONE NO. | | CLOCK NO. |
| POSITION | | RATE | | DATE | | | DATE STARTED | | DATE TERMINATED |
| REMARKS | | | | | | | REASON | | |

**FIRST QUARTER 19** — **SECOND QUARTER 19**

| WEEK # | LINE # | HOURS WORKED REG. | OVER TIME | TOTAL EARNINGS | FED. OLD AGE | WITH. HOLDING TAX | STATE TAX | | | NET PAY |
|---|---|---|---|---|---|---|---|---|---|---|
| 1 | | | | | | | | | | |
| 2 | | | | | | | | | | |
| 3 | | | | | | | | | | |
| 4 | | | | | | | | | | |
| 5 | | | | | | | | | | |
| 6 | | | | | | | | | | |
| 7 | | | | | | | | | | |
| 8 | | | | | | | | | | |
| 9 | | | | | | | | | | |
| 10 | | | | | | | | | | |
| 11 | | | | | | | | | | |
| 12 | | | | | | | | | | |
| 13 | | | | | | | | | | |
| TOTAL 1ST QTR | | | | | | | | | | |
| TOTAL 3 MOS | | | | | | | | | | |

DEDUCTIONS

| WEEK # | LINE # | HOURS WORKED REG. | OVER TIME | TOTAL EARNINGS | FED. OLD AGE | WITH. HOLDING TAX | STATE TAX | | | NET PAY |
|---|---|---|---|---|---|---|---|---|---|---|
| 14 | | | | | | | | | | |
| 15 | | | | | | | | | | |
| 16 | | | | | | | | | | |
| 17 | | | | | | | | | | |
| 18 | | | | | | | | | | |
| 19 | | | | | | | | | | |
| 20 | | | | | | | | | | |
| 21 | | | | | | | | | | |
| 22 | | | | | | | | | | |
| 23 | | | | | | | | | | |
| 24 | | | | | | | | | | |
| 25 | | | | | | | | | | |
| 26 | | | | | | | | | | |
| TOTAL 2ND QTR | | | | | | | | | | |
| TOTAL 6 MOS | | | | | | | | | | |

**THIRD QUARTER 19** — **FOURTH QUARTER 19**

| WEEK # | LINE # | HOURS WORKED REG. | OVER TIME | TOTAL EARNINGS | FED. OLD AGE | WITH. HOLDING TAX | STATE TAX | | | NET PAY |
|---|---|---|---|---|---|---|---|---|---|---|
| 27 | | | | | | | | | | |
| 28 | | | | | | | | | | |
| 29 | | | | | | | | | | |
| 30 | | | | | | | | | | |
| 31 | | | | | | | | | | |
| 32 | | | | | | | | | | |
| 33 | | | | | | | | | | |
| 34 | | | | | | | | | | |
| 35 | | | | | | | | | | |
| 36 | | | | | | | | | | |
| 37 | | | | | | | | | | |
| 38 | | | | | | | | | | |
| 39 | | | | | | | | | | |
| TOTAL 3RD QTR | | | | | | | | | | |
| TOTAL 9 MOS | | | | | | | | | | |

| WEEK # | LINE # | HOURS WORKED REG. | OVER TIME | TOTAL EARNINGS | FED. OLD AGE | WITH. HOLDING TAX | STATE TAX | | | NET PAY |
|---|---|---|---|---|---|---|---|---|---|---|
| 40 | | | | | | | | | | |
| 41 | | | | | | | | | | |
| 42 | | | | | | | | | | |
| 43 | | | | | | | | | | |
| 44 | | | | | | | | | | |
| 45 | | | | | | | | | | |
| 46 | | | | | | | | | | |
| 47 | | | | | | | | | | |
| 48 | | | | | | | | | | |
| 49 | | | | | | | | | | |
| 50 | | | | | | | | | | |
| 51 | | | | | | | | | | |
| 52 | | | | | | | | | | |
| TOTAL 4TH QTR | | | | | | | | | | |
| TOTAL YEAR | | | | | | | | | | |

EMPLOYEE PAYROLL RECORD

is legal and not assumed.

4. *Base salary.* Check the contract with the employee to determine the basic contracted salary. If determined according to hours worked, a separate column should be used in which to enter those hours.
5. *Additional salary.* This should include overtime payments which, of course, are subject to payroll taxes.
6. *Total gross salary.* Total of 4 and 5.
7. *Social Security.* Money withheld for social security, which is determined as a percentage of the total wages.
8. *Federal income tax withheld.* This deduction is based on the gross salary and determined according to Circular "E" (Employer's Tax Guide, IRS Publication Guide No. 15, available from the Internal Revenue Service).
9. *State income tax withheld.* In those states that require such deductions, for those employees who reside therein.
10. *City income tax withheld.*
11. *Other deductions.* A double column should give a brief explanation of any other deductions withheld and an itemized list of such deductions as union dues, loans made to the employee by the employer, room rent, food or other charges.
12. *Total deductions.* Total of 7 through 11.
13. *Net pay.* Amount actually paid to employee.
14. *Other pay received.* This should include nontaxable fees given to the employee, such as travel expense money, rental of his costumes, etc.
15. *Total pay received.* Total of 13 and 14.
16. *Check number* if paid by check or *signature* of employee if paid in cash.

The business of computing overtime payments can be very complicated for a large theatrical organization. It is essential to keep detailed rehearsal schedules and a record of time worked by all union employees. The stage manager is required to submit daily time sheets, showing the hours worked by the performers during both rehearsal and performance periods.

**THE DAY TO PAY ▪**

Civic and educational institutions usually pay their employees on a monthly or bimonthly basis and theatre groups affiliated with them may have no responsibility for salary computation and disbursement. Theatres that employ union laborers, however, will be required to make weekly salary disbursements and to insure that employees receive their pay prior to the commencement of the final weekly performance or work day. This day is usually a Saturday or a Sunday. Because banks are not open on weekends and employees should be allowed to cash or deposit their checks when they receive them, salaries are best paid on the last banking day of the payroll week or period. Actors' Equity Association and other labor organizations require that management enable their members to cash their checks at once, on the premises where the check is issued. (Or, management may be required to pay by certified check.) This means that the employer will have to hold what may be a sizable amount of cash; it is advisable to hold it for the shortest time. The employer should acquire the payroll cash from a bank just prior to its disbursement and then redeposit the remainder im-

SAMPLE PRODUCTION PAYROLL SHEET

NAME OF THEATRE _____

| Salary Code | A. State<br>B. Number of Dependents<br>C. Marital Status | Name | Base Salary | Additional Salary | | Total Gross Pay | Security Tax Withheld | Federal Income Tax Withheld |
|---|---|---|---|---|---|---|---|---|
| | | | | Explanation | Amount | | | |
| | | | | | | | | |
| | | | | | | | | |
| | | | | | | | | |
| | | | | | | | | |

WEEK ENDING _____

SHOW _____

THEATRE _____

| New York Income Tax Withheld | New York City Tax | Other Deductions | | Total Amount of Deductions | Net Pay | Other Payments | | Total Pay Rec'd. | Signature or Check No. |
|---|---|---|---|---|---|---|---|---|---|
| | | Explanation | Amount | | | Explanation | Amount | | |
| | | | | | | | | | |
| | | | | | | | | | |
| | | | | | | | | | |
| | | | | | | | | | |

mediately. Friday, or the last banking day of the week, is the most convenient pay day for both employer and employee.

If payroll cash is sizable, the employer should arrange for the local police to escort it from the bank to the payment place (which they will do without charge) or hire a security agency to transport it. In any case, the people who transport large cash amounts should be bonded with an insurance company and the insurance should be sufficient to cover possible losses due to theft or dishonesty. Many theatres arrange for the box office to carry sufficient cash for payroll purposes and to cash salary checks during a specified time at the box office window.

The banking industry today offers many special services to corporate customers and banks can be especially helpful in assisting a corporation with its payroll obligations. For example, if weekly or monthly gross payroll amounts (plus the employer's tax contributions) are deposited with a bank, it may be able (1) to issue the salaries by check or by cash envelopes, (2) to provide a payroll record, (3) to file the quarterly returns and (4) to issue the W-4 forms at the end of the year.

# ■ METHODS OF ACCOUNTING

### THE ROLE OF THE ACCOUNTANT ■

While increases in theatrical production costs over the past few decades may be attributed in part to inflation and salary increases, the largest single increases relate to legal and accounting costs. The costs of keeping it legal and businesslike are high indeed! An accountant or accounting firm, however, is necessary for theatre operations of any size and permanence. As mentioned earlier, the accountant should be directly responsible to the producer or the board of directors. He should, nonetheless, work closely with the business manager in organizing the financial record-keeping system that best suits the theatre in question. Rather than paying an accountant or firm to do *all* the bookkeeping work, it is usually more economical to hire a bookkeeper or assign most record-keeping duties to a staff member. If this is done, the accountant (preferably a Certified Public Accountant) will be primarily concerned with filing the necessary tax forms and preparing the annual or periodic fiscal reports concerning the organization or the production. He will be concerned with reconciling the checkbooks with bank statements, with box office statements, with ticket income deposits and so forth. Where problems or discrepancies or deviations from standard operating procedures arise, he should report these directly to the producer or the board and recommend action to rectify the problem or to investigate it further. The accountant should personally supervise or conduct periodic box office audits as well as audits of the books and records.

### BOOKKEEPING ■

As we have seen, a record should be kept of all fiscal transactions. This will involve, among other chores, listing all transactions in a journal. A journal is a diary that shows in chronological order all transactions made from checkbooks and petty cash funds and also records deposits made. Working from the journal entries, the bookkeeper then posts each item or listing into a ledger. According to a chart of accounts (described in the following section), the ledger classifies each transaction, showing, for example, that it pertains to a particular type of expenditure for a particular production ("makeup supplies" for Production No. 3). Based on information in the ledger, it is comparatively easy to write variance reports and financial statements both for individual productions or departments in the theatre and for the entire fiscal year when it is over. A helpful technique is to use "railway" ledgers which provide numerous columns running across two wide pages.

### CHART OF ACCOUNTS ■

Every financial asset and liability and every type of income and expenditure for an operation should be assigned a code or line number. The numbering or coding system that is adopted should be tailored to fit the specific organization and, once adopted, should remain uniform throughout the life of that organization. The following list provides one manner in which accounts may be named and coded:

**Assets: Code 100**
To include cash assets, petty cash, accounts receivable from patrons, employees and others, returnable deposits and bonds, prepaid expenses, land, building, machinery supplies, etc.

**Liabilities and Capital: Code 200**
To include all accrued withholding and payroll taxes payable, insurance, bonds, accounts and notes payable, mortgages, capital stock, retained earnings, etc.

**Income: Code 300**
To include box office gross receipts, income from interest, concessions, program advertising, etc.

**Preopening Expenses: Code 400**
This could also be called "Preseason Expenses." It should include categories of expenses that pertain to preopening costs, rehearsal costs (if only one production is being planned; in the event of a multi-production season, rehearsal costs should be included under operating expenses), costs of opening the building, maintenance and repair expenses, general supplies, preopening advertising and publicity, preopening fees and salaries, etc.

**Operating Expenses: Code 500**
Should include all expenses related to the individual or weekly performance and building-operating costs; salaries, fees, royalties, advertising, publicity, printing, entertainment, rentals, transportation, payroll taxes and insurance, auditing and legal, etc.

**Closing Costs: Code 600**
Should include all expenses related to closing the theatre or the production; salaries and fees, legal and auditing, supplies, etc.

This system provides that each code may have one hundred subdivisions and, of course, even more if letters are also used (i.e., Code 105-a, 105-b, etc.). While coding should be specific, it should not be so complicated that to study it is like studying a foreign language. The purpose for establishing different accounts and budget lines is to facilitate fiscal analysis and to provide a clear picture of assets, liabilities, income and costs in each area. Multi-production operations should adopt a letter code for each of their productions, and this letter should be used next to each item listed under Code 500 (operating expenses). The first production would be "A," the second "B" and so forth. Hence, the ledger might show a transaction for the purchase of prop food, next to which the code might read: 567-B, meaning a properties expense (567) related to the second production (B). At the end of the season, all the "A" expenditures can be tallied up, then all the "B" expenditures and so forth, to determine the cost of each production. The totals of all preopening and all closing expenditures may then be combined and equally divided among the season's productions to determine the total operating cost of each production.

**LEGAL REQUIREMENTS** ▪

All businesses are subject to examination by the Internal Revenue Service in connection with tax liabilities and they may on occasion be required to present their fiscal records, including receipts, canceled checks and ticket stubs, to insurance companies, arbitration panels or courts of law in order to establish a claim for theft, embezzlement or bankruptcy or for a number of other similarly depressing reasons. Financial records should always be kept in safe and secure places. Unsold tickets, ticket stubs and receipts should be kept for at least three years before being destroyed and books of account and canceled checks for seven years.

**ANNUAL FISCAL REPORTS** ▪

Most producing companies and theatre organizations are required by law to prepare annual financial reports for distribution among investors, partners, directors, trustees and officers, as the case may be. Usually, such reports will be accompanied by the opinion of a Certified Public Accountant. Even modest community and amateur theatre groups should compile annual reports. The report will be a summation of earlier box office and expense reports as well as a statement of the current assets and liabilities of the organization. It may include audience attendance figures and other such statistics. It may be typewritten or prepared in a costly and elaborate brochure with photographs and illustrations. The latter type is often published by organizations that are seeking to impress investors or donors and to attract new support.

---

There is nothing particularly mysterious about good business management, but it does require special knowledge and experience. Many techniques of business management can be acquired and handled by people with no special training in business and economics, provided they seek sound advice and guidance. Because so many theatrical producers and managers refuse to learn business and accounting procedures, a great many poor decisions are made and a great deal of money is spent unnecessarily to hire accountants and other specialists. On the other hand, any business that pays taxes should retain a good CPA or accounting firm to handle at least the major responsibilities related to finance management.

# CHAPTER ELEVEN

# The Box Office

A box office is the wallet of a theatre. It must be secure, well-organized and managed with reverence for accuracy and detail. It should also be regarded as a primary factor in creating the public image of the theatre, as few things are more conspicuous to the public than the box office and the people who work in it.

## ▪ GENERAL CONSIDERATIONS

### THE LOOK OF THE BOX OFFICE ▪

While theatre architects have applied imagination and new interest to most public areas of theatre buildings constructed over the past decade, the physical layout and "feel" of the box office has remained largely untouched. Even our newest theatres contain box offices that appear small and stingy and have steel bars or glass separating the treasurers from the public, making communication difficult. Such factors reinforce the suspicion and distrust with which customers approach a box office and these feelings are obviously unhealthy for a theatre economy burdened with problems far more difficult to solve.

Perhaps box office design could benefit from an example set by the banking industry. When thousands of banks were being constructed during the Victorian era and earlier, there was need to present a fortress-like appearance in order to change a "better-to-keep-your-money-under-your-mattress" attitude to a feeling that private banking could be safe, responsible and desirable. So banks were constructed with granite and steel, decorated with locks and keys, filled with cages for each worker and with impressive vaults and dark, forbidding chambers. The image worked. Private banking grew until the stock market crash, which wiped out many banks and many bank accounts. To restore public confidence, the Federal Depository Insurance Corporation was established to protect bank accounts and, slowly, banking architecture evolved a new image to attract new business; an image of openness, friendliness, honesty and self-assurance. Down went the cages, the steel bars and the locks and up came the open counters between tellers and customers, brightly lighted interiors, carpeting and even "music to bank by"! Again, the public has confidence in private banks. And, with all the modern security devices now available, banks have confidence that steel bars and granite are simply unnecessary as well as unattractive. The American theatre, from Broadway to Berkeley, has something to learn from this example. Armed robbers will not be put off because of window bars, but customers will be.

### LOCATION ▪

A theatre box office should be easily accessible to the public, located so that customer lines at the window do not obstruct the flow of people into the auditorium at performance times and so it can be operable without having to use the main lobbies or other large areas of the theatre building. Frequently, these requirements mean that the box office must be located off an intermediary lobby between the street and the main theatre lobbies. Precautions should be taken to properly heat or cool this intermediary lobby and to protect treasurers from wind and other elements that may intrude into the box office through constantly opening and closing exterior doors. Obvious? Not to theatre architects, who have ignored such precautions so frequently that pneumonia is a professional hazard for many box office treasurers!

Ideally, the box office should adjoin the business office of the theatre or, at least, connect to an inner room without windows or public access that can be used for banking and clerical work. One public window or service counter is generally sufficient to serve a five-hundred-seat theatre and more should be added according to the same ratio. Two windows can be useful, however, even for small theatres. One may be used exclusively for advance ticket sales, the other for current performance tickets; or an additional window area may be handy for disbursing information or payroll. When the theatre is located off the beaten path, it should consider operating a box office in the local business district and also making its tickets available at various stores and agencies. A checklist of other considerations regarding box office location is provided in chapter 3.

### EQUIPMENT AND SUPPLIES ▪

Depending on the size of the operation, the number of people involved in box office work and the cash systems that are used, the following types of equipment are required for an efficient box office:

1. *Ticket racks*
   Different types are available; descriptive brochures should be obtained

from ticket printing companies, such as Globe Ticket Company in Boston or National Ticket Company in New York City. Several types of racks may may be desirable in the same box office: one for storage of numerous upcoming performances, another for more prominent display of current performance tickets. Generally, seats being held on reservation should always be kept with the other tickets for that performance; a separate rack that permits alphabetical filing of current performance reservation envelopes may be desired if such reservations are numerous.

2. *Cash drawers*
Cash drawers or cash registers, whichever are used, should be located so that the treasurer can make change without turning away from the customer. Drawers with cash and silver compartments can easily be built under the customer counters.

3. *Telephones*
The telephone system should have several lines on a roll-over system which permits only one number to be published but, if it is busy, automatically transfers the call to another of the lines on the same instrument. Again, the treasurer should not have to turn his back to customer windows in order to use the telephone. Also, an automatic answering device should be considered for use when the box office is closed; not to take messages but to give performance information and box office hours.

4. *File cabinets*
For storage of ticket order correspondence, box office statements stationery supplies, etc.

5. *Typewriter*
For business correspondence, typing of statements, etc.

6. *Adding machine.*
For computing box office statements, bank deposits, etc.

7. *Safe*
May be located in manager's office or elsewhere in the building, but should should not require that money be carried through public areas to gain access to it. Also, the safe should be secured to the floor or otherwise made immobile.

8. *Work tables*
Desks, counter spaces or work tables should be sufficient to handle the clerical work so that no box office business has to be done outside the box box office or adjoining work room.

Theatre organizations that present only a few performances each year can easily limit the box office supplies listed below, but ongoing organizations will find that most such items are necessary:

Stationery
Box office statement forms
Group sales forms
Bank deposit forms
General office and clerical supplies

Price scales
Price multiplication charts
Ticket stub boxes for ticket-takers
Calendars
Wastebaskets
Broom

### SECURITY ■

Box offices designed in the traditional manner can usually be secured by closing
the customer windows and locking a single door. If the box office is designed as a
largely open space, sliding doors or panels may be used to secure it or ticket racks
and other equipment may be designed to slide into an adjoining wall or room. Obviously, complete security is required for ticket and cash storage. Burglar alarm systems may be installed and made operative during hours when the box office is closed.
Good protection is also realized if the entire box office and the safe are visible from
a busy street through glass walls, in which case lights should remain on all night. In
one theatre, where the box office is accessible through the business office, the manager keeps a policeman's hat and club lying casually on a desk where everyone entering the office can see them. Strangers assume there is a policeman nearby! Another
inexpensive security device is the installation of a microphone in the box office with
wiring that leads to an amplifier in the night watchman's booth or even in the manager's living quarters, if these are nearby. When the box office is closed, the system is
turned on to pick up the sound of intruders.

Many theatres, especially those in busy, multi-operation facilities, employ a security guard to stand in the area of the box office during business hours and, of course,
policemen or private security agents should be used whenever large payrolls or deposits are being transported to and from the theatre. Most managers, however, stop
short at keeping guns on hand for possible use against burglars. Employees should always be instructed not to resist thieves in the event of a robbery. Naturally, as little
cash as possible should be kept on hand. Box office income should be deposited in a
bank shortly after the curtain goes up on each performance, using daytime or night
deposit bank services, whichever is necessary.

## ■ THE BOX OFFICE TREASURER

### QUALIFICATIONS ■

A box office treasurer, unlike a bank teller and most cashiers, is a salesman. He is
in a position to influence which tickets a customer buys, how many tickets are
bought and other factors that affect income. On Broadway, treasurers belong to
Local 751 (Treasurers and Tickettakers) and are contracted by the landlord, which
is somewhat unfortunate. Broadway treasurers are always anxious to work for a
house that has a smash hit, because this may enable them to earn additional income
from ticket agents and scalpers willing to pay a "commission" over the regular price
of difficult-to-get tickets. When business slows down, this income stops and the treasurer then hopes the show will close so a new hit can be brought into the theatre.
Obviously, he can be a negative influence on business so that the show will close all
the faster—hardly a happy situation for producers or for the economics of the Broad-

way stage. But the situation explains why Broadway treasurers are often less than gracious to window customers. Also, of course, commercial New York productions receive little return business because most customers see a production only once and producers rent a theatre for a single production only. Most seasoned theatregoers have had negative experiences with box office treasurers, as a consequence of which the public image of treasurers is a poor one. The Broadway theatre industry is currently considering a number of proposals that might rectify this situation in New York but, meanwhile, all ongoing theatres (especially those interested in return customer business) can take numerous steps to establish pleasant customer services at the box office.

In most stock, resident, college and community theatres, box office personnel work directly for the producer or the producing organization, so that people who are consonant with the feeling and image of the theatre can be employed. Treasurers should be good salesmen who are also honest, efficient, courteous and well-appearing. Where telephone reservations comprise an important portion of ticket sales, it is important that treasurers have a good phone voice. Treasurers need not have special training in theatre, although they should certainly possess an interest in the productions at theatres where they work. It is seldom wise to hire would-be actors, directors or other theatre workers for box office jobs, because the confinement of the work and its separation from the rest of the theatre will almost certainly increase their frustration and decrease their efficiency. The best treasurers are often year-round residents of the community in which the theatre is located: they have an essential knowledge of the area, of transportation routes and other such things. Too, they are more likely to be trusted by local customers and, when off duty, may help establish the theatre as a permanent and responsible community asset.

A knowledgeable manager can easily train box office treasurers provided they possess the right qualities and potential. A background in cashier work and salesmanship, an ability to learn and think quickly and to handle detail and maintain accuracy are important qualifications, as is a positive, friendly and attractive personality. Previous box office experience may not be essential, depending upon the type of theatre involved. Some theatres prefer to train treasurers from scratch. Experienced treasurers may resist box office systems and styles that are new to them and experience makes dishonesty and embezzlement much more difficult for a theatre to detect. It's rather like hiring a bartender: the experienced ones can serve more customers faster and use less liquor in the process (thereby increasing the profit) but there is a good possibility of dishonesty. Inexperienced bartenders may not have learned how to steal from management, but neither have they learned how to pour drinks accurately or serve quickly. Which is the lesser evil?

This chapter does not intend to imply that most treasurers are dishonest. As a rule, they are not. It is true, however, that treasurers in commercial theatres may make additional and unorthodox income by dealing with scalpers and ticket agents. But this does not constitute robbery or embezzlement in relation to money that belongs to the theatre. Treasurers should be watched, however, just as any type of cashier should be watched and made accountable for the money handled. Theatrical business managers, especially in noncommercial theatres, often display naiveté in regard to box office and accounting procedures and should be cautioned against an overly optimistic belief in the ability of the average man to resist temptation. Stories about producers who have been surprised by dishonesty range all the way from a famous embezzlement case involving ticket income for the New York production of *The Fantasticks* to a stock manager who discovered that his two treasurers—both little old ladies retired as town librarians—had robbed him blind!

Without question, an experienced treasurer can sell the more expensive tickets and in other ways increase box office income. He will know, for example, how to get people to claim their ticket reservations, how to sell every seat in the house, how to sell standing room. For busy theatres in more or less continual operation, he is essential. Smaller theatres may have more leeway in hiring treasurers and less ability to pay high salaries, but this does not mean that any box office should function inefficiently or fail to observe certain fundamental practices.

### DUTIES ▪

Treasurers' duties depend on the size of the box office staff and the type of theatre in which it functions. In all cases, one person should be appointed as head treasurer, directly responsible to the business manager or the general manager. A large theatre operation might include the following box office positions:

Head treasurer
Assistant treasurer(s)
Subscription or season tickets treasurer(s)
Mail-order treasurer(s)
Group sales treasurer(s)
Agency treasurer(s)

Small operations need only one or two treasurers to do all the work, including mail-order correspondence, telephone reservations and information, customer window service, ticket-counting and box office statement computation. Only the smallest of operations will be able to employ less than one full-time treasurer and, even for amateur groups, this is never wise when it can be avoided. Box office hours when tickets are on general sale should be as long as possible (preferably twelve hours daily) and box office workers should be able to give their full concentration to their responsibilities. While no box office business should be carried out of the box office, so, too, no other business should be carried into the box office.

Treasurers must be responsible for keeping the box office clean and well organized (janitors and maintenance personnel should never be allowed into the box office). Treasurers must also keep themselves well informed about productions so they can provide accurate information to the public. It is never advisable to be vague or dishonest about answering questions such as "Is it appropriate for children?" "Is it a comedy?" "Is it risqué?" "What time does the curtain come down?" Information regarding productions should be given to the box office by the publicity director, who should be certain that treasurers receive copies of all news releases, brochures and advertisements. Customer comments, questions or complaints about media publicity and advertising will come to the box office, not to the press office. Surprisingly, many theatres fail to establish communication between these two offices. The house manager or stage manager should provide the box office with exact curtain times, playing time for each act and approximate intermission times.

The box office treasurers, in short, should be responsible for all business related to theatre tickets. Bank deposits should be checked by the business manager, however, and periodic ticket audits should be conducted by the theatre's accountant.

## ▪ THE THEATRE TICKET

What does a ticket represent? A theatre ticket is a legal contract promising that whatever is printed on it will actually occur as printed for the printed price. Should the theatre be unable to furnish what is promised on the ticket, it must offer a refund. It may suggest that invalid tickets be exchanged, but it cannot demand this against customer wishes. It is wise for theatres offering a series of productions to omit the names of these productions, as well as the names of the stars, from the printed ticket and to use the phrase "programs subject to change" on seasonal advertising and on the ticket. If this policy is adopted, refunds and exchanges will not be necessary when events conspire to force programming and performer changes, so long as substitutes are offered at the same time, place, date and price as printed on the ticket.

A ticket for a current or upcoming performance is negotiable. It is worth the exact cash value printed on it. It may be bought or sold anywhere in the world where there is a market for it, although there are laws that regulate where theatre tickets may be sold, by whom and for how much. Such laws are especially stringent in New York State, although they are probably unenforceable and, just as probably, detrimental to the economy of the theatre. The point to remember is that a ticket should be handled with the same care—one hesitates to say reverence—as cash. If a ticket is lost or stolen from a box office, it is exactly the same as if money were lost or stolen. The theatre cannot legally reproduce it or duplicate it. If the theatre cannot account for a ticket, it must pay for it: it must declare it as sold and pay royalty, star and other percentages on it as well as admission sales taxes. A box office may contain tickets that represent, in total value, hundreds or thousands or even millions of dollars. Treasurers must be impressed with this fact and taught to handle every ticket as if it were cash.

### TYPES OF THEATRE TICKETS ▪

The two basic types of tickets are the reserved ticket and the unreserved or general admission ticket. Unreserved tickets are less expensive to buy and easier to sell and account for; they also make house management and ushering simpler and less costly. Unreserved tickets may be ordered in roll form, like those used by most movie theatres, or they may be ordered as separated tickets. They should be numbered from 1 to the capacity number of seats in the house.

Reserved seating tickets may be ordered in a variety of styles. When an annual series of programs is being offered, for example, it is good practice to order the tickets in booklet or sheet form (tickets for the same seat at different dates on the series are bound in a booklet or printed together). This saves the box office the considerable work of having to pull individual tickets for a number of performances out of ticket boxes and then having to arrange them in series style. Tickets should be ordered only in this manner, however, when a majority of seats are sold on a series or subscription basis. The initial ticket sales period should offer series tickets only—when such tickets are sold at all—and publish the date when individual seats will be offered, at which time the unsold series booklets are broken up and arranged according to individual performance dates.

Most reserved tickets come in a standard size and should include the following information:

Name and address of the theatre
Performance date
Title of production (optional)
Seat number
Row number
Section (orchestra, balcony, etc.)
Performance night (Monday, Tuesday, etc.)
Curtain time
Aisle number (optional)
Side of house where seat is located (right or left)
"No refunds or exchanges" (optional, but good practice)
"Program subject to change" (optional, but good practice)

When ordering tickets, care must be taken to insure that all the information is submitted in writing to the printer. The first time reserved seats are ordered from a ticket printing company, the theatre should send a ticket manifest to the printer. This is a detailed floor plan of the auditorium, clearly showing every seat in the house and indicating seat numbers, rows, sections and aisles. The printer retains this seating chart to simplify future orders from the theatre. The printer sends a confirmatory ticket order report to the theatre before tickets are printed to provide a final check against incorrect information. Other factors to consider when ordering tickets are the following:

1. All tickets should be notched to permit easy and uniform tearing by ticket-takers, and to make it easier to rubber-band whole tickets.
2. Each price category should be printed in a different color. When a single admission price is used for a large theatre, different colors may be used to indicate different sections of the theatre. If there are price differences between matinee and evening or week-night and weekend performances, completely different color sets should be ordered to indicate such differences.
3. Ticket colors should be changed from season to season.
4. Tickets should be ordered in pastel colors or white. Printing on dark or vibrant colors is extremely difficult for ushers to read.
5. All vital information should appear twice on each ticket, so that both the stub retained by the customer and the stub retained by the theatre tell the whole story.
6. Ticket-takers should always tear the ticket at the notch (one-fourth of ticket remaining) and give the customer "the short end of the deal," retaining the longer portion to make stub-counting easier for the box office.

### HARDWOOD TICKETS ▪

Special passes used by theatres for special purposes are called "hardwood." The so-called twofer, a publicity gimmick offering two tickets for the price of one, is one type of hardwood. Twofers are distributed throughout the community, to be picked up by potential customers and then presented at the box office in exchange for actual tickets. Special passes or discount offers may also be handled by giving out a ticket-like card that patrons may present at appropriate times. These might be called "man-

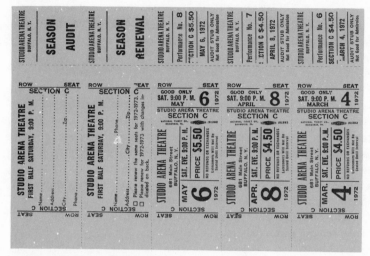

A single ticket

Tickets in series sheet form

Ticket with an audit stub

Ticket with two audit stubs

Tickets in series booklet form

| A62 | STARLIGHT PLAYHOUSE |
| Date _____ | A62 |
| Eve ____ Mat ___ | Date _____ Price _____ |
| Price _____ | Eve _____ Mat _____ |
| Row _____ | |
| Seat _____ | ROW:                    SEAT: |

A hardwood ticket form

ager's pass" or "patron's pass" and might entitle the holder to discounted or free tickets as well as such privileges as use of the coat room, patrons lounge, discount restaurant rates, free parking and so forth. A hardwood ticket may also be printed as a blank form on which treasurers may write the appropriate information and issue it to the customer in lieu of an actual ticket. This allows the box office to retain unpaid tickets, even when they are being used, and may eliminate the mistake of counting complimentary tickets as if they had been paid for. If an unnumbered and unlimited supply of hardwood forms are given to treasurers, management will not be able to check or control how many hardwood tickets are issued and this opens another area for possible dishonesty: the treasurer is able to charge admission for a ticket, write up the transaction as a "complimentary" pass on hardwood, place the actual ticket with the deadwood and pocket the income. To avoid this, hardwood tickets should be prenumbered and given in small quantities to the box office by the business manager. The box office should then be required to keep a list of which hardwood tickets are given out and to whom.

### AUDIT STUBS ■

The foregoing ticket samples show that tickets may be ordered with perforated, detachable portions. These may be left on the ticket for customers to use for parking or coat-room services or they may be removed by the box office when the ticket is sold. In the latter instance, the audit stub serves as a record of ticket sales. When the ticket is sold, the stub is placed in a locked box and all stubs are tallied at the end of the day and checked against window income. This system, however, makes ticket refunds, exchanges and discounts very cumbersome. Also, after constant handling by treasurers, audit stubs tend to loosen and fall off.

### DEADWOOD ■

"Deadwood" is a term used to indicate all unsold tickets that remain after the performance for which they were valid. In the event that actual tickets are substituted by hardwood forms, the actual tickets then become deadwood—representing "dead" seats that have been assigned and may not be sold. When such transactions occur, the actual tickets should immediately be placed in an envelope marked "dead" so there will be no possibility of assigning them to another customer.

### COMPUTERIZED TICKET SYSTEMS ■

During the 1960s there was much talk and speculation about computerized box office systems. Many people were convinced that all professional theatre box offices would eventually be computerized. Three computer ticket companies were formed: Ticketron, Ticket Reservation Systems, Inc., and Computicket. Today, Ticketron is the only one of the original three still in business and speculation about computer tickets is more cautious.

To be successful and economical, computer ticket systems are only feasible for large theatre operations. Tied into a network of computers which serve the theatre as ticket agencies or outlets throughout a city or on a nationwide basis, computerized box offices have the potential of enabling a person in Chicago to purchase Broadway tickets in his home city for a performance he wishes to attend on a trip to New York. Computers also have the potential for bringing ticket marketing into the twentieth century. They are ideal for large sporting events and other activities that

attract live audiences from across the nation and accommodate thousands of spectators. Computers are used by theatres of much smaller than stadium size, in which
case computerized ticket outlets may only be available in the theatre's home city.
Disadvantages of the computer box office system include its high cost (in most cases
it does *not* enable the theatre to employ fewer treasurers) and its poor ability to
handle ticket refunds and exchanges easily, once again foiling the creation of a box
office system that is foolproof against dishonest employees.

A computerized ticket system does possess a number of remarkable advantages.
The system works by electronic tie-in with a central computer terminal that receives
information from as many substations as desired, which may be located throughout a
large area. When the customer requests a ticket at the box office or at a computer
ticket agency, the computer operator feeds the request into the substation which, in
turn, feeds it into the central computer terminal. Within seconds, the substation prints
out information regarding the customer's request. It will tell whether or not the requested ticket is available and, if not, it will give several choices from which the
customer may select. Once a selection is made, the computer substation then prints
the actual ticket and it is sold by the operator to the customer. No tickets are printed
unless and until they are needed. The computer that is located in the main box office
usually has a number of capabilities that other substations do not. For example, it
may be programmed to print complimentary tickets and it can print a box office
statement for any and all performances at any time, so management always knows
exactly how many tickets are sold for a given performance or series of performances.

New theatres and large performance organizations should investigate the possibilities of using a computerized ticket system, if one is available in their area.

Not to be confused with computerized box office systems are tickets that are
printed in bulk by computers. Several ticket companies make it possible for theatre
tickets to be ordered and delivered at very short notice (sometimes less than twenty-
four hours), and for a low price. Like the Ticketron tickets, however, these use a
standard computer printing style that has a rather sterile, technological look to which
some people object.

## ▪ SELLING THE TICKET

### PREPARING THE TICKETS FOR SALE ▪

Before a box office is opened to the public, it should be prepared to operate in
the most efficient manner. It should be thoroughly cleaned and dusted; all tickets,
correspondence and other items unrelated to current operations should be removed.
Fresh filing cards and systems should be organized. Price charts and multiplication
charts should be drawn up, together with seating plans and all the necessary forms.

After the tickets have been ordered and received (providing they are the typical,
reserved seating tickets) the ticket boxes should be lined up in chronological order
and checked against the ticket confirmatory order sheet for accuracy of dates, colors,
prices and numbering. Once tickets have arrived in the box office, nobody except the
people bonded with the insurance company should be allowed to cross the threshold
and the room must be kept either locked or staffed from that point on.

Before placing tickets in the racks, the treasurers should "pull" all permanent locations, that is, all sets of tickets for special purposes that are to be removed for each
and every performance. These may include:

1. *House seats* (A predetermined number of seats held for use by the landlord or producer or, perhaps, by the box office in case of emergency or need upon authorization)
2. *Press seats* (mainly for opening nights, and other performances as authorized)
3. *Dead seats* (seats that may not be sold because they offer an obstructed view of the stage or have been removed to accommodate the orchestra or some special production requirement)
4. *Agency seats* (seats that are permanently assigned for ticket agents to sell, to be paid for by the agency or released for general sale at a specifically arranged time before each performance)
5. *Special seats* (tickets that are to be held, for example, for use or purchase by the star, the designer or others according to their contractual rights)

A master seating plan should be drawn up to indicate which seats have been pulled as permanent locations. Most of these should be prime locations in the orchestra within the first twelve rows and on the aisle where possible. They should also be somewhat scattered, so if most of them are unoccupied at a given performance they will not leave a noticeable group of empty seats all in the same area of the orchestra. (Unused, permanently assigned locations are never released for general sale until the last moment, at which time they may be difficult to sell.)

After the permanent locations have been pulled, the treasurers may begin to assign series tickets, if such tickets are offered for sale. Season or series ticket buyers should be given the seats of their choice whenever possible and, also, the same seats for each production on the series. Transactions of this sort should not only be recorded on the season ticket order forms and customer correspondence, but also upon a separate card which should be filed either alphabetically or according to performance night (or both) and serve as an easy reference for treasurers as well as for mailing list purposes. Seasonal operations should update season ticket-holder cards each year, making the renewal of season ticket orders easier and more efficient.

Once season tickets, permanent locations and large theatre party orders have been pulled from the ticket boxes, then the tickets are "racked" and the box office is ready to open to the general public.

### MAKING UP THE CUSTOMER'S MIND ■

Few people approach a box office with a clear idea of exactly where they wish to sit in the theatre. Their confusion is understandably compounded because they cannot see the seat they are selecting and are probably unfamiliar with the layout of the auditorium. Treasurers should be courteous but positive and firm when discussing seating availability. If, for example, the treasurer asks, "Where would you like to sit?" a long discussion will ensue. If, on the other hand, he says, "I can give you two excellent seats in the tenth row center," the transaction will proceed much more quickly. While treasurers should not mislead customers about seating locations, they should attempt to sell the highest priced tickets. Hence, when the customer approaches the box office and asks, "Do you have three for tonight?" the treasurer might reply, "Yes, I can give you three nice seats in the orchestra," with no mention of the lower-priced balcony seats unless the customer requests such tickets.

As a general policy, tickets should be sold on a first-come, first-served basis, once the necessary press and house seats and agency locations and series tickets have been removed. Customers should be discouraged from walking into the auditorium to study the seating possibilities. The theatre may be poorly lighted during nonperformance periods and this may cause accidents, or it may be cluttered with rehearsal paraphernalia or programs from a previous performance, thereby giving the customer an unfavorable impression. The practice also prolongs ticket transactions. After all, the customer is going to occupy a theatre seat only for several hours, he is not going to build a house on the site!

When quoting ticket prices, the treasurer should always quote the highest price last, since that is the figure the customer will remember first.

## "DRESSING THE HOUSE" ▪

When it appears that a performance is not going to sell out, the treasurer should somewhat scatter the customers throughout each section rather than "pack'em like sardines" into a few rows. Fifty people scattered throughout ten rows appear to be a much larger audience than fifty people squeezed into five rows. Also, if patrons are squeezed into a few rows and then discover an ample number of empty seats, they will move themselves for greater comfort. When "dressing the house," however, treasurers should not scatter the audience so much that the *feeling* of audience is destroyed together with the possibility of unified, group response to the production.

## "PAPERING THE HOUSE" ▪

A house that is "papered" is one in which a number of the seats have been given away. Some producers and managers feel that, when ticket sales are going poorly, it is better to fill the house with nonpaying guests than to allow too many seats to remain empty. Others feel this policy will reduce the number of paying customers in the long run and, more detrimental, will create the impression that business is bad and, therefore, the production must be bad.

All theatres must give away a certain number of tickets—to members of the press, to important visitors and to others who have been or may be helpful to business. These are legitimate complimentary tickets, ones given out for business reasons. On the other hand, theatres will also be asked to give free tickets to special groups and to individuals who merely consider *themselves* special. It is sometimes difficult to convince people that theatre is a business like any other and the only thing it has to sell is the theatre ticket. While the local druggist does not make a habit of dispensing free medicine, or the local innkeeper free rooms, or the local banker free money, these same businessmen seldom hesitate to ask for free theatre tickets—simply because they know the producer or the leading lady. Of course, if the local businessman displays a theatre's publicity material or provides it with free or discounted services, he is more justified in asking for something in return. Nonetheless, complimentary tickets should be handed out very sparingly and selectively. If a person gets a complimentary ticket for one production, he will doubtless expect another for the next production. Even if the chances for this are slim, he will probably keep his hopes alive and refuse to purchase a ticket. Such is the psychology of free "handouts."

When deciding how to "paper the house," then, the theatre should look for individuals and groups who either cannot afford to buy tickets, who are very unlikely to buy tickets or who do not reside in the local community. Residents of senior citizen's homes, noncommissioned military officers, hospital outpatients and school children are among the first groups that a theatre may contact when it wishes to give away blocks of seats.

### MAKING CHANGE AND HANDLING CASH ■

Most box offices do not extend credit or allow tickets to be "charged." Exceptions to this rule include cases when the box office accepts ticket vouchers from authorized ticket agencies for which it is paid later. It also may extend short-term credit to an organization that has agreed to sell a large block of tickets or "charge" tickets to an actor or other salaried employee and then deduct the ticket price from that person's wages. But the fewer such credits allowed, the fewer the mistakes and problems. Many box offices refuse to accept personal checks from customers (except, of course, for mail orders, in which case ten days may be allowed between the time the check is deposited and the time the tickets are mailed, to be certain the check is valid). Traveler's checks and money orders may be accepted with proper identification written on the backs of them, although forgery of such notes does occur.

In recent years, there has been a growing tendency for box offices and ticket agencies to allow customers to pay for tickets with their credit cards. This policy may encourage more impulse ticket buying or make the business easier for customers, but it has its drawbacks. A month or more may elapse before the credit card agency reimburses the theatre for tickets purchased. It also increases the paper work of the box office by an appreciable degree, complicates bookkeeping systems and requires more time to conduct a transaction with a customer. The theatre also must pay a percentage on credit card sales to the credit company. On the other hand, a theatre may gain a considerable amount of advertising by the listings and publicity distributed by credit card companies and it may make tickets more easily available at a large number of stores, banks and other outlets. All Broadway and many Off Broadway theatres now accept major credit cards.

Tickets should not be handed to a customer until he has given his money to the treasurer. The treasurer should leave the money on the counter before him while he makes the necessary change, so there will be no question about the amount of money he has been given. It is surprisingly easy to forget whether you have been given a ten or twenty dollar bill and a surprising number of customers will claim to have been shortchanged. As a matter of protection, a sign near the box office should caution the customer to "check your tickets and your change—no refunds, no exchanges." In some instances, of course, the box office *will* make refunds and exchanges, but a printed warning makes it easier for the theatre to exercise its judgment in such matters. Busy box offices may wish to install change-making machines to facilitate ticket transactions. A ticket multiplication chart like the one that follows should be posted so it is clearly visible to the treasurer as he stands facing the customer. The treasurer should always refer to this chart when quoting prices and making change; he should never rely on memory or on his mathematical abilities.

### TAKING RESERVATIONS ■

The policy of allowing customers to make ticket reservations over the telephone

## SAMPLE TICKET MULTIPLICATION CHART

| | Number of Tickets | | | | | | | | | |
|---|---|---|---|---|---|---|---|---|---|---|
| | 1 | 2 | 3 | 4 | 5 | 6 | 7 | 8 | 9 | 10 |
| **EVENING** | 5.50 | 11.00 | 16.50 | 22.00 | 27.50 | 33.00 | 38.50 | 44.00 | 49.50 | 55.00 |
| | 4.25 | 8.50 | 12.75 | 17.00 | 21.25 | 25.50 | 29.75 | 34.00 | 38.25 | 42.50 |
| | 3.50 | 7.00 | 10.50 | 14.00 | 17.50 | 21.00 | 24.50 | 28.00 | 31.50 | 35.00 |
| **MATINEE** | 4.25 | 8.50 | 12.75 | 17.00 | 21.25 | 25.50 | 29.75 | 34.00 | 38.25 | 42.50 |
| | 3.50 | 7.00 | 10.50 | 14.00 | 17.50 | 21.00 | 24.50 | 28.00 | 31.50 | 35.00 |
| | 2.75 | 5.50 | 8.25 | 11.00 | 13.75 | 16.50 | 19.25 | 22.00 | 24.75 | 27.50 |

or in person makes theatregoing much easier, but it also requires careful control. As a working rule, it must be assumed that at least 10 percent of all ticket reservations will never be claimed and often the figure is higher. People change their minds about theatregoing for such reasons as bad weather, delays in traffic or pretheatre dining or because after making the reservation they heard the production is terrible. The box office should, therefore, strive to keep unpaid reservations at the lowest feasible minimum. When reservations are accepted, customers should be required to claim and pay for their tickets as long in advance of the performance as the theatre can reasonably demand. If there are several weeks between when the order is placed and the performance date, the box office should request the customer to mail his check to the theatre. Or it might require that tickets be claimed a day before the performance. As the performance date approaches, the "pick-up" time may be changed to, say, an hour or half-hour prior to the performance. Unpaid reservations should never be held more than one-half hour before curtain time, to allow the box office to sell unclaimed tickets to last-minute customers. Highly experienced treasurers will know how to create a flexible reservation system and adapt it according to ticket demands. The higher the demand for tickets the more stringent the pick-up policy should be. The ability to sell every seat in the house is difficult to acquire. It may involve taking more reservations than there are tickets available, knowing that a number will never be claimed. But this policy is extremely dangerous and should only be practiced with caution by experienced treasurers. To sell every ticket, or "go clean," will inevitably require some couples or parties of theatregoers to accept seats separated from each other, or it may involve selling some seats that offer a limited view of the stage. While treasurers should be honest about selling such locations, their salesmanship abilities are of particular importance when business is brisk.

All ticket reservation envelopes should carry the following information:

Name and address of theatre
Customer's name and initials
The performance date
Matinee or evening performance

Number of tickets ordered

Price per ticket

The exact time by which customer must claim the tickets

Theatres that do not employ experienced treasurers would do well to order ticket envelopes with a preprinted form on the face of them. This prevents the treasurer from omitting any of the crucial reservation information.

Ticket-size envelopes may be ordered from companies that specialize in stationery and envelope printing and, often, may be acquired at little or no cost to the theatre, provided it allows the printing company to display its advertising on the back of the envelope. Or, the theatre may sell such advertising space itself or print its own ad copy on the envelopes.

In cases when a ticket is paid for and yet held in the box office, it should never be sold or given out for any reason—even if the customer never claims it.

### TELEPHONE PROCEDURES ■

Box office telephones should be answered promptly, courteously and efficiently. Transactions should be brief but clear. As many telephone lines should be installed in the box office as required to handle customer calls and as can be properly serviced by box office personnel. To avoid the risk of having ticket orders taken and then misplaced, box office telephones should never have extensions outside the box office. An answering device should be installed to provide telephone information to callers when the box office is closed. The greater the volume of telephone reservations, the more telephones will be required. If lines are frequently busy, a good percentage of potential customers will get discouraged and give up trying to obtain tickets or information. The manual for box office treasurers (Appendix E) suggests a specific procedure for answering box office phone calls.

### MAIL ORDER SYSTEMS ■

The treasurer's manual also suggests details that must be considered in regard to box office correspondence. As with all box office business, each transaction should be checked and double-checked, preferably by two different people. The publicity department should work with the treasurers in devising ticket order forms for use in advertising and brochures. These should request the customer to include a stamped, large self-addressed envelope with his order. Box office correspondence should only be opened and processed in the box office or an adjacent work room, otherwise orders will be misplaced or lost. All pertinent information should be written on the order form or letter in red ink (price, number of tickets, amount of check, performance date, whether matinee or evening, seat locations, date tickets were mailed) even though the customer may already have provided this information himself. When the order is completed, the correspondence should be filed alphabetically for easy reference by treasurers. Invariably, there will be mistakes and complaints regarding mail orders and many of these will occur during the busy, preshow period when treasurers have little time or patience to rummage through unkempt correspondence files.

### SERIES TICKETS ■

The word "series" (as in play series or concert series) and the term "season ticket" are both clear and meaningful to most customers. On the other hand, they may be uncertain about the meaning of such terms as "subscription series" or "patron ticket." Many people assume that patrons and subscribers donate an amount of money to the theatre over and above the cost of the tickets. In some cases, this is true.

Because it is easier and less expensive to sell ten tickets once than to sell ten tickets ten different times, any system that encourages multi-ticket orders is desirable. The more tickets sold in a single transaction, the better. When a theatre offers a season of nonrepeating productions, each one playing for the same period of time on the same performance schedule, the business of selling a series ticket is simple. The customer merely selects a performance (every Monday night or Wednesday matinee, for example) and buys a series of tickets for the same seat for each production. Ordinarily, though not always, he is given a discount if he buys the whole series. When a repertory system is the policy or when performances are scattered unevenly over a long period of time, then confusion is bound to result. Should the theatre select an arbitrary number of performances to comprise a series or should the customer be allowed freedom of choice in formulating his own series? When the theatre selects the performances, of course, it has greater control and, for example, can select lightly attended performances for the series, knowing that other performances will be supported by individual ticket orders. If the customer selects different performances at random, he probably will not be able to obtain the same seat for each, which is a source of much bickering and confusion. Again, the object should be to make theatregoing as easy as possible.

If the series of performances extends over a long period of time, it is a little unreasonable to expect customers always to plan their activities months in advance. A liberal policy of exchanging tickets may solve the problem to the customer's satisfaction or the theatre may offer an "open series" that permits the customer to order specific tickets for each production up to twenty-four hours prior to the performance of his choice, provided tickets are still available.

#### GROUP SALES ▪

Commercial New York theatre obtains much of its business from theatre parties. Group sales may be handled by the box office directly, by a staff member of the theatre who is assigned to selling theatre parties or by agents who promote and sell theatre parties and take a commission from the sale price. Any large theatre outside New York should employ a person to promote group sales, since agents who specialize in this do not function in most other cities.

Whenever a block of tickets is released from the box office without full payment, a contract should be drawn up between the theatre and the purchasing organization or individual. The contract and terms shown on page 247 are typical, although the style may be formalized with legalistic jargon if desired.

#### TICKET AGENCIES ▪

A ticket agency may be operated by the theatre itself (staffed with theatre employees) or independent ticket agencies may be selected by the theatre to serve as authorized ticket outlets. Ticket agencies in New York and many other states must obtain a special license from the city or state in which they operate and often must conform to a number of laws and regulations. In New York an agent is currently permitted to charge the customer no more than $1.50 over the face value of the ticket. This means that the service charge on a $3.50 balcony ticket is identical to that on $18.00 orchestra tickets—obviously a peculiar regulation. New York ticket brokers are forbidden to sell anything except theatre tickets, thereby severely limiting their potential income. In London and elsewhere, ticket agencies sell theatre books, recordings, posters and other items, which makes their business more lucrative and their shops more interesting and attractive. There is, of course, nothing that prevents a theatre from giving an agent a commission over that which he charges his customers. There is, however, a law forbidding agents to "bribe" box office treasurers with payoffs in exchange for tickets to "hot" shows, although this practice is common and the law is nearly impossible to enforce, as is the law that regulates the $1.50 agency commission. Payoffs and gratuities to agents from ticket buyers are common. Such payoffs are variously referred to as gratuities, commissions, graft and ice. The term "ice" was evidently coined in the last century as an abbreviation for the bookkeeping phrase "Incidental Company Expenses" (ICE). Managers of touring companies, among others, were fond of dipping into box office revenues and then declaring they had done so to pay for unitemized expenses or that they had issued free tickets. The practice came to be regarded as unfortunate but unavoidable. Today, the term "ice" is applied to all shady or under-the-counter dealings in regard to box office monies.

Finally, New York law prevents theatre tickets from being sold (legally) for anything except the price printed on them. Almost no pricing flexibility is possible in theatre as it is in nearly all other retail businesses. While the bookseller and the furniture store may run sales and specials on slow items or during slow periods, the commercial theatre is largely prevented from this by law. The League of New York Theatres has commissioned several studies in past years under the supervision of the highly respected theatrical attorney John Wharton, and most professionals in the theatre now agree that the legitimate theatre industry is over-regulated by law, especially in the area of ticket-pricing and selling. The plain fact is that current laws merely encourage ticket scalpers and payoffs of various kinds and place a lot of potential profit into the hands of middlemen rather than back into the industry itself. If flexible ticket pricing were allowed and could, for example, be based on the laws of supply and demand rather than upon laws concocted by the attorney general's office, the theatre industry might realize an appreciable increase in revenue. If tickets to a production could bring a price of $100 each, that would be the established price. As the production becomes less popular, the price would go down. Or, customers could be given the opportunity to purchase tickets at a low price before the production opens, after which prices might go up or down according to the reviews and the demand for tickets. This type of flexibility, suggested by Wharton in his 1965 report to the Legitimate Theatre Industry Exploratory Commission, recommends that theatre tickets be "floated" in much the same manner that stocks are bought and sold on the stock exchange. It would eliminate the need for scalpers, place all ticket revenues in the hands of the industry and bring in more money much sooner than is now possible. The report also argues that theatregoing is, after all, a luxury and that for this reason the government has no business regulating its pricing policies as if it were in the food or utility business.

While ticket agents of various kinds may be authorized to sell tickets to a produc-

## STAR THEATRE, INC.
## CONTRACT FOR GROUP TICKET PURCHASE:
## TERMS

1. Tickets distributed to organization on sale or return basis.
2. One-third deposit of box office price of tickets required.
3. Final payment must be made no later than one week prior to performance date, until which settlement date tickets may be returned for full value.
4. In order to qualify for a discount, discounted value of tickets sold must exceed amount of deposit.
   ### DEPOSIT NOT RETURNABLE WHETHER OR NOT TICKETS ARE RETURNED
5. Final percentage discount granted is determined by the number of tickets actually sold by the organization.
6. Organizations that sell tickets for more than the price they pay are responsible for the taxation on the excess where taxes apply.
7. In the event of a change in schedule, the liability of the theatre is limited to the return of deposit monies.

_____

_____

Contracting Organization _____

Address _____

Day of Performance _____ Date of Performance _____

Show _____ Settlement Date _____

Agent for Organization _____

Address _____

Phone _____ Date of Contract _____

### NO DISCOUNT ALLOWED UNLESS ORGANIZATION SELLS A MINIMUM OF _____ TICKETS

Accepted for _____ Accepted by _____

(Name of Organization)

Authorized Signature _____Authorized Signature _____

MAKE ALL CHECKS PAYABLE TO _____

### TICKETS RECEIVED BY ORGANIZATION          Box Office Value

Number of Tickets _____ @ _____          _____

_____ @ _____          _____

_____ @ _____          _____

Total No. Tickets _____ Box Office Value of Tickets _____

Tentative Percentage Discount _____Deposit Required _____

Tickets Delivered _____ _____ Deposit Received Date _____ Amt. ___

(date)          (by)          Date _____ Amt. ___

Date _____ Amt. ___

_____

_____

*Contract for Group Ticket Purchase Terms (Cont'd)*

| Tickets Received | Tickets Returned | Tickets Sold | Value |
|---|---|---|---|
| _____ | _____ | _____ @ | _____ |
| _____ | _____ | _____ @ | _____ |
| _____ | _____ | _____ @ | _____ |

Total Tickets Sold _____ Total Value _____

CONTRACTING ORGANIZATION _____ Discount at ___% _____

_____ Discount Value _____

DATE OF PERFORMANCE_____ Deposit Received _____

SHOW _____Balance Received _____

Date _____

By _____

tion, they should not be given the actual tickets. These should remain in the box office and a voucher system devised whereby the customer pays the ticket agent, receives a voucher containing the pertinent ticket information and then exchanges this at the box office for the actual tickets. Prior to each performance, the agency must inform the box office of the exact tickets it has sold for that performance. This is noted, the vouchers are collected from the customers and the two are reconciled. The agent then pays the theatre (on a daily or weekly basis) for the tickets it sold. When agencies do a lot of business for the theatre, the theatre should assign "permanent locations" to that agency. This means that, before any tickets are sold to customers, the treasurers pull specific locations for all performances or a series of performances and hold these at the box office in the agency's name. They do not offer them for sale until the last moment—unless the agency has already sold them, in which case they remain in the envelope until the customer presents his voucher to claim them. This system prevents the necessity of phone calls between the agent and the box office every time the agent has a potential customer.

Many theatres are finding more and more imaginative ways to market their tickets. Large supermarkets in many suburbs, for example, contain an information or customer courtesy booth that can serve as a ticket agency. Stores are usually willing to provide such service merely in exchange for the publicity it will create. Tourist information centers, chambers of commerce, banks and shopping centers are among other possible locations for theatre ticket agencies. Many are already equipped with a Ticketron system. One summer theatre established a mobile box office that, in the form of a beach buggy, was located in different places on different days of the week on a regular schedule.

If customers do not go to the box office, the box office must learn how to go to the customers!

Booklets of numbered vouchers in triplicate sets should be ordered from a printer and issued to the authorized ticket agencies. When a ticket is purchased from the agent, he fills out the voucher and gives a copy to the customer for presentation at the box office. He submits a second copy that day or at the end of that week when he pays the theatre for the tickets he has sold. He keeps the third copy for his own records. Ticket vouchers may appear as follows:

```
┌──────────────────────────────────────────────────────────────┐
│                                                                │
│   TICKET VOUCHER        No. 51176                              │
│                                                                │
│    STAR PLAYHOUSE                                              │
│    Main St., Maplewood, Mass.  577-1000                        │
│                                                                │
│   NAME_____        │
│                                                                │
│                                                                │
│   Performance date_____Eve _____ Mat _____ │
│                                                                │
│                                                                │
│   Seat Numbers and Section:                                    │
│   Number of tickets purchased _____ at  $_____ each  │
│                                                                │
│                                                                │
│   Total paid for tickets  $ _____                    │
│                                                                │
│                                                                │
│   Purchase date _____ Agent _____ │
│                                                                │
│            This voucher represents a confirmed ticket order.   │
│            Please present it at the box office for actual tickets. │
│                      No Refunds—No Exchanges                   │
│                                                                │
└──────────────────────────────────────────────────────────────┘
```

## ■ ACCOUNTING FOR THE TICKET

**TICKET STUBS AND DEADWOOD. ■**

Before each performance, the ticket-taker should be provided with a wooden or steel box into which he must deposit all the stubs torn off from the customers' tickets. The longer portion of the ticket should be placed in the box, the shorter end given back to the customer. If there are different price categories for tickets, the stub box may have different slots and compartments for each price; this will save treasurers a considerable amount of time counting the stubs. The stub boxes may be locked with a key held by the head treasurer or the business manager to prevent others from tampering with the contents. Of course, only in rare instances will all people who purchased tickets actually show up for the performance, especially if it is a large audience. Each theatre should, however, be able to determine an average number who fail to show up for most performances. The number will be small, but it is important to remember this point when stubs are found missing for tickets that were sold.

The deadwood tickets, those remaining in the box office after curtain time, are used to determine the ticket sales. Unsold seats are subtracted from the capacity of seats at that price and entered on the box office statement as the number sold. Ticket stubs should closely correspond with this number. Obviously, the stub count should never *exceed* the capacity. If there is a discrepancy, all tickets should be recounted and the matter should be solved before the statement is finalized. Stubs and deadwood should be counted after curtain time and banded in piles of fifty or one hundred. All counts should be checked by two people. The stub count may or may not appear on the box office statement, depending upon the degree of formality that is desired. After the statement has been finalized, the stubs and dead tickets should be placed in a paper bag or box, labeled with the performance date and stored in a safe place for at least three years.

### DISCOUNTED AND COMPLIMENTARY TICKETS ▪

The fewer discounts or "specials" that are offered, the less chance for mistakes and dishonesty at the box office. It is difficult to avoid the possibility of enabling a treasurer to charge full price for a ticket, declare it as a discounted ticket and pocket the difference. All tickets that are discounted should be stamped or marked in some way so that the returned stubs will indicate which were discounted and to what degree. The treasurers should also keep a written record of all discounts that are made. One method for doing this is to keep a looseleaf notebook in the box office with a separate page for each performance. Every time a discounted or complimentary ticket is issued, it is indicated on the appropriate page and initialed by the treasurer. When the statement is compiled, the page is removed and compared against all the signed house orders for complimentary and discounted tickets that were given to the box office by the producer, manager or press agent. Or, of course, the house order slips alone may serve as the record. All such papers should be stored with the tickets.

### BOX OFFICE STATEMENTS ▪

A box office statement is a form on which the final accounting of tickets and income for each performance will appear. Copies of the statement should be submitted to the accountant, the business manager, the producer and anyone who is receiving a percentage of box office income (the playwright, star, director or their representatives). Obviously, the information on statements should be confidential.

Several types of box office statements may be desirable for use by the same theatre. These might include:

1. *Master statement.* Shows the capacity number of seats at each price and the total potential ticket income.
2. *Daily statement.* A form on which the figures are given for a specific performance.
3. *Weekly box office summary.* A form on which all the box office figures for a given week are summarized.
4. *Seasonal box office statement.* A summation of all box office figures for a given season. Such figures should appear, at least, in the accountant's annual fiscal report.
5. *Ticket stub report.* A form on which the ticket stubs are reported after each performance. May be the responsibility of the house manager or head usher.
6. *Season ticket sales report.* After series or season ticket sales have ended, a complete record of these must be made for each performance in the series to determine the amount that must be discounted for that performance.

For examples that can be adapted to suit the special needs of specific theatres, see Appendix C.

### BOX OFFICE AUDITING ▪

An audit of the box office should be conducted at the end of each production or season and at any time when a notable discrepancy appears between the number of tickets missing and the amount of income. The audit, as mentioned earlier in this chapter, should be conducted by the accountant or the business manager and not by the treasurers, though they may assist in the process. Essentially, an audit involves counting all the unsold tickets on hand, then making up a box office statement showing income to date for all future performances. This total amount, together with income shown on statements for past performances, should be the same as the total of all deposits for ticket sales made into the box office bank account. If income cannot be closely reconciled with the figures shown on the statements, the audit should be done again. It is easy to forget details, like discounted tickets, petty cash money borrowed from the box office and so forth. Also, the audit will virtually never balance exactly. A 1 percent to 5 percent discrepancy (depending upon the professionalism of the box office operation) may be expected and laid to honest human error. If a treasurer makes change for thousands of dollars worth of tickets each week, it stands to reason that he will make a few mistakes. In fact, an audit that balances income with tickets sold to the exact penny is more suspicious than one that shows a small discrepancy. An audit system that can be adapted to suit most theatres is provided in Appendix D.

---

An efficient box office operation requires exacting work, specialized skills and constant scrutiny. Most of all. it requires a system, a system that takes into account every duty and possible type of transaction, yet one that is as little complicated and time-consuming as possible.* Employee dishonesty in the box office is a lesser problem than the fact that many theatregoers regard box offices as places where they, as customers, will be dealt with dishonestly or shabbily. A more imaginative and open design of the physical layout of the box office and a greater insistence upon courteous treasurers could serve as major contributions in improving the image of theatre box offices in the public mind.

Part of a treasurer's negative behavior may stem from the fact that he has a very difficult job. Being locked in a tiny room with constantly ringing telephones and customers making loud demands for hours on end is a situation that would try the patience of a saint. Negative behavior may also stem from the extreme isolation most treasurers have from the rest of the theatre operation. Managers should see to it that treasurers are given an opportunity to watch each production, to meet other staff members and to be included in social activities with other employees. Artistic directors and leading performers (*especially* if they are earning a percentage of box office receipts) should make a point of dropping by the box office and attempting to increase the treasurer's enthusiasm about their production. Yet, such amenities seldom occur and the treasurer all too often becomes a faceless and forgotten member of the staff.

There is no area of theatre operation that can benefit more from innovation than the box office. Repeal or change of state and city laws, of admission tax laws, of ticket marketing and distribution and of ticket pricing and the physical layout of the box office itself are highly desirable and may even be mandatory for the survival of commercial theatre.

---

*A sample box office operations manual is provided in Appendix E.

# CHAPTER TWELVE

# Ways to Generate Additional Revenue

Theatres today depend on revenue not only from ticket sales but, increasingly, also from other sources. This additional revenue, also called subsidiary or contributory income, is of major importance to the total budget of most theatres. The majority of well-established resident theatres and other large, nonprofit theatre organizations may receive as much or more income from grants and donations as from box office ticket sales. And they may spend as much time and effort applying for and administering these grants as they do promoting ticket sales. Small, incipient theatre companies are also frequently dependent on grant monies. Many theatres operate concessions, such as restaurants and souvenir program sales, that generate profits without which they could not survive. Although the business of earning contributory income creates special problems and requires special skills of an apparently nontheatrical nature, few theatres can afford to ignore this area of potential income.

## SETTING GOALS ■

As with all areas of performing arts administration, fund-raising for the theatre is unlikely to succeed unless it is based on a plan. When contributory income is

253

being sought, the organization must first clarify its objectives. This will entail the following:

1. Determine the amount of funding that is necessary.
2. Compose a timetable showing when the goal must be reached.
3. List all sources of income and the amount of money each source is expected to generate during the timetable period.
4. List all possible sources of contributory income.
5. Carefully consider both short-range and long-range deficits, operating expenses, goals and plans.

Many performing arts organizations lack experience when it comes to projecting income and costs over a long period of time. In any case, the nature of the industry probably makes it unwise to attempt projections that extend more than three to five years into the future. But grants agencies of all kinds expect applicants to be able to account for their past *and* make intelligent estimates about their future.

Successful realization of fund-raising goals depends to a very large degree upon the quality of the fund-raising leadership. While the assistance of professional consultants may be obtained, the key to success rests largely with the board of trustees or other volunteer supporters. Together with their close business and personal acquaintances, the trustees or directors of an arts organization often provide the lion's share of donations themselves. But they, too, must be convinced to give their money by a very articulate and knowledgeable artistic director or general manager. Paradoxically, as the size of the funding goal increases, the number of sources often decreases. As commercial theatre producers know, there may be nothing harder than raising a small amount of money—and the $50,000 to $500,000 it takes to produce a play in New York is a small amount of money compared with the multimillion dollar amounts that a major performing arts company must raise to cover three to five years' worth of deficits. Many organizations (including many resident theatres, campus theatres and others) suffer tremendous frustrations and loss of valuable time because they engage in annual appeals to individuals and grants agencies when this burden might be relaxed if they sought funds to cover a longer period. Most individual donors would rather give a large amount once every five years than a small amount every single year. Other factors that influence private giving include the individual's attitudes and interest in the project at hand, his involvement with that project, the impact of the solicitor and the method of solicitation.

As Carl W. Shaver, a respected leader in the fund-raising field and president of his own New York firm, has phrased it, successful fund-raising is when "the right person asks the right prospect for the right amount for the right reason at the right time!"

## ▪ OBTAINING GRANTS AND FINANCIAL AID

### ELIGIBILITY ▪

Generally, only non-profit organizations are eligible for government subsidization, and grants from private foundations are also most likely to be given to nonprofit groups. Financial aid from government agencies is usually assigned to recipients as a "contract" for specified services. Government may buy services but it may not make "gifts" to individuals and organizations as may a private, philanthropic foundation. Hence, a semantic qualification: "grants" are made by the private sector while assistance from public funds is given in the form of a "contract" or, merely, "financial assistance." Gifts from individuals, of course, only qualify as tax-deductible if they are given to a nonprofit organization. But eligibility for aid depends on more than whether the applicant is a profit or nonprofit organization. There are a number of standard factors that most performing arts granting agencies use as criteria in selecting beneficiaries. These generally include:

1. The applicant's seriousness of purpose
2. The ability of the applicant to prove merit, to show a record of honest accomplishment and a realistic potential for development
3. The ability of the applicant to demonstrate responsibility of management and administration
4. Evidence that the applicant is/can serve a wide audience
5. Evidence that the applicant can be self-sustaining in future years if grant money is withdrawn

It should also be noted that government agencies are often prohibited from giving financial aid to organizations that are already supported by tax-levied funds or that are government sponsored; for example, a state university may not be eligible for assistance from the state arts council. Grants are least likely to be awarded for capital expenditures, for short-lived projects, for operating expenses for on-going programs, for inexperienced or mismanaged organizations and for projects with limited public appeal or benefit. The immediate audience size need not always be large, but generally there must be promise that benefit to the public can eventually be widespread (as in the case of providing money to a playwright or to a workshop theatre producing new plays that may someday gain wide recognition). While a specific project may be new and untried, its directors should be able to show sound experience and seriousness. In these early days of government subsidy for the arts, it is especially important that government agencies select their beneficiaries wisely and well in order to establish a clear record of success for the idea of subsidy. Just as the recipient of a grant must be held accountable by the granting agency, so the agency itself is accountable to a board of directors or to the American taxpayer. Interestingly, however, federal and state agencies have tended to support newer, more experimental and less conservative arts projects than those supported by private foundations.

## METHODS OF GRANT AND AID APPLICATION ■

Before approaching a foundation or government agency for financial assistance, an attempt should be made to determine the likelihood of success. What types of projects does the foundation generally support and what types does it automatically reject as a matter of policy? Grants made by government agencies and large foundations are published in leading newspapers and in periodicals dealing with foundations and fund-raising. Annual reports and brochures describing the activities of private foundations are often available upon request. State and local arts councils may be helpful in guiding an applicant to the most appropriate sources of potential funding. The large foundations are inundated with applications, the vast majority of which are rejected because they are poorly presented, do not appear worthwhile, are not the type of project supported by the foundation or because the foundation does not have sufficient resources to support the project. Even though a written application may not be accorded a reply, all requests should be composed in written form and mailed or delivered personally to the foundation office. As the press agent must cultivate personal contacts in the media industries in order to get press coverage, so the "grantsman" must cultivate personal contacts in order to be successful.

Initial letters requesting support for a project should not exceed one or two type-written pages and, in the briefest way possible, should include the following information.

1. Name, address and telephone number of the applicant
2. Whether applicant is profit or nonprofit
3. Name of the project and the director of it
4. Brief description of the goals of the project
5. Brief description of the plans to carry out the project
6. Listing of the leading people to be involved in the project
7. The dates during which the project is planned
8. An estimation of the money required to fund the project, the sources from which the funding is anticipated and the projected deficit. (A budget for the project may be attached to the letter. The projected deficit is probably the amount of money being requested from the foundation.)
9. Main reasons the project is deemed valuable
10. Whether the project or the sponsoring organization has received, is receiving or hopes to receive foundation or government support

If the agency or foundation is interested in the project, it will request more detailed information and personal contact with the project director. It should be stressed that grants are not easy to come by and are never given automatically or automatically renewed from year to year. Interests and priorities of grants agencies change from year to year (often dependent on the personal interests of the grants officers in charge) and the amount of money available may vary. While the arts have enjoyed increased subsidization in recent years, subsidy is still an erratic business and no arts organization yet dares to depend on specific grants over a long period of time. Contingency funding methods should always be held in readiness against the day when an anticipated grant is not given or renewed.

### MATCHING GRANTS ■
Very often, financial aid is assigned to a project or organization on the condition that it be matched by an equal amount of money either by the organization itself of from another outside source. Allocations from the National Endowment to state arts councils must be matched by state funds; many state arts allocations must be matched by equal funds from the recipient organization. In this manner, each dollar allocated from the federal level eventually generates three or four dollars for the arts—a fact guaranteed to impress economically minded congressmen. Also, many grants awarded by private foundations are of the "matching grant" type.

While this means that the recipient must raise matching funds in order to accept the initial grant, the chore may not be as difficult as it seems. Once an organization or project is recognized by one granting agency, others are likely to be more favorable. Matching funds also may be raised from box office receipts. Many civic and educational theatres benefit from salaried personnel or space and services provided without cost to them by their city or by the institution to which they belong. Even though the college theatre department, for example, is not paying rent for its building, a rental value may be determined and is often acceptable as part of the matching contribution, as are salaries and services not paid directly by the grant recipient. On the other hand, once the word is out that an organization has received a large grant, it may be thought that it is financially "out of the woods," a factor that may make it difficult indeed to raise the matching amount.

## ▪ SOURCES OF FINANCIAL ASSISTANCE

Potential sources for funding the performing arts can be divided into four categories: (1) earned income, (2) tax-based revenue or grant income, (3) interest from endowments and investments and (4) private gifts and donations. The commercial theatre depends almost exclusively on the first and last of these—box office income and money invested for profit by private backers. Nonprofit theatre groups often depend heavily on the second and third sources. The almost exclusive reliance that many non-profit performing arts organizations place on aid from foundation and government agencies may be ill-justified. In 1971 the total amount of private philanthropic giving to all causes in the United States exceeded twenty-one billion dollars. Of this amount, over 85 percent came from individuals (gifts, bequests, etc.), less than 10 percent from private foundations and less than 5 percent from corporations. Of the twenty-one billion, the arts received nearly one and a half billion, a figure that represented the single greatest increase to any area in the broad spectrum of philanthropy.

### GOVERNMENT AGENCIES ▪

The National Foundation for the Arts and Humanities is the central governing body for federal subsidy to the arts and humanities. Each area is funded by an endowment granted by Congress through annual presidential requests and each is advised by a national council. Although annual allocations have steadily increased since the formation of the Endowment in 1965, the United States still lags far behind other governments in its support of the arts. In 1971, for example, the United States government was providing as little as fifteen cents per person in support of the arts, while Canada was spending ten times that amount per capita and Austria fifteen times the U. S. amount. Yet, the federal government spends twenty dollars per capita to pay farmers not to grow certain crops! The need for increased federal support for the arts is, however, becoming more widely recognized and, along with it, the need for effective lobbying groups such as the Partnership for the Arts, an organization that functions in numerous communities to rally political influence in favor of federal subsidy.

Under the directorship of Roger Stevens and, later, Nancy Hanks, the National Endowment for the Arts has established a sense of permanence and exerted its influence with remarkable success and good judgment. Much of its budget is directed through well-defined channels that ensure benefits on the grass-roots level. Annual allocations are given to state-controlled arts councils and they, in turn, make direct payments to artists and arts organizations; or, the state councils subsidize community arts councils which make awards on the grass-roots level. Every state in the union has an arts council, and few large cities are without a community arts council. Between government agencies and private, nonprofit agencies concerned with the arts in America, it is safe to say that, since 1960, an enormous power structure and a sizable bureaucracy to operate it has come into existence. So large, in fact, that simply keeping abreast of all the publications, conventions, meetings and other activities of this power structure is a full-time job in itself. Yet, for many arts leaders and organizations, it is a necessary job if financial assistance is to be secured. Personal contact is as important in securing grants as a knowledge of the agencies and monies that may be available to assist a given project. Lobbying activities are also essential, as is a strong and unified attempt by all arts workers to impress the powers that be that the arts are, indeed, central to society.

The New York State Arts Council was the first to be established, preceding even the National Endowment, and has remained the nation's best funded state council. In fact, in 1971 it dispensed more financial support to New York State arts organizations than the National Endowment dispensed to the entire nation. This, of course, has been largely due to the efforts of Governor Nelson Rockefeller, to the strong concentration of arts output in New York City and to the efforts of groups such as the Performing Arts Association of New York State, Inc., that have lobbied the state legislature. More and more politicians are discovering among their constituents a genuine enthusiasm for government support of the arts. An independent poll commissioned in 1970 under Boston's Mayor Kevin White, for example, showed that an overwhelming 97 percent of Boston's taxpayers favored continued city support for "Summerthing," a city-wide summer arts festival that sponsors over fifteen hundred free performances annually. New Yorkers doubtless feel the same enthusiasm in regard to the summer arts programs given in that city's parks and streets. Other cities offer free performances and exhibitions, both publicly and privately sponsored, that are drawing crowds sizable enough to impress even the most conservative politicians.

There are nearly one hundred federal programs other than the National Endowment that offer assistance to artists and arts organizations. A listing of these is available from the Superintendent of Documents Office in Washington. Through the United States Office of Education, for example, theatre groups have benefited from three programs: Title I and Title III of the Elementary and Secondary Education Act of 1965 (which funded special educational arts programs for children in low-income areas and also special programs of an innovative type) and Title I of the Higher Education Act of 1965 (which funded programs in which colleges worked to solve community problems). The Economic Opportunity Act of 1964, administered by the Office of Economic Opportunity, and the Model Cities Program, administered by the Department of Housing and Urban Development, also funded programs that assisted arts organizations of certain types in certain areas.

The allocations received by state arts councils from the National Endowment must be matched by state funds which, where effective state lobbies are at work, may be budgeted well beyond the matching allocation. While lobbying, letter-writing, demonstrating, picketing and arm-twisting in the halls of government consume a big portion of the arts administrator's time and over-crowded schedule, they are activities that no concerned artist or arts worker dare ignore or leave to others. Second only to concern for the quality of the arts in America is the need to increase both public and private subsidy for the arts.

### PRIVATE FOUNDATIONS ∎

While several large, private foundations such as Ford and Carnegie have been active in supporting the arts for over two decades, the number of such foundations increased substantially during the sixties and seventies. *Private Foundations Active in the Arts,* published by the *Washington International Arts Letter,* and other sources provide listings to which a theatre may refer when trying to decide which foundation to approach for which program. When there is no personal contact between a theatre organization and the foundation to which it is applying, an initial letter briefly describing the project in question should be sent to ascertain whether or not the foundation is interested. Personal visits and phone calls are also desirable in many cases. A more detailed application may be composed after the agency expresses interest in a project.

There are several private, nonprofit organizations that offer valuable assistance in keeping arts administrators informed about government and foundation grants activities, that serve as a clearinghouse for information and consultation and that publish frequent newsletters and special material. The busiest of these is probably the Associated Councils of the Arts, located in the Palace Theatre Building in New York. Its paying members are comprised of state and community arts councils as well as arts organizations and individuals. It provides a library of publications and special services for members. Other organizations that serve to promote communication between different agencies and arts organizations include the United States Institute for Theatre Technology, Theatre Communications Group, the American National Theatre and Academy and the American Theatre Association. The *Washington International Arts Letter,* a subsidiary of Allied Business Consultants, is also a helpful source of information.

### SUPPORT BY BUSINESS AND INDUSTRY ∎

Private businesses and corporations have, like the public sector, increased their support of the arts in recent years. A significant attempt to stimulate business and corporate arts support was the formation of the Business Committee for the Arts in 1967 under the chairmanship of C. Douglas Dillon. Membership in BCA is comprised of the heads of over one hundred of the nation's largest corporations. Its objectives are to bring the business and arts communities closer together, to find new sources of private funding for the arts, to disseminate information about business in the arts and to establish standards and criteria for corporate giving to arts projects. Each year it honors business groups that have provided imaginative support for worthwhile arts projects. BCA has been successful in making many "marriages" between specific business and arts organizations.

While most private corporations know that federal law entitles them to make tax-deductible gifts from a certain percentage of their corporate profits, the majority do not exercise this privilege. Often, they must be "sold on the idea" of philanthropy by a group like BCA or by a particular arts organization. Certainly, arts managers should approach the larger business and industrial groups in their locality and attempt to gain their support. Assistance need not always be in the form of a cash gift. The business may supply materials or services, purchase large blocks of tickets to give away or assist the arts organization in a number of other ways.

A factor that often distinguishes corporate philanthropy from foundation and government giving is the element of reciprocity. Public and nonprofit agencies seek to support arts projects primarily on the basis of their merit and their potential benefit to the public. But businesses may ask "what do we get in return for supporting this project?" This is not an unreasonable question although, of course, no arts organization should compromise its objectives or its image merely to obtain a handout. In many cases, a business or corporation may be able to gain favorable publicity by supporting a particular project, secure cultural benefits for its employees or even gain new insights into its operations as the result of a working relationship with artists and arts projects. When approaching a business in order to gain its support, the arts manager should be prepared to reciprocate in some specific manner and should never fail to give recognition to a supporting business group in theatre programs, advertisements or wherever feasible.

INDIVIDUAL GIFTS, DONATIONS AND BEQUESTS ▪

Government and corporate support for the arts has gained increased importance as private philanthropy has diminished during the past half century. *Noblesse oblige,* which traditionally encouraged the aristocracy, the Church and families of vast wealth to support the arts, has declined in proportion to the rise of an increasingly socialistic distribution of wealth. Generally, we now look to governments and corporations for the largesse that used to come from princes and billionaires. Yet, there remain many individuals wealthy enough to make large donations to cultural projects, and the individual inclination is encouraged by tax advantages, by prestige and by the perpetuation of one's name that may accompany philanthropic activities. A theatre group may work to gain small gifts and donations or it may approach individuals for bequests with an eye to the establishment of an endowment fund. The latter idea appeals to many donors, especially if the plan is to leave the principle intact and spend only the interest, thus establishing a kind of permanent memorial to the donor and insuring that maximum value will be derived from the gift.

When soliciting donations from individuals, the first rule to follow is this: Make the amount requested comparable to the donor's ability to give. One should not ask "important" people for unimportant sums, or vice versa.

An ongoing theatre group may sponsor an annual fund-raising campaign by itself or in cooperation with other arts organizations. Community arts councils can be especially valuable in organizing local fund-raising efforts and more effective results are generally achieved when several groups work together. Lincoln Center, for example, recently conducted its first unified fund-raising campaign for all its constituents. It discovered that total contributions were greater than ever before. A reluctance among different arts organizations to join a mutual fund-raising endeavor is understandable but, perhaps, not always wise.

Another method for consolidating fund-raising efforts is for an organization to estimate its financial needs over the years in the immediate future (three to five years, perhaps). One fund-raising drive may then be able to cover deficits for several years. This method cuts down on fund-raising costs (it may also make it possible for the organization to retain the services of professional fund-raising firms) and most donors prefer being approached as seldom as possible. Professional fund-raisers of good reputation provide their services for a set fee, not a percentage of the money raised. Generally, they also insist on conducting a feasibility study prior to launching the actual fund-raising campaign. Their consultation can be extremely valuable and should be considered by all types of nonprofit theatre organizations.

## ■ SELLING ADVERTISING AND RENTING SPACE

### PLAYBILL ADVERTISING ■

Very few theatre groups fail to generate at least some revenue by selling ads in their printed programs. Sometimes the names of contributors are merely listed according to the type and amount of their contribution ("member," "patron," "angel," etc.) and sometimes elaborate display ads are printed. Of course, the more elaborate the printing, the more costly it is to produce the playbill.* When a large number of advertisers are solicited, a full-time ad salesman may be required. The three most common ways of handling playbill advertising are: (1) for the theatre and staff itself to conduct all ad sales and playbill layout work, (2) for the theatre to hire a professional ad agency to do this work on commission and (3) for the theatre to sell the playbill advertising rights to some agency in exchange for a percentage of the profits or a flat fee. The second two methods are appropriate only when a large playbill with numerous advertisements is the goal.

Playbills offer prime space for appropriate advertisers because there is a better-than-usual guarantee that the ads will be seen. Playgoers sitting in a theatre waiting for the curtain to go up comprise a captive audience for the advertiser: they have little else to do except read the program. Advertising rates, therefore, should not be overly modest. They should be based on the total potential audience that can receive a particular playbill; the higher the potential audience, the higher the rates should be. If the number of display ads in a playbill is limited to one or two, these become more valuable and should command higher rates.

The local printer or newspaper is often anxious to obtain the rights to publish playbills for a theatre organization, especially if it is a professional theatre that offers a full season or series of productions. Publishers of other periodicals already have contacts with advertisers as well as printing facilities, making publication much easier for them than for the theatre staff. Whenever contracts are signed giving permission to some other company to print the playbills, the theatre should protect its right of final approval over all editorial copy and always guarantee itself the necessary space in the playbill to print its production information, staff listings, cast biographies and so forth. The theatre should also select the cover design and the general size and look of the playbill, since it is a major factor in creating the public image that a theatre projects.

### OTHER ADVERTISING SPACES ■

Selling ads in the program is an obvious way of earning extra money, but there are other ways to sell advertising space, although the extent to which this is done should always be governed by the desired image of a theatre. Will too many

*See chapter 15.

advertisements in too many places around the theatre building and in its literature create a cluttered or cheap appearance? The answer depends as much on the content and design of the advertisements as on the number of them. Here are a few possible places where a theatre may sell advertising space:

1. *Ticket envelopes*
2. *Printed brochures and performance schedule cards.* Often, one advertiser may pay the cost of such printings in exchange for being the sole advertiser on it.
3. *Newspaper ads for the theatre.* Business may pay for a theatre's newspaper ads, or some of them, thus creating an association with a cultural activity that they may find desirable.
4. *Postage imprints.* The federal post office now permits private advertising on postal imprints; postage meters may be rented and designed to print short ad messages next to the regular postage imprint. A theatre that handles a lot of mail orders may be able to obtain free postage in exchange for using the postage imprint of a local hotel, restaurant or other business. Or, it may exchange imprinters with another business that brings visitors into the area.
5. *Lobby display space.* Most theatre buildings have sufficient space somewhere in the lobbies or on lobby walls to sell advertising display space, although not all theatre groups wish to do so. Nonetheless, an attractive display from a local antique store or art gallery may not only bring in additional revenue, it may also enhance the appearance of the theatre.
6. *The asbestos curtain.* Until the present century, it was commonplace for most theatres to paint advertisements on the asbestos fire curtain—obviously a prime space that no theatregoer fails to see. Although this practice is blatantly commercial, it may still be appropriate for some theatre organizations.
7. *Theatre seats.* As hospitals and many public buildings place names of contributors on rooms and pieces of equipment, there is no reason why theatres may not tastefully place the name of a person or business on the backs or arms of theatre seats to indicate large or sustaining contributors to the theatre.

### RENTING THE AUDITORIUM ▪

Depending on how actively a theatre organization uses its stage and auditorium, the availability of other leasable halls and theatres in the community and the terms of the theatre organization's own lease with a landlord, the business of renting a theatre to outside groups may be a lucrative source of revenue. Most operation and maintenance costs remain constant whether there are five or ten public events in a hall during a given week. When events are sponsored by outside groups, they are likely to attract people to the theatre building for the first time and this may provide an indirect method of boosting ticket sales for regular theatre productions. Once again, a theatre should engage in rentals only when this does not seriously upset its own work or indirectly associate it with outside groups or purposes contrary to its own image and goals. When the volume of rentals is heavy, a theatre staff member should be assigned to supervise rental activities and, perhaps, to solicit rental contracts. The following points suggest the variety of uses to which a theatre may be easily adapted for rental purposes:

1. Stage productions by other local theatre groups
2. Films, concerts and recitals sponsored by outside groups
3. Fund-raising events, such as fashion shows and lectures, sponsored by outside groups
4. Political and municipal rallies and meetings
5. Industrial shows or meetings sponsored in relation to large conventions being held in the area
6. Graduation and commencement exercises
7. Recitals by local music and dance schools

**OPERATING AND LEASING CONCESSIONS** ▪

The more profit a theatre can earn outside the box office, the more secure its economic structure will be. While the majority of theatre managers prefer to spend their time exclusively on theatrical endeavors, few can afford to overlook the additional revenue that various types of concessions can generate. The first question is whether the theatre itself should staff and operate the concession or whether it should rent on a straight payment or commission basis. Campus, community and other theatres that do not offer continuous, daily performances generally operate their own concessions because profit potentials are too small to interest professional concessionaires. Also, many campus and municipally owned theatre buildings are not permitted to operate certain types of concessions, if any at all. In cases where a building is rented from a private owner, the landlord may reserve for himself the sole right to operate concessions or the right to share in concession revenues. Nonetheless, contributory revenue from concessions can be considerable and there are some cases where profit from such revenue exceeds the profit earned from ticket sales.

Nickle and dime profits from vending machines and other coin-operated contrivances can mount up to an appreciable sum over a period of weeks. Most such machines may be rented or simply used on loan from a vending company, thereby requiring no investment by the theatre and no service or maintenance responsibilities. These include:

Public pay phones
Cigarette machines
Candy machines
Softdrink machines
Coin-operated coat lockers
Coin-operated toilet booths
Rest-room vending machines (combs, sanitary napkins, etc.)

Larger concessions that require considerable management but that also offer the lure of larger profits include:

Coat-room checking services
Automobile parking lots
Restaurant
Alcoholic beverage concessions
Soft drink concessions
Gift shops
Art galleries
Souvenir program sales
Candy sales

Inventory and revenue control over such concessions, as discussed in the previous chapter, is time-consuming when the concession is operated directly by the theatre or when the theatre shares profits on a percentage basis. The easiest and often the best solution is for the theatre to charge a fixed rental fee for concession rights and let a professional concessionaire worry about the problems. This way the two parties will not get into disputes regarding honesty and each can go about his business in a comparatively independent manner. It should be remembered, however, that the theatre *per se* is and should remain the major attraction in the building and not be reduced to the status of a sideshow. Assuming that the theatre is the primary attraction that brings customers to the building in the first place, the theatre management must accept overall responsibility for everything that transpires in the building. If a customer is shortchanged in a lobby gift shop, he will complain at the box office or to the theatre manager, as he will if he receives poor service in the theatre restaurant, inadequate drinks at the lobby bar or loses a dime in the public pay phone. This despite the fact that both the theatre and the concessionaire may merely be tenants under the same roof with no other legal or business relationship. When the theatre is itself the landlord and leases out concession space, it should devise agreements with concessionaires that protect the image and the interests of the theatre. The theatre landlord should reserve the right to evict the tenant-concessionaire if, for example, the latter does not maintain certain standards of cleanliness, customer service and product quality. The concessionaire may also be required to carry certain types of insurance, although in most situations it is easier and less expensive if special insurance coverage (such as products liability insurance, coat room theft coverage, etc.) are attached to the theatre's own policy.

When concessions are used by most playgoers, such as coat rooms and parking lots, the theatre may include a detachable stub on its regular theatre ticket which, upon presentation at the concession, entitles the holder to a particular service. Such stubs may also entitle customers to discounted meals in nearby restaurants or other bargains. At the end of each week, the theatre and restaurant managers in this kind of tie-in offer should get together and match those presented to the restaurant with a duplicate set kept by the theatre. Perhaps the agreement is for the restaurant to pay the theatre a certain cash amount for each stub collected. Perhaps the box office collects the full amount for a combined dinner and theatre ticket, in which case the theatre periodically pays the restaurant for all such ticket sales.

Dinner theatres have become increasingly popular in recent years, but both dinner and theatre need not be offered in the same room in order to create a single ticket that features a dinner-theatre bargain. The "declared" breakdown of prices on

package-deal tickets can be important to the businesses concerned from a tax viewpoint. If both the theatre and the food concession are operated by the same company, for example, it may be decided to declare that, out of a $10.50 package price,
$6.50 is the food cost and $4.00 is the theatre cost. The smaller amount is declared
as theatre income because this enables the theatre to avoid paying percentages, royalties and entertainment taxes on a larger amount. Some theatres have even included an automatic service charge on all printed tickets and never show this on
box office statements: the ticket might read, for instance, "this price includes a
50 cents parking charge." So fifty cents is taken off the top of every ticket, thereby
lowering the amount of revenue on which the theatre pays percentages, royalties
and certain taxes. On the other hand, there may be a local tax imposed on parking
lot revenue that is higher than the state entertainment tax. It should be said that
this practice is not altogether ethical, as it shortchanges actors and playwrights and
deprives them of income that is legitimately theirs.

Theatregoing should be enjoyable, convenient and special. By offering a variety
of "extras," the theatre helps make the experience of playgoing a more complete
and interesting one. But these extras, in the form of concessions and gimmicks, can
easily be overdone or create negative impressions. Contributory income is important
but never as important as the fundamental business of a theatre organization which,
after all, is the business of producing plays.

# ▪ SPONSORING EDUCATIONAL PROGRAMS

More and more theatres of every type are sponsoring community, educational
and special programs. Two reasons for this are that most performing arts organizations today recognize an urgent need to develop new audiences, especially young
audiences, and a considerable amount of grant money and financial aid is given for
programs that are essentially educational or community oriented. The federal
government, as already mentioned, has poured millions into such programs through
Title I, Title III and Model Cities appropriations. It is comparatively more difficult
for a theatre to gain grants for building, production, administrative and regular
operating expenses than it is to get outside funding for programs that send performance troupes into public high schools, train young people in theatre crafts, bring
school children to special performances or relate to community-action programs.
Unquestionably, special programs are needed if future audiences are to be developed
and if artistic standards and appreciation of the arts are to be elevated. But just as
the temptation of profit can cause a commercial theatre to turn its lobby into a
circus of concessions, so the temptation of grant monies can cause even the most
artistically dedicated resident theatre to divert its energies into special programs
that detract from the value of its regular work.

## A SPEAKERS BUREAU ▪

As part of a theatre publicity program, it is helpful to have several staff members
or resident artists who are willing and prepared to address local school and community groups. Once aware that such speakers are available, there will be no difficulty in securing speaking engagements—especially, of course, if the theatre is willing
to provide speakers without charge. In that case, the speeches become obviously

promotional in nature and should be supervised by the publicity or public relations department. If resident staff members or artists are prepared to speak to outside audiences, they should be compensated for their time when speeches are given on general topics, and the theatre at which the speaker is employed should receive a booking fee.

## ADULT EDUCATION PROGRAMS ▪

Using the regular staff members of a theatre organization, assisted by one or two clerical workers, it may be possible to offer a series of adult lectures or workshops. The lecturers should be compensated over their regular salary for such duties and an enrollment fee should be charged to participants. Various special series may be designed around productions being offered at the theatre or as drama appreciation courses or they may concern themselves with theatre crafts. In some cases, it is possible for the theatre to cooperate with a local college or university and make facilities available on a rental basis for college workshop classes or to provide the instructors themselves and charge the college a fee for each student enrolled. In the latter case the college handles the administrative chores and students receive college credit for their work. Many adult education programs, university extension programs or internship programs offer ideal opportunities for cooperative ventures between a theatre and a school and provide numerous advantages for both institutions.

## CHILDREN'S THEATRE WORKSHOPS AND SCHOOL PROGRAMS ▪

If a theatre is engaged in producing its own children's theatre productions and has specialists in residence who are qualified to conduct workshops, it may be able to hold weekly theatre classes for children. These may or may not lead to a public performance by the students. In either case, there is a great demand in most communities for such programs. The responsibility of teaching children the art and craft of theatre, however, should not be taken lightly. There are already far too many poorly supervised children's theatre groups, too many unqualified people working in this field and too much damage being done to future audiences to encourage more programs simply because they are profitable or appear easy to sponsor. On the other hand, dedicated artist-instructor-performers can be of great service as an adjunct to public school instruction and can stimulate young people in their artistic, intellectual and emotional development. By working with the local board of education and with school principals in the district, it may be possible to develop officially endorsed programs that relate to regular classroom instruction, bringing lecture-demonstrations to the schools or bringing students to special performances at the theatre or both.

In recent years several elaborate pilot projects have been tested in which professional, resident theatres received large federal grants to produce hundreds of performances for school students, as was the case with "Project Discovery" at the Trinity Square Playhouse in Providence, Rhode Island. Colorful and detailed literature concerning the play performed together with teacher's manuals were made available to reinforce the performance experience. The play was studied in the classroom as drama, as history and as theatre, with special attention given to scenery and costume design. Students were bused to the Trinity Playhouse from all over the state.

Most often, educational theatre programs are organized informally, infrequently and with little if any relation to the curriculum, which is unfortunate. Part of the cause for this is that funding for educational theatre programs is usually erratic as well as limited. But pressure can be applied through parents' associations, principals and school boards to increase budgets for theatre programs and to establish them as part of the regular school curriculum. Large cultural centers, such as Lincoln Center for the Performing Arts, may find fund-raising for "artists-in-the-schools" projects easier to obtain than if a school itself attempted to originate such a project. Cultural centers also are likely to possess a greater number and variety of artistic personnel for such purposes. Small theatres should attempt to establish more intimate, ongoing programs for children within a limited area, working closely with nearby block associations, civic groups, parents and neighborhood councils. One performing arts college, for example, is planning to establish a number of "storefront conservatories" in its city to stimulate performing arts interest and appreciation among young people and to identify outstandingly talented youngsters when they may benefit most from special training.

### APPRENTICE PROGRAMS ▪

Apprentice programs may be established as part of almost any type of theatre. A civic or community theatre may enlist local high school students as junior members or apprentices. A stock theatre may utilize apprentices to supplement its regular staff and acting company. College theatres that operate summer programs may offer college credit for apprenticeships. Professional resident theatres now hire journeymen actors and stage managers, a form of apprenticeship governed by Actors' Equity regulations. Apprentice programs may be informal or they may be centered around a program of formal classes. Apprentices may receive low salaries and living allowances or they may be charged a tuition fee and also pay for their own room and board. In any case, running an apprentice program should not be confused with running a summer camp. The program should offer a valid learning experience for young people seriously interested in becoming professional artists or theatre craftsmen. An apprentice program should not be inaugurated in order for the theatre to "make a profit" on it, although apprentice-workers may slightly reduce overall staff costs.

## ▪ SPONSORING SPECIAL PERFORMANCES

Almost no theatre organization produces its own performances every afternoon and evening of every week. Yet, in one form or another, rent is probably being paid for the theatre space whether it is utilized or not. If the theatre cannot generate additional income by renting available space to outside groups, then it should consider sponsoring or booking special productions. This, of course, carries the risk of losing money on the visiting event, but with good judgment and experience the risk should not be a large one.

### CHILDREN'S THEATRE PRODUCTIONS ▪

If a theatre does not produce its own children's theatre productions, it may select from touring groups that are available across the country. Some are professional, Equity children's theatre companies and some are not. Each year the Producers'

Association of Children's Theatre (PACT) presents a showcase of productions in New York for the benefit of potential bookers. Other touring children's groups are also available, ranging from marionette performances to circus acts. Professional orchestras, opera companies and dance companies sometimes offer special children's productions on tour. In short, most theatres can easily produce an annual children's theatre series. The revenue can be substantial. The quality of such productions, however, can also vary tremendously.

### SPECIAL MUSICAL PERFORMANCES ▪

Most leading colleges today sponsor a concert series comprised of performances given by the world's major symphonic groups and vocalists. Campus concert managers responsible for booking such series generally belong to The Association of College and University Concert Managers, which holds an annual convention and publishes and distributes literature that is helpful to the campus manager. A variety of other organizations and booking agencies are also active in this field, so that advice and guidance is available to those who seek it. Of course, the sponsorship of large musical groups requires a large auditorium. But recitalists and chamber groups are also available in abundance and if a theatre can develop an audience for such events, it may prove to be a good additional source of income. Popular musical groups, rock singers and the like may also bring in large profits.

### FILM SHOWINGS ▪

Given the necessary equipment, it is usually a simple matter to convert a theatre into a film house without disrupting stage sets and the other accouterments being used for live performances. A great variety of films are available on a rental basis, both sixteen and thirty-five millimeter. Although recent releases may not be available if there is a competing movie house in the community, and a union projectionist may be required, a film series may generate additional profits and also attract a younger or different audience to the theatre building than usually attends the regular live productions.

## ▪ INCOME FROM SUBSIDIARY RIGHTS

### ROYALTIES FROM NEW PLAYS ▪

Whenever a theatre of any kind performs the premiere or pre-New York production of a script, it should attempt to negotiate the right to share in future profits that the property may earn. If the producing organization is the only one interested in presenting the script at the moment, it is in a strong bargaining position. On the other hand, if a premiere is being offered to it and other theatres are also vying for the privilege of producing the property, the bargaining position is considerably weakened. Few campus, stock or resident theatres, for example, would not jump at the chance to premiere a new play by one of the nation's leading dramatists. Unless there is a special reason why the dramatist wishes to be produced in a particular theatre, however, he is unlikely to allow that theatre to share in the play's future profits.

There are, however, many cases in which unknown playwrights are given their first productions in campus and regional theatres, and there are a sufficient number of instances in which such plays have earned large royalties after their premieres to make it worthwhile to negotiate for a subsidiary share in them. When new plays are produced in New York or sold for film production, the theatre in which they were originally produced is often a rightful partner to their success. The profits earned from legally negotiated rights can be of major importance in supporting a theatre and enabling it to produce more new plays. The Dramatist's Guild, Inc., or an attorney can advise both playwrights and producing organizations about the legalities of assigning subsidiary rights.

#### SPONSORSHIP OF TOURING PRODUCTIONS •

A theatre may be able to increase both its profit and its reputation by offering tours of productions that have proved successful in its home theatre. Broadway, Off Broadway and large musical performance groups have long earned a major portion of their income by organizing national tours. Smaller and lesser-known theatre groups can also organize touring productions, perhaps within the public schools or colleges over a statewide area, as part of a summer arts program in city parks or elsewhere. The Juilliard School has established a repertory company under the leadership of John Houseman comprised exclusively of recent graduates of the school's theatre program. The company not only has toured on a nationwide basis but also has offered a summer series at the Saratoga Performing Arts Center. Financed by federal and state grants, many resident theatre companies are able to sponsor extensive tours in public schools and in community centers. On a highly informal and shoestring basis, even the smallest theatre groups can organize special tours. A little-known company that grew out of the New York City Street Theatre, for example, rallied around the leadership of Marquetta Kimbrall and spent a summer performing in the ghettos of Chicago, on Indian reservations in Colorado, for the grape pickers in California, for audiences in Appalachia and for prison audiences in Georgia. Not a typical touring circuit, but one which offered a viable and rewarding experience for the company and proof that the conviction to do something can count for more than the budget. The business of going on tour stems from the desire to reach more audiences and, often, the desire to earn greater income. Touring can provide a means of keeping an acting company together on a permanent basis, since few communities can support a company in residence on a year-round basis, and it can provide a wide audience the opportunity to see what theatre in America has to offer.

#### TRANSFER OF PRODUCTIONS TO OTHER THEATRES •

In New York commercial theatre it is sometimes necessary to transfer a production from one theatre to another because the theatre rental license has expired and the landlord has booked another show into the theatre. Or, the producer may feel that his show would be better off artistically and financially in a different house. Resident theatres in the New York area have sometimes decided to transfer a successful production to an Off Broadway or Broadway theatre, as was the case when *Hair, That Championship Season* and *Sticks and Bones* were moved from the Public Theatre to Broadway houses and when *Slaveship* and *Kaddish* moved from the Chelsea Theatre Center in Brooklyn to Off Broadway houses.

The cost of physically transporting a production from one theatre to another is considerable, especially when union contracts are involved, as they are in commercial New York theatres. But there are other instances when transferring a production involves less work and expense. For example, college theatres might move a production from a workshop to a major stage, or community theatres might decide to continue a successful production at another theatre or hall while its regular theatre goes on with the previously announced production schedule. Productions that are artistically or financially successful, or both, are sufficiently rare to warrant their continuation whenever possible, and this often necessitates the transfer of the production to a new location.

## ▪ MISCELLANEOUS SOURCES OF ASSISTANCE

### INTEREST FROM SAVINGS ACCOUNTS ▪
Although most theatre organizations do not have an abundance of money in the bank, many are able to maintain some balance. Through off-season or inactive periods, as much available money as possible should be placed in savings accounts where it can accrue interest. If season or series tickets are offered for sale considerably in advance of the performance dates, this income should also be placed in savings accounts until it is needed. Not making withdrawals until the first of the month, investing in bonds and other simple practices can earn additional income.

### OBTAINING GOVERNMENT AND BUSINESS SURPLUS ITEMS ▪
Nonprofit theatre organizations that offer educational programs are often eligible to receive government surplus items. Such things as office furniture and machines, paints and canvas may be available for only a small service charge. Disbursement of surplus goods is through state agencies, not through a federal agency, and requests for such goods should be directed to the state surplus property official whose exact title and address can be obtained from appropriate state information listings.

Large industries and businesses sometimes maintain a policy of giving surplus or unneeded items to nonprofit organizations, and a survey of local businesses may prove fruitful indeed. Other private businesses, such as airlines and bus companies, may be willing to provide free services to nonprofit theatre groups, especially when the services provided require no actual cost to the business.

### RENTAL OF EQUIPMENT ▪
Seasonal theatre operations may be able to earn extra income by renting their portable lighting, sound and other stage equipment during their "dark" months to outside groups. Or they may make seldom-used equipment available for rental on a year-round basis. Theatres in some communities have formed an equipment pool and made a general practice of sharing equipment and scenery supplies whenever possible and, also, of avoiding the duplication of equipment purchases so that the common stock of items is varied and mutually economical. Renting equipment from other theatres is usually much less expensive than going to a professional stage rental company. Similar cooperation can be advantageous in the areas of costumes, wigs, make-up supplies, sound equipment and tapes.

### THEATRE TICKETS AS PAYMENT ■

Although it is a policy that should be practiced with caution and only to a limited extent, it is sometimes possible for a theatre group to obtain goods and services in exchange for theatre tickets. Of course, many businessmen willingly provide free services without any compensation (free advertising display space in their windows, the loan of items to be used as stage properties, etc.) and few theatres can afford to give away a pair of tickets every time a poster is put up or a prop is borrowed. But a pair of tickets may turn the trick of obtaining a car for a limited period from a car dealer, for example, or something else that would normally represent a large expense. It never hurts to try!

---

Few people actively engaged in producing plays and managing theatres had any inkling, when they first began, that so much of their time would be spent on ostensibly nontheatre business. Hiring bartenders and checking empty bottles, estimating the number of popsicles to order for a kiddie matinee, going to tea with rich old ladies and to businessmen's luncheons and to countless receptions are not activities that readily satisfy an interest in theatre. But they are necessary if theatre is to be made possible. The need for contributory sources of income to support theatre is unfortunate, as is the need for most actors to supplement their income by finding extra employment outside the theatre. Far better for producers and managers to work at building the artistic standards of a company and for actors to study and practice their art. Nobody enjoys the feeling of being a poor relation in a rich society, of constantly looking for handouts and free services, of counting pennies and always asking favors from friends. But such is the state of theatre today.

The greatest danger that may arise from seeking grants and organizing concessions is that such activity may compromise the direction and the goals that a theatre or individual is striving to obtain. When a majority of grant money seems to be going to minority theatre groups or to the production of new plays, it may be difficult to maintain a desire to specialize in the Elizabethan repertory, just as it may be difficult to resist filling an overcrowded lobby with unattractive vending machines. Ironically, however, a strong and unbending conviction to follow a certain course is the greatest asset that a theatre or individual can possess and the refusal to compromise that conviction is probably the quickest path to success. Certainly, it is that quality of enthusiastic faith in a project that most impresses grants organizations, community leaders and audiences alike. Many contributory sources of income can be tapped without the loss of artistic principle and objective. Once these elements of integrity *are* lost, one may as well put vending machines on the stage itself.

# Part IV

# The Theatre and Its Audience

# CHAPTER THIRTEEN

# Community Relations

The community in which a theatre operates is the immediate family to which it belongs. Audiences may include tourists and distant relatives, but there is always a local nucleus of people drawn from the business, social, governmental, educational and political sectors of the community whose support of the organization is critical as audience or ancillary support or both. The theatrical producer or manager in a large city deals with complex and continuously evolving power structures and institutions that he must understand and learn to live with. In smaller communities the producer's business relationships and his grasp of audience tastes may be easier to establish and maintain. But whether located in a Times Square skyscraper or a Kansas barn, a theatre operator must comprehend the boundaries of that theatre's home community and the forces that make the community what it is.

## ▪ THE PRINCIPLE OF RECIPROCITY

The success of a live performance is judged in great measure by the intensity of the audience-performer relationship. A sense of partnership and mutuality between people is at the core of live theatre. Even if the artistic aim is to "alienate" or "aggitate" the audience, that audience must at least be willing to remain in the theatre. In the wider sense, a theatre can only exist when a sufficient portion of the local community is willing to allow its existence. The Yankee proverb that says "you can't fight city hall" may not be precisely true, yet it contains more than a little wisdom. But how can a theatre gain more than mere tolerance from local audiences and authorities? How can it attract the active and enthusiastic support it requires to survive?

Just as the actor can be prepared for his performance through training and rehearsal, so the audience can be prepared for theatregoing. A community can be led to accept the idea and the value of live theatre through broad public and personal relations while, more specifically, it is given information about a theatre's goals, location, production schedule and admission policy. Preparing a community to be receptive to theatre and motivating it to attend theatre does not mean that public relations for the performing arts should be aimed at creating a passive, uncritical audience. Perhaps live theatre owes the mass media a vote of thanks for providing "nonexperience" entertainment for those who seek diversion without emotional or intellectual engagement. The easy availability of such entertainment today makes it all the more clear that live theatre must offer something special, something personal and complete in terms of human experience. It is the promise of emotional or experiential challenge and response that arts promotion should offer and, of course, that the performance itself should fulfill.

The essential reciprocity of theatre is this: in exchange for the special efforts required for theatregoing, the performer provides a special experience for the theatregoer. This reward is promised both implicitly and explicitly by virtually all theatrical publicity and advertising. When performances fail to provide audience satisfaction, either the actors or the audience or both are poorly or improperly prepared. A major responsibility of theatre administration is the analysis of audience reaction and, subsequently, the appropriate correction of administrative or artistic policy. If audience dissatisfaction is apparent, what is the cause of it? Is it faulty audience preparation (an administrative problem) or faulty production preparation (an artistic problem)?

A valid analysis of audience response can seldom be arrived at unilaterally within the theatre organization. Live theatre audiences are much more than faceless herds of cattle randomly roped off the streets and corralled into theatre chairs. Many come to theatre because they feel an identity with the production being offered or the institution or people who are offering it; others come out of curiosity or social commitment; some out of habit. The community in which a theatre is located gives the theatre's audience a special character and, hence, special responses to theatre which are at least partially predictable—but only if administrators keep an ear close to the ground to gauge the community spirit and character.

This chapter is concerned with ways by which a theatre can establish continuing dialogue with representative audience members and community leaders—methods of reciprocity that underscore the living partnership between a theatre and its audience.

# ▪ FORMAL COMMUNITY TIES

### IDENTIFYING COMMUNITY LEADERS ▪

Chapter 3 discusses factors of community life that a producer should consider before establishing a theatre: audience potential, proximity to transportation, the competition, the media, local organizations, economy, climate and attitudes. The charac-

ter of the community can be analyzed informally and intuitively or with the assistance of detailed feasibility reports compiled by professional consultants. Eventually,
however, an intensive effort must be launched to relate a theatre to its community in
a pragmatic, day-to-day manner. A good way to begin is to identify community leaders in terms of their ability to help (or hinder) the success of the venture.

A theatre that hopes to become a permanent part of its community is well-advised
to conduct the bulk of its business within that locale: to establish bank accounts and
financial credit at the local banks rather than out-of-town banks, to buy from local
retailers and wholesalers whenever possible (even if the cost is a little higher than buying out-of-town), to attend social and political functions in the community. Yet,
when the manager or artistic director is new to the community, he may be tempted
to draw from people and business concerns more familiar to him "back home." There
is no quicker way to alienate the local business and banking segment of the community or to establish an image of the theatre as an "intruder" or "parasite," taking what
it can get monetarily while giving back very little.

Permanently based theatre companies should make personal contact with:

1. Business leaders:
    head of the chamber of commerce, bank presidents, heads of local utilities ser-
    vices, industrial leaders, etc.
2. Political leaders:
    the mayor, leading city officials, elected state and federal representatives, politi-
    cally appointed commissioners, etc.
3. Professionals:
    opinion-makers in educational institutions, in the legal profession, etc.
4. Media directors:
    newspaper editors and publishers, arts critics, radio and television heads, colum-
    nists, etc.
5. Social leaders:
    heads of local women's organizations, service clubs, religious and political clubs,
    charitable organizations and self-appointed society leaders and organizers
6. Cultural leaders:
    heads of cultural organizations, directors and administrators of competing thea-
    tres, heads of local arts councils and philanthropic groups, etc.

Letters must be sent, appointments arranged, receptions held and personal contacts
renewed on a regular basis. To formalize this process, a theatre can create one or more
advisory boards to cultivate the friendship and support of local leaders and to benefit
from their experience and position.

## A BOARD OF ADVISERS ▪

Any theatre group may create a board of *advisers* (which has no legal obligation to
the theatre) comprised of thoughtfully selected community leaders. An advisory board
may function separately or in conjunction with a board of trustees. Generally, advisers should be people who are enthusiastic about the theatre that they serve, although, occasionally, "foes" become friends when invited to join such a group. There
may be no quicker way to silence a highly negative or critical voice than by giving that

voice an opportunity to help change what it opposes—most palates still prefer sugar to salt. Also, every community has a few resident kooks, eccentrics, gossip-mongers and "nuts" who should not be ruled out as possible advisers.

An advisory committee should have specific responsibilities, should meet regularly and should change at least part of its membership on an annual basis. Its opinion should be sought (though the theatre administration is not bound to abide by it) regarding such matters as play selection, general policy, public relations, financial problems and long-range planning. The producer or general manager, if not others on the theatre staff, should be present at all general meetings of this board and should know each of its members personally. Sometimes an individual on a board of trustees or advisers, because of his special or personal acquaintances, can be asked to solve a specific problem for the theatre. For instance, a board member might be able to assist the theatre in establishing its banking credit, in obtaining more cooperation from the press or in securing special permission from city officials for such things as placing directional signs on city property or obtaining permits for street theatre festivals.

While advisory committees are too cumbersome for commercial New York productions, they are a helpful asset to most other types of producing organization, both profit and nonprofit. With its growing awareness of community ties, the college theatre can certainly benefit from advisory groups—at least one each comprised of students and community leaders. Stock and resident theatres may also create advisory boards to advantage. Civic performing arts centers may create several advisory committees, each with a specific area of specialization, such as business, public relations and fund-raising. The function of such committees, however, should not be confused with that of volunteer ticket sales committees and other "working" groups or with "patrons" groups or groups of "friends" or sponsors who purchase season or series tickets. Advisers should be called upon primarily to give advice which, if it is well-founded, provides an objective and analytical overview of an operation which may assist its administrators.

INVOLVEMENT IN COMMUNITY PROGRAMS •

Most theatres expect their community to support them at least to the extent of buying tickets. It seems only fair, then, for the theatre to reciprocate by supporting the community. And this should go further than buying an annual ticket to the firemen's ball! The theatre should ask: What local programs, organizations, landmarks and institutions are most highly regarded by local residents? What are the local assets in which the community takes greatest pride? How can the theatre use its special know-how and resources to assist local causes?

While political activities and other partisan efforts should generally be avoided (unless, of course, they relate directly to the objectives of a theatre company), official theatre support for worthwhile, charitable programs may win reciprocal support for the theatre. Aside from benefit performances to raise money for local programs, what methods may be used?

Stock, resident and college theatres that engage well-known performers will find many who have their own pet charity or who are willing to make personal appearances and appeals for worthwhile causes. During a busy week of performances at one stock theatre, for instance, the widely respected actress Helen Hayes spent a day fund-raising for the local hospital (radio appeals, guest of honor at a lawn party that charged $25 per person, guest at a nurses' association cocktail party and visitor to more than a hundred hospital patients). Such appearances are easy to encourage and cost the theatre nothing, although the community benefits extensively.

Government arts agencies have given special grants to professional performing arts companies that tour the campus circuit if they are willing to conduct master classes and lectures at the campuses where they perform. Usually open to the entire student body if not auditors from the general community, these activities stimulate performance attendance while also providing an unusual community service.

Most theatres retain control over the editorial content of their playbills and this offers another opportunity for the support of local causes. An article or story that promotes some nontheatrical program, a free advertisement for a local charity or some similar gesture can usually be published in a playbill at no cost to the theatre.

A theatre may donate the use of its building to outside groups for the purpose of fund-raising, provide a booth or table in its lobby where charitable contributions may be solicited, send out another organization's literature with mail-order tickets and so forth. As with setting up concessions, it is obviously important that a theatre select the causes it supports with care and carry out this support in a manner appropriate to its own objectives and goals.

Finally, a theatre should be an active member of the chamber of commerce, the local business bureau or trade association and neighborhood and civic organizations involved in such areas as ecology, beautification, urban renewal and community-planning. Involvement signifies that a theatre is truly part of the community in which it operates, that it cares about the community and does not shun or ignore the responsibilities of community citizenship.

## THE THEATRE STAFF AND THE COMMUNITY ■

Each person who works for a theatre, whether as a salaried employee or as a volunteer worker, is a representative of that theatre. His actions on the street, at the local pharmacy and in the restaurant next door all contribute to the community's image of the theatre. This fact assumes greater importance in small towns than in large cities, but it can never be overlooked. Even on Broadway a producer depends on staff members to maintain good relations with numerous people who are ostensibly unassociated with the theatre business.

Producers and managers should welcome feedback from employees regarding any ill will that they encounter in the community. A midwestern theatre manager, for example, was aware of a local undercurrent of negativism toward his theatre; yet, he was unable to pinpoint the cause of it. As the opening night of his first season in residence approached, the publicity department armed a bevy of volunteers with posters for distribution in local stores. A few of the volunteers reported that tradesmen refused to display the posters, even when offered complimentary tickets. Some businessmen were openly hostile when the theatre workers appeared and one volunteer was given a severe dressing-down by a pharmacist and nearly thrown bodily out of the store. The manager investigated the matter for himself and learned that the properties mistress of the previous season had returned borrowed props in poor condition or not returned them at all. The pharmacist claimed that the theatre had borrowed a man's pipe some ten months previous but failed to return it. The manager inquired if a bill for the pipe had ever been sent to the theatre. The answer, given rather sheepishly, was no. What was the value of the pipe? The pharmacist placed the retail value at $3.95. The manager gave the man a check, together with an invitation to be his guest at the theatre.

A single, irate person in the community can create thousands of dollars worth of negative publicity. There is an undeniable facet of human psychology that makes many people happier when they are complaining about something than when they are not. Because people are likely to gripe most about their current job or set of circumstances, effort must be taken to dissuade employees from airing dirty linen in public. Dissatisfaction often arises from ignorance, from petty jealousies or from a sense of being ignored or ill-treated. Small theatres can discourage employee griping by creating an atmosphere of openness among staff members and participants. Workers in a large institution find it more difficult to relate to the institution and its leaders and more difficult to vent criticism to the appropriate people—a situation that institutional managers must work diligently to overcome.

## ▪ COMMUNITY RESOURCES

### HUMAN RESOURCES ▪

A theatre's audience, real and potential, is that theatre's primary human resource, its constituency, together with the actors, the staff and others who assist the operation in a myriad ways. All the financial and material resources in the world can't make theatre work if the very considerable human resources it requires are missing.

Who are the potential members of an audience and how can they be reached?

Affluent segments of a community, from which many theatres derive considerable support, tend to be more conspicuously organized than poorer segments. Social, political and business leaders in the affluent sector are generally well known, as are the living habits and leisure-time preferences of that sector. Wealthier citizens belong to more clubs and organizations, are listed in more directories, have more permanent and easily obtained addresses than the middle and lower income groups. As a resource for fund-raising as well as audience support, then, the wealthy segment is comparatively easy to define.

Similarly, large industry, business and educational units are easier to spot than a collection of smaller ones. The former may be important as a market for group ticket sales, as a source of advisory personnel and of financial and material contributions. The city or community with readily identifiable social, political and financial units may be described as having a "high" profile—one from which it is theoretically easier for an incipient theatre group to gain support. Where there is a "low" community profile, it will probably be more difficult and take longer for a theatre to establish itself with any permanency. The Borough of Brooklyn, New York, provides a case in point.

Although it has the fourth largest population of any American city, Brooklyn as a whole presents a low profile. As the "bedroom of Manhattan," the borough contains a large number of commuting residents; there is a marked absence of large industry and large business. Commercially, it is a community of small shopkeepers. Politically, it is a constituent of the City of New York. Ethnic groups within the borough, however, remain fairly self-contained and easily recognizable from neighborhood to neighborhood. But intraneighborhood travel—especially for leisure-time purposes—is rare.

The Coney Island resident is unlikely to visit a Bedford-Stuyvesant theatre, the Flat-bush resident unlikely to visit a Brooklyn Heights theatre and so forth. Consequently, if a Brooklyn theatre group wishes or needs to attract more than neighborhood sup-port, it faces a very discouraging problem indeed; but it is a problem common to many theatres in many different cities. In such cases, publicity must penetrate deep into each neighborhood and, ideally, each neighborhood must feel a sense of identifi-cation with the theatre. This provides a good opportunity for the use of advisory com-mittees, with one each from the larger neighborhoods and each committee represented on a general board of advisers.

But advisory groups are merely one means of opening channels of communication between a theatre and its community. The more such channels that exist, the more a theatre is able to understand its audience and, importantly, its nonaudience. Any con-versation, any meeting, any confrontation between the personnel of a theatre and others provides an opportunity to discover human resources that may be of mutual benefit. Perhaps advisers can suggest how to organize group ticket sales; perhaps the butcher's wife is a seamstress who is willing to assist the costume department from time to time; perhaps the milkman will loan the theatre his truck on weekends; per-haps the local college will provide dormitory space for visiting theatre personnel. Knowledge of such facts is tremendously important to the theatre administrator—and they are all facts that can only be learned through person-to-person contact. When put to use, they also tend to generate interest in the theatre and increase audi-ence support, simply by virtue of involving people directly in the theatre's work. The seamstress tells her family about the costumes she is making, the milkman tells his customers how his truck is converted into a sound stage for street theatre productions. Slowly the theatre becomes known in all segments of the community—known as a place where "something is happening," where there is something that should not be missed.

Most people must be told that they will enjoy something before they will attempt to experience it. Theatre personnel, together with the publicity department, must create favorable word of mouth about the theatre and its productions and this word of mouth serves as a matchmaker, bringing together the public and the production. The more that people are prepared to like something, the more they will actually tend to enjoy it. And the audience attitude of enjoyment can be reinforced while it is at the theatre (program articles, personal contacts and the like) and after it has left the theatre (newspaper reviews, stories, follow-up publicity). There is an old rule about public speech-making that says that all effective speeches should tell the listeners (1) what they're *about* to hear, (2) what they *are* hearing and (3) what they've *just* heard. In other words, any message or theme should be repeated at least three times. If the administration of a theatre can somehow tell audiences they are about to enjoy a pro-duction, tell them again while they are enjoying it and tell them afterwards that they have enjoyed it, the majority will almost certainly enjoy themselves! What is the secret of romantic matchmaking? Pick two strangers and tell each one separately that the other is madly in love with him or her. Arrange for the two strangers to meet and let simple psychology blossom into romance! The public relations director for a thea-tre has a lot in common with a marriage broker.

## MATERIAL RESOURCES ▪

"Where can we find an Oriental cricket cage, a live goat and a beat-up army jeep?" asks the discouraged properties mistress two days before the opening of *Teahouse of the August Moon*. "Where can we get two theatre seats to replace the ones that were broken when the ladder fell off the first balcony?" asks the house manager. "Where can we find a tape splicer before today's rehearsal?" asks the sound engineer.

The theatre manager's life is literally flooded by such questions and the success of his operation depends to a remarkable degree upon how ready he is with the answers. While managers must always keep an ear open for potential human resources, they must also keep an eye open for potential material resources. The enterprising stock or community theatre director never visits a house without memorizing its contents, never looks casually through antique shops and has an insatiable curiosity about who owns what, goes where and knows whom. His memory and the memories of the theatre staff comprise an encyclopedic resource of priceless value. So often in theatre it is not only a matter of low budgets but of severely pressing time limitations that turn otherwise petty problems into crises of gargantuan proportions. Finding a live goat is one thing, but even for the Broadway producer, finding a live goat with a reasonable degree of toilet training is no small challenge!

Knowing the physical and material resources of a community, then, is an essential prerequisite of theatrical producing. Published lists of names, business services and other precious bits of information are certainly helpful. But no printed directory can replace quick-thinking personnel who know the people, places and things that comprise the local community.

## COMMUNICATION RESOURCES ▪

In this electronic age it is tempting to think of "communication" as a process dependent on television, telephones, radios and computers. The very word "communication" suggests something more complicated and mysterious than two people sitting down and talking with each other. Yet, communication is just that—people talking with people. Live theatre reminds us of the humanity in communication. And the "liveness" of live theatre should not occur exclusively during performance time. If "liveness" is the leading component of theatre (its most unique quality in contrast to the electronic media, literature and the visual arts), then it is a quality that should be emphasized in the day-to-day operations of a theatre company: the liveness of a personal visit as opposed to a phone call, the liveness of a personal greeting as opposed to a recorded message, the liveness and imperfection of human behavior—behavior which most of all shuns the impersonal approach. The human and material resources of a community cannot be discovered, much less harnessed for action, without a highly personalized approach to communication: people talking with people.

Theatre remains a localized, community business: a small shopkeeper in a world of chain stores and mass distribution. It competes most effectively by emphasizing its unique attributes rather than by attempting to imitate the "big guys." For example, there would be something distinctly incongruous about walking into the office of a resident theatre company to discover a neatly tailored secretary sitting behind a switchboard, amidst black and chrome furniture, plastic plants and wall-to-wall carpeting and telling people that "so-and-so is 'in conference' right now." Television studios and slick business firms might find this a desirable "front," but it is insufferably sterile when transposed to the environs of live theatre, precisely because it is not very "lively."

The first communication resource a theatre organization can tap is not the news media or some electronic device invented to save time. It is the ability of the theatre's personnel to talk with outsiders and each other on a personal basis in a manner that expresses the purpose and the excitement of live theatre.

In every social unit (the family, the neighborhood, the community at large) there exists an almost tangible communication network. Like sending chain letters, each individual tends to receive and transmit verbal messages along particular interpersonal routes. Person A tells person B, who tells C, D, E, who tell certain others. Community leaders invariably represent major communication "terminals," since no position of leadership can be gained without an ability to make people listen. When the same message is transmitted through a number of "terminals" within the same network, it gains in force and credibility. The object, then, is to study the personal communication network within a given community and to learn how messages are commonly transmitted. The theatre manager must also study the influence of news media upon the community for the purpose of learning which media terminals most strongly influence public opinion, where paid advertising is most effective and so forth. But saturation advertising is outside the budgetary limits of most theatres, so word-of-mouth advertising remains crucial. For some theatres, in fact, it may be virtually the *only* advertising. The community theatre may be able to afford no more than mimeographed fliers. Inner-city theatres may find that their potential audience reads no newspaper at all. Favorable word of mouth, especially from the local opinion-makers, is essential.

Theatre is live people relating to other live people—right now, in person, in the flesh.

# ■ THE AUDIENCE PROFILE

Because so much time, money and effort is spent on getting people to purchase tickets for a production, it is tempting to forget about people once they have purchased a ticket. Yet, the audience attending a production provides the primary resource material for research and analysis regarding the successes and failures of any theatre and any production. Where does the audience come from? Why did they purchase tickets? What do they think? What segments of the community do they represent? What segments are not represented?

## INFORMAL AND INTUITIVE AUDIENCE ANALYSIS ■

Small theatre operations usually enjoy frequent, personal contact between the staff and the audience, making it comparatively easy to gain some understanding of audience characteristics. If, for instance, telephone reservations are taken at the box office, the treasurers will soon learn where the bulk of the audience is coming from, how far in advance they generally reserve their seats, whether they feel that ticket prices are too high and other such things. The treasurers, the house manager and the ushers will hear numerous comments that indicate audience reaction to the performance. One can visually estimate the median age of the audience and guess at its general level of education, taste and affluence.

A theatre administrator must be an "audience-watcher" and make every attempt to know his audience, individually and collectively. But there is a danger in arriving at conclusions too informally or intuitively too much of the time. After all, play selection, advertising and many other decisions are made largely on the basis of how a theatre audience is analyzed. Many myths and faulty generalizations about theatre audiences have been perpetuated because producers and publicists are always seeking quick explanations for poor attendance. "Young people don't support live theatre," "no show can survive a bad review in the *Times*," "people can't afford to go to theatre any more" and "most people prefer comedies" are all common statements in theatre circles, despite the fact that none hold up under close scrutiny.

Several recent studies confirm that the theatre industry knows far less about its audiences than it likes to believe. The first comprehensive, nationwide survey of performing arts audiences was conducted by William J. Baumol and William G. Bowen and reported in their book *Performing Arts: The Economic Dilemma*. On the basis of over twenty-four thousand usable survey returns, they found that audiences have not changed markedly over the past several decades in terms of size, median age, income range, education and the like. They found little indication of a "cultural boom" during the sixties. There appeared to be little difference between Broadway and Off Broadway audiences. The education and income levels for performing arts audiences, they found, were extremely high. Other extensive surveys of arts audiences are currently in progress and will doubtless be of value in further dissipating some favorite myths.

### AUDIENCE SURVEYS ■

While much work remains to be done before arts administrators have a truly scientific evaluation of America's leisure-time activities, administrators can gain specific information about their own audiences by conducting periodic surveys at their own theatres. Questionnaires may be designed to elicit responses regarding special problems or "gray" areas that exist for a certain theatre. Perhaps the manager wishes to know which are the most frequently read newspapers in the community, how effective the direct-mail publicity is, how often audience members attend other live performances or which surrounding neighborhoods support the theatre most heavily.

A common method of conducting an audience survey is to insert questionnaires into the playbills and to provide pencils at convenient locations in the lobbies, along with boxes where completed questionnaires may be deposited. This method assures that everyone in the audience will receive a questionnaire. If there are several ticket prices and sections in the theatre (orchestra, loge, balcony), it may be desirable to use different-colored questionnaires (or some other indication) for each section. This enables the evaluator to learn, for example, if students tend to buy the lowest-priced seats, which sections may or may not object to existing ticket prices and other correlations between audience characteristics and the price paid for tickets.

An alternate means of survey distribution is to instruct ticket-takers and ushers to hand the surveys to customers as they enter the theatre or during intermissions. The most intrusive method is to dispatch a team of interviewers during intermissions to conduct oral interviews with a random sampling of the audience. This may guarantee more honest and detailed results, but it constitutes a serious interruption of the playgoers' evening. When simply given a questionnaire and sufficient time to complete it, the number of returns should be sufficient to obtain valid results. Most people like being asked for their opinion and most cooperate to a remarkable degree in giving honest, thoughtful answers to survey questions.

The survey questionnaire should be designed with the following guidelines in mind:

1. The more personalized questions tend to bring the least reliable answers (i.e., questions dealing with the respondent's income).
2. The fewer the questions on a survey sheet, the better.
3. The less actual writing the respondent must do, the better. (Questions should be followed by answer spaces or boxes in which the respondent simply marks an "x.")
4. The more precise the questions, the less room there will be for misinterpretation.
5. The fewer possible answers to each question, the better (although great care must always be taken not to omit possible responses to a question).

The more usable questionnaires that are completed and returned, of course, the greater the validity of the results (although statisticians consider a 30 percent return on distributed questionnaires to be sufficient in most cases). A common danger in survey-taking is failure to consider all the variables that influence results. Are the questions and answers really measuring what the evaluator *thinks* they are measuring? For example, results are invalid when the audience surveyed is not representative of the theatre's general audience. If a theatre offers eight weekly performances over a twelve-week season, an entire week should be surveyed (matinee and evening or week-night and weekend audiences vary greatly). Performances attended by unusual, non-representative groups should be avoided: large groups of children, students, senior citizens and others easily invalidate survey results. Also, the week selected for the survey should feature a production that is fairly typical of the theatre's usual attractions.

When preparing the questionnaire, close attention should be given to each question. First, is the question necessary? For instance, does the surveyor really need to know the sex of the respondent? (Most people attend theatre in pairs and it is likely that married couples will complete only one questionnaire between them and, furthermore, that the husband will exercise the prerogative of completing it, thereby producing results that show a predominately male audience when this is not the case at all.)

The following chart shows the questions and the results of an audience survey that was conducted by the Theatre Division at Brooklyn College over six performance nights of a major production. Nearly 50 percent of the questionnaires distributed were completed and returned. The answers shown are represented by percentiles computed to the nearest full point.

### RESULTS OF AN AUDIENCE SURVEY CONDUCTED AT GERSHWIN THEATRE, BROOKLYN COLLEGE (MARCH 1970)

A. What is your age?

| | |
|---|---|
| 1. under 12 | 0% |
| 2. 12-17 | 15% |
| 3. 18-21 | 39% |
| 4. 22-30 | 15% |
| 5. 31-40 | 8% |
| 6. over 40 | 23% |

B. Sex:

| | |
|---|---|
| 1. male | 36% |
| 2. female | 64% |

C. Where do you live:

| | |
|---|---|
| 1. Brooklyn | 89.43% |
| 2. Queens | 4% |

3. Manhattan 3%
4. Bronx .55%
5. Staten Island .02%
6. other 3%

B. Are you:
1. married 32%
2. single 68%

E. Are you attending the performance
tonight:
1. alone 9%
2. w/spouse 18%
3. w/friend 73%

F. Do you think the curtain-time tonight is:
1. too early 8%
2. too late 7%
3. just right 85%

G. Are you a:
1. B.C. student 39%
2. student elsewhere 19%
3. B.C. faculty member 4%
4. other 38%

H. Are you a full time:
1. educator 14%
2. student 48%
3. businessman 6%
4. professional 8%
5. retired 2%
6. housewife 10%
7. other 12%

I. If you are self-supporting, what is your income? Or, if not self-supporting, what is
the total income of your family?
1. under $5000 9%
2. $5,000 to $10,000 29%
3. $10,000 to $15,000 25%
4. over $15,000 23%
5. no answer (14%)

J. What is your primary reason for attending this performance?
1. for entertainment 54%
2. a friend or relative is connected
with the production 15%
3. production is related to
classroom study 21%
4. other 10%

K. How did you get here tonight?
1. car 53%
2. bus 19%
3. subway 12%
4. walk 15%
5. other 1%

L. How did you first hear about this production?
1. radio 0%
2. city newspaper 1%
2. posters 13%
4. campus newspaper 3%
5. direct mail 13%
6. word of mouth 50%
7. from an instructor 20%
8. other 0%

M. What publication do you most frequently
read for entertainment information?
1. New York Times 38%
2. New York Post 20%
3. Village Voice 10%
4. Daily News 12%
5. B.C. campus papers 2%
6. Cue Magazine 11%
7. other 7%

N. Have you seen another play in Gershwin
Theatre since September?
1. Yes 41%
2. No 59%

O. Have you ever attended a performance
in the B.C. New Workshop Theatre?
1. Yes 28%
2. No 72%

P. Have you seen a B.C. music department
event since September?
1. 0 40%
2. 1-3 43%
3. over 3 17%

R. How many Off Broadway productions
have you seen since September?
1. 0 54%
2. 1-3 33%
3. over 3 13%

S. About how many films have you
attended since September?
1. 0 6%
2. 1-3 25%
3. 4-10 45%
4. over 10 24%

T. About how many hours do you watch
TV each week?
1. 0 hrs. 9%
2. 1-5 hrs. 47%
3. 6-10 hrs. 26%
4. over 10 hrs. 18%

U. About how far in advance did you
order your ticket(s)?
1. month 15%

| | | | | |
|---|---|---|---|---|
| 2. week | 40% | 2. by phone | 5% |
| 3. day | 23% | 3. in person at B.C. | 48% |
| 4. tonight | 22% | 4. through a friend | 43% |

V. Was your ticket:
   1. full price    36%
   2. discounted    48%
   3. complimentary    16%

W. Do you feel that the price of the ticket is:
   1. too high    9%
   2. too low    2%
   3. fair    89%

X. Did you buy your ticket:
   1. by mail    4%

Y. Which type of theatre production do you prefer?
   1. serious plays    44%
   2. musicals    23%
   3. comedies    19%
   4. all    14%

Z. Would you purchase a season ticket for next year's B.C. theatre productions if you were offered 5 plays for the price of 4?
   1. Yes    24%
   2. No    17%
   3. Maybe    59%

## CHARACTERISTICS    (according to survey results in foregoing chart)

### Most Average Playgoer

*Single, female, age 20
*Brooklyn resident
*$14,000 family income
*Brooklyn College student
*Attended play with friends
*Arrived by car
*Prefers serious plays
*Not a regular B.C. playgoer
*Hasn't seen Music Department concert
*Heard about play from friends
*Bought ticket 5 days in advance in person at the box office at discount rate; thinks price is fair

*Entertainment in past 6 months: 7 films, 2 Broadway shows, 2 Off Broadway shows, 8 hrs. of TV per week
*Would consider buying a season ticket
*Reads the *New York Times* for entertainment information

### Least Average Playgoer

*Married, male, age 35
*Non-Brooklyn resident
*$5,000 family income
*B.C. faculty or no B.C. affiliation
*Attended play alone
*Arrived by subway or walked
*Likes all types of plays
*Has attended play here before
*Has seen Music Department concert
*Heard about play from "other sources"
*Ordered ticket by mail, a month in advance; got complimentary ticket, thinks price is fair but curtain time is too late

*Entertainment in past 6 months: No films, over 3 Broadway shows, over 3 Off Broadway shows, does not watch TV
*Would not consider buying a season ticket
*Reads the *Village Voice* for entertainment information (or the local suburban papers)

### TYPICAL AND ATYPICAL THEATREGOERS ▪

The results in the sample survey shown above enable the evaluator, at a glance, to understand the general characteristics of his audience. A more graphic way of depicting these results would be to determine those characteristics that represent the most average playgoer and the least average playgoer. A cartoonist might picture two hypothetical figures based on the survey results.

It would not be a bad idea for audience survey results to be pictured in a manner similar to the above cartoon and displayed in the office of the theatre to which they pertain. Certainly, theatre administrators should have a clear, well-informed picture in their mind of typical and atypical audience members to facilitate decision-making and continued audience analysis.

Despite high purpose and artistic merit, a theatre group may find it impossible to survive if it is encumbered by bad community relations. Good relations and an atmosphere of good will make the work of theatre much, much easier. A theatre must work hard to create and maintain a positive and cooperative spirit from the community in which it is located. This involves the kind of work that begins long before the curtain rises and continues long after the audience has gone home.

Knowing the audience, individually and collectively, is a big first step in communicating with it. Audiences should be analyzed, formally and informally, and policy decisions should be directly related to the conclusions. Theatre is not produced for its own benefit, it is produced for "the people out front."

# CHAPTER FOURTEEN

# Press Relations and Publicity

The three little words that theatre people most like to hear are "standing room only." Theatrical advertising, publicity and promotion all aim at attracting capacity audiences on a regular basis. But ticket-buyers are elusive and many factors influence the success or failure of a theatrical production, making "SRO" signs a comparatively rare spectacle. The job of the publicity director is, if not the most difficult staff position in a theatre, certainly the most thankless one. Like the proverbial mother's, the publicist's job is never done. Even when a production is sold out, work must continue to improve the image of the theatre in the public eye, to secure grants and other contributions and to strengthen audience support for the future. When audiences are small, the publicity director is first to be criticized. When attendance is high, credit is given to others. It is difficult and perhaps fruitless to speak of "good" publicity as opposed to "bad" publicity. Either promotion succeeds in its goal of attracting audiences or it doesn't. Most theatrical press agents know this and are fond of saying "the only bad publicity is *no* publicity." Or, as a notorious actress once said, "I don't care what people say about me, as long as they keep talking about me!"

# ■ THREE REQUISITES OF ALL PUBLICITY

### GETTING ATTENTION ■

A newspaper advertisement, a press release, a personal appearance, a special gimmick and all other types of promotion must first capture attention. If the potential reader doesn't *see* an ad or the editor doesn't read the press release or nobody shows up when the star makes a personal appearance, then the value of such things is "zero." There are all kinds of ways that promotional material can gain attention. There are endless gimmicks, stunts and activities that can be invented to call attention to a particular theatre or production. Whatever method is used must *itself* be captivating. The simpler techniques are frequently the most effective. A press release, for example, might be printed on brightly colored paper so the editor who receives it and whose desk is cluttered with dozens of other press releases will notice it and be less likely to misplace it. The newspaper advertisement with a border around it or with minimal, uncluttered copy will stand out on the printed page. In other words, the ultimate purpose of theatrical publicity is to call attention to a production or event, but the publicity device employed to do this must first call attention to itself.

### PROVIDING MOTIVATION ■

Once promotional subject matter has captured attention, it must go a second step and motivate the reader or observer to buy tickets or follow whatever other course is advocated by the promotional material (i.e., donating money, volunteering services, etc.). Even the most casual observer of media advertising today is aware that he is being appealed to on many levels. Most advertising does more than say, in effect, "buy me." It says "buy me *because* . . ." The "because" is the advertising element meant to provide enough motivation to convert potential consumers into paying customers. The shoddy and sometimes dishonest techniques invented by Madison Avenue to sell Americans everything from cheesecake to presidents have been exposed in many studies, including Vance Packard's *The Hidden Persuaders*, Alvin Toffler's *The Greening of America* and *The Culture Consumers* and Theodore White's *The Making of the President*. Yet, the advertising assault on the public mind continues without much change.

A majority of advertisements employ what might be called "personal motivating appeals": appeals to an individual's self (often selfish) needs and desires. The desire to be beautiful, rich, popular, famous, successful and sexy appears to dominate the field. Other promotional pieces appeal to selfless interests such as honesty, humanity, religion, patriotism and charity. There is nothing wrong with self or selfless interests as such. What is frequently wrong with the ads, however, is that they make promises that cannot possibly be fulfilled by the product being advertised. How many television commercials, for example, use the "before and after" technique that pictures a miserable-looking girl before she uses some product or other and then shows her looking like a movie star or walking down the aisle toward marital bliss after having used the product? Obviously, no cosmetic or mouthwash can turn a spinster into a happy housewife or a dull coed into a scintillating siren. Unhappily, however, human desire often dominates human intelligence.

It is the nature of advertising to promise the consumer some kind of fulfillment if he uses the product or service being advertised. But responsible advertisers are careful to promise only what their product can deliver, because they want the customer to purchase it more than once. Generally, products will be judged on the basis of how they are advertised: do they live up to the promises made about them or not? And this pertains to the way audiences judge a theatre production just as much as the way people judge a newly purchased mousetrap.

### DELIVERING SATISFACTION ▪

To advertise a warmly touching but nonfarcical play like *Our Town* or *Ah, Wilderness!* as an "uproarious comedy hit" is no less misleading than to advertise a toothpaste for its ability to produce "sex appeal" after the first brushing or a political candidate's ability to bring about world peace if he is elected. Yet, promises like these are made frequently. Aside from creating customer dissatisfaction, they tend to invite the wrong kind of judgment regarding the product. If an audience goes to *Ah, Wilderness!* expecting to swoon from belly-laughter, it will be hard-pressed to respond in a more appropriately appreciative manner even if the production is superb. And disappointment will be justified.

Theatrical advertising can generally be criticized for its lack of imagination and professionalism, but it shouldn't go too far in mimicking flashier and more superficial advertising methods. It should promote the product (the theatrical performance) as the main consumer attraction and underplay or ignore less primary appeals that may entice a few playgoers.

While the performance must deliver the satisfaction promised by advertisements about it, the advertisement or publicity piece itself must provide "information satisfaction." If a reader's eye is attracted to an advertisement on a newspaper page and the copy and graphics of the ad stimulate his desire to attend the performance, then he should be able to learn from the ad the basic information he needs to "follow through." Where and when is the performance being held? How can tickets be obtained and for how much? Strange as it may seem, many advertisements and press releases leave out such information. Is it "chic" to assume that one needn't give out an address, that potential customers will take the trouble of looking it up in the telephone directory? Far wiser to assume that most people are lazy and that the more difficult it is for them to do something, the less likely they will be to do it.

## ▪ THE PUBLICITY DIRECTOR

### QUALITIES ▪

A publicity director is a salesman who should be enthusiastic about the product he is selling. This requires a somewhat outgoing personality, a sense of conviction and the ability to make people sit up and take notice. The experienced publicity director is likely to be more valuable than the person with little experience. It helps considerably to have knowledge of a particular area, to know members of the press, advertising salesmen and local leaders and to know such technical matters as how to write press releases and obtain names for a mailing list. On the other hand, long experience in a job can cause apathy and laziness, so a newcomer may be an enthusiastic go-getter capable of accomplishing more than the old-timer. Writing and typing skills and executive and supervisory abilities are also important in most public relations jobs.

Too, the head of publicity for a theatre must be able to understand the objectives
and qualities of that theatre (or production) and translate them in a manner that will
be meaningful and exciting to the public. When publicity and advertising misrepresent
the true aims and qualities of a theatre, either intentionally or mistakenly, the damage
can be irreparable. The publicity director, above all else, must possess interpretive
talents and techniques.

While it is essential that the public image of a theatre or a production be consonant
with the objectives of that project, it is a mistake to think the public relations director himself must fit some kind of predetermined image. If, to use an extreme example,
a particular theatre wishes to create a fairly conservative and socially snobbish image,
the publicity director himself need not be a conservative snob. The man who has successfully promoted a traveling circus may be just as capable of promoting a traveling
opera company or a chamber music recital. As with most theatrical employees, talent
and ability are far more important than "type."

### REQUIREMENTS ▪

The publicity director can bring a great deal to the theatre project for which he
works, but he cannot succeed unless the management is willing to give him a great
deal to work with. Aside from the basic tools for his work (office space, equipment,
a budget, etc.), he must have access to information regarding the history, goals and
accomplishments of the theatre and its personnel. The advertising and publicity budget, as suggested in chapter 9, should be no less than 10 percent of the total production or operating budget in most cases. The publicity director's salary should reflect
his key position in the theatre's administration. Depending on the type of theatre
project, he may be paid by a predetermined fee, by weekly salary, by a percentage of
the box office gross or by a combination of these. His budget should include an expense account to cover business entertainment and other such costs that are essential
to his work.

Importantly, the producing organization must allow its publicity director a fair
margin for error. He is expected to be an "idea" man, to invent countless promotional devices and gimmicks and to employ imaginative advertising techniques. Not all of
his ideas will work. In the world of publicity the following ratio is probably true:
only one out of ten publicity ideas will be successful and only ten out of a hundred
will even be feasible. If a producer rejects too many publicity ideas or is too quick
to condemn particular ads or promotional techniques, he is denying the publicity
director the flexibility and leeway he requires to do his job. Rarely will a single newspaper ad, however expensive it may be, sell out the house. A single brochure or flyer
seldom "sets the world afire." Repetition, time, variety of approach and word-of-
mouth are the usual ingredients in successful publicity. No publicity director is a
miracle worker. The best, rather, are men and women with a professional way of getting things done efficiently and economically.

### THE ATPAM PRESS AGENT ▪

The Association of Theatrical Press Agents and Managers negotiates minimum employment conditions for press agents, house managers and company managers. Sig-
natories to the tri-annually negotiated agreements include the members of the League
of New York Theatres and various independent producers. The agreement stipulates

that any attraction or production in the United States or Canada that is owned, operated or controlled (directly or indirectly) by any signatory to the Agreement must employ a press agent, a house manager and a company manager at virtually all times. The press agent must be hired four weeks prior to the first paid New York performance (five weeks before, if the production opens first out of town). On tour (after a production has left New York) or after six weeks of a pre-Broadway tour, the press agent may handle only one production. Other regulations cover part-time press agents, local and associate press agents and, of course, establish minimum salaries and other standard demands found in most union employment agreements.

# ■ THE PUBLICITY OFFICE

To organize and dispense public information, certain pieces of equipment and research sources must be available to the publicist. Printing, reproduction and mailing machinery is expensive but necessary. Theatre groups connected with large institutions can usually avail themselves of central printing services. Low-budgeted theatres often rent or borrow reproduction facilities belonging to a neighboring business or someone associated with the theatre organization. However the problem of printing press releases and other promotional material is solved, the result should be neat, professional-looking literature. Messy, illegible or difficult-to-read promotional literature is worthless and should not be distributed under any circumstances. There are simply too many easy and inexpensive ways to produce neat-looking copy for editors or the general public to bother deciphering things that resemble rejected Rorschach tests. A busy and well-organized theatrical publicity office should also possess the following, adapted to its special needs:

## PUBLICITY PRODUCTION MATERIALS ■

**News-release stationery**

**Publicity office stationery**

**Photograph files**
(Standard interior and exterior pictures of the theatre building; photos of leading artistic and administrative employees, of the performers, of past and current productions and rehearsals, of VIP visitors or audience members.)

**Plates and mats**
(Zinc plates—from which printers cast mats and glossy proofs for use in newspaper ads—should be ordered and maintained for all frequently-used pictures, mastheads, logos, graphic designs, etc.)

**Scrapbooks**
(All printed publicity and ads should be collected and placed in scrapbooks, arranged by the production and by year.)

### Press board
(A bulletin board should display all ads, publicity and reviews pertaining to current productions for perusal by staff members and performers.)

### Supplies
(If handmade posters and fliers are produced, an ample supply of construction paper, pens, inks and glue should be kept on hand.)

### Biographies
(A file should be maintained to collect personal data on all performers and leading employees associated with the theatre and its productions.)

### Performers' index
(A file card system should be maintained in which all previous performers are catalogued with the productions, roles and dates when they appeared at the theatre.)

### Addressing machinery
(For typing names on envelopes or labels, for folding and collating addressed mail, etc.)

### Postage meter
(To imprint postage on mailing pieces.)

## SPECIAL LISTS FOR THE PUBLICIST ▪

General mailing list of past and potential ticket-buyers
List of current season-ticket holders
List of special patrons or advisory groups
List of area businesses (hotels, restaurants, etc.)
Organizations list (schools, charities, community centers, etc.)
List of theatre personnel (past and present)
List of appropriate alumni (for school theatres)
List of faculty and administration (for school theatres)
Borrowed lists (supporters of other area theatres, arts organizations, contributors to fund-raising drives, property-owners, members of professional or social organizations, etc.)
General press list to include the following:
    Special press lists (society editors, etc.)
    Press list for printed media only
    Press list for radio and television media
    Local press list
    City-wide press list
    State and national press list

## THE PUBLICIST'S WORKING LIBRARY ▪

All play publishers' catalogues
Copies of all plays in current or imminent production at the theatre
The most recent *Who's Who in the American Theatre*
A good dictionary of the English language
A good desk encyclopedia
A thesaurus and other "word-finder" books
A good "book of quotations"
*New York Critics' Reviews*
One or two theatre histories with New York original production information (casts, dates, etc.)
Playbill collection of all previous productions at the theatre
Area-wide directory of newspapers and periodicals (giving circulation figures and other information, such directories are available from local press-clipping services)
Map collection (of local streets, general area, etc.)
Appropriate periodicals (*Variety*, local newspapers, professional journals, etc.)

A publicist is a strategist and, to plan and execute a publicity campaign, he requires the mind of a field marshal and no small amount of special and ready intelligence. The more preparation that is done in advance of "battle," the more information gathered, the more material prepared and contacts made, the more successful the actual campaign is likely to be.

# ▪ MAILING LISTS

## GATHERING NAMES AND ADDRESSES ▪

Next to person-to-person contact, direct-mail contact is a strong method of attracting potential customers. But the days of the penny postcard are long gone; printing, handling and postage costs for large mailings are high and such advertising is no longer in the "bargain" category. Because direct-mail publicity is expensive, but still effective, a tremendous effort is required to develop and maintain a valuable list of "high-potential" customers.

The best mailing list is comprised of names of "known" customers: people who have attended theatres or productions similar to the one currently being promoted or, better still, people who have previously attended the same theatre in which the currently promoted production is playing. The first source of names and addresses to which the permanent theatre should turn is the mail-order correspondence file in the box office. Whenever a person requests information or orders tickets by mail, that person's name and address should be entered on a 3 x 5 card (easily a duty of the box office clerk handling such correspondence) for placement on the "active" mailing list. The other primary source of names is from audience members who fill out address forms provided for them in the playbill or in the lobby of the theatre. Address forms might resemble the following:

```
┌─────────────────────────────────────────────────────────────────────┐
│              BE THE FIRST TO HEAR ABOUT OUR NEXT PRODUCTION!          │
│                                                                       │
│              (To receive our brochure, please complete this form      │
│               and deposit in the lobby "mailbox" or at the box office.)│
│                                                                       │
│    NAME . . . . . . . . . . . . . . . . . . . . . . . . . . . . . . . │
│                                                                       │
│    ADDRESS . . . . . . . . . . . . . . . . . . . . . . . . . . . . . .│
│                                                                       │
│    . . . . . . . . . . . . . . . . . . . . . . . . . . (Zip) . . . . .│
└─────────────────────────────────────────────────────────────────────┘
```

Or, space may be provided for the customer to write the name and address of "a friend who also might like to receive our brochure." Seasonal operations attended by tourist audiences should design forms that distinguish between seasonal and permanent addresses. Theatres that offer different types of attractions might utilize the following form in order to create mailing lists aimed at specific interests:

```
┌─────────────────────────────────────────────────────────────────────┐
│              PLEASE PLACE MY NAME ON YOUR MAILING LIST.               │
│                                                                       │
│              I would like to be informed about events in the          │
│                  categories that I have checked below:                │
│                                                                       │
│  ☐ Theatre    ☐ Music     ☐ Dance      ☐ Film     ☐ Children's Theatre│
│                                                                       │
│    NAME . . . . . . . . . . . . . . . . . . . . . . . . . . . . . . . │
│                                                                       │
│    ADDRESS . . . . . . . . . . . . . . . . . . . . . . . . . . . . . .│
│                                                                       │
│    . . . . . . . . . . . . . . . . . . . . . . . . (Zip) . . . . . . .│
└─────────────────────────────────────────────────────────────────────┘
```

The address form that is individually inserted into the program, rather than printed as part of the program, is more likely to be filled out and returned. Attractive desks or mailboxes should be placed at convenient places in the lobby for the purpose of filling out and depositing address forms. The playgoer who is already standing in the lobby is the playgoer most likely to return; to miss the opportunity of obtaining his name and address is at best shortsighted.

In cases where a single production is being organized (unassociated with any ongoing theatrical group) the publicist should attempt to borrow mailing lists belonging to other performing arts organizations in the area or include his literature with their regular mailings. One of the most successful and distinguished producers on Broadway, for example, is not above delivering brochures about his shows to box office mail-order clerks for inclusion with the tickets being mailed out for other shows. Once a ticket is ordered for one show, he reasons, why should the competing producer care if the customer receives publicity about another show?

It is also possible to build up a mailing list of good potential customers from the property tax lists in a city hall and from lists obtained from a chamber of commerce, professional organizations and charity groups, professional fund-raisers and the like. These, however, should be kept separate from the list of "known customers" and, probably, used more infrequently. Finally, one may buy or rent mailing lists from companies specializing in that business, although especially for the small theatre group—these lists are expensive and not nearly as valuable as hand-chosen ones. Theatre organizations are often approached to sell their mailing lists to professional mailing houses, a somewhat unethical practice if most names were solicited by the theatre ostensibly for theatre use only.

### MAINTAINING A MAILING LIST ■

The easiest way to collect names is to enter them on 3 x 5 cards and then to file them alphabetically in metal drawers designed for such use. All addresses that come into the box office or from any other source are entered on an index card with the date in the upper righthand corner. Periodically, someone is assigned to file the new cards in the drawers containing the general mailing list. If there is a duplicate card, the old one is removed and the new one inserted. How "current" a theatre wishes to keep its list of names is a policy decision that will vary from theatre to theatre. Perhaps it is decided that no name shall remain on the list for more than five years. Each year, then, all cards dated five years previously are removed and destroyed. This system gives every person on the list five years either to order tickets by mail or to fill out a theatre address card. Of course, the system runs the risk of eliminating the names of people who have been attending theatre but who order their seats in person. But this danger may not be as serious as the budgetary importance of maintaining a meaningful though limited list of active customers.

While bulk postage rates are lower than first-class rates, it may be desirable periodically to send out a general mailing with first-class postage so incorrectly addressed pieces will be returned and the sender can remove those addresses from the list. Or, if bulk mail is labeled "return requested," the invalidly addressed pieces will be returned, but at a cost to the sender of nearly twice the first-class rate.

Large theatre operations may need at least one person working full time to maintain the mailing lists. It may be more economical and efficient to utilize computerized address systems. A computer is able to eliminate duplicate names and to categorize each name according to the particular list(s) specified. The general mailing list (comprised of all names and utilized when an annual calendar of events or similar literature is mailed) may be divided into separate categories (theatre, film, children's theatre, etc.). By a simple adjustment, the computer can be programmed to produce any one of numerous special lists from the general list. New addresses, as they come in, are checked against a computer "print-out" of the general list and added, removed or corrected.

Because postal regulations require that bulk mailings be separated according to zip code categories, file-carded lists should be arranged chronologically by zip number (another advantage of computer lists is that they can be produced either alphabetically or according to zip code).

### UTILIZING THE MAILING LIST ■

When and how often publicity pieces should be sent out depends on the budget available for such purposes and the number of attractions being sponsored. Although Federal postal regulations are published in pamphlets available at any post office, it is wise for the business manager or the publicity director of a theatre to speak personally with the local postmaster. What are the bulk-mailing rates? How should the mail be prepared for delivery to the post office? What are the advantages and disadvantages of various mailing methods? The local post office may be more lenient about regulations than federal rules indicate. As a courtesy gesture, for example, some post offices have even been known to return undelivered bulk mailers (from the same postal district) and ignore the standard additional cost of this service to the sender. In other cases, especially around Christmas, bulk mail piles up undelivered in the post office while first-class mail is processed. But a few kind words to the post-master can sometimes hasten bulk-mail delivery.

Permission to utilize bulk-mail rates is obtained by filing a form with the local post office, paying a fee and receiving a "bulk-mail identification number" which must be printed together with the organization's name on the envelope where the stamp would normally be placed. Bulk-rate permits are valid for only one year. Theatres that send out a limited amount of such mail may find it less expensive to pay first-class rates. Large organizations may find it most economical to employ the services of a professional mailing house to maintain its mailing lists, produce and affix the address labels and send out the mailers. Whenever possible, flyers and bro-chures should be designed as "self-mailers," to eliminate the time and expense of stuffing each one into an envelope.

The number of mailings sent may be decreased when a theatre is able to combine publicity for several events into a single flier or brochure. Timing is always a crucial factor. Enough time must be permitted (1) to prepare, proofread and print the pub-licity material, (2) to address it and deliver it to the post office, (3) to allow for pos-tal delivery, (4) to allow for return, first-class mail orders and (5) to allow time for tickets to be mailed from the box office and received by the customer comfortably before the performance date. If bulk rates are used, this timetable will require a total of no less than six weeks from beginning to end. And, due to the extremely erratic amount of time it takes for bulk mail to be delivered, more time should be allowed when possible. The publicist's nightmare is the producer or organization that makes last-minute production plans or changes that must be publicized and sold in a week or two.

## ▪ GATHERING INFORMATION

### BIOGRAPHIES AND RESUMES ▪

Most theatres traditionally publish brief biographies of the performers and leading artistic personnel in the playbill for the production with which they are associated. Usually entitled "who's who" or "behind the scenes," these write-ups should be prepared literately and with care, and preferably final copy approval should be given to each person listed. Resumes and biographies should be collected as soon as the performer is engaged in a production. Biographical files should also be maintained on other theatre personnel. At leisure, the publicist may read through such files and use them as the basis for special newspaper stories. Aside from listing previous theat-rical credits, jobs, education, travel, hobbies, family data and the like, each resume should indicate the individual's home-town and college newspapers. The publicity department may then devise a standard news-release format to send to such news-papers, informing them that so-and-so ("class of '59" or "daughter of Mr. and Mrs.

Smith of Middletown'') is appearing in a certain production. This is surefire copy for local editors and may stimulate ticket sales for the theatre, even from very distant customers. David Merrick's long-running Broadway musical, *Hello Dolly!* once adapted this technique to audience members and distributed the following card in the theatre lobby:

If you are from out of town, we would like to notify your home-town newspaper that you came to see our show, "HELLO, DOLLY!"

Sincerely,

*David Merrick*

NAME    MR. & MRS.
            MR. .........................................................................
            MRS.
            MISS

ADDRESS............................................................................

CITY AND STATE..............................................................

HOME-TOWN NEWSPAPER....................................................

*Please give card to usher or drop in box in lobby.*    491

Local newspapers all over the country were soon publicizing the show.

If an employee or participant has an unusual hobby, avocation or background, this may provide a good human-interest story. And, of course, theatrical credits should be known for inclusion in regular press releases about the production and the performers.

## HISTORICAL DATA ■

Permanent theatres should maintain a supply of photographs and general news releases about the theatre. These will be useful for distribution to feature-story writers, critics and visiting firemen. A file-card index of all previous performers and all previous productions and events at the theatre is a frequently consulted resource. Scrapbooks should be kept up to date, with paid advertisements separated from freely given newspaper space. At least annually, these scrapbooks should be reviewed by the administrators of the theatre to determine such things as how newspapers are treating the theatre, whether advertising appears to be creating a favorable image of the theatre and whether there is too much or too little of it. To assist in this process and to insure that the theatre receives copies of all printed stories, pictures and advertisements, a professional news-clipping service may be employed. For a nominal charge (which might average less than the cost of buying all the periodicals in which publicity appears), the service will clip all articles in which the name of the theatre or the production (as specified by the theatre) appears, label the article with the name of the periodical and the publication date and send it to the theatre. Services may be directed to clip paid advertisements only, free copy only or both and they may be limited to a city-wide, state-wide, area-wide or national coverage. The busy and ongoing theatre can make few investments that are as helpful, timesaving and economical as that of subscribing to a good press-clipping service.

Because printers and theatrical press agents are usually busy people working in cluttered offices, the theatre business has, to an alarming degree, traditionally ignored record-keeping and the preservation of publicity materials. The number of theatrical productions, both amateur and professional, both recent and remote, for which absolutely no printed or photographic evidence remains is shocking. Every producer or producing organization should assign one person to collect and preserve samples of playbills, posters, newspaper articles, press releases, photographs and the like. These should be safely stored somewhere and a duplicate set of such memorabilia should be deposited with a local library, appropriate museum or theatre collection. It is a childishly simple task to collect records when productions are still playing; but a year later it may be nearly impossible to locate anything unless someone has taken the trouble to preserve it.

### STATISTICAL RECORDS ▪

Working with the business manager of the theatre, the publicity department should create a file pertaining to such things as audience attendance figures, performance records, budgetary expenditures, box office grosses and special gifts or awards won by the theatre. Such statistics may be used (with caution and always with the approval of the theatre's chief administrator) in general literature about the organization and, most certainly, will be helpful in framing requests for financial aid from government and private agencies. In fact, as nonprofit theatre depends more and more on subsidization and good working relations with nontheatrical professions and institutions, its need for "accountability" becomes essential. When a foundation agent or a potential donor asks hard, cold questions about a theatre, he wants and has every right to expect hard, cold answers. Is attendance up or down? Where does most of the audience come from? To what percentage of capacity did performances play last year?

## ▪ PHOTOGRAPHY FOR THE THEATRE

### TYPES OF PHOTOGRAPHS ▪

Theatrical press agents need both general and specific photographs. The former may be released over a long period of time to almost any source and include photos of the theatre, the entire company of performers or individual performers out of costume. Specific photos may have more limited but no less valuable uses: pictures showing a performer with a visiting celebrity, shots taken during the rehearsal period and so forth. The standard photos that performers submit with a resume are almost invariably of the "cheesecake" variety—formally posed, often touched-up by the photographer and frequently taken eons ago. News editors always favor informal, "action" shots over cheesecake unless, of course, the picture is intended for inclusion in a paid ad. To obtain action shots, the publicist will have to commission a photographer and arrange a "picture call." This is usually an expensive proposition, unless the publicist himself is a photographer or someone on the theatre staff can qualify. Time being of the essence, one needs quick developing service as well as a photographer.

When a large number of photographs are taken, it is wise to request a proof or "contact" sheet (a quickly developed print-out of many pictures shown thumb-nail size on a single piece of paper). Specific pictures and quantities of each may then be ordered from the proof, which is labeled and filed for future reference.

## QUALITIES OF GOOD THEATRICAL PHOTOGRAPHY ■

Any good photograph should possess the qualities of clarity, sharpness, good composition and professional development. Photos for use by a theatrical publicity department require several other qualities. Since most are intended for reproduction in newspapers and other publications, they must be developed with a glossy rather than a mat finish. Dark photographs or photographs with very dark backgrounds should generally be avoided because they reproduce badly in newspapers: photographs with sharply contrasted light and dark areas with a predominance of light in the background are ideal. Also, photos should feature uncluttered subject matter (one to three people, a single building, etc.). Portraits should show the full head and shoulders (or the full body). Composition or cropping should never eliminate the top of a head or part of a face. Production shots should look dramatic and exciting. Most photographs released to the press are printed on standard eight-by-ten-inch stock, although the advent of offset printing enables many newspapers to enlarge or reduce photographs very easily. If offset machinery is not available, a printer must order a zinc plate made from the glossy photo and then cast rubber mats to appropriate newspaper column sizes. To insure the use of photos by such publications, the theatre press agent should supply ready-made mats.

## USES OF PHOTOGRAPHY ■

It is still true that "a picture is worth a thousand words." When promoting a theatrical production, it seems that there is nowhere that a publicist can't use a photograph: the brochure, the flyer, the playbill, the houseboard, the poster, the ads, the special displays.

When releasing a photograph to the press, the subjects in the picture should be appropriately labeled (identified from left to right) — but not in writing scribbled on the back of the photo, since this may press through and mar the face of the photograph. Rather, a separate piece of paper should be glued to the bottom back of the photo, then folded so it extends several inches over the face of the picture.

Photographic enlargements, or "blowups," of good pictures serve as a dramatic means of publicizing a production. The desired size may vary, but forty by sixty inches is standard for mounting in typical display cases and on sandwich boards. The cost of these enlargements (which may be ordered unmounted or mounted on heavy cardboard) is minimal if they are put to good use in lobby areas, ticket agencies or other places that may attract customers.

Actual glossy prints of the production and individual performers, whenever possible, should be displayed on lobby houseboards. This seldom involves any cost to the theatre and it is a standard courtesy to display a picture of each principal performer in the current production, whether his contract requires it or not.

When the supply is sufficient, individual performer photographs may be autographed and distributed to ticket agencies, group sales chairmen, volunteer theatre workers or others who may appreciate the gesture.

Well-used pictures are worth thousands of words to the publicist and thousands of dollars to the box office.

## ■ LADIES AND GENTLEMEN OF THE PRESS

### ESTABLISHING GOOD PRESS RELATIONS ■

Producers, like politicians, will probably never stop arguing about the powers and prerogatives of the press. Is that power too strong, is it exercised unfairly, do theatre reviews really represent life-and-death judgments? Should a few journalists—with no formal education in theatre—be given the power to "close a show" that has taken several years to get from script to stage, cost a half-million dollars and employed "some of the biggest talents in the business"? Can any show be all that bad? The answer, of course, is "Yes, it can!" Critics strongly influence public opinion primarily in the commercial segments of the industry. The Broadway show, after all, aims to become a smash hit and earn huge profits. It invites criticism as a consumer commodity with broad entertainment appeal that is worth a viewing price of from $5.00 to $20.00. The newspaper critic, merely in his role as reporter, is commissioned to reflect or anticipate audience response and in a majority of cases for a majority of audiences, critics have served the public well. To minimize the effect of Broadway theatre reviews, Harvey Sabinson, the well-known New York publicist, has suggested that theatrical advertising eliminate entirely the use of play review quotes. In any case, critics are a fact of theatrical life. But just as important as the reviewer are the general editors and journalists who comprise the permanent staffs of area newspapers and magazines.

Names and addresses of periodicals and of radio and television stations may be culled from telephone directories or obtained from special directories published by news-clipping companies. To establish a meaningful press list, the publicity director should devise a return-card mailer to send each publication or media outlet. The returnable portion of this mailer might resemble the specimen on page 303.

When the press list is long and frequently used, questionnaires like the above should be sent out each year to verify addresses and editors' names; most will be completed and returned.

It is customary to invite critics to preview or opening night performances, but preference should be given to those who actually write reviews that are published in daily periodicals. Journalists who work for weekly or monthly publications, feature story writers, general editors and others may be given complimentary press tickets for a later performance. A limited number of other free tickets should be given to people who never write articles themselves but who are influential employees of publications and media outlets: radio station owners, publishers, general editors, advertising executives, typographers, TV cameramen and the like.

A general press list, comprised of all known publications and media outlets within a large, even national, area, should be broken down into separate lists. Obviously not all press releases should be sent to national publications. Some releases may be suitable only for radio and television stations. Other releases may be geared to society columnists, financial editors or sports editors.

### THE PRESS CONFERENCE OR INTERVIEW ■

When establishing a theatre or beginning promotional work on a new production,

Dear editor:

To assist us in sending you news and information in the fastest and most efficient manner, may we request that you complete the following form and return it to us.

Do you wish to receive our general press releases?_____

Do you wish to receive photographs from us?_____

Do you wish to receive only information for your entertainment listings or announcements? _____

Do you wish to be informed about special press conferences and interviews held at the theatre?_____

What is your deadline for receiving news copy?_____

To whom should our general news releases be addressed?
(Specific editor)_____
(Address)_____

If not the same as above, to whom should information for entertainment listings or announcements be sent?_____
_____
_____

We look forward to meeting you in person and, if you will contact this office, would be happy to provide complimentary tickets to one of our performances.

Sincerely,

Joseph Smith, press representative
Big Sur Playhouse, XX Shore Ave., Los Angeles, Calif.
Phone: 971-000-1129

the press agent should invest a considerable amount of time in personal meetings with editors and journalists. Later, when newsworthy activities warrant it, members of the press should be invited to luncheons, parties or conferences. While the ostensible purpose of these gatherings is to generate press stories, they also provide a way of entertaining the press. And such entertainment is traditional; refreshments should be served at most press conferences and, at other times, the press agent should entertain editors individually: at lunch, at dinner or for a cocktail.

The special nature of each producing organization dictates the most logical times when press conferences should be held. The commercial New York production often begins its publicity with a press release announcing that a producer has just purchased an option on a particular play. The press is usually invited to photograph the company when it meets together for the first time to read the play. The stock theatre that produces weekly or biweekly star-package productions may arrange a standard time each week or two for the press to meet the star at a luncheon or other kind of gathering. The resident, community or college theatre must select or fabricate an occasion which at least appears interesting. For example, the press may be invited to remain in the theatre after the opening night performance to meet the cast and the director, take photographs and ask questions. In no case, however, should press conferences be called unless there is something informative and newsworthy to be discussed. The press agent who calls "fake" press conferences, like the man who cries "wolf" too often, will soon discover that he has alienated the press.

Careful preparation is an important ingredient in a successful press conference or interview. The journalists should be invited in writing or by telephone well in advance. The performers and others from the production should also be warned in advance to insure their presence and to allow them to prepare for photographs and interviews. Usually, the "importance" of the occasion and the theatre people involved will dictate the degree of formality at the press conference. The publicity director or press agent should be present during all press conferences. He should serve as host, master of ceremonies and protector of the production and the people he is representing to the press. He should be certain, for example, that a performer is treated to advantage by photographers, by questions asked and by the introductions made. Questions and interviews should not be overly long and no single journalist should dominate the question-and-answer period or receive favored treatment. It is often a good idea to prepare a press "brief" for distribution before the conference. This contains background information regarding the theatre, the production and the people being interviewed. It insures that all members of the press in attendance will get the same basic information, accurately stated and correctly spelled.

Large press conferences can produce a sizable amount of newspaper and media coverage, but journalists are somewhat wary of them because there is a good chance that competing publications will publish similar stories at the same time. For this reason, the private press interview may result in longer stories and happier editors. Of course, a personal interview can easily take up to an hour's time so not many that involve the same performer should be arranged. Newspapers and media outlets with the largest circulation or coverage should generally be given priority when it comes to arranging interviews. Occasionally, however, the small newspaper that provides generous coverage for the theatre should be rewarded with an "exclusive" or an important personal interview. The press agent should always meet or talk with interviewers before making a commitment to them: are they experienced, are they free-lancers or regular staff reporters, will the articles they write be published in time to benefit the production?

### THE PRESS RELEASE ▪

The most standard and often-used way to feed news and information to the mass media is by means of the written press release. Releases may be individually type-written (each copy mailed should be an original, not a carbon) or, if the same release is mailed to a dozen or more publications, the release should be clearly and neatly reproduced on a duplicator or copying machine. Special stationery should be designed and ordered which carries the heading "News!" or "News from: . . ." This should be printed in large, bold letters at the top of the stationery, below which should appear the name of the theatre or production and the address and telephone number of the press office.

The contents of the press release should observe certain formalities:

1. At the beginning or end of the release, the press agent's name should appear after the word "Contact."

2. Strictly speaking, it is the news editor's job to title all stories he prints so that identical headlines will not appear in two different publications. Nonetheless, it is expedient to write a title in capital letters at the beginning of the press release merely to identify the subject matter.

3. At the end of each page of the release should appear the word "more," referring the reader to the next page. At the top of the next page (the reverse side of a page should never be used) should appear: "Con't. - 2 - Theatre."

4. At the very end of the press release should appear, centered on the page on a line by itself, one of the following editorial symbols: # # # or 30 or "end."

5. At the beginning of the release should appear the words "For Immediate Release!" or "Release date: . . .," indicating either that the story should be published as soon as possible or that it should not be used until a specified date.

The copy contained in the press release should observe the following guidelines:

1. Releases should always be written from the editor's point of view. Adjectives should be used very sparingly, if at all. The copy should sound like news or information reported by an objective observer.

2. The most important information (name of production, name of theatre, performance dates, etc.) should be contained in the first paragraph of the release, the least important information in the final paragraphs. When reducing the length of an article, editors traditionally cut from the end backward.

3. Each press release should be limited to one main story or idea. Whenever possible, the entire press release should be contained on a single sheet of paper (to provide more space, releases may be printed on outsize paper that measures eight by fifteen or eight by eighteen inches).

4. Releases should be typewritten with double-spacing and ample margins to allow for editorial notations and changes.

5. Releases sent to radio and television stations should be typed completely in capital letters, triple-spaced, and should indicate the reading time (10 SECONDS, 20 SECONDS, etc.) at the top of each paragraph.

It should be assumed that editors are lazy. The more editorial work the press agent can do, the more likely it is that his releases will get printed or announced. While the larger, more prestigious media outlets have less time and space for most theatrical copy and have more stringent rules about the standards of the copy they print, small outlets are likely to allow more "puffing," more adjectives and more free publicity. Even so, releases should always avoid the use of hackneyed words like "hilarious," "sensational" and "uproarious." The copy should read easily, crisply, accurately and informatively. Short sentences are usually more effective than long ones.

Periodicals known to use stories issued from a particular theatre should be given periodic "exclusives," stories prepared solely for them. These should be marked "Exclusive to:" which indicates to the editor that no other publication will receive the same copy. To alert the press to special events (such as the visit of a famous person, an interesting reception or whatever) the publicity director should send out announcements marked "News-tip!" giving a brief indication of what is about to take place, where and when. Exclusives, which are in the manner of feature stories, may run longer than most news releases and be specially slanted for use in a particular newspaper, or a special section of that newspaper.

In preparing and delivering all types of news stories, the publicity department must have an infallible sense of deadline. Just as "the curtain must go up," so the newspaper must go to print at a definite time. The news release or story that arrives after the editor's deadline need never have been sent at all.

☐ *Sample press release for the print media:* page 307
☐ *Sample press release for the radio and television media:* page 308

### ■ THE PLAYBILL

#### STANDARD CONTENTS ■

The basic purpose of a playbill is to assist the audience in identifying the performers, the roles they are playing, where the action of the play occurs and the arrangement of dramatic time. Some playbills, or programs, are so elaborate that this basic information is almost impossible to find. Whatever material and advertising may appear in a playbill, the information regarding the current performance should be prominently displayed.

The standard contents of a playbill, listed below roughly according to priority, should include:

1. *The cast of characters in order of appearance,* with character names printed on the left, actors' names on the right of the same line.
2. *The synopsis of scenes,* stating the time and place of each act or scene.
3. *The "title page,"* which is often located in the center-fold pages of the playbill. This page should state: the name of the theatre, the producer(s) or producing organization, the date(s) of the performance(s) (unless it is an unlimited-run engagement), the title of the play, the name of the author(s), the name of the director, choreographer, musical director and conductor, scenic, costume and lighting designers and any other leading artistic directors or collaborators. It should also state if the play or production is presented "by special arrangement with" a play-publishing house or subsidized by a government or private foundation, or if a performer appears "by special arrangement with . . ." If the performers are members of AEA, many if not all of their names must also appear on the title page of the playbill according to the provisions of their contracts.
4. *Brief biographies* under the heading of "Who's Who" or some other appropriate title. These should include all the principal players (those with speaking roles), if not the entire cast, as well as the director, conductor, author and

other leading personnel associated with the production and the theatre in which it is being performed.

5. *Production notes* should usually be printed, in article form, especially for plays that are historical, classical or unusual. These will assist audiences and critics and add to their enjoyment of the production.

---

NEWS!
From Falmouth Playhouse
Falmouth, Mass. 02541       For release as of: June 20
Phone: (617) 000-1100

RE: "Man of La Mancha"

    Allan Jones will re-create the legendary misadventures of Don Quixote de la Mancha in the opening week of the Falmouth Playhouse season beginning on Monday, July 5. The popularity of *Man of La Mancha,* currently playing its seventh Broadway season, has been assured by such hit songs as "The Impossible Dream," "Dulcinea" and "Little Bird." This award-winning adaptation of Cervantes' *Don Quixote* has already established its place in the annals of lyric theatre as one of America's best-loved musicals.

    The famous singing voice of Allan Jones will headline a cast of twenty-five Broadway actors, dancers and musicians in the full-scale Falmouth production. Mr. Jones, whose early career in films was guided by MGM studios, quickly rose to stardom in such pictures as *A Night at the Opera, A Day at the Races, Showboat* and his most popular movie, *The Firefly,* in which he sang the famous "Donkey Serenade," the third largest selling record in RCA history. Appearing with Mr. Jones as the earthy Aldonza will be Gerrianne Raphael, fresh from her Broadway triumph in that role, and as the spirited Sancho Panza, Norman Kelley, who has appeared with such leading opera companies as the Metropolitan Opera and the New York City Opera.

    Performances of *Man of La Mancha* at Falmouth Playhouse are scheduled at 8:30 on Monday through Saturday evenings and at 2:30 P.M. for Wednesday and Friday matinees. Ticket information may be obtained by phoning the Playhouse box office at (617) 563-0000.

CONTACT: O. B. Smith

NEWS!
From Falmouth Playhouse
Falmouth, Mass. 02541                    *For immediate announcement*
Phone: (617) 563-1100

RE: "Man of La Mancha"

(20 SECONDS)

THE FALMOUTH PLAYHOUSE OPENS ITS TWENTY-THIRD
SEASON NEXT MONDAY EVENING WITH ALLAN JONES
STARRING IN THE POPULAR MUSICAL *MAN OF LA MANCHA*.
STILL RUNNING ON BROADWAY. THIS ADAPTATION OF
CERVANTES' *DON QUIXOTE* (KEY-HO-TAY) INCLUDES HIT
SONGS LIKE "THE IMPOSSIBLE DREAM," "DULCINEA" AND
"LITTLE BIRD." TICKET RESERVATIONS ARE NOW BEING
ACCEPTED AT THE PLAYHOUSE BOX OFFICE, 563-0000.

(10 SECONDS)

ALLAN JONES, INCIDENTALLY, BEGAN HIS CAREER AS A
POPULAR STAR IN FILMS LIKE *A NIGHT AT THE OPERA*
AND *A DAY AT THE RACES,* BOTH WITH THE MARX
BROTHERS. HE ALSO INTRODUCED "THE DONKEY
SERENADE" IN A PICTURE CALLED *THE FIREFLY.* THE
SONG BECAME THE THIRD LARGEST SELLING RECORD
IN RCA HISTORY!

(15 SECONDS)

GERRIANNE RAPHAEL WILL PLAY ALDONZA IN THE
FALMOUTH PRODUCTION AND NORMAN KELLEY IS CAST
AS THE SPIRITED SANCHO PANZA. BOTH HAVE APPEARED
IN THE NEW YORK PRODUCTION, WHICH IS NOW IN ITS
SEVENTH YEAR. PERFORMANCES OF *LA MANCHA* ARE
SCHEDULED MONDAY THROUGH SATURDAY EVENING
AT 8:30 WITH MATINEES ON WEDNESDAY AND FRIDAY
AT 2:30.

-END-

6. *Credits* should be listed in cases where the production uses borrowed properties, obtains free services of some kind or wishes to acknowledge some
   kind of unusually helpful assistance.
7. *House rules* should list or state as briefly as possible such points as: smok-
   ing and the taking of photographs are not allowed in the theatre.
8. *Staff for the production* should list all the people and their positions
   associated with running the performances (in commercial theatre, this
   list is comprised only of those people who work for the producer), the
   stagehands, the stage managers, the electricians, etc.
9. *The house staff* should list the front-of-house, executive and supportive
   personnel associated with running the theatre building (in commercial
   theatre, this list is comprised of those people who work for the landlord),
   the treasurers, the ticket-takers, the house manager, etc.
10. *An article about the upcoming production(s).* Seasonal operations, college,
    community, repertory and resident theatre should never fail to print stories
    in their playbills that encourage the audience to purchase tickets to future
    productions.

Playbills also feature other contents to further individualize the producing organization. Lists of season-ticket holders, patrons, advisory groups, the board of directors,
membership information and the like might help win friends and loyalty for the
theatre. Feature stories related to the theatre or the production may also be
included when space allows.

Amateur theatres of all types are well-advised to maintain an "everybody or
nobody" policy when it comes to listing names in the playbill. For example, a biography should either appear for every performer or for none. Nonprofessional
theatre should not treat any individual more specially than another, least of all in
the playbill. In professional Equity theatres sensitivities also run high, but they are
dealt with in the performers' contracts. It is the performer's obligation (or his agent's)
to secure billing rights.

Playbill editors cannot be overly meticulous when compiling and proofreading
the program contents. It is incredibly easy to omit a name, to misspell a word or to
misphrase a sentence. Mistakes that seem minor to the editor or general reader can
and frequently do evoke tremors of volcanic force from the person with the unfortunately misspelled name.

## PLAYBILL FORMAT AND LAYOUT ▪

A playbill projects an important visual image of a theatre. It should not only be
in complete visual accord with the objectives of the theatre or producing organization, it should also state the philosophy and objectives of that organization.

Playbills can be produced very inexpensively or in a very costly manner. The
first decision is whether or not outside advertisers should be invited to buy space
in the programs. Such advertising offers a good way of offsetting playbill printing
costs and, in many instances, may be an important source of subsidiary income for
the producing organization. But some organizations believe that advertising will
overly commercialize the desired look of their operation and, therefore, reject the
policy of mixing ads with program copy. In other cases, there may be so little time

and help available that it is just not feasible to solicit advertising.

The second decision to be made in regard to playbill publication is whether the producing organization itself should write, compile and print the publication or enter into an agreement with an independent publisher who is willing to do this for the organization. In New York and other large cities, virtually all playbills for legitimate, commercial productions are published by firms that specialize in that business. An agreement is signed between the producer and the publisher which guarantees the producer control over the "production copy," while the publisher retains control over the advertising copy, the general layout, the size and the editorial copy of the program. This frees the producer or the theatre landlord from the bulk of work entailed in publishing a playbill and also provides a stipulated amount of subsidiary income. Most ongoing theatres that produce plays with any regularity will be able to locate a printer or publisher who is both willing and anxious to "buy" the rights to publish the playbills. Companies that publish periodicals of other kinds are in the best position to publish playbills, since they already have a working staff of ad salesmen, editors and typographers and all the necessary printing machinery. The business of selling program advertisements can be very time-consuming and even small theatre operations might find it necessary to engage a full-time ad salesman. But the investment of a salary or two might be worth it if potential income from program advertisements is high enough. Whoever publishes the playbill, the producing organization should be certain that it retains a goodly amount of control over the copy, layout and design.

Possibilities for program layout and designs are endless; the following styles are the most common:

1. *Uniform cover design.* Theatres that offer a series of different productions during the same year or season should consider designing a single program cover. Because these can be printed in bulk (with inserted contents printed separately for each production), they will be less expensive than separate covers for each production. This may enable the theatre to produce more impressive-looking covers. The inside pages may be devoted to standard information about the theatre, a calendar of events, listing of board members, a statement of the theatre's goals or seasonal advertisements. The disadvantage of a uniform cover is that it may not permit the reader to distinguish which production it pertains to (though this can be avoided if a "window" is cut into the cover, through which one can read the name and date of the current production). Or, the cover may be designed to reveal part of the first inserted page, showing the name and date of the production.

2. *Outsize program design.* Typical, commercial playbills measure eight by ten inches and audiences have come to accept this as standard for all theatrical programs. To reinforce the unique image of a particular theatre or production, however, playbills of unusual sizes and shapes should be considered. Many dinner-theatre playbills, for example, resemble dinner menus. The Chelsea Theatre Center in Brooklyn once offered a workshop theatre series under the banner of "paper bag productions," and its playbill consisted of mimeographed sheets of production information inserted into paperbags donated by a local department store.

3. *Different format for each production.* Often the most desirable playbill, since each playbill is designed to reflect a specific production, this is also the most expensive and time-consuming style for busy production organizations.
4. *Multi-purpose playbills.* To cut expenses, it is sometimes possible to design a theatrical flyer (as a mailing and giveaway piece) that can double as a playbill. Old-fashioned, nineteenth-century handbills provide an interesting style to adapt for some productions.
5. *Souvenir programs.* Elaborately designed and printed, filled with photos of cast members and production shots, souvenir programs may be produced in addition to the regular "giveaway" programs. These may provide additional income for a producing organization that attracts a large audience. The souvenir program may describe one production or an entire season of productions.

Printing costs are high, so a theatre organization should select its printer carefully (inviting bids for each season's playbills) and study the various qualities of paper available and how the format will affect the cost of printing (multi-color printing, printing on outsize stock, graphic and photo reproduction and other such factors all influence printing costs).

## ▪ AEA REGULATIONS PERTAINING TO PUBLICITY AND ADVERTISING

### BILLING REGULATIONS ▪
Agreements negotiated with Actors' Equity Association by the different branches of the industry all contain rulings that cover billing and publicity. Generally, these require that the names of all principal players in the current production (those with speaking roles) be displayed on the houseboard of the theatre, either outside or in the lobby. When a principal leaves the production, his name must be removed and that of his successor substituted by the day of the successor's first performance. Similar corrections must also be made in the playbills and all paid advertising controlled by the theatre. Generally, the actor has the right to approve the biography that appears about him in all playbills and souvenir programs. If a mistake or omission occurs in the playbill, the manager must, upon receipt of a written note, correct this or insert a mimeographed "correction slip" in each faulty program. In cases where an understudy assumes a role at the last minute, a notice must be placed in the lobby stating the name of the substituting actor and the role he is playing and a correction slip to the same effect must be inserted in all programs; *or* an announcement must be made from the stage immediately prior to the commencement of the performance. The names of understudies for principal players must be listed in the programs.

Other billing regulations are covered in the individual contracts between the actor and the manager (producer). The publicity department in a professional operation must carefully check each contract, as billing riders vary greatly from contract to contract. The more well-known an actor is, of course, the more extensively and prominently his name must be used, as specified in his contract. As mentioned previously, some players are willing to decrease their salary demands in exchange for prominent billing. But it must be remembered that billing takes up valuable space in paid advertisements and, in the long run, may be more costly than the payment of higher salaries. A simple but typical billing rider in a star's contract might read as follows:

> Actor shall receive sole star billing on a line by himself above the title of the play, whenever that title appears in advertising controlled by the manager, in type that is no less than 100 percent the size, prominence and boldness of the title.

This means that the manager may not grant any other performer billing above the title. A majority of the players in most Equity productions have billing riders in their contracts. Some will specify exactly where the actor's name must appear in relation to other names, others merely specify that his name must appear wherever and whenever the name of "the first featured actor" appears. The rider may require a name to appear on a line by itself, in a box, of a certain size in relation to the title of the play, preceded by a certain phrase (such as "and," "also starring" or "in the role of . . . ") or whatever else the actor's agent dreams up and the manager is willing to approve.

Breach of billing requirements carries a stiff penalty for the manager, frequently requiring him to pay the actor one-eighth of his weekly salary for each breach and for each week the breach continues after the manager has been notified of it.

### PICTURE CALLS ▪

A picture call refers to times when the manager requires the company or parts of it to pose for photographs. AEA rules limit such calls to regular rehearsal periods, to certain time limits, only *after* performances and only following a twenty-four-hour notice of the call. Picture calls requested at unusual times may require the manager to pay the actor an hourly wage. If an actor's pictures are used to endorse a commercial product, the actor must be paid a specified fee for this purpose. On the other hand, it is the actor's obligation to supply the manager with a standard photograph of himself at his own expense for display on houseboards and elsewhere.

### FILMING OR RECORDING ADVERTISING "SPOTS" AND THE PRODUCTION ▪

An actor may usually participate in a radio or television commercial at no cost to the management, provided that it does not include any material from the show being advertised. When it does, the actor must be paid AFTRA or SAG minimum for such work. If the commercial is over one minute in duration and if it includes material from the show being advertised, all actors involved must be paid the equivalent of one week's salary. If a sound recording is made to cut a record album or a film is made of the production, all actors involved must be paid a full week's salary for every day (or part day) of recording or filming they do or AFTRA or SAG minimum rates, whichever is higher.

### GENERAL PUBLICITY ▪

Any performer (professional or amateur) should be given the courtesy of a day's advance notice of any publicity activity that is required of him, especially if this involves photography. Equity rules concerning personal appearances, press interviews and the like are purposely vague. It is expected that actors will cooperate and agree to assist the theatre in publicizing the production whenever the request is a reasonable one. The publicist should at no time require an actor to perform in an impromptu manner; nor should the actor be asked to wear costumes or undertake anything else that might place him in an embarrassing or professionally compromising position. The actor's time and energy should be respected and, of course, he should be reimbursed for any expenses related to publicity appearances.

It is somewhat difficult to separate the areas of publicity and advertising since both are necessary to any promotional campaign and both must be closely related in terms of their tone, content, purpose and appearance. This chapter, then, serves as a basis for the next.

In most theatres the responsibilities of press-agentry, advertising and promotion all fall on the shoulders of one individual. The publicist may also be the director or manager of the enterprise, as in many amateur theatres. Large operations may be able to afford a full-time press representative as well as a full-time advertising director or agency. All promotional workers, however, should maintain close ties with other personnel in the theatre. Effective publicity requires considerable advance planning and organizing, strict adherence to deadlines and a mode of attack that is frequent, imaginative and yet consistent with the artistic objectives of the theatrical project being promoted.

# CHAPTER FIFTEEN

# Advertising and the Promotion Campaign

Publicity is promotion that is achieved at little or no cost to the promoter: a newspaper story, a party given and financed by a supporter of the theatre and the like. Advertising, on the other hand, is promotion that is paid for inch by inch, minute by minute: the newspaper ad, the radio commercial, the poster or brochure. Both are important if one's aim is to achieve "saturation" coverage. Paid advertising is expensive and, yet, a majority of theatres (amateur and professional) appear to exert little effort and less imagination when it comes to planning the advertising campaign. The phrase "let's run some ads," like the phrase "let's put on a play," sounds deceptively simple. No less time and thought should go into advertising design than goes, say, into scene design.

## ▪ PAID ADVERTISING

### BY THE COLUMN INCH ▪

All periodicals that sell advertising space quote their rates on a "per line" basis. The size of the print and the width of the column vary from publication to publication. To get a clear idea of the value of ad space in a particular publication, one should measure the width of its newsprint columns then ascertain from the publisher how many lines comprise the depth of a column inch. A column inch in the *New York Times,* for example, measures one and three-fourths inches wide and fourteen lines deep. If the advertising rate for a particular section is $4.65 per line, the cost per column inch (14 x $4.65) will be $65.10. An advertisement that measures two columns wide by five inches deep (a total of ten column inches) would cost $611.00. Because rates are traditionally quoted on a "per line" basis and this sounds like a low figure, the inexperienced publicist should always take the trouble to figure out the total cost of an advertisement before it is placed. Otherwise he may be surprised when he receives the bill.

Rate cards may be obtained from any periodical and, for those in which a theatre places regular advertisements, should be collected and kept on hand for quick consultation. The rate card will state the net (paid) circulation of the periodical and the different rates that are charged for the different sections: amusement advertising, financial advertising, legal notices, classified advertisements, preprinted sections and so forth. Rates are determined according to the following factors:

The edition (morning or evening)
Publication day (daily or Sunday)
The section
The circulation (the higher the circulation, the higher the rates)
The amount of space purchased (Rates for large ads may be lower per line than for smaller ones. If ads are purchased regularly over a period of time, a contract providing reduced rates should be signed with the publication.)
Type of copy (Some publications charge extra when required to print photographs, adapt a graphic design, etc.)

### BY THE MINUTE ▪

Radio and television commercials are purchased according to the amount of air time they consume. Electronic media advertising rates vary in much the same manner as do rates for publications: according to length of time, time of day or night broadcast, programming context in which they are broadcast (during the news program, etc.), the strength of the broadcasting signal (how large a geographical area is reached by the station) and the amount of time that is purchased. Radio and television stations are prone to selling "ad packages" which consist of repeating an ad over a certain period, in different time slots. Especially with smaller stations, there is more flexibility of ad pricing than with the printed media. There is also likely to be a more blatant relationship than in the print media between the amount of paid advertising on radio and television and the number of "free mentions" given the advertiser: "Buy this package and we'll mention your production on the five o'clock news" and "Buy twenty spots a week and we'll put you on the morning talk show" are typical "deals" offered by the time salesman.

It pays to give careful attention to the preparation of radio and television ads. Special tapes can be produced that make an advertisement more exciting because background music or special scenery is added, a star speaks the narration instead of a radio announcer or some other device. At very least the station should be given the exact copy which the advertiser wants broadcast so that important information won't be insufficiently emphasized or omitted.

**OUTDOOR ADVERTISING** ▪

While the greatest portion of a theatrical advertising budget is likely to be spent on newspaper and radio ads, there are other advertising outlets that should not be ignored. Outdoor display advertising, for example, is an effective way to reach potential theatregoers. The marquee of the theatre itself and space on nearby buildings or roadways may be rented directly from a property owner. Some cities permit banners to be strung across main streets. Invariably, however, there are local, state and federal laws that regulate where outdoor advertising may and may not be placed and how large it may be. Many resident and stock theatres place large, painted signs on the sides of theatre vehicles or construct billboards that can be pulled behind a car on a small trailer. Or, outdoor display advertising may be purchased from companies that maintain billboards on highways and buildings, although this is comparatively expensive and involves the cost of making the sign as well as the rental charge.

Another unusual method of advertising is that of banner-towing. In areas where it is permitted, the local airport is likely to have an airplane banner-towing company in residence. Especially effective in busy resort areas or metropolitan areas (where crowds gather outdoors at beaches, stadiums and parks) the banner advertising a star or a local theatre production draws attention because most people expect to see standard products employ such advertising (suntan lotion and beer, for instance). The effectiveness of aerial banners, of course, is limited by weather conditions and by the small number of words that can be placed on a single banner.

It should be mentioned that outdoor advertising of most kinds contributes to environmental pollution and is a factor in defacing the nation's highways and scenic resources. In the frequently desperate business of promoting live theatre and in view of all the other outdoor advertising that we see, it may be tempting to forget this fact. But a theatre organization must take care not to create an "advertising backlash" from environmentalists and others.

**ADVERTISING CORRECTNESS AND CUSTOMER RESPONSE** ▪

There is always a possibility that published advertising copy will be faulty or incorrect. It is the advertiser's responsibility to catch mistakes and demand credit or a rebate from the publisher. This is an easier task if the advertiser has hired a clipping service to send him copies of all the ads he has purchased. Of course, if the ad copy and layout submitted to the publisher were faulty to begin with there is no recourse. When time permits, it is wise to request a proof for each ad before it is published (professional advertising agencies supply copy proofs to their clients and otherwise render the whole process of ad placement much easier and more efficient).

The effectiveness of media advertising is difficult to measure with true accuracy. Several methods, such as audience and community surveys, have already been mentioned. Perhaps the most common method of checking the effectiveness of a particular advertisement or series of ads is to print some kind of coupon or giveaway offer as part of the ad. This invites the reader to clip the coupon and present it when he purchases the product being advertised. By collecting the coupons, the advertiser gains some idea of how many customers are responding to a particular ad. Radio and television commercials, in a similar manner, sometimes offer the customer a special gift or sales concession if he mentions the show or station on which he heard the ad. If an advertising campaign involves a number of different publications, all running the same ad and all including a mail-order form for the customer to clip and return with his order, an identifying mark of some kind can be printed on the forms to distinguish the different newspapers and indicate to the advertiser which newspapers have attracted the greatest number of customers. If a brochure is designed for mailing to a wide variety of potential customers (and includes a return-order form) the advertiser may wish to know which of his various mailing lists is drawing the largest response (perhaps he has mailed his brochure to a new list of ten thousand property owners in the community or a list of names borrowed from another institution and wishes to distinguish responses from those on his regular mailing list of active customers). The brochure may be printed in a different color for each list used or otherwise marked to segregate one group of respondents from another. When the number of orders stimulated from a particular mailing list or media advertisement is minimal, the advertiser discontinues its use. Most theatrical advertising budgets are too small to conduct blanket promotional campaigns on a hit-or-miss basis. Techniques to evaluate the effectiveness of advertising should be devised whenever possible.

## ▪ ADVERTISING COMPOSITION AND LAYOUT

As discussed in chapter 14, every promotional device or advertisement should (1) catch the reader's or listener's attention, (2) motivate him to buy the product advertised and (3) supply the information necessary to make the purchase. It's easier said than done. There are, however, a few guidelines that may be helpful.

### THE GRAPHICS IMAGE AND THE LOGO ▪

Printers and publishers can be helpful in suggesting how to design a particular poster, brochure or ad. They have available different styles of lettering, various paper and poster-board qualities and a selection of common graphic symbols and designs (such as border designs, flowers, stars, musical notes and the like). For truly individualized and striking promotional literature, however, one must employ the services of a graphic artist. The cost of professional graphics assistance is well worth it, especially for ongoing theatre operations or for the long-running commercial production. (The low-budgeted community or amateur theatre can obtain ready-designed advertisements and posters for recent, commercially successful plays and musicals from such companies as the Package Publicity Service in New York.)

The first problem that a graphics designer attempts to solve is that of inventing an image or symbol which visually identifies a specific theatre or production. This symbol becomes a trademark that, over a period of time, the public associates almost automatically with the theatre or production. When the trademark incorporates the name of the theatre or production, it is called a logo or logotype (sometimes it is also called a "signature" or, simply, a "sig"). The logo should appear on all literature pertaining to the advertised product: stationery, posters, ads, playbills and so forth. Its style should attempt to capture the feeling and the meaning of the organization or production it symbolizes. In a sense, it is the visual statement of the group's philosophy or goal. A logo not only provides an attention-getting element in promotional literature, it can also—like a picture—serve as a very economical use of space because its design can communicate a feeling, a mood or an excitement

**FESTIVAL THEATRE**

**75 MAIN ST. 781-0000**

**Presents**

**NOV. 17, 18, 19, 20, 8 P.M.**

**William Shakespeare's**

# OTHELLO

**Box Office Open 10-5**

**Tickets: $4.00, $5.00, $6.00**

**Phone Orders Accepted**

**Group Rates Available**

1. Straightforward type and layout.

**Presents**

**SHAKESPEARE'S**

# OTHELLO

**NOV. 17-20**

**8 P.M.**

**Box Office: 75 Main St.**

**Tickets: $4.00, $5.00, $6.00**

**Phone: 781-0000**

2. Curved lettering for logo. More white space, less copy.

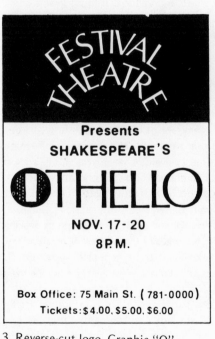

3. Reverse-cut logo. Graphic "O" in title.

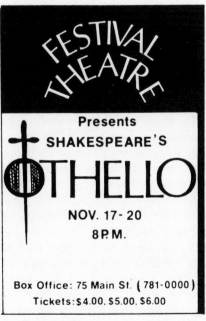

4. Shadow box to tie ad together. More elaborate graphic "O"

that would take many words to convey. Some logotypes are superimposed over a picture or placed next to one. Virtually every Broadway hit has a widely-used logo that the general public immediately associates with the show and that has become a valuable advertising device in itself, whenever and wherever that show is produced.

DISPLAY ADVERTISING ∎

When written out on a piece of plain white paper, any ad design looks good. When clipped out of a newspaper and pasted into a scrapbook, it looks even better. But when the same ad appears on a newspaper page, cluttered with numerous other ads, photographs and news stories, what becomes of it? The *context* in which an ad appears is just as important as the ad itself. When analyzing the effectiveness of printed advertisements one should look at a "tear sheet" of the entire page on which an ad appears. Does it stand out beside others or does it get lost? The upper-outside corner of a page is the strongest position because readers scan a page from the top down and inside spaces may be lost in the fold of the newspaper or magazine.

The advertisement that contains an ample amount of blank space is likely to be the most attention-getting. While it is important to provide the necessary information about a production or theatre, the publicist must develop a strong resistance against overcrowding his ad copy. Letters printed in an unusual style are also attention-getting: script letters, curved letters, letters embroidered with a pattern and so forth. (A wide variety of type and lettering styles may be selected from catalogs available at professional typography or typesetting firms. Or the publicist or graphics designer may purchase ready-made sets of letters which are easily transferred onto an ad layout.) A border or "shadow box" helps to make an advertisement stand out from the page. A photograph or graphics design makes an ad more effective, as does the use of reverse-cut typesetting (a graphics device that surrounds the lettering with inked space, allowing the letters to be formed by the paper itself). These principles are illustrated by examples on the preceding page. Most readers will agree that number 4 is the most attention-getting and effective of the samples shown. The same principles of layout and design, of course, can be applied to posters and brochures, where the introduction of colored paper and inks can further enhance effectiveness.

## HARD SELL VS. SOFT SELL ▪

There is a tendency to associate certain products with certain types of advertising, whether speaking of consumer goods or theatrical productions. "You wouldn't advertise a Shakespearean production as if it were a circus" or "Don't advertise a serious repertory theatre like a Broadway musical" are common kinds of admonishments among naive theatrical promoters. The truth is that what advertising should or should not look like is a matter of opinion that has been influenced by years of conditioning. Just because circus posters usually employ a particular style of their own is no reason why they should continue to do so. Promotion material that follows tradition merely enforces a cliché and runs a strong risk of being ineffective. Serious and high-minded enterprises, such as opera and repertory theatre, usually need customer support just as much (if not more) than profit-oriented projects such as circuses and Broadway musicals. Conversely, if the Broadway musical can attract bigger audiences by utilizing promotional techniques commonly associated with chamber music recitals, for example, all the better.

Most advertising can be classified as either "hard sell" or "soft sell." The former is the variety that attempts to jump off the page and hit the reader face-on. The latter usually employs a more quiet visual impact and is more cerebral in its appeal. Hard-sell advertising *commands* the consumer to do something, soft-sell advertising relies more on suggestion. Both approaches can be equally successful. Using the most "appropriate" advertising style for a specific theatre or production is, perhaps, not as important as selling tickets. Hard-sell advertising is not necessarily in poor taste any more than soft-sell advertising is necessarily unexciting. It is usually a matter of how the contents are organized. For example, a young publicist for a Brooklyn production of *Fidelio* conceived the idea of building his campaign around the slogan "Beethoven Comes to Brooklyn." The artistic director argued that it should be the other way around, that the mountain should go to Allah, as it were. A compromise was reached and the slogan was modified to "Brooklyn Welcomes Beethoven!" Speaking of opera, one of the most successful and long-ranging opera publicity campaigns was organized by Gynn Ross, the energetic manager of the Seattle Opera, who recruited youthful volunteers to saturate the community with bumper stickers that read "Opera Swings" and "Opera Is a Gas!"

While media advertisements and most forms of outdoor advertising must vie for attention against the competition of many other advertisers, direct-mail brochures and other promotional pieces have a good chance of capturing the readers' undivided attention. The brochure, then, may employ the soft-sell approach with less threat of being ignored than if the same approach were used in newspapers. Brochures promoting season ticket sales, benefit performances or special events often use a soft-sell, invitational format. An example is shown on page 322.

If it is printed on high-quality paper and mailed in hand-addressed envelopes, the recipient may at first think that he is receiving a wedding or party invitation, which guarantees that he will open and read the contents (a lot of bulk or "junk" mail goes into the wastebasket unopened). Furthermore, the personalized approach together with the "R.S.V.P." may make many people feel honor-bound to reply, even if in the negative.

Soft-sell newspaper advertisements frequently limit their contents to a few simple words or to a slogan, without even providing ticket information or the name of the theatre. One example, which was meant to entice New Yorkers for some months, read "You've only seen *Man of La Mancha once?*" Of course, several years of harder-sell publicity and advertising preceded this "softened" approach and the public was familiar with the title, the hit songs from the show and considerable word-of-mouth publicity.

An interesting soft-sell campaign was devised by a nonprofessional summer stock theatre that ran a series of ads that merely showed a picture of the week's leading actor above a paragraph of copy that told about the production. After a few weeks, readers began to look forward to the little stories and the "friendly" approach to selling tickets began to·pay off at the box office. For one of the ads they printed in the local newspaper, see page 323.

---

## THE FESTIVAL THEATRE

cordially invites you to become a patron
by purchasing a contribution ticket to the
opening night of William Shakespeare's

## O T H E L L O

November 17 at 8 P. M.
Contribution tickets: $25.00 (tax deductible portion: $20.00)

*Reception immediately following the*
*performance in the Tudor Room.*

R.S.V.P.                                                          Festival Theatre
                                                                 75 Main Street
Card and envelope enclosed                        Avon, S. C.

---

### ORGANIZING THE INFORMATION ▪

The effectiveness of promotional literature is largely dependent on how information is organized. It is easy to say that an ad or a brochure should put "first things first." But what *is* really first or primary: the name of the theatre, the production, the artistic director, the leading performer? Ongoing theatre organizations should probably stress the name of their theatre or organization as the overall, unifying factor in publicity and advertising. Public loyalty should go first to the organization and second to the individual productions so the nucleus of an audience that will support all productions is created. If the individual production is stressed to the near exclusion of the producing organization, then each publicity campaign will have to build an entirely new audience.

Often, contractual billing obligations or old-fashioned ego lead publicists to emphasize a name or title or phrase that is meaningless to the public and deadening to the effectiveness of advertising. Or, a slavish fascination with detail may lead to overly crowded ads, too much copy and uninteresting layout. When composing promotional copy, one should remember the old adage: "Simplify! Simplify! Simplify!"

```
┌─────────────────────────────┐
│       Picture               │
│       of star               │
│                             │
└─────────────────────────────┘
```

### "OWL HOWL"

Once upon a time, a wise owl met a naughty and uncontrollable
pussycat, and that's how all the fun began. Discover the fun of
"The Owl and the Pussycat" at the Theatre-By-the-Sea this week—
the laughs roll on and on, like the waves outside. Timothy Smith
is one of the stars in our production, although he doesn't look
much like an owl—and we are showing you his picture to prove it.
But he is very handsome and very funny in "The Owl and the
Pussycat" every night at 8:30 until Saturday and on Wednesday
afternoon at 2:30. Phone Kathy or Dave at the theatre box office
(522-0000) and ask them to put aside your favorite seats. Have
you ever *been* to an owl howl before?

Hard-core information should be stated once only, clearly and directly and with the
greatest possible economy of words. The most complicated and difficult information
to convey is that which pertains to the play schedule for a repertory theatre. A season
of plays performed in repertory-rotation is a format that ticket-buyers confront only
rarely and when they wish to purchase a season ticket to all the plays find it confus-
ing to select the dates they wish. If productions can be scheduled so that each play
is at some point in the season offered on a Monday, each on a Tuesday and so forth,
then series tickets will at least conform to the same day of the week (though not
necessarily every week of the season). Or, a series might consist of three or four
plays in rapid succession over one or two weeks (an enterprising way to capture playgoers in resort areas where the average tourist spends only a week or two). One of the
most common and effective methods of showing a repertory schedule is to enter the
play titles onto a calendar. Here are several examples that demonstrate progressively
higher degrees of clarity:

## OCTOBER ⊙ MUSIC CENTER of Los Angeles County

Dorothy Chandler Pavilion
Mark Taper Forum
Ahmanson Theatre

| SUNDAY | MONDAY | TUESDAY | WEDNESDAY | THURSDAY | FRIDAY | SATURDAY |
|---|---|---|---|---|---|---|
| 1 Ahmanson 2:30 ANTONIO GADES SPANISH DANCE COMPANY | 2 Pavilion 8:30 THE SOUND OF MUSIC | 3 Pavilion 8:30 THE SOUND OF MUSIC | 4 Pavilion 2:30 & 8:30 THE SOUND OF MUSIC Forum 8:00 NEW THEATRE FOR NOW | 5 Pavilion 8:30 THE SOUND OF MUSIC Forum 8:00 NEW THEATRE FOR NOW | 6 Pavilion 8:30 THE SOUND OF MUSIC Forum 8:00 NEW THEATRE FOR NOW | 7 Pavilion 2:30 & 8:30 THE SOUND OF MUSIC Forum 8:00 NEW THEATRE FOR NOW |
| 8 Pavilion 7:30 ENRICO MACIAS Forum 2:30 & 8:00 NEW THEATRE FOR NOW | 9 Pavilion 8:30 THE SOUND OF MUSIC | 10 Pavilion 8:30 THE SOUND OF MUSIC Ahmanson 8:30 preview performance THE PRISONER OF | 11 Pavilion 2:30 & 8:30 THE SOUND OF MUSIC Ahmanson 8:30 preview performance THE PRISONER OF | 12 Pavilion 8:30 THE SOUND OF MUSIC Ahmanson 8:30 preview performance | 13 Pavilion 8:30 THE SOUND OF MUSIC Ahmanson 8:30 preview performance THE PRISONER OF | 14 Pavilion 2:30 & 8:30 THE SOUND OF MUSIC Forum 8:00 Ahmanson 2:30 & 8:30 HENRY IV PART I preview performance THE PRISONER OF SECOND AVENUE |
| | | | | | 20 | 21 Pavilion 2:30 & 8:30 QUINCY JONES & ROBERTA FLACK |

# 1   2   3

## HENRY IV Part 1
## HENRY IV Part 2
### IN REPERTORY
### JUNE 11 – AUG. 2

by William Shakespeare
Directed by Gerald Freedman
Scenery by Ming Cho Lee
Costumes by Theoni V. Aldredge
Lighting by Martin Aronstein
Music by John Morris

## ROM... and ... JUL... AUG...

by Will...
Direct...
Costu...
Lighti...
Musi...

### SCHEDULE

| SERIES | HENRY IV Part 1 | HENRY IV Part 2 |
|---|---|---|
| A | Tues., June 11 | Wed., June 19 |
| B | Wed., June 12 | Thurs., June 20 |
| C | Fri., June 14 | Fri., June 21 |
| D | Sat., June 15 | Sat., June 22 |
| N | Thurs., July 11 | Fri., July 19 |
| O | Sat., July 13 | Sun., July 21 |
| P | Tues., July 16 | Wed., July 24 |
| R | Thurs., July 18 | Fri., July 26 |
| S | Sat., July 20 | Sun., July 28 |
| T | Tues., July 23 | Wed., July 31 |

Sponsor Department, N. Y. Shakespeare Festival
425 Lafayette Street, New York, N. Y. 10003

Please enroll me as.................................... sponsor(s)
@ $10.00 each. I enclose my check/money order for $.....
N. Y. Shakespeare Festival. I am also enclosing a self-ad...
your convenience in sending me my tickets.

Mr. Mrs. Miss ...................................................
(please print)

Street .................................................................

City ............................................ State ...............

Phone (include area code) Home.............................

Please check: ☐ Renewal ☐ New Sponsor ☐ Su...
If you wish to sit with friends who are sending in the...
us your orders in the same envelope.

Please send me tickets for:

(1st choice) Series #.......... (2nd choice) Series #
As I am unable to attend a series, please send me t...

Henry IV, Part I   (1st choice)...............(2nd cho...
Henry IV, Part II   (1st choice)...............(2nd cho...
Romeo and Juliet  (1st choice)...............(2nd ch...

☐ Please send the best available tickets for any...

---

**Buy 10 or more shows...get 26% off every night,
Monday thru Thursday and Saturday 6 p.m. Friday
& Saturday nights...full price apply.**

All orders must be received by May 30, 1969. Seats on first come, first
served basis.

Every effort will be made to hold the same seats for last year's subscription
ticket holders. However, this courtesy cannot be extended beyond May 25

## HERE'S THE SCHEDULE (subject to change)

Mon. June 2 - 7

### JACK GILFORD    MAUREEN O'SULLIVAN
## "YOU KNOW I CAN'T HEAR YOU WHEN THE WATER IS RUNNING"

Four hilarious short playlets which took Broadway by storm
and catapulted Martin Balsam to stardom

Mon. June 9 - 14

## "JACQUES BREL IS ALIVE AND WELL IN PARIS"

An offbeat musical revisits high on Gallic charm and now on tempo

Mon. June 16 - 21

## "THE SHOW OFF"

By Philadelphia's own George Kelly, whose brother John B. Kelly
founded the Playhouse. Just completed a triumphant national tour.

Mon. June 23 - 28

### JAY GARNER
## "RED, WHITE AND MADDOX"

Hilarious political lampoon. A musical satire poking fun at Georgia's top man.
Follows a highly acclaimed New York run.

Mon. June 30 - July 5

## ...HAWN
### TO BE AN...

Mon. July 28 - Aug. 2

### WILLIAM SHATNER
## "THERE'S A GIRL IN MY SOUP"

A rollicking French bedroom farce
gives a modern twist and an American setting

## 4 MORE EXCITING SHOWS TO COME

SAVE A BIG 25%!    THE BEST SEATS
NO STANDING IN LINE
NO SELL-OUT DISAPPOINTMENTS

### CHOICE OF 4 PLANS 10–11–12–13 shows

| | Single Show Price | Box Off. Price for Season Ticket | You Pay | You Save |
|---|---|---|---|---|
| **13 SHOW PLAN** Mon-Thurs eves & Sat 6 p.m. Rows A | | | | |
| Row 1 | 14.50 | 158.50 | 143.88 | |
| Row 2 | 13.75 | 149.75 | 136.58 | 14.62 |
| | 13.50 | 145.50 | 134.13 | 12.19 |
| | 14.25 | | 185.00 | 211.21 |
| | | | 155.75 | |
| **12 SHOW PLAN** Mon-Thurs eves & Sat 6 p.m. Rows A | | | | |
| Row 1 | 14.50 | 174.00 | 140.50 | |
| | 13.75 | 145.50 | 133.75 | 13.50 |
| | 13.50 | | 131.50 | 277.25 |
| Fri. 8:30 & Sat 9:30 NO DISCOUNT | 14.75 | 180.00 | 150.00 | 170.50 |
| | | | 180.00 | |
| | | | 151.00 | |
| **11 SHOW PLAN** Mon-Thurs eves & Sat 6 p.m. Rows A | | | | |
| Row 1 | 14.50 | 149.50 | 137.13 | 272.37 |
| | 13.75 | 141.75 | 130.95 | |
| | 13.50 | 138.50 | 128.88 | 10.30 |
| Fri. 8:30 & Sat 9:30 NO DISCOUNT | 14.75 | 153.50 | 155.00 | 9.62 |
| | | | 146.75 | |
| **10 SHOW PLAN** Mon-Thurs eves & Sat 6 p.m. Rows A | | | | |
| Row 1 | 14.50 | 140.50 | 133.75 | 271.25 |
| | 13.75 | 137.50 | 128.13 | 9.37 |
| Fri. 8:30 & Sat 9:30 NO DISCOUNT | 14.25 | 135.00 | 128.75 | 8.75 |
| | | | 150.00 | |
| | | | 142.50 | |

I want ................................. seats of tickets for
(10, 11, 12 or 13) ...................... Show Plan.

Make Check or money order payable to Playhouse in the Park and mail to Playhouse in the Park,
West Fairmount Park, Phila., Pa. 19131, or call box office GR 7-1760

Name ........................................... Phone ..................

Address ............................................................

City ........................... State ........................... Zip ..........

Prior subscriber? (Year) ...........................

TICKETS FOR ENTIRE SEASON WILL BE MAILED TO YOU PRIOR TO FIRST PLAY DATE
Please enclose stamped, self-addressed envelope.

When the play series consists of different productions, each offered for a one- or two-week engagement over consecutive weeks, the season can be listed in clear, chronological order. Wherever possible, season scheduling should be printed on pocket-size or easily retained cards to encourage the reader to keep a copy in a wallet or pocketbook. Designing a brochure layout for a season of five plays (consecutive, one-week engagements) seems a simple matter. But compare the following often-used design formats for clarity of information:

1

| Jan. 4-9 <br> The Man Who <br>   Came to Dinner | Jan. 11-16 <br> The Fantasticks |
|---|---|
| Jan. 18-23 <br> The Odd Couple | Jan. 25-30 <br> Dial M for Murder |
| Feb. 1-6 <br> The King and I | Ticket Information: <br> _____ <br> _____ |

2

3

| Jan. 4-9 |
|---|
| Jan. 11-16 |
| Jan. 18-23 |
| Jan. 25-30 |
| Feb. 1-6 |
| Ticket Information: <br> _____ <br> _____ |

4

| Jan. 4-9 | _____ _____ _____ |
|---|---|
| _____ _____ _____ | Jan. 11-16 |
| Jan. 18-23 | _____ _____ _____ |
| _____ _____ _____ | Jan. 25-30 |
| Feb. 1-6 | _____ _____ _____ |
| Ticket Information: <br> _____ <br> _____ | |

Samples 2 and 3 are the most easily readable because they present the information in clear, chronological sequence (sample 2 from left to right and sample 3 from top to bottom. Examples 1 and 4 both confuse the eye. Often, information is muddled because the publicist forces it into a clever or striking graphics format. Design, color and attention-getting techniques should, of course, be present in most promotional literature. But when they have served their purpose of getting the reader's attention, the reader should easily and quickly be able to decipher the information he is seeking. The wise publicist always takes time to "test" his promotion designs on a few people before committing the copy to a printer. Comments made by an outsider often point up weaknesses or omissions which the publicist has overlooked; familiarity can cause "copy blindness."

Most theatrical promotion can abbreviate ticket and schedule information without risking confusion. Usually, the fewer words the better. For example:

Ticket Information:
   Monday through Saturday at 8:30 P.M.
        Orchestra:     $8.00, $7.00
        Mezzanine:     $7.00
        Balcony:     $6.50, $6.00
   Wednesday and Saturday matinee at 2:30 P.M.
        Orchestra:     $7.00, $6.50
        Mezzanine:     $6.00, $5.50
        Balcony:     $5.00, $4.50

may be reduced to:

Tickets:
   Mon thru Fri (8:30) $8.00, 7.50, 7.00, 6.50, 6.00
   Wed & Sat Mat (2:30) $7.00, 6.50, 6.00, 5.50, 5.00, 4.50

Play promotion customarily includes a descriptive phrase above or below the title of the production being advertised. Sometimes a play or a star is so well known that such "blurbs" are unnecessary or even insulting to the reader's intelligence. One need not labor to find adjectives to describe *Hamlet* or Laurence Olivier or Julie Harris, to name a few. In other cases, the "blurb" should provide a clue to the nature of the event as well as a stimulus to attend it. Readers like to know if a production is serious drama or not, musical or non-musical, a new work or a revival, a recent work or not, fully staged or not and so forth. This information can be incorporated into the descriptive phrase that appears in the advertising and should also attempt to emphasize the most interesting or unusual aspect of the production (i.e., "a modern-dress version," "a musical adaptation," "a drama of political corruption," "a comedy of marital errors"). The publicist must ask "who or what is most likely to sell tickets?" Should publicity emphasize the title of the play, the name of the author, the name of the leading performer, the subject matter? The answer is not always easy. A dinner theatre that caters to tourists and "tired businessmen" would probably dampen ticket sales if it emphasized that its production of *Pygmalion* was written by George Bernard Shaw. It might do better to publicize the fact that *Pygmalion* is the play that was adapted into the musical hit *My Fair Lady*. On the other hand, the campus theatre should probably emphasize Shaw's name. Publicity blurbs should be designed to suit the event *and* the audience.

Alliteration has been overly used in theatrical promotion and should be avoided. Phrases like "Marlowe's marvelous melodrama," "Simon's sizzling satire" and the like are certain to turn people off. A straightforward description, a clever play on words, an incisive quote from a review or a single, strong adjective make the most effective blurbs.

## ▪ PROMOTION GIMMICKS

### PROMOTION WITHIN THE THEATRE ▪

No audience member should leave the theatre empty-handed. An audience is comprised of the people most likely to return as members of future audiences. Not to make them aware of future events at the theatre is to lose the theatre's greatest publicity opportunity.

To begin with, there are the obvious and traditional methods of display advertising within a theatre: the marquee, the billboards and display cases, houseboards and the playbill. Box office treasurers can give each ticket-buyer a calendar of events or a flyer (such material should always be enclosed with mail-ordered tickets). Attractive holders for leaflets and other giveaway literature can be attached to lobby walls or near the box office. As mentioned earlier, a deposit box should be placed in the lobby where customers can fill out and leave mailing-address forms.

Giveaways of a great variety can be designed in conjunction with most productions. The Broadway producers of the comedy *Any Wednesday* (the final scene of which employs a great cluster of balloons), nightly handed out free balloons with the title of the play printed on them. Every night for several weeks the after-theatre crowds around Time Square were chatting about this colorful publicity gimmick. Another New York show gave away attractive buttons that read "I Am 'The Me Nobody Knows' " to advertise its title. A suburban theatre gave each lady in the audience a red rose following the opening night of *The Subject Was Roses.* Young audiences can be treated to free lollipops. Although such gimmicks tend to be expensive, giveaways can stimulate considerable word-of-mouth publicity if they are sufficiently unusual and meaningfully distributed.

Finally, there is "spoken" publicity. While many theatres rightly feel that announcements and speeches from the stage tend to disrupt the production, there are cases in which this is an acceptable manner of publicizing future events. Some theatres may be able to increase audience loyalty by appointing the artistic director, the manager or a performer to "plug" future events in a curtain speech before the performance or at the end of an intermission. If the person is articulate, representative of the producing organization and easy to listen to, he may be able to boost advance ticket sales. The spoken word generally has greater impact than the written word.

If curtain speeches are ruled out, there are still many opportunities to speak personally to customers in the theatre. Box office personnel can invite ticket-buyers to purchase or reserve seats for future events. The house manager and the ushers can, without being obtrusive, find opportunities to speak with individual patrons about upcoming events. The publicity director, the manager and others can be on hand as audiences enter a lobby and, while greeting members of the press and people they know or recognize, can chat about current and future productions. Personal contact of this kind intensifies word of mouth about the activities of a theatre and is an important foundation for good audience relations.

### LOCAL TIE-INS AND PERSONAL APPEARANCES ■

A newspaper or radio station will only go so far in providing free space or time to publicize a production per se. But the chances of getting free media coverage are increased a hundredfold when the production, the theatre or the performers can be related to some outside event, local cause or visiting fireman. A photo of the performers greeting a well-known politician backstage after a performance is good copy for local editors. Benefit performances and special groups that attend theatre make good copy. The publicist should keep a sharp lookout for local "clambakes" of one kind or another. When a representative from the theatre participates in a local fund-raising event (a cake sale, a carnival, a sport event, a rally, a parade or whatever) it is often worth a picture and a free mention in local media outlets. Of course, the better known the theatre person is the more likely he is to gain attention.

There is, of course, reason to be cautious about personal appearances. Aside from the danger of cheapening or compromising artistic goals when performers make off-stage appearances, there is also the danger of overexposure. When the manager pays a performer an enormous salary to appear at his theatre, that performer is his drawing card. Expose the performer outside the theatre where people can see him at no cost and perhaps satisfy their curiosity and there is a good possibility that ticket sales will suffer. If the performer not only appears but also performs in some way, the possibility is greater. Even the most celebrated and well-established theatre artists understand that publicity is part of their profession. However, to perform excerpts of a play outside the theatre, to stage public costume parades or simply to parade the artist around outside his professional milieu is not only to risk overexposure but, worse, to risk demeaning the theatre and its true objectives. Personal appearances, in short, should be limited to worthwhile occasions where they can be handled with good taste and to the legitimate benefit of the theatre.

### CONTESTS, BARGAINS AND GIVEAWAYS ■

Supposedly, everybody loves a bargain. But this may not always hold true. If a production offers two tickets for the price of one, for instance, the public may suspect that the show is poor. It may be better to reduce all prices or make available to everyone large numbers of low-price seats. Less suspicious are ticket bargains that offer reduced prices for group sales and season or series tickets.

Bargain tickets may be offered through contests or tie-in offers sponsored by local business firms. Banks may be persuaded to give free tickets to customers who open new accounts and similar arrangements can be made with other businesses (which, of course, must reimburse the theatre for the tickets they dispense). Other kinds of offers may involve giving away autographed photographs, a personal visit with a star and the like. The recent growth of dinner theatres across the nation indicates the popularity of dinner and theatre package offers. Without serving a meal simultaneously with the entertainment, a number of theatres work in cooperation with a neighboring restaurant that offers preshow dining. In this case, a dinner-theatre combination ticket may be offered at an apparently bargain rate while the theatre ticket alone is also available. Similar combination tickets may offer a matinee and luncheon, a cocktail-theatre package, a theatre-buffet ticket or a theatre-supper ticket.

## ▪ FREE ADVERTISING AND PUBLICITY

### TIE-INS WITH OTHER BUSINESSES ▪

The various reciprocal or joint advertising schemes that can be worked out with business firms are endless and often inexpensive. Sometimes, to assist a local non-profit theatre or because theatrical advertising is colorful and unusual, a local business will provide advertising without any cost to the theatre. All stores, for example, dispense shopping bags of some kind and, carried by customers onto streets and buses, these become "walking" ads. Many stores are willing to incorporate theatre publicity in their window displays. The tops of locally manufactured milk bottles, soda bottles and jars of canned goods can be imprinted with theatre advertising. Libraries, schools and book stores are usually willing to dispense bookmarks that carry theatrical advertising. Utility companies, banks and department stores are often willing to support worthwhile, nonprofit theatres by mailing theatre literature with their monthly billing statements. Or, if such companies publish newsletters, they may be persuaded to devote an issue to the local theatre. Using imagination and drive, the theatrical promoter may be surprised at the amount of free advertising co-operation he can obtain from the business community.

### MEDIA APPEARANCES ▪

Virtually all radio and television stations sponsor variety and talk shows that continually seek interesting guests. It is not difficult, then, for the publicist to arrange frequent appearances of theatre personnel on these shows. An attempt should be made to utilize artistic directors, designers, managers and others as well as performers. Naturally, the celebrity is the person whom the media is most interested in interviewing.

The danger of arranging too many personal appearances for theatre performers on local television programs is the danger of overexposure. There is a very old and not illogical school of thought among actors that makes many of them disinclined to appear publicly, except on a stage in a production. That is what they are paid to do and what audiences pay to see. Remove an actor from the magical realm of his theatricality—which is his trade and his art—and you risk doing disservice both to the actor and to the theatre. One need watch very few television talk shows that feature celebrated performers discussing politics and trivia to wish that more actors subscribed to this feeling.

If the television appearance of an actor tends to make him less mysterious, less artistic and less worth the price of admission to see him perform in person, radio exposure, it may be argued, tends to have the opposite effect. The actor's voice without his image tends to increase the listener's curiosity, to whet his appetite for seeing the performer in person—especially the celebrated performer. Radio spots are also much easier for the press agent to arrange than TV appearances. An interview can be conducted over the telephone or the host of the program is often able to tape record the interview at the time and place most convenient for the performer. When arranging the radio or television interview, the press agent should give the announcer or host some background information about the person being interviewed and also the basic facts about the production with which he is currently associated (performance dates, the name of the play and the theatre, etc.). There is nothing more disconcerting than elaborate and time-consuming media arrangements that result in a guest appearance that fails to connect the guest with the theatre at which he is working. Best of all, of course, is a guarantee that the host of the show will begin and end his interview by "plugging" the appropriate theatre and production.

### PUBLIC SERVICE ANNOUNCEMENTS AND LISTINGS ▪

As well as talk shows, most media outlets provide programs or space devoted to free activities announcements. In fact, radio and television stations are required by law to provide a certain amount of public service programming. The format used to present entertainment and cultural information to the public varies from one publication or broadcasting station to the next. The press department, then, should inform itself about format, deadline and manner of presentation for public service announcements offered by each entry on its press list. A specific person should then be assigned to prepare and mail activities announcements. These announcements are much shorter than press releases and often individually prepared. The list to which they are sent should be different from the press release list, which consists of drama editors as opposed to public service or "community bulletin board" editors.

If scrupulous attention is paid to the multitude of sources that provide event listings, a tremendous and a steady barrage of free advertising can be gained. There are no secrets about obtaining such advertising—just a lot of time and effort.

## ▪ A COORDINATED PROMOTIONAL CAMPAIGN

### TIMING, SATURATION, UNITY ▪

Long before actual publicity work begins, the publicity director should be gathering promotional ideas. He should familiarize himself with the script itself, the performers and the artistic personnel associated with the production. He should call at least a few meetings with artistic and administrative personnel for the purpose of batting around promotional possibilities. What, in the artistic director's opinion, is the main theme of the production? What single word best captures the production's significance? Is there one especially powerful moment in the production? Is there a particular character in the play who symbolizes the theme or style or essence of the work? How can such things be depicted on a poster? What segments of the public might be especially interested in attending the production?

Through open discussions of such matters, a number of publicity ideas are bound to emerge. No publicity director can be expected to come up with a sufficient stock of ideas all by himself. And without consulting the artistic personnel he runs a very high risk of developing a promotional campaign that is not in keeping with the spirit of the production being publicized.

Once the advertising and publicity budget is known and the publicist has completed his basic research on the play and the people involved in it and begun to formulate ways of reaching the public, then he may begin to draw up a timetable of deadlines for himself. If he is promoting a theatre that offers a season or series of productions, it will probably be the dual purpose of publicity to sell both discounted series tickets and individual performance tickets. The campaign to sell series tickets, of course, ends with the first performance in the series, while the general campaign to sell individual seats continues to the final performance of the series. Obviously, the more series tickets are sold the easier the publicist's job will be once the season gets under way. In any case, the series ticket campaign can be planned and executed more or less independently from other advertising and publicity.

To impose unity on a publicity campaign is to draw the diverse ads and gimmicks together in the public mind and establish graphics symbols that, over a period of time, become meaningful trademarks. Some uniformity, some identifying factor, should be present in the majority of promotional pieces that concern the same theatre or the same production.

When considering how to spend the advertising budget, the object is usually to reach the greatest volume of potential theatregoers. It is often difficult to decide whether to place a lot of ads in a few important newspapers or a few ads in a lot of newspapers and media outlets. If advance sales are high, it may be wise to advertise in "fringe" newspapers or employ unusual or unproven promotion approaches in order to attract a wider audience. A large amount of preseason or preopening newspaper advertising that brings in a good percentage of ticket-buyers has, in all likelihood, served its purpose of attracting as many sales from that particular readership as it will ever attract. Advertising should then be drastically redistributed and redesigned to reach other ticket-buyers. If a massive advertising campaign fails to stimulate much response at all, there is either something wrong with its content and design or it is not reaching the right potential audience. Saturation advertising, then, means two things: steady and extensive coverage in a few media outlets *and* in a wide number and variety of outlets.

Along with saturation coverage and a unified approach, good timing is a third element necessary to the successful publicity campaign. Like all deadlines in the theatre, the publicist's basic deadline is the curtain time. Working backward from the moment a performance (or series of performances) is scheduled to begin, the publicist sets deadlines for advertisements to appear, for press releases to be mailed, for personal appearances to be scheduled, for brochures to be mailed and so forth. In the early stages of a publicity campaign, the aim should be merely to make the press and the public aware that "something is going to happen." Second, the campaign attempts to build public curiosity and interest in what is going to happen. Third, it accelerates public excitement about the event to stimulate ticket sales. As "curtain time" draws near, the excitement ideally reaches fever intensity. After the opening night (assuming that performances are to continue) the object is to maintain or increase public interest in the production or the theatre, although from this time forward the publicist's ability to achieve this is largely dependent on audience reaction to the production.

Good timing requires, among other things, the coordination of media advertising with direct-mail advertising, and both at a time neither too close nor too distant from the opening night. Potential ticket-buyers should receive mailed brochures at about the same time that they read advertisements and stories about the event. They should be exposed to follow-up promotion either through media ads, telephone calls, another mail piece or by word of mouth. Ideally, each potential ticket-buyer should be given three chances to buy a ticket. The first chance may be a poster or newspaper story he sees. The second chance may be the newspaper ad he reads. The third chance is perhaps the brochure and order form he receives in the mail. Without two or three "teasers" or reminders, the majority of people will never actually purchase a ticket. The strongest motivation to purchase tickets comes from word of mouth publicity. When one or two friends recommend a theatre or a production, it suddenly becomes "the thing to attend," personally guaranteed.

## THE SEASON OR SERIES TICKET CAMPAIGN ▪

The amount and variety of advertising used to promote series ticket sales will depend largely on the available budget. The timetable on page 333 of deadlines suggests the minimum amount of activity that should comprise a season ticket campaign for a typical five-hundred- to seven-hundred-seat multi-production theatre, whether it is a stock, resident, community or campus operation. These activities are exclusive of general promotional duties.

This simplified calendar, of course, does not list the detail or preparatory work that is necessary to arrange each activity that is shown. The promotion department will find it necessary to make countless phone calls and hold numerous meetings to set up the volunteer committees, arrange the telethon and so forth. It should also be noted that the largest budget item listed on the calendar (for newspaper advertising) would be a normal preopening expenditure to promote individual ticket sales even without a season ticket campaign. The main thrust of the campaign, of course, could be centered around a slogan or theme that attempts to make the purchase of a season ticket especially attractive, prestigious, economical or exciting. Since season tickets are usually priced lower per ticket than individually purchased seats, the bargain appeal is an obvious selling point. So, too, is the guarantee to customers that they will receive preferred locations of their choice. To heighten the prestige element, the series ticket holder might be called a "friend," "patron," "subscriber" or member of the "inner circle," "critics' circle," "golden circle" or whatever.

## INDIVIDUAL SHOW LITERATURE ▪

A promotional calendar or timetable should be plotted by the publicist for each production that is offered by his theatre. This set of deadlines will be in addition to those related to the season or series ticket campaign. When deadline notations are not made in writing on a calendar, poor promotion will almost certainly be the result. And a liberal amount of time must always be allowed for unforeseen delays.

The amount of publicity and advertising necessary throughout a multi-production season will depend on the success of the series or preseason ticket campaign. If a sizable number of tickets remains unsold for individual performances, then a vigorous promotional campaign will have to continue throughout the season. To save time and money, the major seasonal brochure or schedule of events should be designed in such manner that it may be reproduced and used throughout the entire season as an information and order form. In addition to this, flyers and media advertisements may be designed for each production as well as special gimmicks. Personal appear-

OPENING NIGHT OF SEASON:  July 4

BOX OFFICE OPENS FOR GENERAL TICKET SALES: June 25

(Prior to this, only series tickets are sold)

| Deadline | Activity | Estimated Cost |
|---|---|---|
| November 20 | Mailing of "holiday greeting" card with season ticket gift certificate order forms (select list of 5,000 names). | $ 195 |
| December 5-15 | Place ads in two leading newspapers with same holiday gift coupons (total of six ads, 2 cols. x 5" each). | 300 |
| March 20 | Annual meeting with board of directors to discuss new season, new advisory councils and annual promotion budget. | — |
| April 13, 14, 15 | Meetings with advisory councils to discuss audience development, new mailing lists, organize regional season ticket sales committees. | 10 |
| May 7-10 | Establish and meet with volunteer heads of the twelve regional season ticket sales committees. Plan strategy, set expense budgets of $50 for each committee, discuss season. | 620 |
| May 15 | Season ticket renewal mailing to past season ticket buyers and new "high potential" prospects. This brochure does not contain actual performance dates, just names of productions, season ticket prices and general information (3000 mailers). | 360 |
| May 20 | Feature stories to press and local media detailing the new volunteer ticket sales committees in each area. Photos of committee meetings to accompany stories where possible. | 10 |
| June 1 | Press release about upcoming season, repeating ticket sales committee names and phone numbers. | 10 |
| June 1-30 | Series of Sunday newspaper ads and ads in local weekly publications listing season performances with season ticket order forms. Limited radio ads from June 20-30. | 2,000 |
| June 1-25 | Series of speeches and appearances by artistic director, publicity director and performers before local clubs and organizations to boost season ticket sales. | — |
| June 3 | Mailing of general seasonal brochure with names and dates of performances, season and individual ticket order forms (15,000 mailers). | 900 |
| June 5 | Artistic director meets with volunteer ticket sales committees for "pep-talks"; discuss season, take photos for press stories. Refreshments. | 50 |
| June 8 | Press release regarding above meeting, response to season ticket orders, etc. | 10 |
| June 10 | Meeting with advisory councils to evaluate season ticket campaign to date, get suggestions, enlist additional support for ticket sales committees. | 10 |
| June 24 | Annual telethon with local radio or TV station. All ticket sales volunteers to participate in massive telephone appeal (use names from mailing list and past ticket-buyers who have not responded to mail offers). Utilize artistic director, current performers, past performers, local VIPs, guest celebrities as M.C.s. Invite phone orders from listener/viewers. Get local industry or business firms to sponsor the air time. | 100 |
| June 25 | Tickets go on general sale at the box office. Seasonal orders accepted until opening night, but without guarantee of preferred locations. | — |
| July 4 | Opening night performance. Special party should be arranged before or after the performance to reward all volunteer ticket workers, introduce them to the performers, present awards for volunteers who brought in the highest sales, certificates of appreciation to all others. Names of all volunteers to be listed in the theatre programs. | 200 |
| | Estimated total cost of season ticket campaign: | $4,775 |

ances, press releases and feature stories must also continue at a steady pace. Even when performances are virtually sold out in advance, information must still be fed to the press and the public must continually be reminded of the theatre's activity. A current season should not grow too old before the publicist begins to plan and promote the next season.

---

Publicity work for the theatre is demanding, thankless and frustrating. But the publicist is the marriage broker between his theatre and the general public. Hopefully, he is able to create a lasting love affair between the theatre and a large, devoted audience. To accomplish this, the seasonal or multi-production operation should promote first the producing organization and second the individual productions. If the overall image and reputation of the organization can be established successfully, a large percentage of the audience will support all its productions. Audiences should be encouraged to enjoy theatregoing in general and not only to see favorite or well-known plays and performers. To promote the producing organization, the publicist depends on the support of everyone in that organization—the kind of support that makes attendance at a theatre enjoyable in itself, quite apart from the performance being offered. Are customers treated well by the treasurers and ushers? Is the theatre well maintained? Do playbills and lobby displays enhance the excitement of theatregoing? The atmosphere, the physical setting and the circumstances around which plays are produced usually make the difference between one-time visitors and steady customers. There is much, much more to audience development and theatrical promotion than a few ads in the local newspaper!

# CHAPTER SIXTEEN

# Audience Engineering and Psychology

The idea, the place, the actors, the staff, the money and the materials for a theatrical production are brought together and organized for the benefit of an audience. If the organization has been effective, it will appear to the audience that the performance "just happened—as easy as pie!" The audience will never know that the ingenue was replaced by another actress just last week, that the musical conductor walked out on the dress rehearsal, that the kettledrums are borrowed from the local high school, that the roof leaks when it rains, that mechanics are still trying to repair the air-conditioning, that the police chief has been asked to halt performances on grounds of obscenity or that the director donated his salary when no funds were available to pay for costume materials. The audience arrives, the performance takes place—and nothing should intrude between these two elements. To prevent intrusions that may influence or interrupt audience enjoyment of a performance is the fundamental obligation of house management.

- ## THE HOUSE MANAGER

### QUALIFICATIONS ■
As the term implies, the "house manager" works for the "house," which is to say

335

for the landlord. At least this is true in commercial New York theatre, Las Vegas and road theatres. The house manager is the landlord's resident representative. He is not only responsible for supervising the "resident staff" of treasurers, ticket-takers, ushers, doormen, maintenance personnel and others, but also checks box office statements and is the counterpart of the company manager, who is the producer's resident representative. In unionized theatres both the house manager and the company manager must be members of the Association of Theatrical Press Agents and Managers (ATPAM). Employment terms and conditions are determined through periodic contract negotiations between ATPAM and the League of New York Theatres. Typical of all union contracts, these embrace such points as salary, benefits, minimum length of employment and union jurisdiction. The majority of professional theatres that employ Equity actors, however, do *not* fall under the jurisdiction of ATPAM: most summer and winter stock theatres, tent theatres, dinner theatres and resident and repertory theatres are not required to hire ATPAM managers. For this reason the definition and duties of a house manager vary considerably from theatre to theatre. Where non-union managers are permitted, it is not unusual for the house manager to fulfill other jobs in the press office, the box office or elsewhere as the employer requires.

Ideally, a house manager should regard his position as much more than head janitor or chief ticket-taker. A good house manager is, in effect, an audience engineer. By supervising such factors as house maintenance, house temperature and house personnel he is really supervising audience comfort and audience attitude. He is a public service employee in the truest sense. He should be aware of audience needs, of public safety and of comfort. He should be capable of handling emergency situations with authority and dispatch (such as fire or the illness of an audience member), possess good judgment and be representative of the type of producing organization for which he works. An ostensibly small and insignificant oversight or mistake on the part of the house manager can easily disrupt or destroy objectives that have taken the artistic staff months to realize. It is not an exaggeration to claim that the house staff holds the artistic product in the palm of its hands during performance periods.

Many stock theatres assign the job of house management to an apprentice, and campus theatres often utilize a student house manager. When the entire front-of-house staff during performance time is comprised of inexperienced or volunteer help, a staff or faculty supervisor should at least be present in case difficult or emergency circumstances arise. The responsibility and potential liability of gathering a large group of people together is simply too great to be entrusted to inexperienced supervisors.

### STANDARD HOUSE MANAGEMENT DUTIES ∎
Dependent on whether the house manager is a member of ATPAM, on the type and size of theatre operation in which he is employed and whether or not he also performs other jobs, the following are the twelve responsibilities most likely to fall under the aegis of the house manager:

1. Hire and supervise front of house personnel, i.e.:
   a) assistant house manager
   b) ticket-takers
   c) ushers

        d) doormen

        e) parking attendants

        f) chief-plant engineer

        g) janitorial staff

        h) public rest room matrons

        i) security guards

        j) checkroom and other concessions attendants

2. Contract and supervise maintenance services, i.e.:

        a) plumbers

        b) electricians

        c) heat and air-conditioning services

        d) vending machine companies

        e) landscape gardeners, exterminators, etc.

3. Arrange for a house physician.

4. Verify hours worked by part-time help for payroll purposes.

5. Coordinate ticket-taking with box office systems and needs.

6. Supervise cleanliness and sanitary conditions of the plant.

7. Maintain safety and fire laws.

8. Oversee condition of plant machinery (heat, water, etc.).

9. Oversee special customer services (water fountains, etc.).

10. Coordinate curtain times with stage manager (through house warning bells and communications system with backstage).

11. Handle special customer problems regarding seating, etc.

12. Check opening and closing of auditorium and public areas before and after performances.

Nearly all these responsibilities, of course, may be delegated to a staff member, but a goodly amount of personal supervision by the house manager is always desirable. Before each performance, the house manager should personally tour all the public areas of the building *as if he were a customer seeing it for the first time.* Are the cigarette receptacles empty? Is the floor clear of all papers? Is there a musky odor in the auditorium? Are the rest rooms in spotless condition? Is the lobby furniture dusted and polished? Are curtains, seat covers and draperies neatly arranged? What is the auditorium temperature? Are all light bulbs working? Are there any "accident traps" (such as loose carpeting, unlighted steps, insecure railings, sharp edges on seats or cigarette dispensers, etc.)? Theatres tend to use soft, interior lighting and janitorial staffs tend toward blindness! Older theatres, especially, require scrupulous cleaning if they are to look fresh and neat. And, without an ample air-conditioning system, a theatre must be continually "aired out" to avoid building up a musky, unpleasant smell of heavy air, particularly between matinee and evening performances and after long rehearsal periods.

# ▪ GREETING THE AUDIENCE

## LOBBY ATMOSPHERE ▪

    Chapter 3 considers how the architectural and decorative features of a theatre space contribute to the general feeling and atmosphere that an audience will derive from it. Such elements as the volume of open space, the arrangement of the seats, the colors and the materials used in decorating the theatre will determine the psychological degree of warmth or coldness that is created. Seemingly minor factors may contribute significantly to the manner in which customers respond to the physical setting of a theatre: flower arrangements in lobbies and rest rooms, paintings and other wall decorations, lobby and lounge furniture, the type of general illumination (fluorescent lighting fixtures produce a very hard, cold illumination while amber or tinted electric bulbs create a warm, complimentary illumination). In virtually all cases, the ideal lobby or theatre atmosphere is warm and relaxing: carpet as opposed to marble, cotton as opposed to plastic, upholstered as opposed to hard surfaces, wood as opposed to steel, candle-like glow as opposed to fluorescent harshness. All this seems obvious enough—except, evidently, to theatre architects and decorators. Fortunately, the occupant of a cold and hostile-appearing theatre can take quick and inexpensive corrective measures which will dramatically improve and "warm up" the public areas.

### FRONT OF HOUSE STAFF ATTITUDE ▪

General qualifications for administrative personnel in theatre and, especially, the behavior of all those who deal with the public have been discussed in chapter 4. But the importance of how a theatre staff greets the public cannot be overemphasized. Almost as soon as a visitor walks into a theatre, he can sense the kind of operation it is. Staff members with whom he is confronted (from doormen to managers, from performers to ushers) immediately convey an attitude toward the theatre and that attitude invariably emanates from the top administrator: confidence, arrogance, vitality, informality, confusion, pride, professionalism, amateurism or a combination of these begin to condition the theatregoer's reaction to a performance even before the curtain goes up. Staff attitudes are also reflected in staff behavior and dress. Employee uniforms for ushers, ticket-takers and others are becoming a thing of the past, at least for small operations. In very large auditoriums, uniformed service employees are helpful simply because they are easy for customers to recognize. Where full uniforms are not used, some standard, identifying garment may be worn, such as a vest, jacket, apron or sash. Whether the ushering staff is dressed in semiformal or informal attire should be determined by the objectives and attitudes of the producing organization. Standards of attire may well change from production to production within the same theatre in order to suit each production and best prepare the audience for it. The total experience of theatregoing, to repeat an earlier theme, begins long before the curtain rises and continues after it falls.

Especially when the style or content of a production represents a severe break with tradition, when it attempts something that the general audience will find highly unusual, the artistic director should encourage front-of-house behavior, attire and decoration that help prepare the audience for what is about to transpire on stage. For instance, when the Seattle Opera Association produced the American premiere of the rock opera *Tommy,* it was presented in a suitably informal theatre rather than the organization's more plush opera house where barefoot hippies and matinee matrons alike would have felt alienated either by the production or by the theatre atmosphere. Of course, this is an extreme example. Generally, it is sufficient if

front-of-house employees are courteous, efficient and appropriately attired. To insure these qualities, however, close supervision by a house manager or other staff
member is necessary. A well-known producer in one repertory theatre personally
lines up the entire front-of-house staff before each performance to check everyone's grooming from shoeshine to fingernails. This may prove an effective technique
for insuring a well-appearing staff and for instilling in that staff high and meticulous
standards of operation. When supervisors show personal concern with the staff, the
staff will almost certainly respond in kind by showing greater concern with the
customers.

### AUDIENCE SEATING SYSTEMS ■

The larger the audience, the more supervision and control that will be required
over the flow of human traffic. But even with an audience of fifty or a hundred
people, patrons need guidance in getting from the street through the lobbies and
into the correct theatre chair. Care must be taken to insure that public transportation and automobile parking systems are adequate to handle the entire audience in
the half hour or hour before the performance begins. Are there comfortable places
where early-arriving customers can wait? What is the policy regarding latecomers?
When should the lobbies be opened, when should the auditorium be opened, when
should the curtain go up? Questions like these should be decided well in advance in
consultation with the artistic staff. Knowing that many customers arrive late for a
performance (especially at theatres where transportation or parking causes delays
that new customers will not anticipate), many theatres maintain a policy of beginning performances ten or fifteen minutes *after* the advertised curtain time. (As a
professional courtesy, newspaper critics and VIPs should be told the exact curtain
time.) Other managements make a point of taking the curtain up on time, exactly
as advertised. Lengthy curtain delays, of course, seriously and negatively affect
audience psychology.

Usually, the flow of audience traffic should be easy and comfortable, although
it is important to aim for a certain "crowding effect." Nothing is more deadly than
a handful of people standing around a cavernous lobby or scattered around a huge
auditorium. When this happens, the whole concept of "audience" is destroyed and,
hence, the possibility of group reaction to a performance. An experienced house
manager will be able to sense when a crowd of people in a lobby is psychologically
ready to assume their seats in the theatre. A healthy amount of lobby crowding
creates an excitement and anticipation which peaks at a given moment—and that
is the moment when the house should be opened. Theatres that contain public
restaurants, cocktail lounges and other concessions will find that concession sales
decrease as soon as the house opens and, if audience members are busily patronizing
the concessions, should open the house later than theatres without such facilities.

Along with staff attitude and behavior, theatre lobby activities and concessions
help determine audience reaction both to the theatre in general and to the performance. The type and the management of concessions can dampen or enhance the
experience of theatregoing. If displays and concessions are attractive, interesting,
fun and even exciting, they constitute a major asset for the theatre. The sound of a
piano playing, of glasses clinking, of champagne bottles being opened and the sight
of camera flashbulbs going off are things that put most people in a festive, relaxed

mood, in a frame of mind that helps them enjoy themselves. Of course such festivity is not appropriate to every type of theatre operation, but some kind of pre-performance atmosphere *is* appropriate and that should be determined and even fabricated where it does not exist automatically (the staff member exploding flash bulbs needn't use a *loaded* camera and the champagne bottles needn't contain the real stuff). In short, theatricality need not be confined to the stage.

The architecture of a theatre will dictate how many ticket-takers, directors and ushers will be necessary to seat an audience quickly and efficiently. The physical point at which a customer must make a decision about how next to proceed is exactly the point where a staff director must be stationed. Customers should never have to guess whether they should go upstairs or down, right or left, whether they should proceed or wait for an usher. Most of all, when reserved seating is used, theatregoers should never be left alone to find their correct seats. Too many will occupy incorrect seats and create embarrassing problems when people with tickets for those seats arrive. There is a peculiar quirk of human nature that seems to compel people to hold their ground once they have established it as their own. Call it "squatter's rights" or the "territorial imperative," the theatregoer is loath to move once having settled down in a theatre seat. And, it seems, those most loath to move are those who are asked to do so after the curtain has gone up. Far easier to seat people correctly in the first place.

More and more theatres are adopting a policy of not seating latecomers until appropriate intervals in the performance. Some productions begin with particularly quiet or sensitive moments and this situation should always prohibit people from being seated late. Theatres with continental seating, where each row may contain as many as seventy or eighty seats without aisle separations, almost automatically prohibit seating of latecomers except during scene breaks or other appropriate moments during the production. If it is the policy not to accommodate latecomers immediately this fact should be stated on a lobby sign, on the printed ticket and in advertising wherever possible.

A signal system should be installed to warn audiences that the performance is about to begin or resume. The least expensive and crudest warning system is that of flashing lobby lights on and off in rapid succession. An electronically operated gong or bell that can be controlled by the house manager and heard in the public lounges, concession areas and the general lobby is standard theatre equipment. A house phone should be installed to enable the head usher or house manager to speak with the stage manager. This will prevent the house manager from seating the audience too early if there are delays backstage, and likewise prevent the stage manager from calling "places" if there is a delay in seating the house. Under no circumstances should the curtain rise before the house manager instructs the stage manager to proceed with the performance.

The length of intermission will vary according to:

1. How many intermissions are scheduled during a given performance. (Usually the more that are scheduled, the shorter they should be. And the first intermission should usually be the longest.)

2. The length of performance time before the intermission (the longer the performance time, the longer the intermission should be).

3. The size of the audience (the smaller the audience, the shorter the inter-

missions should be. This should hold true during the run of a production if and when audience size varies from performance to performance.)

4. The availability of concessions and rest room facilities (not until some
minutes after candy and beverage concessions have served all customers
and after rest room facilities have been emptied should the performance
resume).

5. Extenuating circumstances (more intermission time may be required for
complicated scenery or costume changes. Intermissions may be shortened
or eliminated at certain performances to avoid paying union employee
overtime rates, to allow sufficient time between two closely consecutive
performances on the same day and for other such reasons.)

When a playgoer moves from the lobby into the house, the first person he should
encounter is the ticket-taker. To insure that torn ticket stubs will be obtained from
all customers, the first entrance through which the customer passes should be no
larger than the width of two standard doors. The ticket-taker should greet each customer verbally and might also instruct customers where to proceed next ("inside to
your right," "up the stairs to your left," "please wait at the top of the aisle for an
usher to seat you" and so forth). If the customer must walk more than a few yards
before making his next turn or decision, a director should be stationed at that point
to examine the ticket stubs and instruct the customer where to go next. Usually, it
is more efficient if playgoers wait at the top of aisles for ushers to seat them. Large
theatres may station ushers at two or three points progressively further down an
aisle. All ushers should keep an eye out for customers who are trying to seat themselves without assistance. One good way to prevent this is to make programs available only from the ushers. If customers can take programs for themselves in the lobby
or behind the last row of seats, they will be more tempted to seat themselves without an usher. In European theatres it is often the custom to reward ushers and box
office treasurers with gratuities and sometimes this occurs in American theatres. In
such instances, of course, the staff employee should be allowed to keep the gratuity.

Before each performance, the ushering staff should be given individual intermission assignments for opening and closing doors, for turning on and off manually
operated house lights and other such chores. Similarly, the house staff must be
thoroughly familiar with procedures to follow in case of emergency or unusual
occurrence. And it is wise to caution the entire front and backstage theatre staff
about deportment during performance hours, especially emphasizing such rules as:

1. Never run or shout in audience areas because of the danger of creating
panic or public alarm—especially in the event of a real emergency.

2. Never use the auditorium to gain access to or exit from the backstage area.

3. Performers and backstage personnel should always use the stage door, never
lobby or house entrances.

4. Backstage employees should always report the presence of strangers or unauthorized visitors.

5. Backstage personnel should never be seen in audience areas during performance hours except in cases of emergency.

Just as it might be said that the best manager is the one with nothing on his desk, so it may be said that the best management is usually the least conspicuous management. Theatregoers like to be serviced efficiently but unobtrusively. The front-of-house staff can be friendly without being obnoxious or pushy. It can be present without being obvious and it can serve the public without pressuring the public. The house manager and his staff really comprise the official host of an event, of an evening out. Like the host at a good cocktail party, the house manager must keep things going, must keep people moving, must cover for mistakes or deficiencies of all kinds, must try to see that each guest feels like the most honored guest and must help each guest to go away thinking he has enjoyed a perfectly smashing time. This takes sobriety, diplomacy, great organization and an awareness of others. The truly accomplished theatrical house manager, like the accomplished hotel manager and maitre d', is a rarity.

# ▪ SPECIAL AUDIENCE CONDITIONS AND EMERGENCIES

The frequency with which special problems arise during public performances is high. Latecomers loudly argue with the head usher, someone in the audience causes a disturbance because he is under the influence of alcohol or drugs, a member of the audience becomes ill, the air-conditioning system suddenly develops a case of whooping cough, someone begins using a flash camera: these and countless other occurrences are common and someone from the theatre staff must be there to handle them immediately.

### IN CASE OF FIRE ▪

The most serious and potentially dangerous threat to an audience is fire. History has recorded a long series of theatre fires that have killed thousands of people and have made the public rightfully aware of danger when smoke invades a public gathering. Following the Brooklyn Theatre fire in 1876, which killed over three hundred people, Steele MacKaye and other innovators developed fireproofing methods for stage scenery and invented folding safety seats for the audience and other devices to help prevent such tragedies. Modern technology, of course, has vastly improved upon materials, devices and structuring and greatly reduced the threat of fire in public buildings. But the threat has yet to be eliminated and, of course, countless plays continue to be produced in antiquated or wooden buildings which are hardly less susceptible to fire than those constructed a hundred years ago. Even the truly fireproof theatre (if such a building exists) is not immune from the disaster and loss of life that can result from mass panic. For good reason, it is illegal to shout "Fire!" in a public place unless there actually is a fire. Still, all it takes is a smoldering cigarette to cause panic and disaster.

Insurance companies and fire department inspectors are extremely strict about enforcing public safety laws and regulations, but complete enforcement depends upon the theatre management itself. When a producing organization enjoys a sell-out, for instance, it is almost unbearably tempting to place extra chairs in the aisles, to overcrowd the standing-room space and to allow people to sit on aisle steps. When stage properties are added at the last minute or scenery is late in construction, it is easy to overlook fireproofing laws. When stage directions call for a completely dark theatre in order to create or enhance some special effect (as in the mystery-melodrama *Wait Until Dark),* there is a temptation to cover or extinguish the aisle and exit lights. In New York, Chicago and Los Angeles, the fire inspector virtually sits on the scene designer's shoulder. But this is not usually the case elsewhere. Just as the theatre manager holds the customer's advance sale ticket money in trust, so he holds the customer's safety in trust. Theatre management has no greater responsibility than this.

While no one likes to anticipate a theatre fire, it is foolhardy for management not to formulate procedures for its staff to follow in the event of fire or other threats to public safety. Fire rules should be posted on the actors' call-board and backstage and distributed to all front-of-house personnel. Sometime before the first performance, the stage manager should assemble the entire cast and production company to review emergency regulations. The house manager should review emergency regulations with the house staff before *each* performance. Ushers should be stationed throughout the house so that each exit can be assigned to a specific usher who can open it quickly during a performance if necessary. It is, however, extremely important that the stage manager and the house manager be the *only* two people authorized to institute emergency measures during performance hours and that they communicate any such intentions to each other. Obviously, a very cool head is required. When does a threat become a true emergency? When does a potential problem become a real problem? What should be done to protect the public, when should it be done, how should it be done?

It is not unusual in theatre for some harmless occurrence to appear a pending disaster. For example, a broken fan-belt in a heating or air-conditioning system may suddenly flood the air in an auditorium with smoke-like fumes. If cigarette receptacles are not cleaned out constantly before and during performance hours, they will begin smoldering. If ushers do not scrutinize all customers as they enter the auditorium (both at the beginning of the performance and as they return from intermissions), somebody will get through with a burning cigarette or cigar. The worst offenders are likely to be producers, directors and playwrights nervously puffing away in the last rows of the house. They should not be treated as exceptions.

When an audience *believes* there is some threat to its safety, however innocent the cause may be, its fears should be allayed at once. The quickest and most direct way of doing this is for the stage manager to make an announcement from the stage or over the public address system. This should be done in a calm, reassuringly apathetic voice and the message should minimize the danger: "Ladies and gentlemen, it seems the fan-belt that operates our stage revolve has developed difficulty and is creating the odor you smell in the air. But we'll endeavor to go on with the performance while our stagehands repair it, if you'll just bear with us." Much better than something like: "Don't panic, ladies and gentlemen. There is no fire in the theatre, just a little difficulty with some of our machinery." Panic words themselves can sometimes cause panic because they are *suggestive* of danger. If such announcements can be delayed until an intermission or scene break, all the better. The house manager is in the best position to judge the audience mood and determine whether or not such an interruption is desirable, so he should be consulted before the stage manager takes any action. As often as not, the situation will seem much worse backstage than it seems to the audience.

When the emergency is a real one and it is advisable to get the audience out of the theatre quickly, it is even more important to follow a cool and relaxed procedure. If the performers can be alerted to the situation, they will be able to bring the performance to a normal-appearing halt and the curtain can be brought down as if it were a scheduled intermission or scene break. The house lights should come up at once and the house manager and his staff should immediately open all exit doors. Many people will leave automatically and others should be coaxed out in quick but orderly fashion by ushers telling them, "Please clear the auditorium for this intermission—please clear the theatre."

Often, a performer is more reassuring than a staff member when it comes to announcing difficulties or emergencies, especially if he speaks from the front of the auditorium itself and not from the stage or in front of the stage curtain. It is difficult to say why this is true, but perhaps a complete break from character and the curiosity factor of seeing a performer in the house somehow creates audience security. In any case, it is the exact antithesis of someone running onto the stage during a performance and shouting "Fire!" There is no emergency that requires *that* kind of announcement, but a well-prepared staff is the only assurance against the occurrence of such an insane deed.

### POWER FAILURE ■

The advent of a power failure that plunges a crowded theatre into sudden darkness is a major threat to public safety. New and elaborate theatre complexes often have emergency generator equipment capable of supplying the whole electric power system if public utilities fail. All theatres, of course, are required by law to install and maintain emergency lighting devices in the public areas of the building. These may be simple, battery-operated spotlights or they may be connected to an emergency generator. In either case, they must be rigged to become operative immediately when normal electric power fails. The presence of emergency lighting precludes the possibility of an audience suddenly being thrown into total darkness. But any sudden change can be terrifying and, for a theatre audience in what is potentially a claustrophobic setting, can create mass hysteria.

During the past few years, America has experienced public power failures often enough for most people to have become conditioned to expect them or, at least, not to panic when the lights go out. Knowing that power failures are likely to continue for some years ahead, theatre managers should make advance preparations to cope with them unless they are fortunate enough to work in plants with full generating equipment. As Broadway producers found after the famous blackout of '65, there is no regular insurance or legal recourse for recovering income lost due to blackouts or for not paying union employees for work losses during such periods. Small theatres, by stocking up on candles or battery-operated lights, might be able to continue performances without normal lighting equipment. Most people are indulgent, if not secretly amused, when technology proves fallible. Large theatres have greater difficulty in protecting audiences and should remember that there are times when "the curtain must go *down*." Often, a power failure is of short duration, so a pause or intermission should be allowed to continue for at least twenty minutes before any decision is made about cancelling the performance. In the event that the performance is cancelled and the audience sent home, it should be instructed to retain ticket stubs for refund or exchange at the box office. It is unwise to keep on hand the cash equivalent of a night's receipts, so extensive refunds are usually impossible at short notice.

NATIONAL EMERGENCY ▪

During the 1960s, America was the victim of a demonic series of political assassinations. Within memory, this nation has also been the target of foreign military attack and, sadly, has mobilized surprise military attacks on other nations. There is no one alive today who does not know the meaning of the phrase "national emergency." And to know its meaning is to realize that little can be done to prepare for the emotional impact such an event invariably has on the public. Perhaps the best that one can do initially, as a helpless bystander, is to respond in a human way and to acknowledge that response publicly if one is the representative of a public business or institution.

In the live theatre, as in any other situation involving live participants, adherence to a prestructured script or format has its limitations. If someone throws a rotten tomato at a speaker or performer, the audience expects him to react like a living person not like a mechanical doll or the image on a motion picture screen. When the audience is exposed to a major disruption or occurrence so is the performer and the "pretense" of performance must then be broken. This principle holds equally true for both comic and dangerous or tragic occurrences. When a play is interrupted by the sound of a jet flying over the theatre or an actor's trousers accidently split up the back in plain view of the audience, it is best for the performer to acknowledge the situation with a pause or an *ad lib*. Such acknowledgment is the *only* way to erase the occurrence from the mind of the audience or, at least, to assure the audience that it is not alone in its knowledge of the occurrence.

It is much easier for management to react to a national emergency when it occurs before or after a performance than during one. Whether or not to cancel subsequent performances can be deliberated with the performers and staff and with the managers of other theatres and concert halls. But what if the emergency occurs during the first act of a performance and the audience will be certain to learn about it during the intermission? In this case, the manager has a responsibility to uphold public trust by announcing the situation at the conclusion of the act. In the event of a presidential assassination or some other equally momentous occurrence, the audience should be sent home. Refunds will not be required or demanded. The alternative is merely to inform the audience of the situation and to announce that the performance will continue after, perhaps, observing a moment of silence. Traditionally, most producing organizations remain closed on days that have been designated for national mourning.

ILLNESS OF A PERFORMER ▪

The reason for employing understudies in the theatre is to prevent performance cancellations when actors and singers are taken ill, either before or during a performance. Whenever a performer is replaced, however, an announcement to that effect should be made from the stage (in professional theatre, this is a union regulation).* Theatrical tradition dictates that the illness or death of a performer shall not, unless

---

*See Chapter 14.

absolutely necessary, cause the cancellation of a performance. Understandably, there have been cases when this tradition has been broken. When Leonard Warren died during a performance at the New York Metropolitan Opera House, Rudolf Bing stopped the performance and dismissed the audience. But in most other similar situations, which fortunately are rare, the performance has continued, even when there was no understudy and the replacement has had to read lines from a script.

The major precaution that management can take in regard to illness of a performer or a member of the audience is to retain a house physician who can be reached quickly in case he is needed. The theatre should also have a list of other physicians and their phone numbers. Several staff members should know how to drive to the nearest hospital and police emergency and ambulance emergency numbers should be known and posted in all offices of the theatre. First aid equipment should be located both backstage and in the front-of-house where it is easily accessible at all times. There should be an emergency cot or couch backstage (a union requirement) and another in the public lounge area. Also, it is wise for the theatre to invest in a stretcher and a wheelchair, either of which may suddenly be required to remove an ill person from the audience or the backstage area. (Although the Good Samaritan law protects laymen against prosecution for medical malpractice, only a minimum amount of first aid should be applied until a doctor arrives, and a seriously ill or injured person should never be moved more than is absolutely necessary.)

### ILLNESS OF AN AUDIENCE MEMBER ▪

During the pre-performance instruction of the ushering staff, the house manager should remind personnel about the location of first aid supplies and equipment, the location of fire extinguishers and the procedures to follow in case of emergency. In theatres seating upwards of six hundred people, it is safe to estimate that some kind of emergency will arise at least once during each eight-performance period. If debilitating illness of performers is rare, illness of audience members is quite common. This may be true because so many theatregoers arrive having indulged in too much food, sun, exercise or liquor. Heart attacks, epileptic seizures, drug reactions and even childbirth are phenomena known to seasoned house managers.

When a customer becomes so ill during a performance that he must be carried from the theatre, this should be accomplished as quickly and unobtrusively as possible. If there is no wheelchair available, several staff members should place the patient in a simple, armless chair for the easiest and safest transportation up the theatre aisle. Then the patient should be placed on a lobby couch until a physician arrives.

When anyone on the theatre premises is involved in an accident, however minor, that person should complete an accident report form. Theatrical unions and Workmen's Compensation laws require specific forms for this purpose which are available either through the union office or through insurance companies. Insurance companies will also supply accident report forms for completion by audience members involved in accidents. If such forms are not completed soon after an accident occurs, the theatre may be exposing itself to liabilities and law suits that could have been avoided. Similarly, it is always wise to require an accident victim of any kind to receive immediate medical attention so that the nature of his injury can be legally established at a later time.

Finally, it is a good policy to instruct box office treasurers to make a list of the

seating locations of all physicians who happen to be attending the performance.
This may only be possible when a large number of tickets have been reserved by
telephone or mail and doctors can thereby be identified. When the box office closes
before the performance has ended, the treasurer should then give the list to the
house manager. We have come to make jokes about the question "Is there a doctor
in the house?" But it is no joking matter when the life of a performer or a customer
suddenly depends on such knowledge. Too, the doctor's office or a hospital may
need to reach him.

## CONTACTING MEMBERS OF THE AUDIENCE ■

A sudden or unexpected occurrence may cause an individual to panic, just as it
might unsettle an entire audience. If it is necessary for management to locate a member of the audience during a performance, some methods for doing this are better
than others. When a theatregoer is tapped on the shoulder by an usher and told that
he has a phone call in the front office, the unexpected nature of this news will make
the customer think the worst: his house is on fire, something has happened to his
children, his wife has had an accident. It is highly probable that the customer will
react by shouting "What?" or "Oh, my God!" or some similar exclamation. To receive an unexpected telephone call in a public place where one least expects it carries an unavoidable implication of emergency. On the other hand, if the customer
is told that someone outside wishes to speak with him, he will probably regard this
as curious but not especially threatening. The point is to get the customer out of the
audience before telling him anything about a telephone call, instructing him to phone
his home at once or relating any other kind of personal news to him.

Unlike many movie theatres, live theatres virtually never interrupt a performance
to page an individual from the stage. Very few emergencies related to individual audience members are great enough to require action before the next intermission, at
which time ushers may be stationed at each exit to page the individual concerned.
During a performance or, preferably, before the curtain rises, ushers may also be instructed to page a person orally but quietly as they walk slowly down the aisles.

The biggest problem related to telephone calls that request that someone in the
audience be paged is usually that of trying to determine how important the matter
is. Frequently, there are phone calls from children who are merely lonely or fright-
ened about something or can't find their toothbrush! If the caller is reporting a serious accident, management must try to determine if the customer's *immediate* knowledge of the accident is necessary. Chances are there is nothing he can do anyway.
The nature of the decision about whether or not to interrupt somebody during a
performance is a matter of weighing an individual's welfare against the welfare of
the entire audience.

## DRUNKS, DEMONSTRATORS AND DISSIDENTS ■

Unhappily, public exhibitionism in a theatre is not always confined to the stage.
Disturbances caused by individuals in the audience are common, although the causes
vary. As often as not, rowdiness stems from drunkenness. An exceedingly drunken
customer is not an easy problem to handle. If the drunk becomes noisy and talka-
tive during a performance, customers around him will probably ask him to be quiet,
which is likely to have the effect of making him even noisier. Characteristically, the

public drunk has no friends: his companions suddenly disown him and pretend never to have seen him before. How does the usher or house manager get him out of the audience? One method that often works effectively is to wait until it is necessary to remove him, having no staff member approach him until that time. Then the usher should inform him that someone is waiting to see him at the back of the theatre and he may respond by following the usher up the aisle. But the situation should be handled with caution, since the violent drunk is quite capable of inflicting physical harm if he is angered. Public drunkenness, of course, is not limited to the male sex. Released for a "day in town," many a housewife has enjoyed her romp with a vengeance and wound up at a matinee quite thoroughly soused!

More serious than drunken rowdiness is organized disruption. Foreign artists and touring companies from overseas have frequently been the target of protesters who seek publicity by staging a demonstration during a performance. The news media would do a great favor to the cause of culture and international relations by refusing to report such disturbances. Time and again, audiences are denied their privilege of enjoying visiting artists because performances are interrupted by hecklers and demonstrators. Leaflets are thrown from the balconies, demonstrators line up to chant slogans from the stage and even bomb threats are made to terrorize audiences and intimidate managements. When disruptions such as these can be anticipated, it is the obligation of management to arrange for security guards and police protection. In some cases the State Department has ordered federal agents to accompany and protect foreign artists and, if management expects serious trouble, it should request the best and fullest protection available. No member of a resident theatre staff is trained to handle organized demonstrators and none should be asked or allowed to attempt this. As soon as a demonstration of any serious intensity begins, the performance should be stopped and the police called in at once to remove the demonstrators. An intermission should then take place, following an announcement from the stage that everything is under control and allowing the audience and the performers to regain their composure.

The one characteristic that drunks, rowdies and demonstrators share in common is their inability or refusal to listen to reason. Once such people begin a disturbance, the best and only course of action for management to follow is to get them out of the theatre as quickly and unobtrusively as possible. The action taken should be swift and decisive and absolutely no time should be wasted on trying to placate or calm the disrupter.

### WHEN THERE'S NO HOUSE TO MANAGE ■

For the most part this chapter concerns itself with house management in relation to traditional indoor theatres. What about street theatre or performances given in parks and other open spaces? Is a house manager required under these circumstances? The answer is yes, except for instances where the audience is a mere handful of bystanders.

The audience watching a street theatre production needs guidance in where to stand or sit and the performers may, at times, need protection from overly enthusiastic or rowdy onlookers. If there are no assigned tickets or seating places, the "house manager" must unobtrusively coax people into the desired positions, telling them that they should sit down so people behind them can see and so forth. He must assist in gathering donations or collections of money, if this is the policy. He must help in assembling the audience in the first place (something that is especially difficult if there is little or no advance publicity about the performance, in which case he may "plant" a small group of people as decoys to attract other people). He may have to reassure police officials who wander by that his company has received official permission to perform. Play festivals that are presented in large city parks and recreation areas are more formally organized and may involve near-traditional seating arrangements, but whatever the situation is, some type of audience manager will be necessary.

## ■ INSURANCE FOR THE THEATRE

### PURPOSES AND LIMITATIONS OF INSURANCE ■

One of the most flexible and often vexing items in the theatrical budget is the cost of insurance. Some producing organizations are not concerned with this matter because they are insured through the institution to which they are attached or because they are "self-insured." Most city and government buildings, for example, carry no insurance because it is less expensive to absorb property damage costs and law suits than it is to carry expensive insurance policies. Private organizations may be self-insured to a degree, although law requires certain conditions and limitations. For example, a building must always be insured against fire or destruction at least to the financial extent to which it is mortgaged. All producing organizations must pay in full or in part certain employee insurance, beginning with Workmen's Compensation, plus additional employee insurance as mandated by union contracts and agreements.

Like any contract, an insurance policy is only valid in the areas it defines and qualifies. The special jargon used in insurance policies is difficult for the layman to comprehend and may even be subject to wide-ranging legal interpretation. The word "occurrence," for instance, provides much broader coverage than the word "accident." Limitations often nullify coverage under specified conditions. For example, a policy may cover damage to stage properties while they are on the stage but not while they are being moved to and from the stage. Coverage is withheld in cases where the insurance company can prove that damage or accident occurred as the result of "willful neglect" on behalf of the policy holder.

The landlord of a building usually carries certain types of insurance, while the tenant is responsible for securing additional coverage. Such matters should be clearly spelled out in the lease or rental agreement between the landlord and the renting organization. In order to operate as safely as possible and within the realms of insurance protection, theatrical managers must thoroughly familiarize themselves with their policies. They should be fully cognizant that liability insurance seldom applies when exits and passageways are obstructed, when steps and railings are in poor repair and when an insured area is used for "atypical purposes" (such as parties held backstage or in dressing rooms). Care must be taken about the unauthorized use of company vehicles, power tools and the like. What kind of insurance protection, if any, exists to cover minors, apprentices and volunteer workers?

To expedite insurance claims and provide the best legal protection, the leading supervisors of a theatrical operation (company manager, stage manager, technical director and house manager) should be provided with an insurance claim kit that instructs them what to do in the event of accident or other emergencies. (See Appendix F.)

TYPES OF INSURANCE COVERAGE ▪

Following is a list of the most standard types of insurance related to the operation of a theatre. Needless to say, management should consult a variety of insurance companies before buying a policy and the organization's attorney should be included in such negotiations.

WORKMEN'S COMPENSATION: mandatory for all salaried personnel

EMPLOYEE HEALTH AND LIFE INSURANCE: or contributions to Blue Cross-Blue Shield, Hospital Insurance Plan or other group health coverage and pension fund may be mandated by union contracts

DISABILITY INSURANCE: may be included in the above, but is mandatory in certain cases

COMPREHENSIVE LIABILITY INSURANCE: covers injuries to the public and to employees; also covers property damage; rates may be based on the seating capacity of the theatre

AUTOMOBILE LIABILITY AND PROPERTY DAMAGE: minimum amount of coverage is mandated by each state; may be extended to include vehicles used but not owned by the company or to cover drivers under age twenty-one; provides coverage for claims *against* the theatre

FIRE INSURANCE: and extended types of coverage to protect buildings and their contents; rates determined by location and condition of property; mandatory to extent of mortgage payments due

BOILER AND MACHINERY INSURANCE: covering large, expensive building machinery

THEATRICAL PROPERTY FLOATER: often short-term insurance to cover risks on costumes, lighting equipment, etc.

PROP BREAKAGE INSURANCE: may be short-term; especially important to cover valuable rented or borrowed props

MARINE INSURANCE: to cover risks on canvas tents, movable theatre chairs, etc.

BUSINESS INTERRUPTION: offers coverage against loss of business under certain, carefully qualified conditions

RAIN INSURANCE: a specific type of business interruption insurance to cover outdoor performances

3 D BOND AND THEFT INSURANCE: coverage against dishonest employees, embezzlement, depositor's forgery and the like

FIDELITY BOND: same as above

MONEY AND SECURITIES COVERAGE: to protect against holdup and theft of money whether in the building or in the possession of bonded employees outside the building

CHECK FORGER INSURANCE: an inexpensive protection against forged or falsified checks from customers

PAYROLL HOLDUP INSURANCE: to cover payroll money lost or stolen inside or outside the building

PERSONAL EFFECTS INSURANCE: required by Actors' Equity to cover personal property, clothing and jewelry of actors and stagehands in the theatre during hours of employment

EXTRAORDINARY AND ORDINARY RISK COMPENSATION INSURANCE: required by Actors' Equity when a performer is required to execute some unusual physical feat and to cover him for ordinary risks of employment

TRAVEL INSURANCE: required by Equity to cover members en route to and from their contracted places of employment; management is responsible for theft, loss or damage of actors' property during such travel; special insurance should also be taken to cover the shipping of valuable stage props, costumes and other items

PRODUCTS LIABILITY INSURANCE: to cover theft or damage of concescession inventories and to protect against public liabilities in relation to such products; the concession operator or lessor should pay for this type of insurance

COAT ROOM INSURANCE: to protect against loss or theft of checkroom holdings, for which management is held liable

SPECIAL PROPERTY FLOATER: should be taken to protect landlord or manager against losses of or damage to special exhibits, art works or other things on loan to the theatre or displayed on the premises

NONAPPEARANCE COVERAGE: to compensate the producer in the event a star does not appear or a unit attraction does not perform as contracted

Theatrical insurance is somewhat unusual and may be difficult to secure. City and state employment divisions and building departments may be of assistance in providing information about insurance requirements. Some states operate an insurance "pool" for small or unusual businesses. This provides low-rate group protection for participants who are otherwise unable to qualify for coverage.

## ■ AUDIENCE PSYCHOLOGY

A theatrical performance creates a special set of psychological requirements. The manner in which an audience accepts and responds to these often determines the success of the performance. First, the performer must have the attention of his audience and the audience must usually be polarized to respond as a whole, not merely as a number of different individuals. The way an audience is managed before the curtain goes up, as already shown in this chapter, can go a long way in establishing group psychology and "oneness" of response. Second, it is usually necessary for an audience to suspend many of its normal standards of reality; it must accept a special kind of theatrical reality. Even a circus clown cannot entertain unless the audience accepts his "clownness."

The very business of attending a theatre production is unreal and the liveness of it makes it more unreal to a contemporary audience accustomed to electronic media entertainment. More and more, it is necessary to train audiences how to enjoy and respond to live performances—as anyone who has watched a young audience seeing its first live production can attest. Strange as it seems, the electronically oriented audience (which includes just about everybody) has difficulty in accepting the live performance. Jean Dalrymple, a professional of long experience in the theatre, came to the conclusion that it is necessary to use electronic amplifiers to project the voices of performers in all musical plays and introduced this technique while she was director of the theatre program at New York's City Center. It is not that performers cannot be heard without amplification, but that their voices sound thin or "unnatural" to the electronically oriented listener, even when performances are held in small theatres. Strangely, too, the uninitiated live theatre audience appears slow to comprehend that there is no mechanical separation between the performer and the audience. The talking, the commotion, the moving in and out of seats that one witnesses may not stem from rudeness or disinterest in a performance but from a slowness to grasp the nature of live performance, to understand that it cannot be turned on and off like a television set. And TV viewing habits, conditioned by frequent commercial interruptions, may also be dictating the attention span that audiences bring to the theatre. Certainly, with its one-to-one ratio (the medium and the single viewer), television is making unified group response more difficult to establish.

### FACTORS THAT INFLUENCE AUDIENCE RESPONSE ■

Most performers, producers and theatre managers are "audience watchers" and must be if they are to thrive in their profession. The audience, after all, is the raw material of a performance. How it is shaped, how it is managed and how it responds determines the final nature of the product. One need not observe too many audiences before discovering that many factors, ostensibly unrelated to the performance, contribute substantially to audience psychology.

Before it arrives at the theatre, for instance, the audience may be exposed to a common experience that is difficult to "shake off" and which therefore makes the audience less receptive—a simple case of divided attention. A surprising or disturbing national or local news incident can have this effect, as can a bad storm prior to or during the performance or an accident or some other occurrence outside the theatre or in the lobby just prior to curtain time. If the situation is truly serious or important, management might announce that it will inform the audience of developments during intermissions. This would be an extreme action, but certain situations warrant it. A more casual method of attempting to negate audience reaction to an outside event is for front-of-house staff members to discuss and hopefully negate the concern of audience members informally and individually in the lobby before the performance and during intermissions. It would be common sense, for example, for the house manager to reassure the crowd in a lobby that the person who became seriously ill in full view of the crowd is now "all right."

Once inside the auditorium, an audience will be influenced by other factors. Temperature, for example. An ideal room temperature of sixty-seven degrees should usually be the aim. It may be necessary, where temperature control systems are inadequate, to cool an auditorium to a temperature considerably below this before the audience is admitted, since the body temperature of a large group of people will quickly and substantially increase room temperature. When the temperature is cool, audience response will also tend to be cool. When temperature is allowed to increase slightly along with the increasing intensity of dramatic action on stage, audience response will also become increasingly warmer. It may be desirable, then, to allow the temperature to rise as high as eighty degrees towards the end of each act or toward the end of the performance.

Often, theatres contain air-conditioning systems that produce a noise that is audible to the spectator. When such sounds seriously interfere with acoustics, the system must be kept inoperative during the performance. When machinery produces a low, steady hum it may be tolerable; but only if it is steady. If the machinery is stopped or started during quiet moments in the performance, it becomes unacceptably obtrusive. For this reason, it may be advisable to install an air-conditioning system that can be manually controlled by the house manager from a location where the audience and the performance can be seen and heard. Any mechanical, noice-producing system that cuts on and off automatically presents a major problem because the sudden presence or absense of a steady noise seriously affects audience response.

Another important factor in preparing an audience for a performance is the question of pre-performance music in the auditorium, a decision that should be made in consultation with the artistic director. Whether or not to use pre-performance music of some kind should depend on the nature of the theatre and the production. Often, recorded music (nonvocal) can help relax an audience and establish a mood appropriate to the production, in much the same way that the overture to a musical accomplishes this. If the production is, in fact, a musical one, then no other preshow music should be introduced. The preshow music (however softly it may be amplified, should always coincide with the mood and atmosphere of the production it precedes. Announcements made over a public address system or from the stage prior to a performance, of course, seriously interfere with audience concentration; although, as we have seen, there are times when such announcements are appropriate or necessary.

At the ancient Greek theatre festivals, players and playwrights vying for prizes used to hire a claque, a group of spectators paid to applaud their work or to show disapproval of their competitors' work. Present-day opera stars have been known to cultivate a few of their most enthusiastic fans and support a claque in this manner. In the commercial theatre at least one famous star is known to station her spouse in the auditorium throughout all her performances so the loyal husband-claque can initiate each round of laughter and applause.

The business of manipulating audience reaction is an ancient and, perhaps, not dishonorable one. Indeed, it is quite remarkable how easily audience reaction can be manipulated. One good claque standing at the back of an auditorium near the temperature-control devices can determine audience reaction (for better or for worse) regardless of what is happening on the stage! This is true because a crowd is highly susceptible to the power of suggestion. Any stand-up comedian will testify that one good belly-laugher in the audience is worth his weight in gold. Laughter, silence, coughing and applause are all infectious; when one person sets a strong example, the majority of others in the audience are likely to follow. But while it is comparatively easy for a claque—official or unofficial— to stimulate laughter and applause, it is very difficult to inspire a restless, coughing, fidgeting audience to settle down. These symptoms are usually caused by boredom and indicate that unity of group reaction has been lost or was never established. Sometimes, one good "SHHHHHH!" from the back of the house will do the trick. Audience restlessness may also be symptomatic of an uncomfortable house temperature, so that air-conditioning should be either turned on or off at once. If such machinery is turned on and is accompanied by a low, mechanical humming sound, the sound itself might help reestablish audience unity and contentment. Eugene O'Neill dramatizes the psychological validity of this point in his play *Dynamo,* in which a mechanical generator becomes a mother-substitute figure.

Often the performer is unable to analyze why an audience is responding in one way or another. The performer cannot usually be aware of the temperature in the house or minor disturbances and many times he cannot gauge the effectiveness of his performance. If the audience is reacting in a peculiar or unusual manner, the house manager should send a word of explanation back to the stage manager so that he, in turn, may enlighten the players. Certainly, performers should always be told if they are inaudible or difficult to hear. Similarly, the stage manager should be informed if a stage lighting instrument ceases to work or if something that he may not be able to see goes wrong on stage.

When a performance is over, the manner in which people leave the theatre gives a strong indication of overall audience reaction. As part of the science of audience analysis, the house manager and artistic director should at least occasionally station themselves somewhere in the lobby to overhear customer comments at the end of performances. There will be some spot in the lobby or just outside the theatre where the majority of customers will begin to comment on the production. They seldom do so until they have left the auditorium itself, until they reach that spot where they can light a cigarette, get their coats on and regroup in social pairs or small parties with others with whom they attended the performance. Find that "comment-release spot" and a valid consensus of critical reaction can be learned in minutes.

Naturally, a few patrons will always leave a theatre before the final ovations are over. But the number and enthusiasm of the curtain calls probably remain the quickest gauge of audience enjoyment, although, of course, it is plain courtesy for patrons to remain in their seats and applaud the performers. There is a little-known story about one audience that began leaving the theatre *en masse* as soon as the final curtain came down. It happened that a large portion of this audience was comprised of paraplegics from a local veterans' hospital and those sitting in wheelchairs had to leave before others in the audience could follow. When he saw the audience leaving during his curtain call, the temperamental star said to a fellow actor, "They're walking out! They're walking out on my curtain call!" Of the opinion that the star was getting his just reward, the fellow actor said, "And *some* of them haven't walked in years!"

The dedicated house manager or theatre operator performs a service that might well carry the title of "audience engineer." Certainly, he is an audience psychologist and many decisions that are made in regard to theatre architecture, decoration and management should be based on the principles of group psychology. It is the audience for which theatre is organized in the first place; not for the playwright, the director or the actor alone; not merely to "show off," to gain prestige or to make money. All the ingredients that go into a theatrical production are easy to acquire in comparison to the acquisition of the desired audience response. A production may run for many performances without once achieving the response its directors and performers work to elicit or it may only "work" once in a hundred performances. Why? There are seldom any simple answers, although theatre people will never tire of inventing them. And it is even more difficult to explain the magic and excitement of total audience-performer collaboration when it does happen. All we know is that it happens—once in a while. And if we have shared this unique and overwhelmingly satisfying human experience just once, then we are motivated by one means or another to seek it out again and again: as a performer, a producer, a manager, an usher or a spectator.

# CONCLUSION

# The Integrated Arts

No single book could possibly give comprehensive treatment to the administrative aspects of both live and electronic performing arts, much less include management of fine arts organizations. Yet, this should not be allowed to disguise the great need and justification for an integrated approach to the arts. Happily, this concept is gaining recognition on several fronts: the trend on the college campus is toward integrating the "academic" and "applied" aspects of arts instruction and toward the unification of artistic disciplines into performing arts departments, fine arts schools and arts or cultural centers. Numerous, newly created service organizations and nationally distributed publications address themselves to the performing arts as a whole and, in some cases, to all the arts. Increased mobility and the volume of television production on the doorstep of Broadway have greatly increased the partnership between the live and electronic branches of the industry.

No professional actively working in the arts today is likely to survive in the vacuum of one segment of the arts, for what has been long apparent to some is now apparent to many: no art form itself exists in a vacuum. The scene designer needs the knowledge of the art historian, the lyricist needs the poet, the dancer needs the actor, the cameraman needs the visual artist. The producer, the director and many others draw from all the arts, as well as from an understanding of the dynamic relationship between the arts and the world in which we live. And the relationship between our world and the arts is changing rapidly. No longer the luxury of the few, the arts have become a right of the many.

In his foreword to the *Rockefeller Panel Report. The Performing Arts: Problems and Prospects*, John D. Rockefeller III states that "only in our time have we begun to recognize the arts as a community concern." This concern has, among other things, brought art out of the museum, plays out of the theatre and musicians out of the pit. How extensive this movement will become is difficult to estimate, but it is significant that the National Endowment for the Arts has established a separate office to assist what it terms "The Expansion Arts." It is obvious that the arts administrator must, as never before, be a man of the community. Once only dependent on a world of backers, press agents, talent agents and theatre owners, the performing arts impresario today is also in close touch with leaders in government, education, industry and politics.

As the amount of arts activity in America continues to grow in volume, it becomes increasingly difficult to draw a clear line between the amateur and the professional artist. There are a remarkable number of highly talented producers, directors, actors, singers, dancers and visual artists who are working full time in their chosen field without earning a living wage at it and without union membership and yet are "professional" in their artistic output. The achievements of these men and women stand as a healthy reminder that art does not depend on organized labor, big business, government, institutionalized education or expensive real estate. On the contrary, *those* segments of society need the artist.

A community hears fewer sounds of discontent as it resounds more to the rhythms of art. Where the creative artist is successful in his work, supportive laborers will be required, business will benefit, government will be remembered, educational institutions will be justified and real estate values will go up. Proof of this may be found by reversing the process: remove the theatre, concert hall or museum from a neighborhood or city and the tangible qualities of life in that area will register a decline that is swift and penetrating. Examples of how the arts have upgraded life both in the immediate and distant past, for a neighborhood or for a nation, make it difficult not to concur with Shelley's claim that "poets are the unacknowledged legislators of the world." Certainly, the service that the arts provide for society continues, in America, to be largely unacknowledged—at least until the service has already been provided and everyone has been "paid off" except, in most cases, the artist himself. While government and private support for the arts has certainly increased over the past few decades, it remains far below that provided by many other nations. The frequently poor image of this nation abroad is, in this writer's opinion, substantially reflective of this fact. That the United States cannot "afford" to sponsor representatives to enter some of the world's leading performing arts festivals, for example, must surely indicate to the foreigner either that our priorities are grossly confused or that we have no outstanding artists to represent us. Neither conclusion is very complimentary and both have some validity. America is just beginning to wake up to her cultural resources and her artists are just beginning to find the ways and means to work and contribute to their full potential.

As native American artists and art forms evolve, as a democratically American regard for the arts continues its sudden, if delayed, awakening and as the American genius for marketing is applied to the arts, time becomes increasingly full with challenge and reward, both for the arts worker and for the arts patron.

What can be done to hasten this process in the realm of theatre?

For one thing, theatre participants and organizations could pool their collective knowledge and resources to a much greater extent than they have managed to date. The tremendous vitality and voluminous activity of nonprofessional community theatre, for example, remains largely invisible because no regional or national organizations have succeeded in attracting a truly representative membership. Similarly, communication between campus theatres is little more than tokenistic. Communication between professional resident theatres has been helped by the formation of several service organizations and recent attempts have been made to arrange touring and exchange productions between such groups, but this is only a start.

The desire for communication, of course, begins with the individual. The unfortunate fact is that many people in the arts apply the mudpack of provincialism and remain self-satisfied with outlooks and accomplishments far below their abilities. And it should be added that nowhere is this more true than among aspiring beginners and working professionals in New York City and Los Angeles. As America familiarizes herself with the arts, her artists must familiarize themselves with America.

The average citizen's growing familiarity with the arts is going to increase the demand for higher artistic standards. The under-achiever in the arts world is about to experience a rude awakening! As the good becomes known, the bad will be more and more relegated to its rightful place. Standards of performance in the theatre can someday be as clear to the average American as standards of performance in sports and athletics. But nobody should believe for a minute that this will happen automatically. No one is a "natural" sports enthusiast, any more than a "natural" opera buff. While such comparisons can be misleading, they may, nonetheless, suggest certain goals. As the arts move to a more central position in American life, the hot force of nonartistic influences will grow hotter—either to the benefit or the detriment of the arts, depending on the quality of arts leadership during this, the most crucial period for arts development in America.

Organizations that assist theatres in sharing their knowledge and resources are necessary to the growth of theatre, but a warning should be voiced against centralized sources of power. If regional or campus theatres, for example, began to create touring "circuits" or to centralize play production, they would be setting themselves up for the same tragedy that befell the nineteenth-century stock theatres. Communication does not mean centralization; real strength lies, as always, in diversity.

Juxtaposed with the need for strong arts management organizations whose members can benefit each other and whose combined strength can lobby support for the whole membership, is the need for meaningful leadership within the performing arts labor unions. No responsible producing manager would deny the need for unions in the performing arts field and no responsible labor leader would deny the impossibility of admitting performer members according to audition or some similar test. Artistic achievement cannot be judged in advance: the potential for achievement may be dormant within anyone. While membership policy for certain performing arts technical and craft unions could probably stand scrutinizing by government and civil liberties agencies, the performers' unions in both live and electronic branches of the industry maintain an "open-door" membership policy. One need only be offered a job by a professional producing organization to gain membership. Obviously, the right to work as a performer wherever the opportunity presents itself should not be questioned or legislated by anyone. What should be questioned, however, is the union's responsibility toward the performer and toward the profession.

Although Actors' Equity Association and other performers' unions publish newsletters, journals and rulebooks and provide several other services, the value of such activity, especially for new members, is dubious. There are virtually no formally organized apprenticeship or "junior membership" orientation requirements aside from the journeyman system in resident theatres. Other than what he is able to garner from union rulebooks that read as if they were written by babbling barristers, the young professional has little idea of his obligations to management and less idea of management's obligations to him. Anything resembling what might be called "professional deportment" among performers, it appears, can only be learned in the school of hard knocks. Yet, this need not be the case. If college and school theatre programs, on the one hand, and professional managements, on the other hand, are ill-suited and inappropriate places—and they are—for a performer to learn the meaning of the word "professional," then this obligation must be passed on to the unions and their senior performer members. Initiation seminars could easily be conducted by senior members, and orientation literature that is comprehensible to a person without legal training could easily be prepared.

In regard to its obligation toward the profession, the performers' unions should examine and probably reform a number of their regulations. For example, the AEA policy that limits showcase productions off-Off Broadway to ten days should be liberalized. Its policies regarding alien actors should again be examined. Its policies that make the teletaping of short segments of stage shows for advertising or publicity purposes financially impossible should be changed as should its entire attitude toward the encouragement, training and development of performance talent.

More flexibility is needed in regard to rehearsal regulations, especially rehearsals for resident and repertory theatre productions. No truly distinguished and outstanding theatre company in the world would dream of limiting rehearsals to a four-to-six-week period and America will not possess such a company of its own until this superficial limitation is lifted. But salary demands together with lack of sufficient subsidy presently make it nearly impossible for either profit or nonprofit theatrical enterprises to exceed the four-to-six-week period established by the unions. Two principles are in conflict here: (1) a play should not be performed until it is ready for an audience and (2) a performer should not rehearse without reasonable compensation. Both are valid. Until more subsidy is available, however, some degree of union flexibility is desirable. Actors who wish to opt voluntarily for extra rehearsals should be allowed such rehearsals without overtime penalties being imposed on management. The concept of journeymen actors in resident theatre should be expanded to apply to other branches of the industry and made more attractive to senior members who wish to polish their craft, as well as to more beginners. Every possible measure should be taken to encourage the development of ensemble acting and strong resident acting companies. Most theatrical union offices themselves should be run more professionally, headed by "third-century managers" of the variety described in this book, people of broad commitment and even broader vision. Special programs instituted by performing arts unions should aggressively seek public and private funding, should join management in this pursuit, should assist management in lobbying activities that seek fiscal and audience support and in all other ways work more closely with management for the betterment of the professional arts in America. Both sides have been equally guilty of communicating with each other only when contract negotiations fall due or when special problems arise. The positive aspects and goals of the labor-management relationship in the arts should be vigorously explored and mutually pursued.

Far from being "easier" in the enforcement of their regulations, performers' unions should be more stringent when it comes to requiring both performers and managers to maintain certain minimum standards of employment. Not that Equity should "close" a theatre if the dressing-room temperature falls below the stipulated minimum once or twice a year. But when less than the minimum number of professional actors is employed, when actors consistently fail to report on time for rehearsals and performances, when the general working conditions in a theatre are below par, then the defaulting parties should be labeled as the amateurs they are. Finally, stage managers are ill-placed as members of AEA and should probably transfer their allegiance to another union or bargaining association, probably the Association of Theatrical Press Agents and Managers (to join company managers) or the Society of Stage Directors and Choreographers (to join ranks with stage directors, which many stage managers aspire to become).

To rally the substantial support necessary for the continued growth of the arts in America, a great deal of data-gathering will be necessary. At present, lack of information makes it impossible even to define what "the arts in America" represent. The Ford Foundation has launched an ambitious project toward this end and smaller organizations are also at work. Objective and responsible information, scientifically gathered and presented, will be of inestimable value to many people and organizations. In my own opinion, however, the establishment of anything resembling "data banks" that contain personalized and identifiable information about individuals in the arts and arts organizations is an infringement of human rights. The arts manager or the arts institution, like the artist himself, must be allowed the opportunity to make mistakes, to learn and to try again. Any system of information-banking that would superficially prejudice a foundation, for example, against a particular organization is to be viewed with extreme skepticism.

The conclusions made by John Wharton regarding ticket pricing and theatrical financing in New York State, published by the League of New York Theatres, appear to me very important to the future of commercial theatre and worthy of much more serious attention among producers and lawmakers than they have received. Broadway is, indeed, the "Fabulous Invalid" it has often been called. Despite a few shady characters, neighboring smut parlors and numerous complexities beyond the grasp of the uninitiated, however, it has managed to survive as the central showcase for the entertainment industry. Self-seeking politicians, journalists and others have often taken perverse pleasure in attacking the Invalid—but they, too, have failed to kill the beast.

Under the sympathetic leadership of Mayor John V. Lindsay, beginnings were made to chase out the smut industry, make the streets safer with more policemen and stronger street lamps, silence irresponsible critics on the national media, change building codes to stimulate the construction of new theatres and improve public transportation to and from the Broadway area.

The arts in America—which very much include the arts on Broadway and other main streets of the nation—need all the help and understanding that local officials can be convinced to provide. But they must be convinced and it is up to administrators of the arts to do the convincing. Where they exist, city and state sales taxes on theatre tickets must be removed, tickets must be marketed in a broader and more imaginative manner with flexibility of ticket pricing. Discounted and free theatre tickets must be more generally available to appropriate individuals. Direct lines of communication must be established between local arts organizations and local government, education and business agencies. Most of all, interested parties within the professional entertainment industry must themselves unite and work together for the improvement of their lot—and this means toward the improvement of the nonprofessional branches of the industry as well. The seasoned professional recognizes his obligation toward the amateur and the beginner. But this spirit of generosity and concern so often displayed by individual artists and arts leaders could be organized in a manner that would have a wonderfully meaningful impact on the future. The increased employment of guest artists and artists-in-residence on college campuses is a good move in that direction.

One of the difficulties in writing a book about theatre today is that theatre today, as never before, is rapidly changing. By the time this book is in print the Appendix will be out of date and who knows how much of the rest? But thank heavens this is true! Audiences were allowed for much too long to buy their tickets with the smug realization that "the curtain would go up" on a "nice show" that would leave everybody feeling "much better." Today, there is often no curtain to go up and one may find himself an audience member quite unexpectedly—in the classroom, on a street corner, in the park. What is the theatre coming to? It is coming to the people. But this is such a revolutionary occurrence that the casualty list is high, both for audience members and for producers. As often as not, the practicing arts manager today is concerned not with the organization of new groups but with the *re*organization of existing ones, which is a decidedly more difficult task—and a good topic for another book. But theatre institutions, like the concepts that provided their founding principles, are now in a state of reorganization. This is mainly in response to the reconstitution of their audiences.

As one who has never altogether left the classroom—either as a student, as a student-teacher or as a teacher-student—I have observed several generations of learners, but none quite so alert to the opportunities of meaningful change as the learners who currently occupy what I must call the "defoliated halls of ivy." Like Emerson, young people today seem to have a healthy understanding that institutions—

> ". . . are not aboriginal, though they existed before we were born: that they are not superior to the citizen: that every one of them was once the act of a single man: every law and usage was a man's expedient to meet a particular case: that they are all imitable, all alterable: we may make as good; we may make better."

Reorganization without retrenchment and rededication without retreat are the highest order of our day.

This new order has not evolved without considerable assistance from the old. It took the cultures of European, African, Asian and Indian civilizations to feed the virgin springs of America. It took the sweat of your father and mine to place works of man-made beauty in our sight. And it took the unrewarded investment of many people's faith to establish what, I am convinced, are only the beginnings of America's contribution to the spirit of mankind.

In his final speech as president of the United States, Dwight Eisenhower warned against the dominance of "the military-industrial complex" and a society that emphasized the scientist to the exclusion of the philosopher and the artist. His successor, John F. Kennedy, said "I see little of more importance to the future of our country and our civilization than full recognition of the place of the artist." Well, things began to happen for the arts in America, and they will continue to happen for some time at a positively alarming rate of acceleration—for better or for worse, for richer or for poorer: a contract between the American people and the arts has been sealed.

In this volume I have tried to describe the workings of the American theatre—a small corner in the total output of man's artistic industry. I have sometimes interjected my own opinions in regard to the machinations of this extraordinary contrivance. Always, I could only describe things as I understand them with the grateful assistance of my teachers and colleagues. But one thing does seem clear to me. Systems, methods and ways of doing things will always evolve and change; but the humanity, the excitement and the joy that lies at the foundation of a timeless fascination with the art of theatre will never change. Electronic inventions that do the work of fifty stagehands, computerized box office systems that do what Lee Shubert used to do in his head, public agencies that organize what private impresarios used to organize, actors-turned-politicians and politicians-turned-actors, do not change the basic ingredient of joy that keeps us fascinated with the art of theatre.

# APPENDICES

# Appendix A

## Suggested Syllabus for an Undergraduate Course in Theatre Management and Supervision

### Aims of the Course

This course is designed to provide an introduction to economic and administrative aspects of American theatre, especially as they apply to repertory,
community and educational organizations. It is assumed that the student has
fulfilled the prerequisites in theatre history and production but that he is
comparatively untutored in economics and business administration. Classroom
work will be supplemented by a minimum of thirty hours of administrative
assignments related to the department's stage productions.

### Required Reading

Bernheim, Alfred. *The Business of the Theatre: 1750-1932*. Reprint. New
York: Benjamin Blom, 1964.
Baumol, William J., and Bowen, William G. *Performing Arts: The Economic
Dilemma*. New York: The Twentieth Century Fund. 1966.

### Written Assignments:

1. A report on a publicity or advertising project actually executed for a department stage production with samples of the work accomplished
2. A sample budget for one of the productions being considered for presentation at the college next year
3. A house manager's report on the performance this semester for which you
   served in that capacity
4. A book report that relates the required reading material to the problems and
   complexities of operating our college theatre

### Units of Study:

1. Introduction to the course: aims, definitions, scope
2. A brief history of theatre economics in America
3. Economic principles: labor, capital, management
4. Legal procedures: laws, contracts, agreements, copyrights
5. Operational procedures: the physical plant
6. Policy-making and the implementation of artistic goals
7. Staffing and casting
8. Financing, budgeting and budget-control
9. Public relations and publicity
10. Advertising and press relations
11. Ticket-pricing and box office procedures
12. House management
13. Supplemental sources of income: concessions, program advertising, grants,
    fund-raising
14. Future prospects and directions in theatrical producing and administration
15. Discussion and evaluation of student projects and laboratory work

# Appendix B

## Suggested Core of Courses
## for a Master's Degree Program in Performing Arts Administration*

### I. First Semester

1. *Economic History of the Performing Arts I*
   (Studies in economic structures and management procedures in performing arts history from ancient Greece through the eighteenth century)
2. *Principles of Theatre Administration*
   (An introduction to economic, administrative and legal principles as they apply to the performing arts)
3. *Philosophy and Aesthetics in the Theatre*
   (A survey of artistic theories and concepts behind the great leaders and movements in the performing arts)
4. *Management Practicum I*
   (An introduction to the various departments of the campus theatre and laboratory assignments; emphasis: box office)

### II. Second Semester

1. *Economic History of the Performing Arts II*
   (Studies in economic structures and management procedures in the performing arts in Europe and America from the eighteenth century to the present)
2. *Theatre Engineering*
   (Studies in basic architectural problems and needs for the construction of contemporary theatres and concert halls; analysis of existing plants, survey of types of theatrical machinery)
3. *The Performing Arts and Society*
   (A survey of present day activity in each of the performing arts; comparative analysis of their economic and administrative structure; discussion of their relationship to society, government and politics)
4. *Management Practicum II*
   (Tutorial and laboratory assignments in connection with the campus theatre; emphasis: house management)

---

* The student should be required to take "general knowledge" courses without credit to make up any deficiencies he may have in such areas as theatre history, accounting and business management. Other courses taken for credit should be tailored to fit his special aims and, certainly, a strong selection should be made from the field of economics. Each student should serve a six-to-twelve month internship with an outstanding performing arts organization, with faculty approval and consultation.

## III. Third Semester

1. *Performing Arts and the Law*
   (Studies in legal problems and procedures related to the performing arts: copyright laws, royalties, contracts and agreements, federal and local regulations)
2. *Repertory Theatre Seminar*
   (Problems, studies and projects related to the establishment and operation of resident and repertory opera and theatre companies)
3. *Community and Press Relations*
   (A study of the performing arts in relation to the press and advertising media; problems in media relations)
4. *Theatre Publicity and Promotion*
   (A laboratory in publicity and advertising methods for the performing arts)
5. *Management Practicum III*
   (Tutorial and laboratory assignments; emphasis: publicity and advertising)

## IV. Fourth Semester

1. *Labor Relations and the Performing Arts*
   (Studies and problems dealing with labor unions in the performing arts; evaluation of management and professional societies and organizations)
2. *Methods of Pricing and Budgeting for the Theatre*
   (Bookkeeping, accounting, payroll and banking procedures for the performing arts and a review of price estimation, bidding, budgets and budget-control procedures)
3. *Producing for Educational Institutions*
   (A survey of the performing arts for children, in public schools and on the campus from the administrative viewpoint)

## Appendix C

### Sample 1
### Box Office Report

DATE: _____          cc: _____

ATTRACTION: _____ DATE OF PERFORMANCE _____

THEATER _____ CURTAIN TIME _____

| Location | Capacity | On Hand | Sold | Price | Total |
|----------|----------|---------|------|-------|-------|
| _____ | _____ | _____ | ____ | ____ | _____ |
| _____ | _____ | _____ | ____ | ____ | _____ |
| _____ | _____ | _____ | ____ | ____ | _____ |
| _____ | _____ | _____ | ____ | ____ | _____ |
| _____ | _____ | _____ | ____ | ____ | _____ |

Specials:

| | | | | | |
|----------|----------|---------|------|-------|-------|
| _____ | | | ____ | ____ | _____ |
| _____ | | | ____ | ____ | _____ |
| _____ | | | ____ | ____ | _____ |
| _____ | | | ____ | ____ | _____ |
| _____ | | | ____ | ____ | _____ |

Less Subscription Discounts:

Totals _____  _____  _____            _____

(total used)

Gross forwarded: _____

Gross to date:     _____

Remarks:

Total receipts transfered or credited to:

## Sample 2
## Box Office Statement

DATE . . . . . . . . . . . . . . . . . . . . . ATTRACTION . . . . . . . . . . . . . . . . . . . . . .

EVENING . . . . . . . . . . . . . . . . . . . . MATINEE . . . . . . . . . . . . . . . . . . . . . . . . .

| | Capacity | On Hand | Sold | Gross Per Ticket | Gross Amount | Tax Per Ticket | Tax |
|---|---|---|---|---|---|---|---|
| Orch. . . . . . . | . . . . . . . | . . . . . | 4.09 | . . . . . . . | .31 | . . . . . . . |
| Orch. . . . . . . | . . . . . . . | . . . . . | 3.50 | . . . . . . . | .25 | . . . . . . . |
| Orch. . . . . . . | . . . . . . . | . . . . . | 2.36 | . . . . . . . | .14 | . . . . . . . |
| Balc. . . . . . . | . . . . . . . | . . . . . | 3.50 | . . . . . . . | .25 | . . . . . . . |
| Balc. . . . . . . | . . . . . . . | . . . . . | 2.36 | . . . . . . . | .14 | . . . . . . . |
| Balc. . . . . . . | . . . . . . . | . . . . . | 1.45 | . . . . . . . | .05 | . . . . . . . |

Matinee luncheon special:

. . . . . . . . . . . . . . .     . . . . .    . . . . . . . . . . . . . . . . . .     . . . . . . .     . . . . . . .

Other specials:

. . . . . . . . . . . . . . .     . . . . .    . . . . . .     . . . . . . .     . . . . . . .     . . . . . . .
. . . . . . . . . . . . . . .     . . . . .    . . . . . .     . . . . . . .     . . . . . . .     . . . . . . .

*Less*: Subscription discount:

. . . . . . . . . . . . . . .     . . . . .    . . . . . .     . . . . . . .     . . . . . . .     . . . . . . .

Standees . . . . . . . . . . .     . . . . .    . . . . . .     . . . . . . .     . . . . . . .     . . . . . . .

Gross this performance          . . . . . . . . . . . . . . . .     . . . . . . .

Gross forward          . . . . . . . . . . . . . . . .     . . . . . . .

Gross to date          . . . . . . . . . . . . . . . .     . . . . . . .

## Sample 3
## Box Office Statement

ATTRACTION _____

DATE _____ MATINEE _____ EVENING _____

WEATHER: SUNNY _____ CLOUDY _____ STORMY _____

|  | CAPACITY | ON HAND | SOLD | TICKET PRICE | GROSS AMOUNT |
|---|---|---|---|---|---|
| Orch. | _____ | _____ | _____ | 4.75 | _____ |
| Orch. | _____ | _____ | _____ | 3.95 | _____ |
| Orch. | _____ | _____ | _____ | 2.75 | _____ |
| Balc. | _____ | _____ | _____ | 3.95 | _____ |
| Balc. | _____ | _____ | _____ | 2.75 | _____ |
| Balc. | _____ | _____ | _____ | 1.75 | _____ |

Dinner-Theatre Specials _____ _____

Matinee-Luncheon Specials _____ _____

Other Specials _____ _____

_____ _____

LESS Season Ticket Discount: _____ _____

| (For Use on Playhouse Copy Only) | Gross this performance _____ |
|---|---|
| Mail Order Income Today _____ | Gross forward _____ |
| Window Income Today _____ | Gross for this |
| Agency Income Tdoay _____ | Attraction to date _____ |
| Total Bank Deposit Today _____ | |

## Sample 4
## Box Office STatement

_____ PERF. OF _____ DATE _____ MAT EVE

WEATHER _____SERIES _____ DAY _____

| | ORCH. | BALC. | PRICE EACH | TOTAL |
|---|---|---|---|---|
| SUBSCRIPTION | | | | |
| REG. SALE | | | | |
| CO-OP SALE | | | | |
| GROUP | | | | |
| GROUP | | | | |
| GROUP | | | | |
| COMP | | | | |
| STUDENT COMP | | | | |
| DEADWOOD | | | | |
| TOTAL | | | | |
| CAPACITY | | | | |
| DIFFERENCE | | | | |
| TOTAL PAID THIS PERF. | | | | |
| PREVIOUS TOTAL | | | | |
| TOTAL TO DATE | | | | |

ATTENDANCE _____

_____
TREASURER

REMARKS:

# Sample 5

BOX OFFICE STATEMENT _____ THEATRE.  SHOW _____

DAY _____ DATE _____ AT _____ PM.  WEATHER _____

| Price | Capacity | Theatre | Agency Allot. | Pass | Spec | Total Dead | Sold | Amount | Loc. Tax | Fed. Tax |
|-------|----------|---------|---------------|------|------|------------|------|--------|----------|----------|
|       |          |         |               |      |      |            |      |        |          |          |
|       |          |         |               |      |      |            |      |        |          |          |
|       |          |         |               |      |      |            |      |        |          |          |
| Total |          |         |               |      |      |            |      |        |          |          |

SPECIALS: (Seasons, Industrials, Groups, Disc.)

| | Price | No. Sold | Amount | Loc. Tax | Reg. Price | Disc. % | | | | |
|--|-------|----------|--------|----------|------------|---------|--|--|--|--|
| Season |  |  |  |  |  |  |  |  |  | Total |
| Groups |  |  |  |  |  |  |  |  |  | Total |
| Discnts |  |  |  |  |  |  |  |  |  | Total |
| Indust |  |  |  |  |  |  |  |  |  | Total |

THEATRE PARTY AGENTS' & BROKERS' FEES
AGENCIES:

| Price | Sold | Amount | Loc. Tax | Agency Dead | | | | |
|-------|------|--------|----------|-------------|--|--|--|--|
|       |      |        |          |             |  |  |  |  |
|       |      |        |          |             |  |  |  |  |
|       |      |        |          |             |  |  |  |  |
| Total |      |        |          |             |  |  |  | Total |

HARDWOOD:

| Price | Sold | Amount | Loc. Tax | Serial Numbers | | | | |
|-------|------|--------|----------|----------------|--|--|--|--|
|       |      |        |          |                |  |  |  |  |
|       |      |        |          |                |  |  |  |  |
|       |      |        |          |                |  |  |  |  |
|       |      |        |          |                |  |  |  | Total |

We hereby certify that
the undersigned have          This Performance _____
personally checked the
above statement and it is        Total to Date _____
in every respect correct.
                                       Total _____

TREASURER _____          Adjustment _____

MANAGER _____            TOTAL _____

## Sample 6

THEATRE _____      WEEK ENDING _____

### WEEKLY SUMMARY OF BOX OFFICE STATEMENTS

|  | Admissions | Amount | Tax | Show |
|---|---|---|---|---|
| Theatre | | | | |
| Seasons | | | | |
| Industrial | | | | |
| Groups | | | | |
| Agencies | | | | |
| Hardwood | | | | |
| Adjustments | | | | |
| Total This Week | | | | |
| Less Commissions-A | | | | |
| Total This Week - 1 | | | | |
| This Week's Total | | | | |
| Plus Commissions | | | | |
| Grand Total This Week | | | | |
| Total Carried Forward | | | | |
| Grand Total to Date | | | | |

*Bank Deposits this week    $ _____    Net of Refund

Bank Deposits to date    _____    Net of Refund

Grand Total Bank Deposits    _____    Net of Refund

*Do not include re-deposits

Must correspond to Ticket Account Report
for this week

Includes Weekend Deposit

# Appendix D

## A Box Office Audit System

1. Clean out all money due box office (by check from regular account; include I.O.U.s, petty-cash advances, etc.).
2. Prepare a statement of all money due the box office for tickets (from agencies, benefit groups, etc.) *if* the actual tickets are in the hands of the agent.
3. Deposit all checks and monies on hand (except required cash for change).
4. Transfer all "tax-admission" monies from box office account to tax bureau , if there are any such taxes.
5. Compute the checkbook balance; deduct all checks paid out. Deduct all refunds made through the last performance.
6. Compute total gross forward (minus tax) to last performance.
7. Arrange to pick up bank statement and canceled checks of box office account on the Friday prior to audit; notify bank in advance. Reconcile these with checkbook balance as of audit date.
8. Count all cash on hand (include cash-box advances to playhouse agencies).
9. Count all UNPAID tickets on hand, both in rack and reservation envelopes.
10. In counting tickets, each group must be checked by another counter. Recount where there are discrepancies.
11. Prepare audit statement as follows:

**Add Column**

1. Advance sales monies received from agencies
2. Advance monies due from agencies for actual tickets in their hands
3. Cash on hand
4. Agency cash on hand

**Subtract Column**

1. Any monies due box office, *not* already paid to box office account
2. Beginning-of-the-season box office balance

**Compute**

Add column, minus the subtract column will equal the advance sales for the remainder of the season. Add this to the price represented by all UNPAID tickets on hand and you *should* get the total potential gross for the remainder of the season. This is, of course, only if you have transferred all monies from the box office account as determined by the gross shown on statements up to the last performance. Your remainder, then, should equal the cash sales advance which you have just computed.

Prepare a statement as follows:

## Calculation of Box Office Shortage or Overage

Per Reconciliation performed on_____.

at _____(A.M.) (P.M.)

| | |
|---|---:|
| Box office checkbook balance (including deposit in transit) | $xxxxx |
| *Add:* Cash fund left in box office | xxxx |
| *Add:* Accounts receivable (agencies, hotels, I.O.U.s, etc.) | xxxx |
| **Total Adjusted Cash Balance** | $xxxxx |

| | | |
|---|---:|---:|
| Capacity of house (in printed tickets for last week) | $xxxxx | |
| *Less:* Unsold tickets on hand (in racks, at agencies, reservations unpaid for) | xxxx | |
| **Net Advance Sales of Last Week** | | xxxxx |
| **Cash Over or Under Advance Sales** | | $_____ |

AUDIT MANAGER:_____

**ASSISTING:**

_____

_____

_____

DO NOT DEPOSIT ANY OF NEXT YEAR'S TICKET SALES INCOME, BUT KEEP
IN SEPARATE FOLDER OR BANK ACCOUNT, PENDING COMPLETION OF
BOX OFFICE AUDIT.

# Appendix E

## A Manual for Box Office Treasurers

### Cardinal Rules of Box Office Behavior
1. *Never* leave the box office unattended.
2. *Never* allow an unpaid ticket to leave the box office.
3. *Never* allow anyone into the box office unless he is bonded.
4. *Never* take any box office business across the threshold.
5. *Never* discuss box office grosses or numbers of tickets sold with anyone. (If people inquire about business, your answer should be: "Business is very good" and absolutely nothing more.)
6. *Never* show a statement to anyone: never prepare a statement in front of customers; never count money or prepare bank deposits in view of customers.
7. *Never* bring food or beverages of any kind into the box office.
8. *Never* issue free or discounted tickets without a written order from the producer or the manager.
9. *Never* make personal promises to the customer or encourage him to deal only with you. Anyone in the box office should be able to help any customer.
10. *Never* tie up the box office phones with personal or unnecessarily long conversations.
11. *Never* hesitate to ask questions if you are uncertain about some policy or problem.
12. *Never* hesitate to hand over all monies in the event of a robbery.

*P.S.*

Remember that you control the lifeline of the theatre. In the eyes of the customers you, more than any other person, *are* the theatre. Remember that a ticket is negotiable and, therefore, must be regarded as cash. Treat each ticket as if it were a twenty dollar bill.

### Daily Duties of the Treasurers
1. Report on time and have the customer windows open and ready for business from the stroke of 10 A.M. until the stroke of 10 P.M.
2. Keep the box office clean and neat at all times. Since the janitor is not allowed into the room, you will be required to sweep the floor daily.
3. Process all mail orders daily (see below).
4. Maintain and enlarge the mailing list:
    a) *Every* name and address that comes into the box office on a ticket order, information request or mailing-list form must be checked against the mailing list.
    b) If the name is *not* already on the list, make out a new card, write the year in the upper right corner and file it.
    c) If the name *is* on the mailing list, enter the current date and refile the card.

5. Compute a box office statement for each performance:
   - *a)* Each treasurer will complete his own statement and only then will these statements be compared for correctness. Only when all statements agree may a final copy be given to the business manager: no treasurer will end his time shift until all the statements agree.
   - *b)* Each finalized statement will be signed by the head treasurer who is responsible for its accuracy.
   - *c)* All deadwood and stubs, counted and numbered, will be boxed, labeled with the performance date, then stored.
6. "Rack" all tickets by date and keep the current ticket rack filled with the tickets for the next, immediate performance.
7. Make out two daily bank deposits:
   - *a)* One listing mail-order checks only.
   - *b)* One listing all other checks and cash (minus the precise amount of cash to be kept on hand for sales and payroll purposes. The business manager will dictate these amounts.)
   - *c)* The treasurer shall also give the business manager a daily "silver and bill" cash order when this is required.
8. "Check out" the returned agency tickets and income each day when the agency treasurer(s) report to the box office. The agency treasurer will not leave the theatre until his daily receipts and cash are correct and accounted for.
9. "Phone in" unsold ticket locations for other theatres and record unsold ticket numbers which they, if acting as your agent, did not sell. Return these unsold agency tickets to the rack: retain the sold tickets under the name of the agency and mark them "sold."
10. Report any problems, discrepancies or helpful information to the business or general manager.

### General Sales Procedures

1. Always be courteous—but firm! Keep each transaction as brief and efficient as possible.
2. Every seat in the house is a "good" seat.
3. If phone or window customers ask for tickets and you are SRO, encourage them to return just before curtain time for cancellations.
   - *a)* Cancellation lists are started an hour and a half before curtain time.
   - *b)* Customers must be in the lobby and remain there to get on the list (no phone listings).
   - *c)* Write the name, number and price of tickets desired and where the customer is waiting.
4. All ticket reservation envelopes shall carry the following, clearly written information:
   - *a)* Customer's name and initials.
   - *b)* Performance date: mat. or eve.
   - *c)* Number of tickets: price per ticket (2 x $4.95). Do not ever write the total amount due.
   - *d)* Write the *exact* time when you told customer that tickets, if not claimed, would be canceled.

5. Any ticket that is reserved *and* paid for will be held eternally.
6. Unpaid reservation policy:
     a) If the order is made more than a week in advance of the show, en-
        courage customer to send a check and, if he agrees, write "Ck. in
        mail" on ticket envelope.
     b) Otherwise: we hold unpaid tickets until 12:30 (matinees) or 6:30
        (evenings) on the performance day. If customer can't claim tickets
        by then, he must phone again to reconfirm the reservation. Then
        tell him that we hold tickets until 2:00 (matinees) or 8:00 (evenings)
        NEVER longer.
     c) Cancel and return to the rack all unpaid reservations not claimed
        within ten minutes after the "hold" time. This policy will be carried
        out whether we are sold out or not.
7. All tickets are to be sold on a "first come, first served" basis.
8. "Dress the house." Don't pack 'em in unless necessary.
9. Double-check every transaction. *Handle only one transaction at a time.*
10. Traveler's checks and personal checks in the exact amount due are always
    acceptable, with driver's license or other identification on back.
11. Credit is never extended; unpaid tickets never leave the box office.
12. Press and complimentary tickets will be issued on numbered hardwood
    forms provided by the business manager and the actual tickets then
    placed in the "dead" rack. Record the number printed on the hardwood
    form on the back of the corresponding theatre ticket.
13. When making change:
     a) Don't give out tickets until the money is in your hand.
     b) Leave the customer's money on the counter until he has his change
        in his hands.
14. Until one half hour prior to curtain, only the producer or general manager
    may assign or use house seats. At half-hour, the head treasurer may release
    the remaining house seats for general sale.
15. Do not put house seats on sale until the last feasible moment. If they are
    needed to cover an emergency or a mistake, only the head treasurer may
    authorize their use.

## Procedure for Handling Mail Orders

1. All mail must be processed daily.
2. All mail work must be kept in a separate place, away from other business.
3. Wire baskets will be provided to hold: "Information Requests," "Unproc-
   essed ticket orders," "Problem Orders," "Mailing List Additions," "Checker
   Basket."
4. Open each piece of mail and:
     a) Staple all contents to the customer's envelope with the check on
        top—throw nothing away!
     b) Separate ticket orders from information requests.
     c) Stamp the order form with the PAID stamp and enter the amount of
        the check in the "mail-order income box".
     d) When all letters have been opened and checks removed, make out the
        bank deposit and place it, along with the checks, in the safe.

5. Process each piece of mail individually as follows:

    *a)* Read entire letter or form and underline in red: date, number of tickets and location desired.

    *b)* Pull the tickets, giving the customer what he wants if possible, and write the date of the tickets, location and price per ticket on the letter in red. Be certain he has sent in the right amount for the tickets.

    *c)* Stamp and address an envelope to the customer.

    *d)* Attach all this together and place in the "checker" basket.

6. Checker duties:

    *a)* Reread each letter.

    b) Check order against tickets pulled.

    *c)* Write "tickets mailed" and today's date on letter.

    *d)* Place tickets in envelope, blanket them, weigh envelope to determine postage, scotch-tape the envelope seal, place letter in outgoing mail box.

    *e)* Place the customer's letter or order in "mailing list" basket.

7. After customer letters have been checked against the mailing list, file them alphabetically in the "customer correspondence" file.

    *a)* If customer phones to inquire about his order, check this letter file immediately.

    *b)* If customer complains that he didn't get what he asked for, locate his order. Chances are he forgot what he ordered.

## Possible Mail-Order Problems and Policy Regarding Them:

1. If check is insufficient to cover tickets ordered:

    *a)* Pull the tickets anyway.

    *b)* Deposit the check.

    *c)* Hold tickets and notify the customer of the balance due.

2. If the check is for *more* than the amount due:

    *a)* Process mail as usual, enter refundable amount on letter.

    *b)* Mail the tickets.

    *c)* Enclose a letter signed by the head treasurer saying that "upon presentation of this letter at box office, a refund will be made."

3. If tickets are sold out for the performance requested by customer:

    *a)* Return the letter and the check to the customer.

    *b)* Notify him when tickets are available.

4. If the customer returns tickets by mail for a refund, refer the case to the business manager for a decision.

5. If the mail order is incomplete and does not include all the necessary information:

    *a)* Place the letter and check in the "problem basket."

    *b)* Notify the customer of his negligence (by phone, if a local call, otherwise by postcard).

6. When possible, use the postcard form shown as follows to notify the customer when an order cannot be filled:

We are unable to complete your ticket order due to the following reason:

_____ We are sold out for the (price)(date) you requested.

_____ Seats available, but not the specific locations.

_____ Incorrect payment. You sent $_____ Should be $_____

_____ Failed to state date_____matinee_____evening_____

_____ Check returned for your signature.

_____ Number of tickets and price were not indicated.

_____ Tickets requested not available until _____.

_____ The performance you requested is not scheduled.

We are returning your check. _____

We are holding your check for further instructions. _____

We are holding your tickets at the box office. _____

## Procedure for Answering the Box Office Phones'

1. Salutation: "Good morning. Playhouse box office."
2. If the call is not box office business, refer it to the correct number. Do not take messages or accept nonbusiness calls.
3. If you are speaking on one line and another line rings:
    a) Ask your party to "hold on, please" and push the "hold" button.
    b) Next, push the flashing button, ask that person to "hold on, please." If he is phoning long distance he will probably tell you, in which case deal with him immediately.
    c) Push "hold" button again, return to original call and finish that before going on to the next.
4. Long distance calls take priority over local calls.
5. Phone calls take priority over window customers.
6. Learn immediately how to give clear directions (car and public transportation) to the playhouse from all points within a fifty mile radius.
7. When an order is taken, repeat the number of tickets, location and date and *emphasize* the cancellation time.
8. If a customer requests your name, give him your first name only.
9. Keep yourself informed about the intermission and show-break times.
10. Make a note about the seat numbers occupied by medical doctors. Inform the manager if any VIP or celebrity ticket orders are made.

## Procedure When Customer Has Lost His Tickets

1. If tickets were ordered by mail:
    a) If they were season tickets, check his file card and issue a pass for correct locations, signed by head treasurer.
    b) If ordered by mail, check mail file and issue a pass for correct locations, signed by head treasurer.
    c) If there is no record of customer's order, head treasurer may cross-examine customer and use his own judgment as to whether or not a pass should be issued.

2. If correspondence shows that the tickets ordered were for another perform-ance than the one remembered by the customer, issue a pass for that per-formance only.

3. Always issue passes for lost or stolen tickets by writing the locations on a ticket envelope, not on hardwood, as that would represent a duplicate ticket if the actual ticket shows up.

4. Always clearly explain to customers that, if a pass is issued for lost or stolen tickets and they arrive at their seats to find someone sitting in them with the real tickets, the customer with the pass must relinquish the seats.

5. No theatre staff member is to enter into any dispute between customers in regard to found or stolen tickets: this matter is strictly between the two customers.

# Appendix F

## Sample Insurance Claim Kit

### To Theatre Administrators and Supervisors

This claim kit has been prepared to assure standardization of processing all in-surance claim matters. Prompt and careful attention will insure that all claims will receive proper and efficient consideration by the insurance company.

### General Instructions

1. Each claim, of whatever nature, should be reported promptly, using forms provided with this kit or furnished by the insurance company.

2. Liaison should be established with the office of our insurance company. Other information is furnished elsewhere in this kit. Arrangements have been made for a representative of the company to contact you, to dis-cuss procedures and to provide for close cooperation.

3. Should unusual difficulties arise, with respect to any claim, notification should immediately be made to John Doe, Claims Supervisor of our insurance company, tel: 000-555-0001.

4. In the event that any claim appears to be of a serious nature, verbal con-tact should be made immediately with the insurance office. This should be followed by the regular written report.

5. Additional copies of all report forms may be obtained from the insurance office.

6. Feel free to consult with the managing director of the theatre with respect to any claim matter.

7. Supervisors should be careful not to commit themselves on liability matters (injuries to patrons), nor to commit themselves for any expenses on their compensation cases.

8. Insurance company offices and representatives:

    1._____

    2._____

    3._____

## Specific Instructions

### A. Employee's Injuries (Workmen's Compensation)

1. Employees should be directed to report any injury incurred during the course of employment to the manager immediately.
2. All bills for treatment of injuries should be forwarded to the insurance company's attention: John Doe, and should contain the following information:
    a) Name of employee
    b) Place where injury occurred
    c) Date of injury
3. *Classes of Employees:*
    a) Performers are considered to be New York State employees and are subject to New York laws. Forms provided for New York should, therefore, be used and distributed as set forth later in this kit.
    b) Nonperformers are considered to be employees in the state where employed. Forms provided for the state in which your theatre is located should be used and distributed as set forth later in this kit.
4. It is vital that a copy of all reports be forwarded to the insurance company.

### B. Injuries to Patrons

1. First aid should be rendered as quickly as possible.
2. Employees should be directed to report any injury to a patron, no matter how minor, to the manager.
3. Manager should obtain all data pertaining to the accident, including area where accident occurred, names and addresses of witnesses, if possible, and all information pertinent to the injured patron.
4. Report should be prepared as quickly as possible and distributed as follows:
    a) Original to servicing office
    b) One (1) copy to the insurance company
    c) One (1) copy to the manager
    d) One (1) copy for your file
5. Details of injuries of an apparently serious nature should be telephoned to the insurance office as soon as possible. Written report, distributed as above, should follow.

### C. Automobile Accidents

1. Report of accident should be prepared as quickly as possible, on forms provided, and distributed as follows:
    a) Original to servicing office
    b) One (1) copy to the insurance company
    c) One (1) copy to the manager
    d) One (1) copy for your file.
2. State reports, when required, should be prepared and forwarded as follows:
    a) Proper state authority, as indicated on forms
    b) Copy to the manager

3. Where damage to vehicle, either theatre-owned or leased or other party's, or injury to parties, appears to be of a serious nature, immediate telephone report should be made to insurance office. Written report should follow.

4. Where damage to theatre vehicle is involved, report should contain information as to where vehicle may be inspected.

## Direct Damage to Theatre Property

1. All information pertaining to direct damage to theatre property should be reported to the manager immediately.

2. With respect to burglary or vandalism claims, report at once to local police, giving all details except with regard to values or extent of dollar loss sustained.

3. Great care should be taken to protect undamaged property when a loss occurs, and losses should be reported promptly.

## Performers

1. All performers are considered to be New York State employees.

2. Use Form C-2 to report all injuries to employees in this category: form should be completed as fully as possible.

3. All bills should be sent to the insurance company, attention: John Doe, containing information set forth previously in this kit.

### LIABILITY ACCIDENT NOTICE
#### (Not Automobile)

| | Name of Company | | | | Name and Location of Agent | | |
|---|---|---|---|---|---|---|---|
| Policy No. | | | Policy Period | | | Nature of Business | |
| Limits | Liab. | Med. Pay. | Elevator | Products | Contr. | Other (Specify) | |
| B. I. | | | | | | | |
| P. D. | | | | | | | |
| Insured | Name | | | | | | Phone |
| | Address | | | | | | |
| | Location of Insured Premises | | | | | | |
| Time and Place | Date and Time of Accident | | | | | | |
| | Location | | | | | | |
| Injured Person | Name | | | | | Age | Phone |
| | Address | | | | | | |
| | Occupation | | | | | | |
| | Employed by: | | | | | | |
| | What was injured doing when hurt? | | | | | | |
| The Injury | Nature and extent of injury | | | | | | |
| | Where was injured taken after accident? | | | | | | |
| | Probable disability | | | | | Has injured resumed work? | |
| Property Damage | Owner | | Address | | | Phone | |
| | List damage | | | | | Estimated cost of repair $ | |
| | Name | | | Address | | Phone | |

## AUTOMOBILE ACCIDENT OR LOSS NOTICE

| Name of Company | Name and Location of Agent | Agent's Code |
|---|---|---|

**Coverage Data**

**To Be Completed By Agent**

| Policy No. | | Policy Period | | Loss Payee | | | | |
|---|---|---|---|---|---|---|---|---|
| Limits | B. I. | P. D. | Med. Pay. | Comprehensive | Ded. | Coll. | Ded. | Other (Specify) |
| Auto Rating Class | Driver Class | Symbol | Casualty Territory | Physical Territory | Compact Car | Driver Training Credit | Class | Age | Spec | Sym |

**Insured**

| Name | Phone |
|---|---|
| Address | |

**Time and Place**

| Date and Time of Loss or Accident | Location |
|---|---|

**Insured Automobile**

**Give Age of Driver**

| Year | Make | Model | Serial No. | Motor No. | License No. and State |
|---|---|---|---|---|---|

| Owner of Insured Vehicle and Address | Other Insurance |
|---|---|

| Name of Driver and Address | Age | Driver's License No. and State | Phone |
|---|---|---|---|

For What Purpose Was Automobile Being Used at Time of Accident?

| Where May Auto Be Seen (Address) | Estimated Cost of Repairs |
|---|---|

If Theft, Specify Property Stolen:  If Collision or Comprehensive Specify Damage.

| Have Police Been Notified? | Location and Date |
|---|---|

**Damage To Property Of Others**

| Owner and Address | Phone |
|---|---|
| Other Driver and Address | Phone |
| List Damage | Estimated Cost of Repairs |
| If Automobile, Make and Year | License No. and State |
| Was Other Car Insured? | Name of Company and Policy No. |

| Name of Injured | Address | Passenger Insd's/Other Car/Car Ped. (Check One) | Age and Extent of Injuries |
|---|---|---|---|

Address

---

**Description Of Accident (Cont'd)**

Complete the Following Diagram Showing Direction and Positions of Automobiles Involved, Designating Clearly Point of Contact.

Indicate by arrow  N
direction of north ⟶

Instructions:
(1) Use solid line to show path of vehicle before accident ⟶  1
        ⟶  2  dotted line after accident
(2) Number each vehicle and show direction of travel ⟶  2
(3) Show motorcycle by ⟶ O-O
(4) Show pedestrian by ⟶ O
(5) Show railroad by ---|---|---|---|---

**Damage To Property Of Others (Cont'd)**

| Owner and Address | Phone |
|---|---|
| Other Driver and Address | Phone |
| List Damage | Estimated Cost of Repairs |
| If Automobile, Make and Year | License No. and State |
| Was Other Car Insured? | Name of Company and Policy No. |

## Appendix G


### Offering Circular for the Broadway Production of
### "And Miss Reardon Drinks a Little"

OFFERING CIRCULAR - DATED AS OF NOVEMBER 30, 1970

$125,000 in Limited Partnership Interests *

MISS REARDON COMPANY

a limited partnership to be formed to

finance the play

"AND MISS REARDON DRINKS A LITTLE"

(tentative title)


THESE SECURITIES ARE OFFERED PURSUANT TO AN EXEMPTION FROM
REGISTRATION WITH THE UNITED STATES SECURITIES AND EXCHANGE
COMMISSION. THE COMMISSION DOES NOT PASS UPON THE MERITS OF
ANY SECURITIES NOR DOES IT PASS UPON THE ACCURACY OR COM-
PLETENESS OF ANY OFFERING CIRCULAR OR OTHER SELLING
LITERATURE.


### THE OFFERING

PRODUCING MANAGERS COMPANY, INC. , (a New York corporation whose principal shareholders are James B. McKenzie and Spofford J.
Beadle) and SETH L. SCHAPIRO intend to produce the play "AND MISS
REARDON DRINKS A LITTLE" (hereinafter referred to as the "Play").
They offer limited partnership interests in a partnership to be formed for
that purpose (hereinafter referred to as the "Partnership"), of which they
will be the general partners (hereinafter referred to as the "General
Partners"). The General Partners will make no financial contribution
but will receive 50% of any Net Profits. (See caption entitled "NET PROFITS.")
Net Profits are the excess of gross receipts over all "Production",
"Running" and "Other" Expenses, as these terms are defined in the
limited partnership agreement for the Partnership. If there are no Net
Profits, Limited Partners will bear the entire risk of loss to the extent
of their respective contributions. Any losses in excess of that amount will
be borne by the General Partners. It is presently contemplated that the
Partners' share in Net Profits, if any, will be computed only after payment
to others of approximately 54% of the gross weekly box office receipts and

---

* Subject to a 10% involuntary overcall. If the entire overcall
  is exercised, an additional $12,500 would be contributed and
  the total offering would be $137,500.

deduction of all other expenses from the balance of such gross receipts (see caption entitled "NET PROFITS").

There is no minimum fixed amount that each individual Limited Partner must contribute, but the General Partners reserve the right to refuse contributions of less than $500. An initial contribution of $2,500.00 entitles a Limited Partner to a 1% share of any Net Profits, if the overcall is not made, and if the full overcall is made, an initial contribution of $2,750.00 will entitle a Limited Partner to a 1% share of any Net Profits. The amount to be raised hereunder is $125,000 subject to a 10% overcall, which, if made, will raise the aggregate amount to be raised to $137,500. The Partnership will be formed when and if $125,000 has been raised.

The rights and obligations of the General and Limited Partners are set forth in the limited partnership agreement for Miss Reardon Company (hereinafter referred to as the "Partnership Agreement"). This must be signed by all subscribers to limited partnership interests and may be obtained from the General Partners, whose address is 330 West 45th Street, New York, New York 10036. Telephone: (212) LT 1-2620.

## TABLE OF CONTENTS

## THE RISK TO INVESTORS

(1)     The sole business of the Partnership will be the production of the Play and the exploitation of the subsidiary rights therein. In such a venture the risk of loss is especially high in contrast with the prospects for any profit. These securities should not be purchased unless the investor is prepared for the possibility of total loss.

(2)     While no accurate industry statistics are available, it has been claimed that of the plays produced for the New York stage in the 1969-1970 season, a vast majority resulted in loss to investors.

(3)     On the basis of estimated expenses, if the Partnership is capitalized at $125,000, and no overcall is made, the Play would have to run for a minimum of 9 weeks (approximately 72 performances) on Broadway to a full capacity house in order to return to Limited Partners their initial contribution. A vast majority of the plays produced for the New York stage in the 1969-1970 season failed to run this long. Of those that did, a mere handful played to capacity audiences.

## SUBSCRIPTIONS

Offers to subscribe to limited partnership interests are subject to acceptance by the General Partners. Contributions must be paid in cash, except for a Limited Partner who furnishes a theatre, Actors' Equity Association, or similar bond, at the time of signing the Partnership Agreement. All cash contributions will be kept in a special bank account(s), in trust, until actually employed for pre-production or production purposes of this production or returned to the Partners. It is presently intended that the account(s) will be at the Chemical Bank and that the General Partners will be the Trustees. The Partnership will not be formed, and, except as hereinafter provided, all contributions will be returned in full if $125,000 has not been received by May 31, 1971, the date presently provided by which the Play must be produced; provided, however, that if said date is extended to October 31, 1971, or to any later date, pursuant to the agreement referred to under caption entitled "PRODUCTION AND SUBSIDIARY RIGHTS", the date by which contributions must be received or returned will be similarly extended.

The General Partners shall have the right to use a Limited Partner's contribution prior to the formation of the Partnership, provided they shall have obtained written authorization therefor. However, in the event of an abandonment of production prior to formation of the Partnership, the contributions of Partners who shall have authorized the use of their contributions prior to formation of the Partnership will be returned in full without interest thereon.

A Partner whose contribution is used prior to the formation of the Partnership, may, under certain circumstances, be personally liable as a general partner for production debts incurred prior to the date of formation of the Partnership. The General Partners agree to indemnify such Partner to the extent of his liability, if any, as a general partner.

## OVERCALL

Each Limited Partner's contribution is subject to a 10% involuntary overcall which may be exercised in the General Partners' sole discretion if they believe that additional moneys are necessary to carry on the business of the Partnership or pay unpaid debts thereof. In the event of an overcall, it should be recognized that any Limited Partner failing to contribute his share of such overcall will be in breach of the Partnership Agreement, vesting in the Partnership a cause of action against him for such breach.

## THE PRODUCERS

Producing Managers Company, Inc., and Seth L. Schapiro will produce the Play. They will be the promoters and the General Partners of the Partnership with exclusive control of the production of the Play. They shall have the right to abandon the production at any time and for any reason whatsoever. Their address is 330 West 45th Street, New York, New York.

Producing Managers Company, Inc. was incorporated under the laws of the State of New York on April 22, 1963 for the purpose of producing and managing theatrical interests. It has produced 87 plays at the Westport Country Playhouse in Connecticut, 12 plays at the Bucks County Playhouse in Pennsylvania, 17 plays at the Mineola Theatre on Long Island, New York and 11 North American road tours of plays originally presented on Broadway, which included "Cactus Flower", "Forty Carats" and "The Price". The company has also supplied general management services for other productions and theatres.

James B. McKenzie and Spofford J. Beadle are the principal stockholders of Producing Managers Company, Inc. Mr. McKenzie co-produced on Broadway, "The Girl in the Freudian Slip". Said play opened on May 18, 1967, played four performances, closed on May 20, 1967 and was a 73% loss to investors. Except for the aforesaid production, neither Producing Managers Company, Inc., nor its principal stockholders have ever produced a show on Broadway.

Seth L. Schapiro has been connected with the theatre as a general manager, music publishing executive, company manager, and booking company executive. Most recently, Mr. Schapiro was co-producer at the Westport Country Playhouse in Connecticut. Seth L. Schapiro has never before produced a play on Broadway.

## THE PLAY

"And Miss Reardon Drinks A Little" is a drama about three sisters -- school teachers who assemble for dinner one evening to thrash out a lifetime of hate. The thrust of the Play is in the obsession of one of the sisters who has recurrent visions of "Doom".

## THE AUTHOR

"And Miss Reardon Drinks a Little" is the first play Paul Zindel has had produced on Broadway. Mr. Zindel authored "The Effect of Gamma Rays on Man in the Moon Marigolds" which was produced off-Broadway and won the 1970 Drama Critics Award as the Best American Play. Mr. Zindel has also written teleplays and three novels. His novels have been published by Harper & Row and his teleplays are scheduled to be produced for "The Children's Hour", which is a presentation of the Columbia Broadcasting System.

Mr. Zindel will receive 5% of the first $5,000 of gross weekly box office receipts plus 7-1/2 % of the next $2,000 of such receipts, plus 10% of all such receipts in excess of $7,000 of each company presenting the Play and additional compensation in respect of the disposition, if any, of so-called "subsidiary rights" in the Play.

## THE DIRECTOR

Melvin Bernhardt has been engaged to direct the Play. Mr. Bernhardt will receive a fee of $5,000 and a royalty of 2% of the gross weekly box office receipts until recoupment of production costs and 3% of such receipts thereafter; plus additional compensation with respect to additional companies of the Play.

Mr. Bernhardt has previously directed the play "Cop-Out" on Broadway. Mr. Bernhardt's direction of the off-Broadway production of "The Effect of Gamma Rays on Man in the Moon Marigolds" earned him an Obie Award in 1970.

## THE CAST

Julie Harris has been engaged to play one of the principal roles in the Play. Miss Harris will receive 10% of the gross weekly box office receipts of the Play against a guarantee of $2,500 plus $500 if such receipts exceed $40,000, but are less than $41,000; and an additional $500 if such receipts equal or exceed $41,000.

Miss Harris has previously been starred or co-starred on Broadway in "Forty Carats", "Skyscraper", "Member of the Wedding", "A Shot in the Dark", "The Lark", "I Am a Camera" and "Warm Peninsula". Miss Harris received an award for her outstanding performance in "The Lark", and the New York Drama Critics and Donaldson's Awards for her performance in "Member of the Wedding". Negotiations are underway to sign six remaining actors and actresses for the other parts in the Play.

## THE THEATRE

Although as of the date of this Offering Circular no contract for a theatre has been entered into, it is presently anticipated that the theatre rental will be between 25% and 30% of gross weekly box office receipts depending upon the amount of gross weekly box office receipts, with a two week guarantee of $12,000.

## COMPENSATION OF GENERAL PARTNERS

In addition to their 50% share of Net Profits, the General Partners will receive the following compensation and advantages whether or not the Partnership returns a Net Profit:

(a) As a management fee, 1% of the gross weekly box office receipts of each company presenting the Play.

(b) In respect of furnishing, or causing to be furnished, to the Partnership, office space and secretarial services, $350 per week as to each company presenting the Play. Said office charge shall commence two weeks before the beginning of rehearsals and end one week after the close of each company. The office use for this purpose will be located at 330 West 45th Street, New York, New York or such other place as the General Partners may designate, and may be used for other business activities of the General Partners.

To the extent that charges received from the Partnership by the General Partners for office space or other items furnished by them exceed the cost thereof to the General Partners, they will receive additional compensation. The General Partners will receive no compensation other than that stated above for any services, equipment or facilities customarily rendered or furnished by general partners or producers of theatrical ventures, nor will they receive concessions of cash, property or anything of value from persons rendering services or supplying goods to the production.

The General Partners, a company controlled by the General Partners, or either or both of the principal stockholders of Producing Managers Company, Inc., may perform services or furnish materials to the Partnership which are not customarily performed or furnished by general partners of theatrical limited partnerships (including, but not limited to, services as general and company manager and press agent for the Partnership). They may acquire for their own behalf from the Partnership, and/or the Author, further production rights in the Play, such as second company rights and motion picture or television rights, or may be associated as producer, director or in any other capacity with the purchaser of said rights.

## USE OF PROCEEDS

The present estimated allocation of proceeds is as follows:

PHYSICAL PRODUCTION

| | | |
|---|---|---|
| Scenery - Build & Paint | $7,500. | |
| Scenic Designer Fee | 2,250. | |
| Electrics (Rental & Purchase) | 1,500. | |
| Lighting Designer Fee | 1,250. | |
| Properties (Rental & Purchase) | 2,000. | |
| Costumes | 2,000. | |
| Costume Designer Fee | 1,250. | |
| Miscellaneous | 250. | $ 18,000. |

REHEARSAL EXPENSES & PRE-PRODUCTION

| | | | |
|---|---|---|---|
| Director's Fee | | $3,000. | |
| Rehearsal Salaries: | | | |
| Cast, ASM, Understudies | $6,500. | | |
| Stage Manager | 2,100. | | |
| General Manager | 2,400. | | |
| Company Manager | 1,200. | | |
| Press Agent | 1,750. | | |
| Crew & Wardrobe | 2,250. | 16,200. | |
| Payroll Taxes | | 1,620. | |
| Pension & Welfare | | 1,800. | |
| Rehearsal Hall | | 2,000. | |
| Scripts | | 150. | |
| Office Expense | | 2,100. | |
| Insurance (Pre-Paid) | | 1,500. | |
| Legal Fees | | 5,000. | |
| Auditing | | 1,000. | |
| Per Diem Expenses Out of Town | | 1,000. | |
| Company Transportation | | 1,000. | |
| Trucking | | 1,000. | |
| Take-In, Hang, Rehearse Out of Town | | 3,000. | |
| Take-In, Hang, Rehearse NYC | | 5,000. | |
| Miscellaneous | | 630. | 46,000. |

PUBLICITY AND PROMOTION

| | | |
|---|---|---|
| Newspaper and Other Media | $12,000. | |
| Photos | 1,000. | |
| Signs & Marquees | 2,000. | |
| Printing | 2,000. | |
| Press Agent's Expenses | 500. | |
| Opening Night Expense | 1,000. | |
| Miscellaneous | 500. | 19,000. |

BONDS AND DEPOSITS

| | | |
|---|---|---|
| Actors' Equity Association Bond | $16,000. | |
| ATPAM Bond | 1,300. | |
| IATSE Bond | 1,600. | |
| Advance to Author | 1,000. | |
| Theatre Guarantee | 12,000. | 31,900. |

CONTINGENCY AND RESERVE                                      10,100.

| | | |
|---|---|---|
| TOTAL | | $125,000. |

Plus 10% Overcall

To the extent the General Partners advance their own funds for pre-production expenses, they will be reimbursed upon formation of the Partnership. The General Partners have advanced $2,000.00 to date.

## ESTIMATED WEEKLY BUDGET

Based upon the present weekly budget, it is estimated that once the Play opens in New York City, it will have to gross approximately $25,000 per week to break even. The maximum weekly gross of the Play is estimated at about $55,000. Based upon present estimates, approximately 51% of gross weekly box office receipts in excess of $25,000 will accrue to the Partnership as profits. Accordingly, at prevailing ticket prices, taking into consideration the payments to the author, theatre, director, a star(s) and others out of gross weekly box office receipts, the Play would have to run a minimum of nine weeks at full capacity to return to Partners their contributions, if the Partnership is capitalized at $125,000 and no overcall is made.

## NET PROFITS

"Net Profits" consist of the excess of gross receipts over all "Production," "Running" and "Other" Expenses, as those terms are defined in the Partnership Agreement. (See caption entitled "THE OFFERING".)

As of the date hereof, projected Running Expenses include payments to the author, director, star(s), theatre and General Partners of a maximum of 54% of gross weekly box office receipts. The effect of the foregoing is to reduce the Limited Partners' share of Net Profits to 50% of Net Profits attributable to approximately 46% of gross weekly box office receipts. Additional payments based on a percentage of gross weekly box office receipts and/or net profits, may be paid to anyone else contributing services to the Partnership which will further reduce the Partners' share of Net Profits.

## RETURN OF CONTRIBUTIONS - SHARE OF PROFITS

The Limited Partners as a group will receive 50% of any Net Profits, each in the proportion his contribution bears to the total limited partnership contributions. Any Net Profits will be distributed only after the Broadway opening and after all contributions have been repaid and when such distributions will still leave the Partnership with a $20,000 reserve (plus any amounts which the General Partners wish to accumulate for the formation of additional companies to present the Play) and after payment or provision for payment of all debts, liabilities, taxes and contingent liabilities.

Before Net Profits are earned, all losses will be borne by the Limited Partners to the extent of their respective contributions. After Net Profits are earned, the General and Limited Partners will bear losses to the extent of the Net Profits in proportion to their respective interests. If the Partnership liabilities exceed its assets, all Partners will be required to return pro rata any Net Profits distributed to them and, if a shortage remains, any repaid contributions, all with interest thereon, if the General Partner shall so determine.

Net Profits and return of contributions will be distributed bi-monthly, except as provided above.

## PRODUCTION AND SUBSIDIARY RIGHTS

Pursuant to the contract Producing Managers Company, Inc. has entered into with Paul Zindel, which will be assigned to the Partnership, the Play may be presented in the United States, and elsewhere throughout the world. If the Partnership shall have presented the Play for the number of performances set forth in Section 2 of Article II of the Schedule of Additional Production Terms of said contract, the Partnership shall have the right to share in the proceeds from certain subsidiary rights, including motion picture, radio and television rights. Subject to the terms of the contract, Mr. Zindel has the right to dispose of subsidiary rights as he chooses. The Partnership's interest in any sale of subsidiary rights is 40% of the net receipts derived therefrom during the first ten years after the close of the last first-class run of the Play and decreases to nothing during the next 8 years.

## OTHER FINANCING

The General Partners reserve the right to pay to anyone else, for any reason whatsoever, a participation in Net Profits, solely from their share of Net Profits.

## FINANCIAL STATEMENTS

The ultimate issuer of these securities will be the Partnership to be formed. Accordingly, no financial statements are presently available. After formation of the Partnership and so long as the Play is being presented by the Partnership, the General Partners shall furnish the Limited Partners annually with a statement of operations prepared by an independent public accountant with bi-monthly statements of operations and with such other financial statements as may be from time to time required by law. In addition, the Limited Partners shall have the right to examine the Partnership books.

# Bibliography

## 1. Background Reading

Adams, W. Howard. *The Politics of Art.* New York: Associated Councils of the Arts, 1966.

Artaud, Antonin. *The Theatre and Its Double.* Translated by Mary Caroline Richards. New York: Grove Press, 1958.

*The Arts: A Central Element of a Good Society.* New York: Arts Councils of America, 1965.

*The Arts: Planning for Change.* New York: Associated Councils of the Arts, 1966.

Berg, Iva, ed. *The Business of America.* New York: Harcourt, Brace & World, 1968.

Baumol, William J., and Bowen, William G. *Performing Arts: The Economic Dilemma.* (A study of problems common to theatre, opera, music and dance.) New York: The Twentieth Century Fund, 1966.

Blau, Herbert. *The Impossible Theatre: A Manifesto.* New York: Macmillan, 1964.

Brook, Peter. *The Empty Space.* New York: Atheneum, 1968.

Brustein, Robert. *Revolution As Theatre,* New York: Liveright, 1971.

———. *Seasons of Discontent.* New York: Simon & Schuster, 1967.

———. *The Third Theatre.* New York: Alfred A. Knopf, 1969.

de Grazia, Sebastian. *Of Time, Work, and Leisure.* New York: The Twentieth Century Fund, 1962.

Dewey, John. *Art as Experience.* New York: Minton, Balch & Co., 1934.

Dorian, Frederick. *Commitment to Culture: Art Patronage in Europe. Its Significance for America.* Pittsburgh: University of Pittsburgh Press, 1964.

Engel, Lehman. *The American Musical Theatre: A Consideration.* New York: Macmillan, 1967.

Farnsworth, P. R. *Musical Taste: Its Measurement and Cultural Nature.* Stanford: Stanford University Press, 1950.

Fischer, Ernst. *The Necessity of Art.* Baltimore: Penguin Books, 1965.

Golden, Joseph. *The Death of Tinker Bell: The American Theatre in the 20th Century.* Syracuse: Syracuse University Press, 1967.

Grau, Robert. *The Stage in the Twentieth Century.* Reprint. New York: Benjamin Blom, 1968.

Grotowski, Jerzy. *Towards a Poor Theatre.* New York: Simon & Schuster, 1969.

Guerard, Albert L. *Art for Art's Sake.* New York: Schocken Books, 1965.

Heckscher, August. *The Public Happiness.* New York: Atheneum, 1962.

Hofstadter, Richard. *Anti-intellectualism in American Life.* New York: Alfred A. Knopf, 1963.

Houghton, Norris. *The Exploding Stage.* New York: Weybright, 1971.

Kirby, Michael. *Art of Time: Essays on the Avant Garde.* New York: Dutton, 1969.

Koestler, Arthur. *The Act of Creation.* New York: Macmillan, 1965.

Kostelanetz, Richard, ed. *The New American Arts.* New York: Horizon Press, 1965.

MacDonald, Dwight. *Against the American Grain: Essays on the Effects of Mass Culture.* New York: Random House, 1962.

McLuhan, Marshall. *Understanding Media: The Extensions of Man.* New York: Signet, 1964.

McMullen, Roy. *Art, Affluence and Alienation: The Fine Arts Today.* New York: Frederick A. Praeger, 1968.

Myers, Bernard S. *Problems of the Younger American Artist.* New York: The City College Press, 1957.

Rockefeller Panel Report. *The Performing Arts: Problems and Prospects.* New York: McGraw-Hill, 1965.

Rosenberg, Bernard, and White, David Manning, eds. *The Popular Arts in America.* New York: The Free Press, 1964.

Snaith, William. *The Irresponsible Arts.* New York: Atheneum, 1964.

Vaughan, Stuart. *A Possible Theatre.* New York: McGraw-Hill, 1969.

Wilson, Robert N., ed. *The Arts in Society.* Englewood Cliffs,N.J.: Prentice-Hall, 1964

## II. General Histories of the American Theatre

Anderson, John. *The American Theatre.* New York: Dial Press, 1938.

Blum, Daniel. *A Pictorial History of the American Theatre: 1860-1960.* New York: Chilton, 1960.

Burian, K. V. *The Story of World Opera.* New York: Spring Press, 1961.

Dunlap, William. *History of the American Theatre.* Reprint. New York: Burt Franklin Co., 1963.

Freedley, George, and Reeves, John A. *A History of the Theatre.* rev. ed. New York: Crown Publishers, 1968.

Grout, Donald Jay. *A Short History of Opera.* New York: Spring Press, 1961.

Hewitt, Barnard. *Theatre U.S.A.: 1668 to 1957.* New York: McGraw-Hill, 1959.

Hornblow, Arthur. *A History of the Theatre in America.* 2 vols. Philadelphia: Lippincott, 1919.

Houghton, Norris. *Advance from Broadway: 19,000 Miles of American Theatre.* New York: Harcourt, Brace & Co., 1941.

Hughes, Glenn. *A History of the American Theatre, 1700-1950.* New York: Samuel French, 1951.

Mueller, John H. *The American Symphony Orchestra.* Bloomington, Indiana: Indiana University Press, 1951.

Nicoll, Allardyce. *The Development of the Theatre.* New York: Harcourt, Brace & Co., 1946.

Quinn, Arthur Hobson. *A History of American Drama, from the Beginning to the Civil War.* New York: Appleton-Century-Crofts, 1951.

—. *A History of the American Drama from the Civil War to the Present Day.* rev. ed. in 1 vol. New York: Crofts, 1945.

Reyna, Ferdenando. *A Concise History of Ballet.* New York: Grosset & Dunlap, 1965.

Seilhamer, George. *History of the American Theatre.* Reprint. 3 vols. New York: Benjamin Blom, 1968.

Sonneck, Oscar G. *Early Opera in America.* Reprint. New York: Benjamin Blom, 1967.

## III. Regional Theatre and Studies
## of Individual Theatre Groups and Managers

Atkinson, Brooks. *Broadway.* New York: Macmillan, 1970.

*The Awkward Stage* (The Ontario Theatre Study Report). Toronto: Methuen Publications, 1969.

Barck, Oscar T., Jr. *New York City During the War for Independence.* New York: Columbia University Press, 1931.

Bing, Rudolf. *5000 Nights at the Opera.* Garden City, New York: Doubleday & Co., 1972.

Bloomfield, Arthur J. *The San Francisco Opera: 1923-1961.* New York: Appleton-Century-Crofts, 1961.

Carson, William G. B. *Managers in Distress: The St. Louis Stage, 1840-1844.* New York: Benjamin Blom, n.d.

Churchill, Allen. *The Great White Way: A Re-Creation of Broadway's Golden Age of Theatrical Entertainment.* New York: Dutton, 1962.

Clapp, William Warland. *Record of the Boston Stage.* Reprint. New York: Benjamin Blom, 1968.

Clurman, Harold. *The Fervent Years.* New York: Alfred A. Knopf, 1945. (Reprint. New York: Hill & Wang, 1964.)

Crowley, Alice Lewisohn. *The Neighborhood Playhouse: Leaves from a Theatre Scrapbook.* New York: Theatre Arts Books, 1959.

Deutsch, Helen, and Hanau, Stella. *The Provincetown: A Story of the Theatre.* New York: Farrar & Rinehart, 1931.

Donohue, Joseph W., Jr., ed. *The Theatrical Manager in England and America.* Princeton, New Jersey: Princeton University Press, 1971.

Eaton, Walter Prichard. *The Theatre Guild: The First Ten Years.* New York, 1926.

Elliott, Eugene C. *A History of Variety-Vaudeville in Seattle from the Beginnings to 1914.* Seattle, Washington: University of Washington Press, 1944.

Enders, John. *Survey of New York Theatre.* New York: Playbill, 1959.

Erskine, Hohn. *The Philharmonic-Symphony Society of New York: Its First Hundred Years.* New York: Macmillan, 1943.

Flanagan, Hallie. *Arena.* New York: Duell, Sloan, & Pearce, 1940.

Freedley, George. *Broadway Playhouses.* New York: New York Public Library, 1943.

Gard, Robert E. *Grassroots Theatre.* Madison, Wisconsin: University of Wisconsin Press, 1955.

Gard, Robert E., and Burley, Gertrude S. *Community Theatre.* New York: Duell, Sloan, & Pearce, 1959.

Goldman, William. *The Season: A Candid Look at Broadway.* New York: Harcourt, Brace & World, 1969.

Graham, Philip. *Showboats: The History of an American Institution.* Dallas: University of Texas, 1951.

Green, Abel, and Laurie, Joe, Jr. *Show Biz: From Vaudeville to Video.* New York: Henry Holt & Co., 1951.

Greenberger, Howard. *The Off-Broadway Experience.* Englewood Cliffs, New Jersey: Prentice-Hall, 1971.

Harding, Alfred. *The Revolt of the Actors.* New York: William Morrow & Co., 1929.

Harrison, Harry P. *Culture Under Canvas: The Story of Tent Chautauqua.* New York: Hastings House, 1958.

Hodge, Francis. *Yankee Theatre.* Austin: University of Texas Press, 1964.

Houghton, Norris. *But Not Forgotten: The Adventures of the University Players.* New York: Sloan, 1951.

Ireland, Joseph N. *Records of the New York Stage 1750-1860.* Reprint. New York: Benjamin Blom, 1968.

James, Reese David. *Cradle of Culture: 1800-1810, The Philadelphia Stage.* Philadelphia: University of Pennsylvania Press, 1957.

Kendall, John S. *The Golden Age of the New Orleans Theatre.* Baton Rouge: Louisiana State University Press, 1952.

Kinne, Wisner Payne. *George Pierce Baker and the American Theatre.* Cambridge, Massachusetts: Harvard University Press, 1954.

Krehbiel, Henry Edward. *The Philharmonic Society of New York.* New York and London: Novello, Ewer & Co., 1892.

Laufe, Abe. *Anatomy of a Hit: Long-run Plays on Broadway from 1900 to the Present Day.* New York: Hawthorn Books, 1966.

Leavitt, M. B. *Fifty Years in Theatrical Management.* New York: Broadway Publishing, 1912.

Little, Stuart W. *Off-Broadway, The Prophetic Theatre.* New York: Coward, McCann & Geoghegan, 1972.

Ludlow, Noah. *Dramatic Life As I Found It.* Reprint. New York: Benjamin Blom, n.d.

MacKay, Constance Darcy. *The Little Theatre in the United States.* New York: T. Holt, 1917.

Marcosson, Isaac F., and Frohman, Daniel, *Charles Frohman, Manager and Man.* New York: Harper, 1916.

McCleary, Albert, and Glick, Carl. *Curtains Going Up.* Chicago and New York: Pitman, 1939.

McLean, Albert F., Jr. *American Vaudeville As Ritual.* Lexington: University Press of Kentucky, 1965.

Merkling, Frank; Freeman, John W. and Fitzgerald, Gerald, *The Golden Horseshoe: The Life and Times of the Metropolitan Opera House.* New York: The Viking Press, 1965.

Moody, Richard. *The Astor Place Riot.* Bloomington, Indiana: Indiana University Press, 1958.

Newton, Michael, and Hatley, Scott, *Persuade and Provide: The Story of the Arts and Education Council in St. Louis.* New York: Associated Councils of the Arts, 1970.

*The New Theatre.* Souvenir Booklet (no publisher listed). New York: 1909. Theatre Collection, New York Public Library.

O'Connor, Francis V., ed. *The New Deal Art Projects: An Anthology of Memoirs.* Washington, D. C.: Smithsonian Institution Press, 1972.

Patrick, J. Max. *Savannah's Pioneer Theatre: From Its Origins to 1810.* Atlanta: University of Georgia Press, 1953.

Pearson, Talbot. *Encores on Main Street: Successful Community Theatre Leadership.* Pittsburgh: Carnegie Institute of Technology Press, and New Brunswick, New Jersey: Rutgers University Press, 1948.

Pollock, Thomas Clark. *The Philadelphia Theatre in the Eighteenth Century.* Philadelphia: University of Pennsylvania Press, 1933.

Price, Julia S. *The Off-Broadway Theatre.* New York: Scarecrow Press, 1962.

Smith, Sol. *Theatrical Management in the West and South for 30 Years.* Reprint. New York: Benjamin Blom, n.d.

Smither, Nelle. *A History of the English Theatre at New Orleans, 1806-1842.* Reprint. New York: Benjamin Blom, 1967.

Sobel, Bernard. *Broadway Heartbeat: Memoirs of a Press Agent.* New York: Heritage, 1953.

Stagg, Jerry. *The Brothers Shubert.* New York: Random House, 1968.

Taoer, Bernard. *The Arts in Boston.* New York: Drama Book Specialists/Publishers, 1969.

Willard, George O. *History of the Providence Stage 1762-1891.* Providence: The Rhode Island News Company, 1891.

## IV. Performing Arts Producing and Administration

Anderson, John. *Box Office.* New York: Jonathan Cape & Harrison Smith, 1929.

Bailey, Howard. *The A. B. C.s of Play Producing.* New York: David McKay Co., 1954.

Baker, Hendrik. *Stage Management and Theatrecraft.* New York: Theatre Arts Books, 1968.

Beckhard, Richard, and Effrat, John. *Blueprint for Summer Theatre.* New York: J. Richard Press, 1948.

Bernheim, Alfred. *The Business of the Theatre: 1750-1932.* Reprint. New York: Benjamin Blom, 1964.

Bradbury, A. J., et al. *Production and Staging of Plays.* New York: Arc Books, 1963.

Burgard, Ralph. *Arts in the City: Organizing and Programming Community Arts Councils.* New York: Associated Councils of the Arts, n.d.

Cavanaugh, Jim. *Organization and Management of Non-Professional Theatre.* New York: Rosen Press, 1972.

Clark, Barrett H. *How to Produce Amateur Plays.* Boston: Little, Brown & Co., 1925.

Cullman, Marguerite. *Occupation: Angel.* New York: W. W. Norton, 1963.

Cutler, Bruce. *The Arts at the Grassroots.* Lawrence, Kansas: University of Kansas Press, 1968.

Engel, Lehman. *Planning and Producing the Musical Show.* New York: Crown Publishers, 1967.

Eustis, Morton. *B'way, Inc! The Theatre as a Business.* New York: Dodd, Mead, 1934.

Farber, Donald C. *Actors' Guide: What You Should Know About the Contracts You Sign.* New York: Drama Book Specialists/Publishers, 1971.

———.*From Option to Opening* (A Guide for the Off-Broadway producer). New York: Drama Book Specialists/Publishers, 1968.

———*Producing on Broadway: A Comprehensive Guide.* New York: Drama Book Specialists/Publishers. 1969.

Ferber, Henry. *Reserved Seat Box-Office.* New York: National Ticket Company, n.d.

Gard, Robert E.; Balch, Marston; and Temkin, Pauline. *Theatre in America: Appraisal and Challenge,* New York: Theatre Arts Books, 1968.

Gassner, John. *Producing the Play.* New York: Dryden Press, 1953.

Graf, Herbert. *Producing Opera for America.* New York: Atlantis Books, 1961.

Gruver, Bert. *The Stage Manager's Handbook.* New York: Drama Book Specialists/Publishers, 1972.

Hinsdell, Oliver. *Making the Little Theatre Pay: A Practical Handbook.* New York: Samuel French, 1925.

Jones, Margo. *Theatre-in-the-Round.* New York: McGraw-Hill Paperbacks, 1965.

Lounsbury, Warren C. *Theatre Backstage from A to Z.* rev. ed. Seattle, Washington: University of Washington Press, 1967.

McCalmon, George, and Moe, Christian, *Creating Historical Drama: A Guide for the Community and Interested Individuals.* Carbondale, Illinois: Southern Illinois University Press, 1965.

Moore, Thomas Gale, *The Economics of the American Theatre.* Durham, North Carolina: Duke University Press, 1968.

Moskow, Michael H. *Labor Relations in the Performing Arts.* New York: Associated Councils of the Arts, 1969.

Pearson, Talbot. *Encores on Main Street: Successful Community Theatre Leadership.* Pittsburgh: Carnegie Institute of Technology Press, 1948.

Plummer, Gail. *The Business of Show Business.* New York: Harper & Brothers, 1961.

Poggi, Jack. *Theatre in America: The Impact of Economic Forces, 1870-1967.* Ithaca, New York: Cornell University Press, 1968.

Reiss, Alvin H., ed. *The Arts Management Handbook.* New York: Law-Arts Publishers, 1970.

Seldon, Samuel, ed. *Organizing a Community Theatre.* Cleveland: National Theatre Conference, 1945.

Smith, Milton. *Play Production.* New York: Appleton-Century-Crofts, 1948.

Stanton, Sanford E. *Theatre Management.* New York: Appleton-Century, 1929.

Sweeting, Elizabeth. *Theatre Administration.* London: Sir Isaac Pittman and Sons, 1969.

Taubman, Joseph, ed. *Financing a Theatrical Production.* New York: Federal Legal Publications, 1964.

Volbach, Walther B. *Problems of Opera Production.* 2nd ed. Hamden, Connecticut: Shoe String Press, 1967.

Wharton, John F. *A Fresh Look at Theatre Tickets* (Report to the Legitimate Theatre Industry Exploratory Commission). New York: League of New York Theatres, 1965.

———. *Some Forgotten Facets of Theatrical Financing* (A Report to the Legitimate Theatre Industry Exploratory Commission). New York: League of New York Theatres, n.d.

Young, John Wray. *The Community Theatre and How It Works.* New York: Harper & Brothers, 1957.

## V. Theatre Architecture and the Physical Plant

Beranek, Leo L. *Acoustics.* New York: McGraw-Hill, 1954.

—. *Music, Acoustics and Architecture.* New York: John Wiley & Sons, 1962.

*Bricks, Mortar and the Performing Arts: Report on the Twentieth Century Fund Task Force on Performing Arts Centers.* New York: The Twentieth Century Fund, 1970.

Burris-Meyer, Harold, Cole, Edward C. *Theatres and Auditoriums.* New York: Reinhold Publishing Co., 1949.

Burris-Meyer, Harold, and Goodfriend, L. S. *Acoustics for the Architect.* New York: Reinhold Publishing Co., 1957.

Cogswell, Margaret, ed. *The Ideal Theatre: Eight Concepts.* New York: American Federation of the Arts, 1962.

Gascoigne, Bamber. *World Theatre: An Illustrated History.* Boston: Little, Brown & Co., 1968.

Joseph, Stephen. *New Theatre Forms.* New York: Theatre Arts Books, 1968.

Knudsen, V. O., and Harris, C. N., *Acoustical Designing in Architecture.* New York: Wiley, 1950.

Merrill, Robert H. *The School Theatre Is a Laboratory.* 3rd ed, Indianapolis, Indiana: R. H. Merrill, 1967.

Mielziner, Jo, and Smith, C. Ray, *The Shapes of Our Theatre.* New York: Clarkson N. Potter, 1970.

Mullin, Donald C. *The Development of the Playhouse: A Survey of Theatre Architecture from the Renaissance to the Present.* Berkeley, California: University of California Press, 1970.

Parkin, P. H., and Humphreys, H. R., *Acoustics, Noise and Buildings.* New York: Humanities Press, 1958.

Penn, Herman J. *Encyclopedic Guide to Planning and Establishing an Auditorium, Arena, Coliseum or Multi-Purpose Building.* Greenville, South Carolina: Penn-Fleming, 1963.

Robinson, Horace W. *Architecture for the Educational Theatre.* Eugene, Oregon: University of Oregon Books, 1970.

Schubert, Hanne Lore. *Modern Theatre Buildings: Architecture, Stage Design, Lighting.* New York: Praeger, 1971.

Silverman, Maxwell, and Bowman, Ned A. *Contemporary Theatre Architecture: An Illustrated Survey and a Checklist of Publications, 1946-1964.* New York: New York Public Library, 1965.

*Theatre Check List: A Guide to the Planning and Construction of Proscenium and Open Stage Theatres.* Prepared by and published for The American Theatre Planning Board, Middletown, Connecticut: Wesleyan University Press, 1969.

## VI. Career Guidance in Theatre

Dalrymple, Jean. *Careers and Opportunities in the Theatre.* New York: E. P. Dutton & Co., 1969.

Hirschfeld, Burt. *Stagestruck. New York: Julian* Messner, 1963.

Joels, Merrill E. *How to Get into Show Business.* rev. ed. New York: Hastings House, 1969.

Lord, William J., Jr. *How Authors Make a Living.* New York.

Savan, Bruce. *Your Career in the Theatre.* Garden City, New York: Doubleday & Co., 1961.


## VII. The Performing Arts in Education

*The Arts and the University.* New York: Council on Higher Education in the American Republics, Institute of International Education, 1964.

Dennis, Lawrence, and Jacobs, Renate, eds. *The Arts in Higher Education.* San Francisco: Jossey-Boss, 1968.

Mahoney, Margaret, et al., eds. *The Arts on Campus: The Necessity for Change.* Greenwich, Connecticut: New York Graphic Society, 1970.

Ommanney, Katherine. *The Stage and the School.* New York: Harper & Co., 1932.

Sponselor, Whitney R. *A Manual for High School and College Theatrical Administration.* Hollywood: American Legitimate Theatre Service, 1957.


## VIII. Fund-Raising, Philanthropy and Subsidy for the Performing Arts

Bridges (Lord). *The State and the Arts.* Romanes Lecture, Oxford, June 3, 1958. Oxford: Clarendon Press, 1958.

Business Committee for the Arts, *Approaching Business for Support of the Arts.* New York, 1971.

Chagy, Gideon, ed. *Business in the Arts '70.* New York: Paul S. Eriksson, 1970.

———.*The State of the Arts and Corporate Support.* New York: Paul S. Eriksson, 1971. (Original title: *Business in the Arts, 1971*).

Cunninggim, Merrimon. *The Role of Foundations in American Society.* New York: McGraw-Hill, 1972.

Dermer, Joseph. *How to Raise Funds from Foundations.* New York: Public Service Materials Center, 1968.

———.ed. *Where America's Large Foundations Make Their Grants.* New York: Public Service Materials Center, 1971.

Dewhurst, J. Frederic, and Associates. *America's Needs and Resources.* New York: The Twentieth Century Fund, 1955.

Dorian, Frederick. *Commitment to Culture.* Pittsburgh: University of Pittsburgh Press, 1964.

Eells, Richard. *Corporation Giving in Free Society.* New York: Macmillan, 1967.

———.*The Corporation and the Arts.* New York: Macmillan, 1967.

Gingrich, Arnold. *Business and the Arts.* New York: Paul S. Eriksson, 1969.

Grau, Robert. *The Business Man in the Amusement World.* New York: Broadway Publishing, 1910.

Heckscher, August. *The Foundations and the Arts.* New York: The Twentieth Century Fund, 1966.

Landstone, Charles. *Off-Stage: A Personal Record of the First Twelve Years of State Sponsored Drama in Great Britain.* London: Elek, 1953.

Lewis, Marianna O., ed. *The Foundation Directory.* New York: Columbia University Press, 1971.

Nielsen, Waldemar A. *The Big Foundations.* New York: The Twentieth Century Fund, 1972.

Noe, Lee, ed. *The Foundation Grants Index, 1970-71.* New York: Columbia University Press, 1972.

Overmyer, Grace. *Government and the Arts.* New York: W. W. Norton, 1939.

Purcell, Ralph. *Government and Art.* Washington, D. C.: Public Affairs Press, 1953.

Reiss, Alvin H. *Culture and Company.* New York: Twayne Publishers, 1972.

Seymour, Harold J. *Designs for Fund Raising.* New York: McGraw-Hill 1966.

Stoddard, Hope. *Subsidy Makes Sense.* Newark, New Jersey International Press, n.d.

Taft, J. Richard. *Understanding Foundations: Dimensions in Fund Raising.* New York: McGraw-Hill Paperbacks, 1967.

Thomas, Ralph Lingo. *Policies Underlying Corporate Giving.* Englewood Cliffs, New Jersey: Prentice-Hall, 1966.

Toffler, Alvin. *The Culture Consumers: A Study of Art and Affluence in America.* New York: St. Martin's Press, 1964. 1964.

Urgo, Louis A., and Corcoran, Robert J. *A Manual for Obtaining Government Grants.* Boston: Robert J. Corcoran Co., Fund Raising Council, 1972.

Weaver, Warren. *U. S. Philanthropic Foundations: Their History, Structure, Management and Record.* New York: Harper & Row, 1967.

Young, Donald R., and Moore, Wilbert E. *Trusteeship and the Management of Foundations.* New York: Russell Sage Foundation, 1969.

## IX. Theatrical Promotion and Publicity

Barry, John F., and Sargent, Epes W. *Building Theatre Patronage.* New York: Chalmers Co., 1927.

Baus, Herbert. *Publicity in Action.* New York: Harper & Brothers, 1954.

Capbern, A. Martial. *The Drama Publicist.* New York: Pageant Press, 1968.

Clay, Roberta. *Promotion in Print: A Guide for Publicity Chairmen.* South Brunswich and New York: A. S. Barnes & Co., 1970. 1970.

Mitchell, Arnold. *Marketing the Arts.* Menlo Park, California: Stanford Research Institute, 1962.

Weiner, Richard, ed. *News Bureaus in the U.S.* New York: Richard Weiner Press, 1972.

——— *Professional's Guide to Public Relations Services.* Englewood Cliffs, New Jersey: Prentice-Hall, 1971.

# X. Reference Works
## for the Performing Arts Administrators

Alexander, J. H., ed. *Early American Theatrical Posters.* Hollywood, California: Cherokee Books, n.d.

Ayers, Richard G., ed. *Directory of American College Theatre.* 2nd ed. Washington, D. C.: American Educational Theatre Association, 1967.

Baker, Blanch M. *Theatre and Allied Arts* (An annotated bibliography). Reprint. New York: Benjamin Blom, 1968.

Belknap, S. Yancey, ed. *Guide to the Performing Arts.* New York: Scarecrow Press, 1965.

*The Billboard Index of the New York Legitimate Stage.* New York: Billboard Publishing, annual editions, 1921 through 1941.

Bowman, Walter P., ed. *Theatre Language: A Dictionary of Terms in English.* New York: Theatre Arts Books, 1961.

Burton, Jack. *The Blue Book of Broadway Musicals.* New York: Century House, 1952.

Cahn, Julius. *Official Theatrical Guide.* 20 vols. New York: Empire State Building, 1896-1921.

*Directory of Community Arts Councils.* 2nd ed. New York: Associated Arts Councils, 1972.

*Directory of National Arts Organizations.* New York: Associated Arts Councils, 1972.

*Directory of National Arts Service Organizations.* New York: Associated Councils of the Arts, 1969.

Enders, John. *Survey of New York Theatre.* New York: Playbill, 1959.

Ewen, David. *Complete Book of the American Musical Theatre.* New York: Holt, Rinehart & Winston, 1970.

—. *Encyclopedia of the Opera.* New York: Hill & Wang., 1955.

*Federal Funds and Services for the Arts,* Document No. FS 5.250: 50050. Washington, D. C.: U. S. Government Printing Office, 1967.

Finley, Robert. *Who's Who in the Theatre.* 15th ed. New York: Pitman Publishing Co., 1972.

Free, William, and Lower, Charles *History into Drama. A Source Book on Symphonic Drama.* New York: Odyssey Press, 1967.

Gohdes, Clarence. *Literature and Theatre of the States and Regions of the U. S. A.: An Historical Bibliography.* Durham, North Carolina: Duke University Press, 1967.

*Grants and Aid to Individuals in the Arts.* Washington, D. C.: *Washington International Arts Letter.*

Hartnoll, Phyllis, ed. *The Oxford Companion to the Theatre.* 2nd ed. Oxford: Oxford University Press, 1957.

Lewis, Marianna O., and Bowers, Patricia, eds. *The Foundation Directory.* 4th ed. New York: The Foundation Center (Columbia University Press), 1971.

Lindey, Alexander. *Entertainment, Publishing and the Arts: Agreements and the Law.* 2 vols., with a 1972 supplement. New York: Clark Boardman Co., 1963.

Nicholson, Margaret. *A Manual of Copyright Practice for Writers, Publishers and Agents.* New York: Oxford University Press, 1956.

Odell, George C. *Annals of the New York Stage.* 15 vols. New York: Columbia University Press, 1927-1949.

*Private Foundations Active in the Arts.* Washington, D. C.: *Washington International Arts Letter.*

Rae, Kenneth, Southern, Richard, eds. *An International Vocabulary of Technical Theatre Terms in Eight Languages.* New York: Theatre Arts Books, 1960.

Rigdon, Walter, ed. *The Biographical Encyclopedia and Who's Who of the American Theatre.* New York: James H. Heineman, 1966.

Rockefeller Brothers Fund. *Directory of National Organizations in the Arts and Education.* New York, 1967.

Santaniello, A. E. *Theatre Books in Print.* New York: Drama Book Shop, 1963.

Sharp, Harold S., and Sharp, Marjorie Z., *Index to Characters in the Performing Arts.* 2 vols. New York: Scarecrow Press, 1966.

*Simon's Directory of Theatrical Materials, Services and Information.* New York: Package Publicity Service, 1970.

Slonimsky, Nicholas, ed. *Baker's Biographical Encyclopedia of Musicians.* 5th ed. New York: G. Schirmer, 1958.

*State Arts Councils.* New York: Associated Arts Councils, 1972.

Stratman, Carl J. *Bibliography of the American Theatre Excluding New York City.* Loyola University Press, 1965.

Taubman, Joseph. *Performing Arts Management and Law.* 4 vols. New York: Law-Arts Publishers, 1972.

Veinstein, Andre; Gilder, Rosamond; Freedley, George; and Myers, Paul, eds. *Performing Arts Collections: An International Handbook.* New York: Theatre Arts Books, 1960.

*Washington and the Arts.* New York: Associated Arts Councils, 1971 1971.